Cuauhtémoc's Bones

SERIES ADVISORY EDITOR:
Lyman L. Johnson,
University of North Carolina at Charlotte

CUAUHTÉMOC'S BONES

Forging National Identity in Modern Mexico

PAUL GILLINGHAM

UNIVERSITY OF NEW MEXICO PRESS | ALBUQUERQUE

Library of Congress Cataloging-in-Publication Data

Gillingham, Paul, 1973–

Cuauhtémoc's bones : forging national identity in modern Mexico /
Paul Gillingham.

    p. cm.

    Includes bibliographical references and index.

    ISBN 978-0-8263-5037-4 (pbk. : alk. paper)

1. Cuauhtemoc, Emperor of Mexico, 1495?–1525—Tomb.

2. Cuauhtemoc, Emperor of Mexico, 1495?–1525—Tomb—Social aspects.

3. National characteristics, Mexican.

4. Nationalism—Mexico.

5. Mexico—Civilization—20th century.

6. Mexico—Politics and government—20th century.

I. Title.

    F1210.G49 2011

    972—dc22

2010051923

Design and composition: Melissa Tandysh

Text is composed in Minion Pro 10.25/14.

Display type is Stempel Schneidler Std.

Frontispiece

Cuauhtémoc hanged, 1525 (detail). Codex Vaticanus A, reproduced in Viscount Kingsborough, *Antiquities of Mexico: Comprising facsimiles of ancient Mexican paintings and hieroglyphics,* vol. 2 (London, 1830–48); courtesy of the Butler Library, Columbia University.

For Alastair Kirkwood
and
Bill Gillingham

Contents

Acknowledgments

This book began life as an undergraduate thesis, so there has been time enough to rack up debts in writing it. From that start in Oxford I am particularly grateful to Alan Knight, who provided the germ of this book and consistent, critical support across the subsequent years, and to John Blair, who first suggested that I write a thesis on Mexico.

Those years were made possible by the training, stimulation, facilities, and funding afforded by diverse institutions: the Queen's College, Oxford; the Instituto Mora, Mexico City; St. Antony's College, Oxford; the Institute of Historical Research in London; the University of North Carolina (UNC), Wilmington; and Columbia University. Grants and fellowships from the Arts and Humanities Research Board, the Scouloudi Foundation, and the Past and Present Society provided critical time to research and write. The project would never have progressed past an extended essay were it not for the original leap of faith of the Leverhulme Trust, which offered a graduate without plans for postgraduate degrees the means for an appreciable period of research in Mexico. It might never have ended were it not for the very generous support offered in interesting times by my colleagues at UNC Wilmington, in particular Sue MacCaffray, Paul Townend, Kathy Berkeley, Bill Atwill, and Lynn Mollenauer. It is a pleasure finally to thank them all.

The archival work this required was frequently eased by the archivists who helped me in the Archivo Diocesano de Chilapa, the Archivo General de la Nación, the Archivo Histórico del Estado de Guerrero, the Archivo Histórico de la Secretaría de Hacienda, the Public Records Office, the Instituto Nacional de Antropología e Historia, the Secretaría de Educación Pública, and the Universidad Nacional Autónoma de México. The impromptu archivists of Ixcateopan, municipal policemen who carried the contents of the town hall basement up to the Registro Civil, deserve particular recognition. I have also worked in some extraordinary libraries—the Bodleian, the Randall Library in Wilmington, the Butler Library in Columbia, and those of the Colegio de México and the Universidad Nacional Autónoma de México—and have been helped in sourcing this book's illustrations by the staff of these and several other institutions, including the Getty Research Institute, the Newberry Library of Chicago, the Arts Institute of Chicago, the Library of Congress, the Benson Latin American Collection at the University of Texas at Austin, and the Smithsonian Institution. There would be half as many illustrations were it not for the tireless work Roberto Soto put in tracking many of them down. I would like to thank all of these people very much and, above all, to offer my warm thanks to Ruth Hodges, Elvira Ryan, and Laura Salinas, who made Oxford's Latin American Centre such a congenial place to work.

One of the bonuses of writing this book was the range of people to whom it introduced me. To read about Ixcateopan is to discover the work of the finest Mexican archaeologists, anthropologists, and historians, ranging across the twentieth century from Manuel Gamio to Eduardo Matos Moctezuma. Those of them who could meet me gave generous time and advice to someone considerably their junior. The enthusiasm of Salvador Rueda, director of Estudios Históricos at the Instituto Nacional de Antropología e Historia and one of the leading experts on Ixcateopan, particularly influenced me. The forger's rationale central to this book was originally his idea; without it the book would not have been undertaken. The work of two other historians was fundamental, namely, José Ortiz Monasterio's studies of Vicente Riva Palacio and Román Parra Terán's histories of his home, Ixcateopan. The extent to which my work draws on theirs is very clear. In Chilpancingo Tomás Bustamante, Renato Ravelo, Hermilio Castorena, and Juan Pablo Leyva were gracious with time and advice. Finally, I would like to offer many thanks to the people of Ixcateopan, who extended me hospitality and kindness. This version of their past is one many of them would not have chosen. I hope they will find at least parts of that past, however, as impressive as I do.

Outside Mexico, I am grateful to those who offered questions, comments, and criticism during relevant presentations at Berlin, Colby, Michigan State University, Oxford, and the University of Texas at Austin. I particularly appreciated the questions raised by Thomas Benjamin, Malcolm Deas, Ben Fallaw, Seth Garfield, Alan Knight, Ben Smith, and Ann Twinam. The anonymous readers from the Journal of Latin American Studies, in which parts of this appeared, and at the University of New Mexico Press provided scrupulous revision, from which the final draft benefited greatly. Bill Atwill, Rob Davies, Ben Fallaw, Alastair Kirkwood, Alan Knight, Pablo Piccato, Barry Carr, Sam Brunk, and Lyman Johnson extended me the same courtesy at different points of the writing process. Lyman, the book's commissioning editor, brought considerable enthusiasm, support, and patience to that process, as well as excellent photos. He and Clark Whitehorn made me glad to be with the University of New Mexico Press.

Not all the debts behind this book are professional. I greatly appreciate the welcome and the varied education afforded in Mexico by Paco Hernández and Andrea; José Ortiz Monasterio; Anvy, Angélica, and Vicente Guzmán; Cris, Luis, Jorge, and Herta Altamirano; Chusais; Rafael Cue, who gave me a job and designed me a cover that I like very much; and José Antonio Trueba, Mario del Olmo, and the rest of the *peña*. Oscar Altamirano taught me more than any book. My family and friends offered me support, a range of interesting examples, and sometimes even company. A visit with Josh to Chiapas, a road trip with my mother through Michoacán, a swim with my father in Ixtapa, a series of broken-down cars with Matthew, and an earthquake with my sister in Veracruz all stick in my mind. Later on, Snjezana and Alastair gave me invaluable inspiration and the best reasons to finish writing. Last of all, I am very grateful to my grandfathers, who gave me so much, and to whom this book is dedicated.

Introduction

Who Makes Nations?

The more outré and grotesque an incident is the more carefully it deserves to be examined, and the very point which appears to complicate a case is, when duly considered and scientifically handled, the one which is most likely to elucidate it.

—Arthur Conan Doyle, *The Hound of the Baskervilles*

The mystery of Cuauhtémoc's burial place is one of our obsessions. To discover it would mean nothing less than to return to our origins, to reunite ourselves with our ancestry, or break out of our solitude. It would be a resurrection.

—Octavio Paz, *The Labyrinth of Solitude*

THIS IS A HISTORY, NOT A DETECTIVE STORY, BUT IT DOES AT LEAST start with a body. It was a distinguished body: that of the last Aztec emperor, Cuauhtémoc. He had fought heroically and hopelessly against the indigenous allies, the microbes, and the steel of the Spanish, who captured him, tortured him, and finally hanged him, far to the south of his hometown, somewhere in the watery vastness of the Tabasco Plain. The last record of his body dates back to February 1525, when Hernán Cortés's soldiers trooped wearily out of a place called Izankanac, leaving Cuauhtémoc hanging from a large silk-cotton tree. In 1949 a group of villagers and ad hoc archaeologists dug up what they took to be the body, buried beneath the altar of the parish church in Ixcateopan, a remote village in the mountains of central Mexico. Their discovery led to intense nationalist celebrations: in the village, in the main square and boule-vards of Mexico City, and all the way to distant places in the northern border-lands. Mexico's professional archaeologists, however, quickly denied that the body was that of Cuauhtémoc. This gave Mexico's nationalists serious problems, and the discovery set off the greatest scandal in the cultural politics of twentieth-century Mexico. The first problem was self-evident: whose bones were actually nestled in the narrow hole beneath the church of Santa María de la Asunción? If Cuauhtémoc's tomb was forged, could a forgery still trigger the sentiments of national identity? If it was a fraud, whodunit? That, finally, was bound up with a bigger question. To ask who made the fake tomb was also to ask what sorts of people make a bigger thing: the set of ideas, beliefs, and dreams that bind societ-ies to the main form of modern political organisation, the nation-state.[1]

The answers to that question matter a long way outside Mexico. In the early 1990s European governments watched as genocide was carried out in former Yugoslavia, justifying inaction on the grounds that a murderous ethnic nation-alism was endemic to the Balkans, entrenched in everyday people since forever, and consequently too difficult to stop through intervention. This was bad his-tory and worse policy.[2] In Africa similar atavistic appreciations of "national culture" dominated early international responses to another genocidal nation-alism, which left half a million Tutsis dead in Rwanda.[3] After the shock of 9/11, Anatol Lieven argues, a "wounded and vengeful nationalism" underpinned actions, including indefinite detention without trial and torture, fundamen-tally at odds with America's laws, civic traditions, and idealist self-image.[4] In Southeast Asia, by contrast, popular nationalist beliefs could be profoundly liberating, hastening the end of Western empires and the birth of indepen-dent states. Even the most successful alternate ideologies have quickly adopted some nationalist components. The Bolshevik Revolution began with an explicit rejection of national identity in favour of social class as the main bond between humans; that internationalist idea lasted less than twenty years, and in the 1930s Stalin blended communism with a powerful, resuscitated Russian cul-tural nationalism.[5] Over the last two centuries nationalism has replaced earlier solidarities such as kin, locality, or religion as the main way that people identify themselves, organise themselves, and mobilise themselves.

Historians are both the analysts and authors of this idea.[6] In the late twen-tieth century social scientists took an increased interest in nationalism, which generated two main schools of thought.[7] One is the primordialist, which holds that nations "exist in the first order of time, and lie at the root of subsequent processes and developments," or are at the least of extremely long standing, "formed on the basis of attachments to the 'cultural givens' of social existence."[8] The other—and the more influential—is the instrumentalist school, which sees the nation as "an invented category . . . [with] roots in neither nature nor history."[9] In this interpretation the nation has four key characteristics. It is a claim that a territory and its people, culture, and polity are closely and naturally interrelated; it is a recent, mythical creation, forged by modern elites as a tool of power to make, preserve, and expand nation-states; while encoded in a series of "invented traditions," it in reality requires an advanced level of technology to be disseminated; and it develops unevenly, both within any given country and around the world.[10] Politicians and cultural managers, in other words, knowingly use public space, print capitalism, and mass education to fill everyday life with nationalist versions of what T. S. Eliot called "the objective correlative": "a set of objects, a situation, a chain of events which shall be the formula of [a] particular emotion; such that when the external facts . . . are given, the emotion is immediately released."[11] Elites try to make flags, statues, pictures, rites, dead people, gestures, military drills, tunes, and words into these objective correlatives, triggers for deeply emotive national stories of common origins, triumphs, and tragedies. Such stories are written to produce a Pavlovian reflex in the ruled: a powerful attachment to a platonic ideal of the *vaterland, la patria,* or the homeland, and its culture. Thus, Ernst Gellner argues, "Culture, which had once resembled the air men breathed, and of which they were seldom properly aware, suddenly becomes perceptible and significant. The wrong and alien culture becomes menacing. Culture, like prose, becomes visible, and a source of pride and pleasure to boot. The age of nationalism is born."[12] And with that attachment, that pride, that pleasure, and that sense of external threat should come obedience—elites are held to calculate—to the nation-state's avatar, the political leadership of the day.

Latin America has been a critical place for understanding nationalism. The republics that Latin Americans made after they ended Spanish colonial rule constituted some of the earliest attempts at democratic nation-states in the world. A very particular reading of Latin American history underpins the classic definition of what a nation actually is, namely, the anthropologist Benedict Anderson's description of the nation as "an imagined political community."[13] According to Anderson, Latin American nationalism preceded Latin American nation-states. Their geographical borders were shaped by the circuits that colonial bureaucrats travelled, their mental borders by print gazettes, early newspapers that helped creoles to imagine a different, non-Spanish community of interests and, by implication, politics. Anderson's "pilgrim creole functionaries and provincial creole printmen" have, however, proved difficult for subsequent historians to find.[14] Furthermore, there was no explosive growth of locally oriented newspapers before independence. Caracas got its first press in 1808; Chile, in 1812.[15] And where there was a press, in the territory that became Mexico (which most resembles the model) it reflected a Spanish as well as a creole sense of community. (The merchants who formed a key readership were, after all, often Spanish.)[16] Historians now tend to agree that nationalism in Latin America was a nineteenth-century creation that tended to follow rather than fuel state formation.[17] Yet, while the body of evidence for Anderson's theory has disappeared, the basic concept of nationalism as "a hegemonic, commonsensical, and tacitly shared cultural construct . . . a kind of cultural successor to the universalism of premodern (European) religion," lingers on like the Cheshire Cat's smile.[18]

This divorce of evidence and theory is emblematic of the problems in studies of nationalism. As Anderson points out, "Nation, nationality, nationalism—all have proved notoriously difficult to define, let alone to analyse."[19] There are three basic agreements in studies of cultural nationalism in Mexico. Writers generally concur on a broad metanarrative of Mexican nationalism: a story of self-sacrificing, popular, pluralist identity; rooted far back in the high urban cultures of the prehispanic past; shaped through the miscegenation of *mestizaje* and a long series of heroic, one-sided defeats; and made whole by popular stoicism, struggle, and victory, whether against the colonial power of the Spanish, the would-be colonial power of the French, or the neocolonial regimes of Porfirio Díaz and the oil companies. Within that story there are a handful of critical symbols: Cuauhtémoc, the Virgen de Guadalupe, the leaders of independence, the soldiers who fought the American invasion of 1848, the liberal leader Benito Juárez, and the popular revolutionaries—Emiliano Zapata, Pancho Villa, and Lázaro Cárdenas.[20] These ingredients are obvious, although their relative weight is open to some debate, and more than one Mexican sociologist has undertaken survey research to draw up league tables of national heroes.[21] The oldest—the prehispanic cultures, Our Lady of Guadalupe—seem to have been influential signifiers for the people who became Mexicans well before the age of nationalism began.[22] Finally, most who have studied Mexican nationalism agree on its comparative success as a modern belief system of clear and widespread affective power.[23]

Thereafter agreement declines. While many of the symbols and stories seem self-evident, the mechanisms of that nationalism are often obscure, and different analyses give different versions of what Mexican nationalism might be. Uncertainty persists around five key questions. First, who makes the nation—a single group of the powerful or cultural authors from across a whole society? Second, should national identity have multiple creators, must they have a broadly similar, coherent idea of what that identity is? Or does "Mexico" mean very different things across different ethnicities, social classes, religious denominations, genders, and places? Third, if there are multiple nationalisms, are they distinguished by different degrees of "authenticity"; are popular nationalisms any more primordial, less Machiavellian, than elite nationalisms? Fourth, how convincingly can historians reconstruct the motives of different actors and groups for making nationalist constructs? And fifth, where is the material for materialist—as opposed to purely cultural or political—readings of nationalism?

Mexican nationalism was long seen in strongly instrumentalist terms, as a belief system made up by a few to dominate a very diverse many. Nineteenth-century politicians frequently complained of the lack of patriotism of their compatriots, seeing themselves, as a contemporary writer put it, as foreigners in their own land.[24] They sought to remedy this problem, rooted in the diversity and the disunity of the newly invented Mexican population, with acts that ranged from promoting intensive European immigration to the production of novels and histories that shaped clear, inspirational lessons from Mexico's exotic past.[25] After 1857 liberals in particular understood themselves quite consciously to be elite instrumentalists, and in doing so they started an interpretive tradition that lasted for over a century. Foreign scholars after the revolution inherited the concept that Mexico was the idea of a few—the "middle class intellectuals," "an insignificant part of the population"—and were sceptical about both its magnetism and its penetration.[26] Mexican public intellectuals continued this Machiavellian analysis through the mid-century: Octavio Paz found the geographical, ethnic, and ideological differences between Mexicans to be so great that only a small group were self-consciously Mexican at all.[27] Some historians agree. Enrique Florescano argues that Mexican elites across the nineteenth and twentieth centuries manipulated the past far beyond the enthusiasms of the ruled, creating "symbols and myths that might unify a nation that does not exist except for the minorities who seek to build it."[28] Mauricio Tenorio-Trillo views the Porfirian nation as "solely for those who created it"; Adrian Bantjes finds even revolutionary nation building to be "inevitably the work of the political elites."[29] Such interpretations square well with broader judgments on Latin American nationalism, which is seen as overwhelmingly elite until well into the twentieth century.[30] It also squares well with the self-representations of Mexican elites themselves, who consistently wrote and spoke of themselves as bulwarks of the civilisation that modern metropolitan nationhood represented in a land of parochial countrymen.

Rather more historians and anthropologists, however, think that nation builders are to be found across society. Nationalism may well be a bourgeois project, but it is not just a bourgeois project. The past, as Arjun Appadurai and others have noted, is a universal tactical resource.[31] The peasants who until the mid-twentieth century formed the overwhelming majority of the population also busily imagined communities: their villages and lands, certainly, but also bigger visions of Mexico in which those villages were of central historic importance. Peter Guardino's work on the nineteenth century, for example, stresses the extent to which villagers in the state of Guerrero turned the organisations of central control and the nationalist ideology that infused them against those very same centralizing projects.[32] Michael Ducey's history of riot and revolt in the early national Huasteca details how "the nationalist idiom became part of the political vocabulary of rural indigenous villagers in a remote corner of Mexico," as rebellious peasants "played politics on the national level . . . to protect their interests and local traditions . . . [inviting] themselves to participate in the process of state formation."[33] Guy Thomson and Patrick McNamara's studies of the *serranos*, the mountain men of Puebla and Oaxaca, respectively, likewise emphasise how adeptly villagers in the later nineteenth century deployed their histories, framed in the rhetorics of nationalist ideology, in pursuit of local goals.[34] Claudio Lomnitz has provided several case studies of contemporary local intellectuals who engage in sophisticated symbolic manipulation to claim privileged places for their communities in national historical narrative.[35] Such work sidesteps what Florencia Mallon calls the "simple celebration of subaltern agency," charting instead how peasants "actively struggled and thought in national terms . . . [even if they] never emerged as influential members of the political coalitions that took control of the state."[36] Yet by participating, by using the language and ideas of the nation, peasants endorsed and reinforced those ideas and to some extent made them their own. As Alan Knight concludes, nationalism can originate at all levels of society and in all places, and "a 'nationalist' or patriotic commitment to Mexico [is] quite compatible with a 'localist' attachment to community and repudiation of the overweening central government."[37]

Yet are these nationalist collages really all that similar? Is Mexico much the same ideal for an indigenous villager in the Huasteca, a market vendor in Tepito, a rancher in Sonora, a lady who lunches in the Colonia Roma, a Zapatista in Morelos or Chiapas, and the abbot of the Basilica de Guadalupe? Most scholars posit the existence of several strands of nationalism across Mexico's modern history. There are, they argue, class divisions in nationalist ideology. At the very beginning, Eric Van Young argues, the independence movement was fractured between profoundly different elite and popular ideas of what exactly rebels were fighting for. These grew over the nineteenth century into parallel ideas of national identity: a popular nationalism, or patriotic liberalism, rooted in the "little fatherlands" of the villages and their contemporary histories of warfare against Spanish, conservatives, and French; and an elite version rooted in more abstract notions of *mestizaje*, distant pasts, and immediate futures of export-led progress.[38] Mexico's peasant nationalists tapped, Mallon believes, into the intense mobilizing power of the "universal promise of a national-democratic project," an essentially alternative project to that of the metropolitan elites.[39] There were also status divisions in nationalist ideology. From the late nineteenth century onward an alternative Catholic nationalism emerged, stressing the role of Church, Mary (both as the Virgen de Guadalupe and as older incarnations such as the Virgen de Covadonga), the Emperor Iturbide, and the centrality of the family.[40] It seems clear that quite different nationalist canons, cosmologies, and pragmatic goals exist side by side in Mexico.

Yet these mental worlds are not discrete but, rather, closely interrelated in "a dialectic of cultural struggle" and by the "circularity" between elite and popular cultures that theorists such as Norbert Elias and Mikhail Bakhtin have identified: "a circular relationship composed of reciprocal influences, which travelled from low to high as well as from high to low."[41] In brute terms, different nationalists shamelessly compete for and pirate each other's material. They also censor or redefine whatever competing stories or symbols they can. Thus conservative Catholic nationalists also drew on two of the key liberal symbols, Morelos and Hidalgo, and adopted the forms of modern science to endorse miracles, endowing university chairs for hopefully sympathetic physicists.[42] Liberal and revolutionary nationalists adopted many of the forms of Catholic celebration, such as altars and carnivals for independence heroes, and—after the disastrous anticlericalism of the 1920s and 1930s—insinuated their own religious beliefs. In 1940 the winning presidential candidate advertised his faith; in 1951 the chairman of the ruling Partido Revolucionario Institucional toured churches to demonstrate the party's "profoundly respectful" attitudes toward Catholicism; in 1959 the political boss of Oaxaca's Región Mixe ordered municipal bands to come to the city and celebrate the Virgen de la Soledad.[43] And in a striking example of how fundamentally opposed belief systems can be articulated, some P'urhépecha communities reportedly conflated Christ and Saint Joseph into a single deity who worked his miracles through the intercession of the anticlerical President Benito Juárez.[44]

Such syncretism also operated across, and blurred, the class lines between popular and elite nationalisms.[45] Mexican elites attacked the genuinely popular revolutionaries while alive—Zapata was the "Attila of the South," Villa was a "gorilla" and a "troglodyte"—and adopted them as key nationalist icons once dead.[46] Indigenous villagers in Guerrero's eastern highlands invited a government school inspector to their hamlet for their Independence Day celebrations in 1927 and wept as he gave them one of those great abstractions, a national flag, to mark their first ever patriotic festival.[47] By the 1940s, Mary Kay Vaughan argues, such ubiquitous festivals "did not simply disseminate ideology from above nor merely legitimate local, regional and national powerholders. . . . The symbols, values and behaviours celebrated in the festival fused in a hegemonic discourse."[48] Different users of nationalism may have started with very different aims and assumptions, but they tended strongly to end up moving in the same symbolic neighbourhood. Whether this adds up to a single, "real" nationalism or not is a matter of stress more than substance.

The mechanisms of invention, plagiarism, and piracy that go into nationalist beliefs are often relatively visible at the top of societies. Newspapers and government papers record the births of monuments, ceremonies, texts, behaviours, and rhetorics. Some of the motives of elite nation builders are also often on display, whether directly, through their own testimonies in speeches or memoirs, or circumstantially, through the uncoincidental coincidence of political crisis and nationalist initiative. Even their basic legwork can be seen: the nation-building politician Vicente Riva Palacio, for example, busily collecting popular folklore; or the great media magnate Emilio Azcárraga, asking the masses queuing up to be studio audiences for ideas on what should happen in his soap operas; or the enthusiastic bureaucrats in charge of censorship, debating which comics were good for national culture; or the spies monitoring cinema audiences, singling out the newsreel segments that those audiences booed for the scissors.[49] All three of these component stages in nationalist creation—motivation, conceptualisation, and execution—are far more difficult to reconstruct at the grassroots. And in large part because of this difficulty, historians have frequently been unsure whether popular nationalism is as knowing a mechanism for domination at the village or regional level as they assume elite nationalism to be at the national level.

Do peasants believe deeply in peasant nationalism? Or is it a similarly cynical resource for them as it is for their Machiavellian superiors? Is popular nationalism "simply one option among many that are open to political entrepreneurs—a politically convenient self-classification to obtain material resources rather than a social movement with an intrinsic and unique cultural substance?"[50] Such questions are at the heart of the instrumentalist/primordialist distinction, the answers drawing the border between the transcendental and the transactional politics of nationalism.[51] The language historians often use—"popular nationalism," "patriotic liberalism," "authentic nationalism"—is itself a normative judgment, hinting that the nationalism of the masses is of a different, less fictitious, more straightforwardly emotional, psychologically deeper nature than that of their rulers. Yet there are few empirical studies to support such assumptions, for the obvious reason that the heads and wallets of most people leave few traces. Both the cultural and the material drives of everyday nationalists are consequently problematic for historians: difficult to reconstruct, yet central to understanding what nationalism is and why it works.

Cuauhtémoc's tomb affords unusual possibilities for considering this problem. More than one intellectual recognised that the scandal offered extraordinary insight into the politics, imaging, and mechanisms of Mexican national identity. Miguel Angel Cevallos wrote of the "fervour" he had seen in autumn 1949, among congressmen, villagers, Indians, bureaucrats, and bourgeois, and concluded, only half ironically, that "the alleged discovery of the mortal remains of Cuauhtémoc, last king of the Aztecs . . . is producing a surprising social phenomenon, worthy of a sociologist's attention; and which leads to the unveiling, in this chance experiment underway in the vast laboratory of the whole Republic, of the fundamental outlines of the Mexican people."[52] The "new industry of tomb raiders" would do nothing for history, one historian noted acerbically, but "they [would] help us to understand better many of our contemporaries."[53] The last emperor's memory and his fake tomb produced pride and excitement and disappointment and neurosis and anger and the realisation of opportunity across a broad range of Mexicans. Cuauhtémoc's bones came to lie at the nexus of both elite and popular ideas about the transcendental and the tactical meanings of national identity. They are consequently an ideal place to study the relationships between these phenomena.

There is also an extraordinary quantity of evidence regarding the forgery and the responses it evoked, dispersed among Mexican and foreign archives. The scandal surrounding the tomb's authenticity ensured historians copious sources, spanning personal papers, municipal archives, newspapers, ethnographies, the work of diplomats and spies, and the reports of three academic commissions. The Ixcateopan tomb was carefully analysed by several generations of the finest Mexican scholars, ranging from the first professional anthropologist, Manuel Gamio, to the senior archaeologists, historians, and anthropologists of the last forty years.[54] Their work and these rich archival materials enable a comparatively empirical reconstruction of the rise and fall of a nationalist symbol. They do not allow us to wholly bypass the critical methodological hurdle to any study of nationalism, namely, the paucity of evidence for everyday reactions to such symbols. Given material such as the interviews of Mexican anthropologists with some sixty villagers from the tomb site, however, Cuauhtémoc's bones make useful tools to tackle what Harold Pinter has called "the immense difficulty, if not the impossibility, of verifying the past."[55]

This is not to understate the reliance on deduction and comparative method in much of what follows. As Clifford Geertz noted, "Cultural analysis is (or should be) guessing at meanings, assessing the guesses, and drawing explanatory conclusions from the better guesses."[56] The reconstruction of popular nationalism in particular relies heavily on circumstantial evidence—the cumulative meaning extracted from as many indirect pointers as possible—rather than the direct evidence of historical actors stating precisely what they did and why they did it.[57] The governor of Guerrero left no record of why the tomb was so important to him; the handful of villagers who opposed the tomb's authenticity left no explanations for their risky idiosyncrasy. What evidence exists is sometimes pushed hard in the story that follows; but it is a story rooted in evidence that can be reexamined, its conclusions supported, criticised, or nullified. Some of the weaknesses common to histories and detective stories, such as unreliable narrators and their over-neat conclusions, can thus be countered.[58] And in the strange meeting around a remote grave of a huge cast of Mexicans—ranging over time from colonial archaeologists, devil-worshipping ranchers, and pulp fiction novelists through indigenous dancers, field hands, and schoolteachers to petty bureaucrats, presidents, and Maoist guerrillas—there may be some insight into the vexed, vitally important question of who forges the nation.

Chapter 1

Cuauhtémoc

Because so little
Is known about you from history,
I could fashion you more freely in my mind.
—C. P. Cavafy, "Kaisarion"

A BIOGRAPHY CONVENTIONALLY STARTS WITH A DATE OF BIRTH AND a flourish. Rhetorically elaborate treatments of the life of Cuauhtémoc, last emperor of the Mexica, abound. Yet any biography of Cuauhtémoc should start with the most basic confessions of ignorance: that we cannot know when, or where, he was born. Nor do we know with the greatest certainty where or why he died, and neither is the identity of his mother established beyond question. In terms of written remains, he passed the majority of his life without leaving much of a trace at all.

Cuauhtémoc moves elusively through the texts that did endure to describe the late Mexica Empire and its defeat by the conquistadors. For all his significance, references to his character and life are sparse, terse, and frequently contradictory. Inside the handful of relevant indigenous texts that survived the vicissitudes of war, Cuauhtémoc's life only extends beyond the minimal outlines of chronicle at the moments of his capture, torture, and death. For the Spanish, Cuauhtémoc did not exist until he became emperor; and even then he existed as a largely abstract enemy. In describing his epic and bloody siege of the Mexica capital, Tenochtitlán, the Spanish leader Hernán Cortés mentioned its last emperor by name a mere eight times.[1]

Cuauhtémoc's life, and particularly his death, provoked bitter controversy among the few contemporaries and near-contemporaries who wrote of it. Even when on apparently neutral ground, early accounts of the conquest are characterised by the bitter disagreements of their authors. Bernal Díaz del Castillo, the soldier whose bluff simplicity masks a sophisticated sense of narrative, set out to write his "true history" inspired by what he claimed was disgust at everyone else's mendacity. Francisco López de Gómara, Cortés's chaplain and tame historian, had, Bernal Díaz accused, penned his hagiographic *Historia General de las Indias* under the amnesiac influence of bribes from Cortés's son; Bartolomé de las Casas's account flatly "contradicts the facts"; and as for Gonzalo de Illescas, his narrative was truthful "neither in the beginning, nor the middle, nor the end."[2] Against this background of historiographical bloodletting it is no surprise to find considerable divergence in Spanish memories of Cuauhtémoc.

Indigenous historians present different problems, although they too were perfectly capable of partisanship. Working in part from remembered tradition, men such as Álvaro Tezozómoc and Fernando de Alva Ixtlilxóchitl pieced together encyclopaedic reconstructions of their ancestors' histories nearly a century after their abrupt end. Yet frequently they were pushed to admit defeat and conclude a genealogy with such eloquently bald statements as "the names of the other two men are not well known."[3] Earlier attempts to record and defend a besieged and predominantly oral history, such as the anonymously authored *Anales de Tlatelolco*, faced a context of censorship severe to the point of paranoia. Even Spanish authors' output was implacably controlled. Cortés's collected reports on the conquest, the *Cartas de Relación*, were banned (and burned) in 1527 and not reprinted until the eighteenth century; Cortés's first biography, written by the Sicilian Lucio Marineo Sículo, was finished by 1530 and similarly, immediately, prohibited; even Gómara's work met with an initial ban. In a royal decree of 1577, Philip II explicitly prohibited "that on any account, any person should write things which deal with the superstitions and ways of life which these Indians had."[4] For the indigenous elites matters were further complicated by powerful religious opposition to attempts at registering (and hence perpetuating) prehispanic culture. The efforts of bishops such as Zumárraga or de Landa, who collected and burned thousands of codices, were all too effective in erasing wide tracts of memory both sacred and profane.[5]

Yet in addition to the numerous Zumárragas, there were men such as Bernardino de Sahagún, Franciscan witch-hunter turned ethnographer, who set out to describe prehispanic Mexico all the better to bury its remains and ended by assembling a text of rich detail that not only describes but frequently eulogises a dying culture.[6] From Sahagún and his indigenous informants alone one could reconstruct a complex vision of the Mexica world and its eclipse. When these are read in conjunction with what documentation did survive the rigours of the sixteenth century, Cuauhtémoc may remain in many ways shadowy, but the backdrop of his life comes to light and throws him into some relief. As an individual we have mere glimpses of who he might have been through his few recorded words and actions; as just another Mexica noble, however, we have a vivid idea of the outlines of his life.[7]

Figure 1.
Cuauhtémoc as emperor, 1521. Codex Vaticanus A, reproduced in Viscount Kingsborough, *Antiquities of Mexico: Comprising facsimiles of ancient Mexican paintings and hieroglyphics,* vol. 2 (London, 1830–48); courtesy of the Butler Library, Columbia University.

Cuauhtémoc, the falling eagle, was the firstborn legitimate son of the emperor Ahuitzótl and as such scion of the clan that had ruled Tenochtitlán and the Mexica since the late fourteenth century.[8] At the same time he was, quite literally, just another noble, because that clan was extensive and the political gene pool of those eligible to become emperor was broad. Baroque levels of disposable wealth combined with polygyny to create vast households: some lords maintained over two hundred consorts at the same time, while Moctezuma II kept over three thousand noblewomen at his pleasure in the royal palace—with the result, claimed Torquemada, of once having 150 of them simultaneously pregnant. (On that particular occasion, Torquemada continued pruriently, they all aborted "to give solace to Moctezuma.")[9] Such conscientious family planning was not, however, the norm: Moctezuma had fourteen, and Cuauhtémoc nineteen, legitimate siblings.[10]

Given this profusion of imperial consorts, it is perhaps understandable that they should figure fleetingly if at all in remaining records and that the identity of Cuauhtémoc's mother should be consequently unclear. Bernal Díaz held that she was one of Moctezuma's sisters, whom Chavero later named as Tiyacapantzin.[11] The tradition recovered by Ixtlilxóchitl and Torquemada contradicts this, however, making Tiyacapantzin a daughter of Moquiuixtli, last king of the neighbouring city-state of Tlatelolco.[12] The latter seems more feasible, if only because of Cuauhtémoc's later lordship of Tlatelolco, suggestive of some prior association such as that offered by a Tlatelolca mother.[13] Tlatelolca or Mexica, she gave birth to Cuauhtémoc at some point prior to 1502, the year of his father's death, most probably in the mid- to late 1490s. Various chroniclers have it that Cuauhtémoc was eighteen years old when he came to the throne in 1521, dating his birth to 1502 or 1503.[14] Yet for all his title of Xocoyotzin, the Young One, this seems unlikely; it would require his father to have practised virtual abstinence for fifteen of the sixteen years of his reign and then to have fathered some twenty children in the last months of his life.[15] And although once more certainty is an unrealistic goal, it is probable that Bernal Díaz is nearer the mark when he estimates Cuauhtémoc to have been twenty-five or twenty-six when they first met, placing his birth date around 1495.[16]

Cuauhtémoc was born into a culture characterised by a peculiar blend of imperial arrogance and existential insecurity. By the late fifteenth century the Mexica had become the hegemonic power of central Mexico: their area of tribute, comprising thirty-eight lordships and approximately half a million square kilometres, had been extended by Cuauhtémoc's father as far south as Soconusco in modern Chiapas.[17] Of the principal cities of their valley, only Texcoco maintained a nominally independent monarchy in 1500 (and not for much longer), the Mexica having replaced the kings of Tlatelolco and Tacuba with centrally appointed governors.[18] The flow of tribute from this empire into the coffers of the capital funded increasingly elaborate displays of wealth: Nezahualcóyotl's palace in Texcoco covered nearly a square kilometre and contained over three hundred rooms. In such palaces, said Ixtlilxóchitl, the elite consumed more than one hundred turkeys a day.[19] At a more mundane level, imperial wealth enabled the city to expand beyond its immediate ecological potential and, by importing foodstuffs from the lake borderlands and beyond, sustain its growth until it was considerably bigger than any contemporary Spanish city.[20]

And yet despite this unmatched power the Mexica were continually and uncomfortably conscious of their status as *arrivistes*. They rewrote history and blustered about the antiquity of their achievements—one passed the main temple off on Bernal Díaz as dating back thousands of years; it was, in reality, all of thirty-two years old—precisely through insecurity concerning their impermanence.[21] Their own meteoric rise from obscurity had impressed upon them the perishability of political power: they had, after all, been tributaries of neighbouring Azcapotzalco until 1428 and had only taken firm control over the Valley of Mexico in 1500.[22] At the same time as they remembered instability, they inherited from earlier Mesoamerican cultures an ontology of cyclical cataclysm. Four earlier epochs, they believed, had come violently and unswervingly to their respective ends; the Fifth Sun, whose end was foretold in earthquakes, was equally finite. Man was an unwelcome, ephemeral presence in a world that fate had ranged against him.

As soon as he was born, therefore, a Mexica child like Cuauhtémoc was ritually informed of the predictable harshness of his life and of his only viable reactions, stoicism and the appeasement of hostile destiny through the intertwining mechanisms of religion and war. "My dearly beloved son," he would have been instructed, "know you and understand that your home is not here where you were born, because you are a soldier and a servant, you are a bird called *quecholli*. . . . [T]his house where you were born is no more than a nest. . . . [Y]our duty is to give the sun the blood of your enemies to drink, and to feed the earth, which is called *Tlaltecuhtli*, the bodies of your enemies."[23] War was essential to generate the sacrificial victims that religion demanded, to the extent that in the absence of a real war, a phony, so-called flowery war would be arranged with a convenient neighbour, to the formal end of providing prisoners

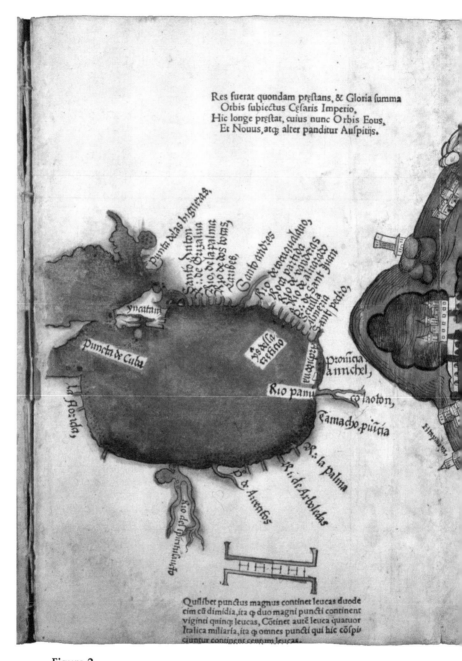

Res fuerat quondam preſtans, & Gloria ſumma
Orbis ſubieċtus Cæſaris Imperio,
Hic longe preſtat, cuius nunc Orbis Eous,
Et Nouus, atq̃ alter panditur Auſpitijs.

Punta delas higueras,
Santo Anton
de Gruzalua
Rio de la palma
Rio de los tonos
Larribes
Santo andres
Rio de aguaqualquo,
Rio de partida
Rio de baudeas
Rio de aliuatado
uculla de Sant Juan
almeria
almeria
Sant pedro,
yucatan
ysla de nefluo
Puncta de Cuba
prouincia
anuchel,
La florida,
Rio panu
co laoton,
Camacho puicia
R: la palma
R: de Astoledas
B de Auentos
Rio del ſpiritúſancto
ilipuicho

Quiſlibet punctus magnus continet leucas duode
cim cū dimidia, ita q̃ duo magni puncti continent
viginti quinq̃ leucas, Cötinet autē leuca quatuor
Italica miliaria, ita q̃ omnes puncti qui hic cöſpi
ciuntur continent centum leucas.

Figure 2.
A 1524 map of Tenochtitlán as depicted in Cortés's second letter to Charles V;
by permission of the Newberry Library, Chicago.

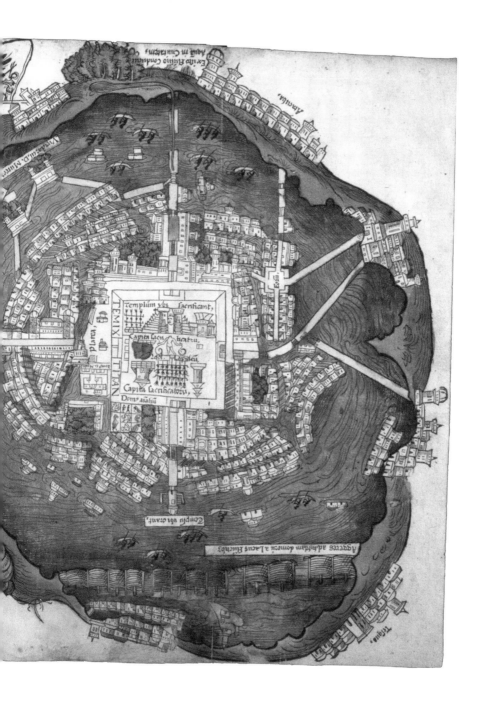

for later offerings. This religious impulse was, however, so fervently met during the Mexica expansionist drive that periods of peace were rare. During his eighteen-year reign Moctezuma II fought forty-three campaigns; at least two of these were launched for no graver reason than the emperor's coveting of certain flowering trees possessed by his rivals.[24] War was a structural constant of Mexica society, its successful prosecution "the foremost duty of a lord."[25]

Yet after the bellicose injunctions and the gifts of weapons attendant upon a baptism, religious training for Cuauhtémoc would have initially implied austerity and intensive study. The patchwork pantheon of divinities worshiped by the Mexica was for a start difficult to master through its sheer size. Their neighbours scoffed at the Mexica as having more gods than they could count, recognizing as they did four hundred gods of cactus alcohol and drunkenness alone. At the same time the generalised conviction, and fear, of human frailty that dogged Mexica thought translated into spartan educational norms.[26]

Figure 3. Mexica warfare: the critical battle against their former overlords, Aztcapotzalco. From Juan de Tovar, *Historia de México* (ca. 1585); courtesy of the Kislak Collection of the Rare Book Division of the Library of Congress.

Cuauhtémoc from an early age would have received the instruction afforded the elite in the complexities of the tribe's religion and official history, encoded in the aide-mémoires of the codices. At the same time he would be taught the same essential drudgeries as any other child: gathering firewood, fishing, attending market, and cultivating the floating gardens of the *chinampas*. From boyhood to early adolescence he would subsist on an ascetically meagre diet while learning to worship the gods through strict penance: tapping his blood with maguey spines, rising in the middle of the night to bathe in cold springs, and sleeping on the bare earth. And at some stage, possibly very early, he would be sent away from his family to the *calmecac*, the monastery school of the nobility, with the admonition to forget parents and privilege and to devote himself to his own advancement.[27]

That Cuauhtémoc listened is evident, for in 1515 he became lord of Tlatelolco.[28] This was a signal honour; the Mexica had not named a king to that city in forty-two years.[29] In the formally meritocratic military hierarchy of the Mexica his new rank implied not just high birth and talent as a leader but also that he had personally captured several prisoners for sacrifice. Once lord of Tlatelolco he is further mentioned as serving with distinction in Nezahualpilli's campaigns against Quetzaltepec and Iztactlalocan.[30] Such early feats of arms would have placed him among the frontrunners of the extended family from which the *tlatocan*, or state council, would select the next emperor.[31] His father, Ahuitzótl, had been *tlacatecatl*, or captain-general, before reaching the throne; his cousin Moctezuma II had distinguished himself, particularly in the wars against Cuautla, during Ahuitzótl's reign; a brother of Moctezuma's named Cuitláhuac had recently come to the fore in wars against Atlixco and the Mixtecs.[32] Proven military ability was a sine qua non of Mexica lordship. Cuauhtémoc displayed it, and claimed his status as contender in the eventual imperial succession, at an early stage. By 1519 and the arrival of the third Spanish expedition to Mexico he was held in considerable prestige, not just as lord of Tlatelolco but also as one of the high priests and "a very famous captain."[33]

It was, then, as a member of the inner circle that Cuauhtémoc would have experienced the society-wide terror incurred by the Spanish landing on the Gulf Coast. According to the postconquest accounts of Sahagún's informants, the Cortés expedition was prefigured by nearly twenty years of auguries of disaster, ranging from the farcical death of Ahuitzótl, who banged his head on the lintel of his bedroom while fleeing a flood of his own creation, to a menacing series of atmospheric and supernatural phenomena. Comets, solar eclipses, temple fires, inexplicable storms, and a long string of biological freaks formed the backdrop to the repeated prophecy uttered by a mysterious wailing woman in the night: "O my sons! We are about to perish."[34] These may be pure post hoc literary embellishments, as Nahua writers followed the Mexica's (and, of course, the Franciscans') apocalyptic mythos and invented the traditional signs of impending doom. It is notable that there are eight such signs, a number of magical significance in prehispanic culture. They may, however, have been at least part-experienced, reflecting the growing pressures of ecological overload or rumours from the islands and Yucatán of alien invaders and the catastrophes they caused. The arrival of Cortés may well have placed these harbingers within what was for the Mexica a rational context, that of one of their oldest and central myths: the return of the god Quetzalcóatl, the feathered serpent. The Spaniard was white and bearded and came from the East with bewildering technological superiority; Quetzalcóatl, similarly white and bearded, had disappeared to the East on a raft following his fall from grace, vowing eventual return. In a world where the gods were ever present, the mistaken identification of Cortés as an avatar of Quetzalcóatl was an eminently empirical deduction.[35] Faced with such a cosmological fait accompli, Moctezuma sent Cortés "the priestly trappings which befitted him" and sat back in indecisive despair, awaiting his arrival in Tenochtitlán to reclaim the throne: "He conceived within himself a feeling that great ills were coming upon him and his kingdom, and not just he, but all those who knew of these tidings, began to fear mightily."[36]

Moctezuma's lurch into ineffectuality was a surprising shift in character. After an initial—and perhaps ceremonially assumed—reluctance to accept the position of *tlatoani* (he who talks; the emperor), he had rapidly become a forceful and absolutist ruler.[37] On accession he removed all of Ahuitzótl's officials from his service, replacing them with noble-born candidates and sending those who had served the last emperor to execution.[38] Spearheading what has been portrayed as an aristocratic reaction, he went on to enforce draconian protocol in his relations with the Mexica. It was forbidden to look directly at his face or to wear shoes or anything but the coarsest clothing in his presence, and when he proceeded through the streets everyone bowed before him.[39] This authoritarianism was far more than a question of style: Moctezuma lived up to the literal meaning of his name, the man who is angered, making repeated use of arbitrary terror as an instrument of government. During one early campaign in Soconusco he sent instructions back to Tenochtitlán to behead all the tutors

Figure 4. Moctezuma II. From Juan de Tovar, *Historia de México* (ca. 1585); courtesy of the Kislak Collection of the Rare Book Division of the Library of Congress.

and attendants of his sons and wives.[40] His people, he explained to Cortés, "did not like being treated with love but with fear."[41] His people were not so sure; indigenous informants of Sahagún and Motolinía repeatedly condemned Moctezuma as extraordinarily cruel.[42]

Yet he could not be criticised as weak or incompetent—at least until 1519, when, confronted with the Spanish, he underwent psychological collapse. As Cortés made his way up from the coast, defeating the renowned Otomí, allying with the Mexica's traditional enemies the Tlaxcalans, descending into the valley and massacring the first city dwellers they encountered, his entire progress reinforced Moctezuma's worst suspicions. The Spanish, whatever they might be, were evidently obsessed with meeting the emperor in person: they had insisted on it from the first encounter.[43] And they had overwhelming magical allies in the form of cavalry and cannon, which the indigenous peoples believed (and were consistently encouraged to believe by Cortés) to be both sentient and intrinsically hostile.[44] The only viable defence against such aliens, Moctezuma seems to have reasoned, was itself magical. Yet when he dispatched his necromancers on a last-ditch attempt to keep Cortés out of his city, they met a drunk from Chalco who prophesied their abandonment by the gods and the fiery destruction of Tenochtitlán. And so he considered flight, and he attempted to pass off another noble as emperor on the first encounter with the Spanish, but he never organised a coherent resistance; rather, both evasiveness and magicians failing him, Moctezuma invited the Spanish into the city and lodged them in his father's palace.[45]

The following eight months, from November 1519 to June 1520, were characterised by a surreal relationship between invaders and invaded. A front stage display of labyrinthine courtesy covered the backstage reality of mutual ignorance, suspicion, and mistrust. And, constantly, fear. Neither side, each highly militarily able, held particular confidence in its chances of victory should the tense, constantly shifting modus vivendi collapse. The Mexica, inspired by both mythological and pragmatic concerns, their emperor verging on the useless as a source of effective leadership, saw Cortés's presence in the city as the advance guard of destruction long foretold. "They were," said Sahagún's informants, "awaiting death, and they talked of this among themselves, saying 'What can we do? Go where we may, we shall be destroyed. Let us await death here.'"[46] Meanwhile the Spanish, as soon as they had settled inside Tenochtitlán, began to consider the trap into which they had marched: a handful of men, perhaps as few as 250 foot soldiers and fifteen horsemen, in the heart of an unknown and intensely militarised society that was possessed of a vast army and, according to their indigenous allies, the decision to use it to annihilate them.[47]

And so, with that brilliant, improvisational thuggishness that underwrote much of Spanish success in the conquest, Cortés and his captains decided to kidnap Moctezuma. They had been in the city perhaps a week. Armed, and with the excuse of a Mexica attack on their coastal settlement, Veracruz, Cortés and a small escort visited Moctezuma's palace and presented him with the choice of accompanying them as prisoner or being killed on the spot. It was one of several critical moments that revealed Moctezuma's helplessness. Not only did he accompany them, but he also went along with Cortés's fiction that he was doing so freely on advice from his priests. He became, at a stroke, a puppet: a collaborator who still legislated in petty affairs of the Mexica but whose lack of real authority was rapidly demonstrated when Cortés put him in chains and publicly burned the captains who had attacked Veracruz.[48]

In the aftermath of that execution Cortés offered the emperor the chance to return to his palace, and he refused, in fear, says Torquemada, of his own people. Whether this is the case or whether, as Bernal Díaz claims, he recognised the speciousness of the offer is irrelevant.[49] What is clear is that the imprisonment of Moctezuma brought to the surface dormant tensions in the Mexica polity. Opposition to the emperor's policy of appeasement rapidly crystallised in a hawkish faction of nobility and priesthood; given Cuauhtémoc's later intransigence in the face of the Spanish, it seems likely that he was among them.[50] These hawks stayed initially within the discourse of absolute loyalty to the sovereign, restricting themselves to daily visits to Moctezuma in the Spanish quarters to urge war. But the emperor's acts of collaboration grew increasingly compromising. When the Spanish discovered the great treasure of Ahuitzótl concealed within their quarters, Moctezuma did not just give it to them but sent his silversmiths to assist in breaking it down. Provoked by first the kidnapping and then this imminent robbery, Cacama, king of Texcoco, began organizing a surprise attack on the Spanish; Moctezuma had the king arrested and handed over to Cortés, who garrotted him.[51] He appeared desperately eager for approval from his jailers; as Torquemada put it, "He would have done anything to make Cortés happy."[52]

Finally, in spring 1520, his people presented the still-captive Moctezuma with what seems to have been an ultimatum, couched again in the language of divine command, to make war on the Spanish. He warned Cortés and temporised, negotiating the Spanish time to build ships in which to depart. Whether they would actually have left is a moot point: before the ships were completed a second Spanish expedition arrived. With nineteen ships, over a thousand men, and nearly a hundred horses, it far outnumbered that of Cortés; and dispatched by his powerful enemy Diego Velázquez, governor of Cuba, it was hostile.[53] But it was commanded by the uninspiring Pánfilo de Nárvaez. Cortés directed a skillful campaign of subversion against Nárvaez's men, winning over with gold and promises several commanders and key parts of the army, such as the artillerymen. Then, at the end of May, he made a forced march from Tenochtitlán to the coast, fell on the new arrivals by night, and swiftly defeated them. There were very few casualties, and Cortés was able to incorporate Nárvaez's men into his own expedition, trebling his forces; it should have been a moment of both triumph and relief for Cortés.[54] But "just at the moment of victory news came from Mexico that Pedro de Alvarado was besieged in his quarters."[55] The Mexica had finally risen.

It was, of course, bound to happen: the most radical counterfactual cannot include peaceful coexistence between Spanish and Mexica. The two cultures were almost utterly antithetical, save in theocracy and deep-seated expansionism.[56] It was, however, no coincidence that the final rupture should come in Cortés's absence. He was a gifted Machiavellian, a born political juggler who had steadily increased his demands on the Mexica while maintaining an improbable peace. When he left for the coast he handed over command to Alvarado, who had Cortesian pretensions without (bar charm and courage) the corresponding abilities. It was an error, as Cortés recognised on his return.[57] Alvarado received rumours of a Mexica attack—nothing new for the Spanish—and, finesse failing him, eschewed diplomacy for terrorism. The Mexica had asked his leave to celebrate the festival of Huitzilopochtli, the god of war, in the main temple; he gave his permission and then, at the height of the celebration, launched an attack that carefully turned the temple compound into a killing ground. There were at the time six hundred dancers present, "the flower of the nobility," and almost all were killed.[58] The reaction, a disorderly but furious attack on the Spanish barracks, was immediate; it would have been terminal had Moctezuma not ordered the attackers to withdraw.[59]

At that point his people still obeyed him. When Cortés reentered the city on June 24, bolstered by Nárvaez's men and two thousand Tlaxcalans, he found the streets empty and the market closed but the fighting paused. He then compounded Alvarado's error by insulting Moctezuma, the only possible mediator, and releasing his brother Cuitláhuac as a messenger. Cuitláhuac was king of Iztapalapa and one of the hawks, imprisoned by Cortés for his part in Cacama's failed attack. Predictably enough, he never came back; the Mexica appointed him their leader, effectively deposing Moctezuma, and launched a massive assault on the Spanish quarters. After a short period of intense fighting Cortés tried once more to use Moctezuma, sending him onto the roof to urge the Mexica to cease their attacks and let the Spanish leave in peace.[60] But they were having none of it, and it was, according to the Codex Ramírez, Cuauhtémoc who was the first to defy his cousin the emperor, denouncing him as a scoundrel and a homosexual.[61] The Mexica then rained darts and stones onto the roof, wounding Moctezuma in the head, arm, and leg. The next day, "quite unexpectedly," he died.[62]

Their diplomacy in tatters, the only option left to the Spanish was retreat. Botello, the expedition's soothsayer, claimed to have foreseen total annihilation if they did not leave immediately; this was not a prediction that required second sight.[63] Facing the Spanish were some 150,000 to 200,000 indigenous soldiers; they themselves numbered around 1,450, accompanied by several thousand Tlaxcalans.[64] On the night of June 30 they attempted to sneak out of the city, bearing what they could of the treasure and a large portable bridge. The latter was vital, for Tenochtitlán was an island city, linked to the lakeshore by causeways punctuated by canals, from which the Mexica had removed the bridges. The withdrawal began in a light rain, the column heading west along the Tacuba causeway.[65] They managed to cross the first canal in safety, but the alert was given, and at the second canal the fighting began. The night turned to bloody chaos: the Spanish rapidly lost their bridge, and retreat became rout. At the canal of the Toltecs, attacked on both sides by canoes and pressured by the Mexica following them down the causeway, the panicking Spanish were forced to the water and were either drowned or killed in such numbers that the survivors found the gap bridged by corpses. Once on land, it took a week to fight their way back to the safe haven of Tlaxcala, where, decimated, they took stock.[66]

Cortés later claimed that he lost a mere 150 countrymen on that slaughterous night, which became known as the Noche Triste, the Sad Night. Other chroniclers' estimates vary wildly, with Bernal Díaz reporting 860, and Cano, 1,170 deaths; it would be tempting to take the 450 losses registered by Gómara, Ixtlilxóchitl, and Camargo as a useful average. But when Cortés mustered his men in late December his force totalled 590 men, and that after receiving at least 150 reinforcements in the autumn. He commanded by all accounts over fourteen hundred men before the outbreak of war; it would, consequently, seem evident that the Mexica killed toward nine hundred Spanish during the Noche Triste and its immediate aftermath.[67]

This indigenous victory was, however, short-lived. As the Spanish regrouped in Tlaxcala they gained a further advantage over the Mexica, a new, microbial ally: smallpox. The disease had been brought ashore in Veracruz by Francisco de Eguía, one of Nárvaez's black slaves; it broke out in epidemic at the end of September in Chalco.[68] Smallpox was common in Europe, and the Spanish had a correspondingly high degree of resistance, whereas the indigenous peoples had none whatsoever. As a result, "among them the sickness and pestilence was so great throughout the land that in most provinces more than half the people died, and in the others little less. . . . [T]hey died like flies."[69] This extensive mortality obviously weakened the Mexica's military strength and caused a generational shift in political leaders across central Mexico. In

Cholula, Tlaxcala, and various other towns it was Cortés who chose successors for the dead caciques, tightening his grip on the region.[70] In the valley of Tenochtitlán, it was the Mexica state council, because among the dead was their emperor, Cuitláhuac.[71]

In his place they chose Cuauhtémoc. The ritual admonition to a new tlatoani, if the Mexica priest gave it, must have rung particularly threatening:

> Perchance you will bear for a while the burden entrusted you, or perchance death will attack you and this your election to this kingdom will be but a dream. . . . [P]erchance God will permit that there be discord and riot in your kingdom, that you might be scorned and laid low, or perchance other kings who despise you will wage war on you, and you will be defeated and detested, or perchance God will permit that hunger and dearth fall upon your kingdom. What will you do if in your time your kingdom is destroyed, or our lord God unleashes his wrath upon you, sending plague? What will you do if in your time your kingdom is destroyed and your splendour becomes darkness?[72]

The Mexica's recent history had been disastrous, and Cortés was successfully recruiting allies among their neighbours for a further attack on the city. So the new emperor continued his predecessor's preparations for war. He sent emissaries to both subjects and sworn enemies, including the Tarascans and even the Tlaxcalans, offering new and favourable relationships in return for support. Meanwhile he gathered troops and strengthened Tenochtitlán's fortifications, deepening the canals, building walls, digging trenches, and sowing stakes underwater to defend against boats.[73] As captured Mexica told Cortés before the city was invested, "Cuauhtémoc's intentions . . . were that they would never make peace, but either kill us or die to the last person."[74]

The siege began on May 30, 1521.[75] The Spanish divided their forces, blockaded the three main causeways into Tenochtitlán, and cut the Chapultepec aqueduct, ending the city's fresh water supply. Cortés at first followed a raider's strategy, sallying daily down the causeways toward the city centre, burning houses and defences, and then retreating for the night. This was, however, painfully slow; the Mexica had sufficient manpower to rebuild many of the defences destroyed; and the Spanish, sleeping in half-ruined huts, eating grasshoppers, oppressed by the heavy rains and continuous fighting, grew impatient. The failure of their initial plan seemed confirmed on June 24, 25, and 26, when

Cuauhtémoc gathered his entire force for simultaneous night attacks on the Spanish camps and then launched all his men against Alvarado's camp. The Spanish, very nearly overrun, took heavy losses. In the aftermath they decided to attempt to end the siege rapidly with a three-pronged attack on the marketplace. It ended disastrously: Cuauhtémoc lured Cortés's contingent deep into the city and ambushed them. In addition to the many deaths, the Mexica took sixty-six Spanish alive—once more at one of the bridges—and sacrificed them.[76] The effect on Cortés was critical, and in defeat he decided to act on his earlier conclusion: "Seeing that those of the city were rebellious and showing such determination to defend themselves or die, I gathered from them two things: first, that we would have little or none of the wealth that they had taken from us, and second, that they . . . were forcing us to destroy them utterly."[77] Henceforth the war would be one of blockade, hunger, and attrition.

Cuauhtémoc's personalist leadership, sometimes fighting, sometimes directing operations from the top of one of the temples, was initially effective.[78] His men very nearly captured Cortés in the defeat of the bridge; in the aftermath, the combination of Mexica victory and subsequent propaganda succeeded in briefly scaring off many of Cortés's indigenous allies.[79] The Mexica, sometimes portrayed as condemned to lose through sheer incomprehension of their situation, were all too aware of the novelty—and gravity—of confrontation with the Spanish.[80] They fought not just with mass courage but also with the habitual sophistication of Mexica warfare, making use of spies, saboteurs, and complex ambushes. They adapted to the new weapons and tactics imported by the invaders: warriors learned to run in zigzags to confuse the aim of the bowmen and arquebusiers or to throw themselves to the ground and take cover from cannon fire. Indigenous armourers beat captured swords into scythes and lances, more effective weapons than anything they had made before. Commanders used the cover of night to strew boulders across open spaces such as the marketplace, hindering the deployment of cavalry inside the city.[81] And yet for all that Cuauhtémoc faced certain structural disadvantages that made defeat the most probable ending.

There was for a start a technological abyss separating the two sides. The Mexica fought with shield and *macquahuitl*, a wooden sword edged with obsidian; for projectiles they used spear-throwers, bows, and hand-thrown stones.[82] These were weapons that tended to disable rather than kill. They were mismatched against the lethal early modern arms that the Spanish used: steel swords and armour, crossbows and arquebuses, cannon and cavalry. The horsemen, in particular, were extraordinarily difficult to combat. Their value to the Spanish was such that Cortés, in reporting the death of a mare, expressed more grief than he did in describing some human deaths.[83] In addition to the weapons they imported, the Spanish also fabricated more in the course of the war. Some, such as the trebuchet (a siege catapult) put together by a veteran of the Italian wars, were useless.[84] But others, such as the replacement gunpowder made with sulphur extracted from the crater of Popocatepétl or the thousands of arrows shaped by the indigenous allies, were essential.[85] One of these improvised weapons, wrote Cortés, was "the key to the entire war": the brigantines.[86]

These thirteen small ships, heavily manned and armed with gunners (and later cannon), gave Cortés control of the lake. He had the hulls built in Tlaxcala in the winter and spring and then carried by eight thousand porters more than fifty miles from that kingdom to the lakeshore.[87] Cuauhtémoc quickly realised their significance, and before they were even launched he had three times sent in saboteurs to try to burn them.[88] The Mexica fleets found themselves hopelessly overpowered by these ships, far larger, faster, and more heavily armed than their canoes. Consequently, the Spanish were able to raid the outskirts of the city with relative impunity and to send reinforcements rapidly to any camp that came under attack. Most important of all, the brigantines converted Tenochtitlán's great advantage as a fortress, its isolation by a vast natural moat, into strategic weakness. The city was densely populated and utterly dependent on imported food for survival. By patrolling the lake night and day the Spanish cut the Mexica supply lines, and by mid-July the city began to starve.[89]

To attribute Cuauhtémoc's eventual defeat to this technological superiority and the blockade it enabled would be, however, to miss the point. The blockade could never have worked were it not for the conversion of the lakeside towns and villages to the Spanish cause; and the brigantines could never have been built and transported without Tlaxcalan manpower. The entire Spanish campaign is, in fact, unthinkable without the very active indigenous alliances, which began in the mountains of Tlaxcala and steadily expanded until they encompassed virtually all of the central Mexican peoples. The Mexica Empire, as much as submitting to conquest, fell apart as soon as its subjects understood the centre's weakness.

Perhaps terms such as *empire* and *hegemony* are in themselves overstatements. The Mexica dominated an extensive area by force, demanding privileges and tribute in return for peace; there is scant evidence of much consent. They did not incorporate those who submitted into any overarching cultural system, and they did not create strong affective bonds with their subject peoples. They were, rather, despised by those they had conquered. From the coast to the central valley the Spanish found people who professed nothing but enmity toward their overlords. The Cempoalans, on first meeting with Cortés, "broke into bitter complaints," proclaiming themselves "grievously oppressed" by Moctezuma. The Tlaxcalans called the Mexica "wicked traitors," while farther south in Oaxaca they "were so heartily loathed . . . for the robberies they committed that no one could bear to see them or mention them by name." In fact, Bernal Díaz concluded, "all the towns and provinces that Moctezuma had raided and subdued were very hostile to the Mexicans, and their people were forced into battle and fought against their will."[90] As Moctezuma himself said, they were ruled by fear. When the calculus of fear shifted in favour of the Spanish, loyalties followed. By the end of June 1521 Cortés was backed by well over one hundred thousand indigenous troops, with more arriving as more towns went over to the Spanish. Meanwhile, inside Tenochtitlán, transmuted from one of the world's great cities into a crumbling, packed prison camp, Cuauhtémoc faced desertions, betrayals, and a steady sapping of strength.[91]

It was not just on the periphery that the inherent fragility of their political system weighed against the Mexica. Their closest neighbours were equally quick to turn on them. Early in the siege Cuauhtémoc called for reinforcements from the lakeside towns such as Mixcoac and Xochimilco: the latter sent canoe-loads of warriors into the city, where, instead of joining the defence, they took the opportunity to rob houses and to carry off slaves.[92] They then went over to the Spanish, completing the capital's isolation.[93] Disunity was endemic even within the cities of the Triple Alliance, the Mexicas' partners in empire. There the outbreak of war with the Spanish had been followed by a violent power struggle. In Texcoco Cacama's successor, suspected (unjustly says Cortés, who ought to know) of pro-Spanish sympathies, was assassinated by his younger brother Cohuanacotzin.[94] In Tenochtitlán Cuauhtémoc ruthlessly purged Moctezuma's closest associates, hunting down his servants and executing as many of the former emperor's—his cousin's—male children as he could lay hands on. The bloody Shakespearean strife peaked, according to the *Anales de Tlatelolco*, immediately before the siege began: its effects on the Mexica were catastrophic.[95] While Cohuanacotzin and the more intransigent Texcocans joined Cuauhtémoc in the defence of Tenochtitlán, Cortés's puppet ruler in Texcoco sent seventy thousand Texcocan troops to join the Spanish attack. "Your Majesty might well consider," Cortés wrote to his emperor, ". . . what

Figure 5. Unknown artist, *The Conquest of Tenochtitlán*, seventeenth century; courtesy of the Kislak Collection of the Rare Book Division of the Library of Congress.

POR CORTES. N° 7

31

the people of Tenochtitlán would feel to see coming against them those whom they held to be vassals and friends, relatives and brothers, and even fathers and sons."[96] The illegitimacy of the system that Cuauhtémoc inherited left him facing, as much as an invasion, a civil war.

It was also a total war. The Spanish were shocked at the intensity of the fighting, even in the dying days of the siege: "The arrows and darts were so thick," related Sahagún, "that the whole sky seemed yellow."[97] The indigenous allies "knew of nothing but killing."[98] The standard-bearers were changed daily, for they came off "so badly battered that no one could carry the standards into battle a second time."[99] And yet, while Spanish casualties were high, mortality was low. The Mexica, on the other hand, suffered enormous losses from the start. The first skirmish in Iztapalapa cost them some six thousand dead. By mid-July the combination of bad water, hunger, and disease was killing people on a scale approaching that of the fighting; Cortés later attributed fifty thousand deaths to their joint action. When under cover of darkness the Mexica began to forage on the city borderlands, Cortés planned a dawn ambush that killed and captured over eight hundred of what he described as the most miserable, mostly unarmed, women and children.[100] By the end of the siege, broad estimates of Mexica deaths from the fighting alone were upward of a hundred thousand.[101] Such decimation was off the scale of contemporary European warfare. The Battle of Stoke of 1487, which effectively ended the Wars of the Roses, was fought with a total of four thousand casualties.[102] The destruction of Tenochtitlán, for several chroniclers, could only be compared to the Roman destruction of Jerusalem.[103]

Inside the city Cuauhtémoc received regular offers of peace from the Spanish; what he made of them is unclear. While later, hagiographic accounts of his life stress his unflagging resistance, contemporary accounts offer a more nuanced version. He had, according to Gómara, considered treating with the Spanish at the beginning of the siege but had met opposition from his counsellors.[104] The timing is improbable; far more believable is Bernal Díaz's detailed account of a meeting with his leading warriors and priests mid-siege, when Cuauhtémoc had tried everything and was facing the realisation of predetermined defeat. He advocated peace; the council advised him to keep fighting. Cuauhtémoc told them, "somewhat angrily," that if that was their decision, they would fight to the end.[105] He was as good as his word and used further parleys with Cortés as mere opportunities to reinforce defences and make arrows. On July 26 Cortés linked up with Alvarado in the city centre and burned Cuauhtémoc's palaces;

they controlled, by then, over three-quarters of the city.[106] The emperor continued to refuse to negotiate, even as the remaining Mexica began to waver. "I knew well," wrote Cortés, "that only the king and three or four more of the city's principal men were not giving in, because the other people, dead or alive, already wanted out of there." When he sent a Texcocan nobleman as a further peace emissary, Cuauhtémoc had him sacrificed immediately.[107]

The siege was consequently fought to the bitter end. The surviving Mexica were driven to a final stand in a small enclave in the north of the city. For weeks they had eaten whatever came to hand, and not much did: rats, lizards, worms, and marsh grass. They had dug up roots and stripped the bark from the trees in the search for food.[108] Running out of warriors, Cuauhtémoc had resorted to arming the women and children and sending them out to the rooftops to fight.[109] The streets and the houses were filled with corpses; it was impossible to walk without treading them underfoot.[110] A contemporary elegy gives some of the horror of the last days:

Worms swarm through the streets and squares,
and the walls are splattered with our brains.
Red run the waters, red as if dyed;
And when we drink of them,
It is as though we drank
Salt water.[111]

On August 12, after waiting two days for Cuauhtémoc to come to peace talks, Cortés sent his indigenous allies in once more. "There followed," in Inga Clendinnen's description, "a massacre, of men who no longer had arrows, javelins, or stones; of women and children stumbling and falling on the bodies of their own dead."[112] His forces killed and captured more than forty thousand; "the screaming and weeping of the women and children were so great," wrote Cortés, "that there was no one whose heart it would not break."[113] Cuauhtémoc, however, still refused to surrender. Finally, on August 13, the Spanish stormed the last stronghold. Cuauhtémoc and his leading noblemen tried to escape, in a large canoe; but before they could make the safety of the reed beds they were intercepted by a brigantine. Its captain, García de Holguín, took the emperor back to Cortés in Tlatelolco. He met the Spaniard and said, weeping, "Lord Malinche, I have assuredly done my duty in defence of my city and vassals, and I can do no more. I am brought by force into your presence and beneath your power. Take the dagger you have in your belt, and strike me dead immediately."[114]

Cortés's reply was conciliatory: that he respected Cuauhtémoc's defence of Tenochtitlán, that he only wished peace had come earlier, and that Cuauhtémoc should continue as ruler of Mexico. He had nothing to fear. This was, however, more oratory than reality. Soldiers combing the ruined city for gold turned up little Mexica treasure. After two years of living in hardship, uncertainty, and often mortal danger, the haul was so paltry that the ordinary foot soldier was promised fifty or sixty pesos in the division of spoils.[115] This was plainly unacceptable, to both the soldiers and the king's treasurers; and the rumour spread that Cortés had instructed Cuauhtémoc to hide the majority of the gold for his own profit. Cortés was not a man who took kindly to auditors, and he had a long history of enmity with the officers of the Royal Treasury. They had accused him of abstracting part of Ahuitzótl's hoard in 1520; he, in turn, blamed his worst defeat during the siege on the disobedience of the treasurer Julián de Alderete.[116] The royal officials were consequently willing to believe that Cortés had plotted to steal the lion's share of the gold, and to prove their hypothesis they tortured Cuauhtémoc.[117]

He was tied down, and his hands and feet were burned with oil.[118] Beside him, and in a similar fashion, they tortured his cousin Tetlepanquetzal, lord of Tacuba and a particular favourite of the emperor. Exactly what happened next is obscure; the Spanish seem retrospectively ashamed of their violent shabbiness, preferring to gloss over the incident whenever possible. Cortés, in his detailed letters to Charles V, avoided any reference whatsoever to the torture.[119] It seems, however, that Tetlepanquetzal was the first to break; according to Gómara's mythopoeic version, he looked across pleadingly at Cuauhtémoc for relief, at which sign of weakness the emperor asked him if he thought that he himself was enjoying his bath.

But Bernal Díaz, who had the incomparable advantage of actually being there, remembers none of this set piece grandeur in adversity. From Bernal Díaz's account there is nothing redemptive about the scene at all: the men were tortured and talked. Tetlepanquetzal made a false confession, claiming to have treasure hidden in Tacuba. Taken there by Alvarado and the author himself, Tetlepanquetzal, evidently in agonizing pain, "said that he had only told us this story in the hopes of dying on the road, and invited us to kill him, for he possessed neither gold nor jewels."[120] Cuauhtémoc in turn divulged the resting place of some minor articles in a pond in his palace grounds and claimed

Figure 6. Bas relief of Cuauhtémoc's torture from the Avenida Reforma monument in Mexico City; photograph by Lyman Johnson.

that everything else had been cast into the lake when defeat became imminent. With that the torture ended, leaving Bernal Díaz, Cortés, and certain other Spaniards "very much distressed" and Cuauhtémoc crippled.[121]

The next three years must have been bitter for Cuauhtémoc. He was initially used by Cortés as an intermediary between victors and vanquished, transmitting the Spaniard's orders to the Mexica and, with markedly less effect, the Mexicas' complaints to Cortés.[122] The early glib promise of continued power for the emperor, a satrapy of sorts, was, however, betrayed. His only future political role would be as object lesson to other leaders of the cost of noncooperation: when the lord of Michoacán was brought to Mexico, Cortés intimidated him by sending him to see the results of torture on Cuauhtémoc.[123] Excluding the last emperor from any position of influence was, in terms of realpolitik, eminently understandable. In the immediate postconquest period the Spanish were nervously conscious of the improbable fragility, and reversibility, of their victory. Hence, perhaps, the peculiar cruelty with which some of the high guardians of

Mexica culture were treated, torn apart by the dogs that the Spanish bred for war.[124] Cuauhtémoc was the most threatening of the remaining Mexica elite. He had been the centre, real and symbolic, of resistance and continued to be so even in defeat: it is his relatives whom Gómara identifies as leading guerrilla warfare against the Spanish in the early reconstruction period.[125] And so, just as he had done before and during the war, Cortés exploited preexisting political divisions to achieve control. Cuauhtémoc's second-in-command, Tlacotzin, the man who held the position of *cihuacóatl*, the "woman snake," was a survivor from the reign of Moctezuma, well known by Cortés. He had signalled himself on various occasions as more malleable than the last emperor in treating with the Spanish; he seems to have been prime material for a quisling.[126] He became one, reappointed to his former title by Cortés and given sole authority over the Mexica barrio of Tlatelolco in the reemerging, ethnically segregated city. Pedro de Moctezuma, one of the former emperor's few surviving sons and hence an automatic enemy of Cuauhtémoc, was given another barrio.[127] Cuauhtémoc, meanwhile, was given what amounted to a perpetual prison sentence, brought out for ceremonial purposes—accompanying Cortés on his processions through the city or joining the delegation to greet the first Franciscan missionaries in 1523—and incarcerated the rest of the time.[128] It was no conciliatory peace, and it is no surprise that even as the process of conversion to Christianity began to gain momentum, Cuauhtémoc remained unbaptised and a source of fear to the Spanish. There is no evidence that he was in any way assimilated to the new order. He was, rather, perpetually a rebellion in potential, a threat waiting to be realised, "a troublesome man" to Cortés; and so when Cortés decided to leave the city for the lengthy expedition south to Hibueras, it was natural that he should take Cuauhtémoc with him.[129]

Cortés never meant to go to Hibueras, the new Spanish colony in what is now Honduras; he had instead dispatched one of his captains, Cristóbal de Olid. Olid had set out in early 1524 with a powerful fleet of six ships and four hundred men, funded by thirty-six thousand pesos of Cortés's personal fortune.[130] He was ordered to sail to Cuba to purchase horses and arms; to round Cape Catoche, the northeastern point of the Yucatán Peninsula; and then to head south to settle the Cape of Honduras. His expedition was part of the ambitious project of expansion that occupied Cortés and—perhaps more important—his commanders in the immediate postconquest years. But Olid had other ideas. Like almost all of Cortés's men, he undoubtedly felt deceived by the paucity of profits from the sack of Tenochtitlán. He had already disobeyed

Cortés in 1522 and led an expedition to Michoacán into defeat in Colima, causing Cortés to briefly imprison him.[131] He may have felt passed over in favour of other commanders whom Cortés seemed to prefer, such as Sandoval and Alvarado; he may also have felt himself to be Cortés's equal (which in terms of social caste, he was) and been, by a fine stroke of irony, inspired by Cortés's own desperate gamble of disobedience to Diego Velázquez. Whatever his exact blend of motives, he made contact in Cuba with Cortés's principal enemy, the same Velázquez, and made a pact with him to place the new colony under his, and not Cortés's, jurisdiction.[132]

In Cortés's eyes this was evident rebellion and, most galling, rebellion funded by his own money. He sent a punitive expedition, which he considered leading personally before appointing a cousin, Francisco de las Casas, as commander. It failed: after the first skirmish de las Casas's fleet was wrecked in the night by a northerly, and the survivors were pressed into service with Olid.[133] Cortés ("blinded by rage," says Aguilar) then decided to send a further expedition, this time overland, and to lead it himself.[134] Even at the time it appeared irresponsible, near-certain folly: chroniclers such as Gómara, Aguilar, and Durán all stressed how depleted Mexico's defences would be left after Cortés's departure.[135] But it was not just those left behind who had good reason to doubt. The expedition itself was unbalanced: a journey of some fifteen hundred miles, much of it through unexplored swamplands, where "there was no path to be found on any side, nor even a trace of anybody having travelled by land, because they all [the local peoples] make use of the water because of the great rivers and swamps." For navigation they relied on what Cortés described as "a diagram on a cloth" that the rulers of Tabasco and Xicalango had sent him.[136] His plan was so self-evidently weak that Cortés did not even make it public, claiming that the official aim was to conquer the Zapotecs. No one, however, was taken in.[137] Bernal Díaz, co-opted like the majority of the available Spanish veterans, left a disgusted summary of the expedition: "At a time when we should have been recovering from our great labours and trying to get together some properties and farms, he sent us on a journey of more than five hundred leagues, and most of the land we were passing through at war, and we left for lost whatever we had."[138]

The hubris that seemed to underlie Cortés's plan was also suggested in the composition of the expedition. The army was formed by at least 250 foot soldiers and 130 horsemen, backed by three thousand Mexica auxiliaries, comforted by a herd of pigs, two falconers, a band of musicians, a tumbler, and a puppeteer.[139]

They left Tenochtitlán on October 12, 1524, taking with them (for the security of that city) many of its former nobles, including Cuauhtémoc, Tetlepanquetzal, Cohuanacotzin, and the cihuacóatl, Tlacotzin.[140] It was, initially, a triumphant procession, which must have appeared more a royal progress than any serious military expedition. Every village through which this exotic party passed on their march southeast greeted them with a formal reception and a fiesta.[141] The farther they travelled, however, the more hostile the environment became and the more obstacles they met, particularly among the intermeshed swamps and rivers of the Gulf Coast. Even before reaching Espíritu Santo, the last Spanish settlement of any importance on their route and the expedition's forward camp in Tabasco, they had begun to suffer the effects of travelling through such waterlogged country: in crossing a river Cortés lost some personal baggage and was unable to recover it, intimidated by the size of the caimans.[142] After Espíritu Santo the terrain grew more difficult, and their progress slowed further as they struggled across a watery landscape, wading where they could and bridging the rest. At one point, before they had even reached the Río Grijalva, they were forced to construct fifty bridges within sixty miles.[143]

It was after crossing the Grijalva that the expedition really ran into trouble. Cortés sent a party downriver to meet the ships that he had dispatched from Coatzalcoalcos; they returned with a small amount of food and the news that only one of the three caravels had arrived at the rendezvous. His supply line had failed.[144] This left him dependent on the local Maya, but they vanished, leaving the expedition bereft of provisions and—equally importantly—guides. Cortés, congenitally incapable of turning back, floundered along a dismal trail of deserted and burned-out villages eastward across the Tabasco Plain. When the Spanish did capture guides or receive directions, they were frequently inaccurate or misleading, the local ruler having ordered his people to obstruct the intruders wherever possible. In Iztapa, one of the few populated villages they found, Cortés asked the Maya to build bridges and supply him with canoes; they refused and encouraged his departure with the news that it was a mere three days' march to the next settlement.[145] It was instead seven days, which Cortés describes in a litany emblematic of the whole journey:

> On leaving the village I came upon a very large swamp, which goes on for more than half a league, and with many branches and greenery which the Indians our friends [the Mexica auxiliaries] threw into it, we were able to cross, and then we came to a deep estuary where it

was necessary to make a bridge over which we might pass the baggage and the saddles, with the horses swimming across; and once past this estuary we came to another half swamp, which goes on for a good league and never fell below the horses' knees, and often came up to the cinches; but as there was some ground underneath, we went on without danger until we came to the woodland, in which we spent two days opening a path in the direction signalled us by the guides, up until the point that they said they were mistaken, that they did not know where they were going; and the bush was such that one saw no further than where one put one's feet on the ground, or looking up, the brightness of the sky; such was the density and height of the trees that even though some were climbed, [the men] saw no further than a stone's throw.[146]

By the time they found the next village and some paltry supplies, four Spaniards, including the tumbler, had died.[147]

Cortés's solution was to push as hard as possible south toward the next province, Acalán, sending a scout party ahead to persuade its people of his peaceful intentions and to solicit food. His situation was increasingly desperate. The combination of hunger, disease, and fatigue was killing his army, particularly the Mexica auxiliaries. Cannibalism emerged, among both the Mexica, who trapped local Indians—including, unfortunately, two of the guides—and roasted them in pit ovens, and the Spanish. It was the musicians, who had long since stopped playing from hunger, who are recorded as experimenting: "Medrano, flautist of the church of Toledo, claimed to have eaten the brains of Medina, trombonist, a native of Seville, and the tripe and brains of Bernaldo Caldera and a cousin of his, for they were dying of hunger."[148] When Cortés sent out a requisitioning party of Spaniards, they disappeared, either dying or deserting.[149] His men had lost faith in his leadership and in their chances of survival, and finally, foreseeably, they mutinied. Cortés ordered them to build yet another bridge, to pass a particularly formidable estuary, and they refused. It was eventually the Mexica who built it, obeying their own lords.[150] On crossing it, the army met the scout party from Acalán, which had succeeded in bringing back some maize and hens. Far from restoring order, this exacerbated Spanish divisions: the soldiers mobbed the supplies, depriving Cortés and his commanders of any food at all. Their suggestion, when he remonstrated with them, was that he eat his herd of swine. Cortés was furious; he must, also, have been disturbed by the evident contrast between the cohesive discipline of the Mexica and the rebelliousness of the Spanish.[151]

It was consequently a weakened and demoralised expedition that arrived in late February 1525 to the town of Izankanak, capital of Acalán, somewhere in the Río Candelaria basin where Mexico meets Guatemala.[152] What Cuauhtémoc must have been thinking by then is unknowable, but the Spanish already feared the worst: an indigenous rising. The Mexica "raised by night an uproar with their drums, bones, shells and horns, and as it was greater and more frequent than before, the Spanish became suspicious and asked the cause. They became wary of them [the Mexica], whether from hints or hard proof I know not, and went about permanently armed."[153] It was then, in the night, that a traitor came to Cortés. He gave the Spaniard a piece of paper that detailed a conspiracy of the kings, led by Cuauhtémoc, to fall on the battered Spanish army and wipe it out. The rebels would then raise forces among the Maya and attack Olid's settlement in Honduras, while a simultaneous rising in Tenochtitlán would easily overcome the inexperienced skeleton garrison. With Cortés dead and Tenochtitlán resurgent, the remaining scattered Spanish outposts could be readily mopped up, while the ports would be heavily garrisoned to prevent both escape and reinforcement. The idea was complex, long-discussed, and eminently realisable.[154]

So at least said Cortés. But without falling into interpretative extremes— one modern account creatively posits that the entire Hibueras expedition was an elaborate Spanish design to do away with Cuauhtémoc—there are suggestive differences between this and other narratives.[155] There is, for a start, no real agreement as to whether the plot genuinely existed. As Jorge Gurría Lacroix observes, with the exception of Ixtlilxóchitl and Torquemada, all contemporary or near-contemporary authors who treat the events in Acalán mention some form of Mexica conspiracy.[156] There is, however, an important cleavage between those who accepted Cortés's claim of a serious threat and those who perceived the entire affair as maliciously constructed out of idle asides and meaningless gossip between the Mexica leaders. For Tezozómoc the accusation was evidently false, the product of simple calumny by the Tlatelolcas. Ixtlilxóchitl traced the entire plot to an innocuous conversation between Cuauhtémoc and the kings of Tacuba and Texcoco, in which they ironically discussed which of them should rule the provinces they were so successfully conquering and which Cortés overheard and paranoiacally misinterpreted. But belief in Cuauhtémoc's innocence was not confined to indigenous historiography. Durán diplomatically related that the emperor was "accused" of conspiracy, leaving his actual guilt open to question. Torquemada went further and acquitted Cuauhtémoc of any responsibility whatsoever, denying the existence of any intention of rebellion.[157] Most convincing of all, Bernal Díaz believed that the Mexica had discussed the possibility of rising but that Cuauhtémoc had neither originated nor agreed with the idea. And he was not, he added, alone in this opinion: Cuauhtémoc's condemnation "appeared wrong to all of us who were on that expedition."[158]

Aside from the tangibility of the conspiracy, the other central question raised by the diversity of memories surrounding the events in Acalán is the identity of the traitor. In the Chontal Text's version, the local cacique, Paxbolonacha, betrays Cuauhtémoc; yet this is unsubstantiated and suspiciously politically convenient for its authors in the new colonial order. Discounting it as unreliable, the remaining contemporary sources tell two superficially conflicting stories. According to Cortés, Gómara, Torquemada, Tezozómoc, Ixtlilxóchitl, and Chimalpahín, a man called either Mexicatzincatl or Coztemexi emerged from anonymity to inform the Spanish of his people's plans. In Bernal Díaz's and Martín Ecatzin's accounts, however, the traitor is far from an embittered or opportunistic nobody: it is instead Tlacotzin, the cihuacóatl and Cortés's puppet in Tenochtitlán. Cortés's grandson further supports this explanation, with the brief yet telling claim that the traitor was one of the kings themselves.[159] Cortés went on, while still in Acalán, to make Tlacotzin, baptised Juan Velázquez, king of Tenochtitlán. This might well have been a reward for services rendered.[160] The cihuacóatl's motivation, additionally, seems clear. He had long since thrown his lot in with the Spanish, and their overthrow would have been for him at the best prejudicial and at the worst—and most likely—fatal. As for the other informer, Mexicatzincatl, he need not be discarded; as Barlow suggests, it is probable that there was more than one traitor (Bernal Díaz himself records two).[161] That Cortés and most indigenous historians should choose to overlook the most important of them is understandable. Men such as Tezozómoc and Ixtlilxóchitl wanted to cast the blame as unequivocally as possible on Cortés, and the revelation that Cuauhtémoc had been betrayed by one of the Mexica elite and a close relative (his nephew) would have undermined their case.[162] As for Cortés, to have revealed that he judged Cuauhtémoc on the basis of information provided by the last emperor's political rival would have cast that judgment into further disrepute.

While we cannot ever make Cuauhtémoc's implication or innocence in the alleged plot more than a hypothesis, it is not just his contemporaries and later

Figure 7.
*Cuauhtémoc hanged,
1525.* Codex
Vaticanus A,
reproduced
in Viscount
Kingsborough,
*Antiquities of
Mexico: Comprising
facsimiles of ancient
Mexican paintings
and hieroglyphics,*
vol. 2 (London,
1830–48); courtesy
of the Butler Library,
Columbia University.

historians who viewed his condemnation as at best tendentious and at worst plain murderous. Cortés himself quickly regretted his actions. After Acalán he could not sleep, "ill humoured, and still very reflective and unhappy with the gruelling route we had taken, and with how he had ordered Cuauhtémoc and his cousin the lord of Tacuba hanged without justice."[163] It could be that he received the news of the conspiracy, his expedition in chaos, and panicked. It could equally be that he was presented with an opportunity to reinforce his shaken authority and to rid himself of a turbulent priest-king and took it.[164] Whatever the case, on February 28, 1525, he ordered the dawn arrests of the principal indigenous leaders and after cursory interrogation condemned Cuauhtémoc to death. Cuauhtémoc and Tetlepanquetzal, the lord of Tacuba, were hanged from a silk-cotton tree in the dark.[165] Eloquence did not desert Cuauhtémoc at the end, and before he died he left an indictment of Cortés. "O Malinche," he told the Spaniard, "for many days I have understood that you would condemn me to this death, and have known your false words. . . . [W]hy do you kill me unjustly? God will demand it of you."[166] Cuauhtémoc's body was left hanging from the tree as the expedition moved out; and then it disappeared.

Chapter 2

Resurrection

Puebla de los Angeles 1537 By the Holy grace of God I Leave to my sons that
Remembrance and blessing to my beloved Sons in Jesus Christ which is the
immortal Record that in 1529 Ychicatupan I buried Lord King Cuatemo.
—The letter of the reliquary, attributed to the Franciscan Motolinía,
discovered in Ixcateopan, Guerrero, 1949

OVER FOUR CENTURIES LATER A HITHERTO UNKNOWN PARISH PRIEST
delivered a sermon that within days reached the president and the front pages
of the Mexico City papers.[1] On February 2, 1949, in place of the predictable
pieties of the Sunday address, Padre David Salgado surprised his congregation.
He claimed to have proof that Cuauhtémoc was buried beneath the altar of his
church, in a village so remote that men argued over the spelling of its name:
Ixcateopan.[2]

Ixcateopan was a small, bleakly picturesque settlement in the arid northern sierra of Guerrero, historically one of the poorest states in Mexico. In 1950
the state had the lowest rates of literacy, urban employment, industrialisation,
and capital investment; the second lowest rural salaries; and what was said to be
the highest murder rate in the federation.[3] The law, one hack wrote, "was represented by the rifle, the .45 and the machete"; life, in the Hobbesian paraphrase of
the governor, was "semicolonial, impoverished and ruinous."[4] Ixcateopan was
admittedly the cabecera, the administrative centre, of its eponymous municipality. Yet that was one of the poorer municipalities in Guerrero: its annual tax
revenues were lower than all but six of the state's other municipalities, summing

Figure 8. The village of Ixcateopan in 1949. Photograph by Armando Salmerón Moctezuma; by permission of the Salmerón family.

under a quarter the national average.[5] The land had always been poor: the colonial official who surveyed it in 1579 told King Philip II that "there is no flat land, all is hills, and very rocky ones. . . . [T]he earth is chalky and infertile."[6] Particularly in the rainy season, the village looked misleadingly lush from a distance. A simple, well-proportioned colonial church formed its centre, on the long crest of a low hill. Around the church, the main square was bordered by the houses of the village rich, well-sized tiled rectangles enclosing small patios, islands of cool in the hot months. Abundant trees covered the slopes as the land fell away from the *barrio de arriba*, "the barrio at the top," and covered the smaller, poorer, more ramshackle adobe houses of the *barrio de abajo*, the "barrio below" in terms of both space and class. Yet the trees thinned across the mountains that surrounded the village for miles, exposing the dry slopes of thinly cultivated cornfields, grazing pastures, and scrubland. Good land was scarce, limited to the narrow valley floors, and farming was hard and unrewarding. Tax returns do not generally overstate wealth. Yet even allowing for

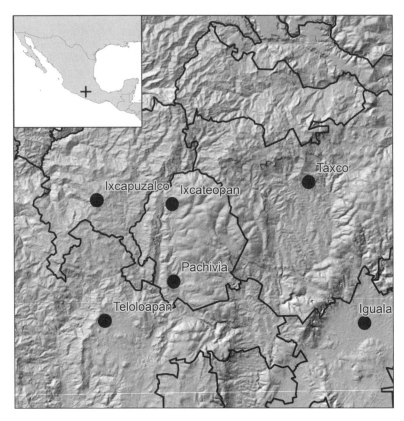

Figure 9. Ixcateopan and its immediate surroundings, with topography, main settlements, and municipal divisions; courtesy of Eric Glass, Electronic Data Service, Columbia University.

considerable exaggerations of poverty, the tax returns for Ixcateopan's ranchers outline an unforgiving place, where most people's small properties were scrubland or barren and where corn could only be planted every two, eight, or even ten years.[7] Wealth was a relative, localised concept: land in the valleys, livestock on the uplands, a shop in the village, and some local trade. This was enough to set apart the elite, a small bourgeoisie, from the poor whom they dominated and whose only way out was quite often the literal one of leaving. In the village archives, a poster from 1929 warned villagers of the dangers of emigrating to Depression-era America; by 1950, though, more people were leaving this relatively small municipio than anywhere else in Guerrero bar Acapulco.[8]

The villagers who stayed, some 1,385 of them by the 1950 census, were in the main accustomed to eking out a subsistence livelihood as smallholders, sharecroppers, and day labourers.[9] Commerce was basic, reflected in a handful of shops and a handful of artisans: four cobblers, two tailors, one ironmonger. The village itself did not have a cornmill, one of the most basic industries in rural Mexico, and so poor women continued to rise well before dawn to grind corn for tortillas. (Although many villagers also said that they ate wheat bread, a claim to the superior status of modern urbanites.)[10] Families could be riven by quarrels, but family networks were critical sources of labour, credit, and comfort, and people extended them through compadrazgo, the "fictive kinship" of godparenting. Government was a distant, sporadically present, and usually unwelcome visitor, whose agents turned up to tax, to conscript, or to prevent logging. Crime—the only reason countrypeople ever wanted more rather than less state—was generally petty, and bar the occasional cantina shootout or peasant ambush, Ixcateopan was relatively peaceful.[11] The symbols of modern life were sparse: the developmentalist dictatorship of Porfirio Díaz had provided a town clock and a telephone, but the telephone worked erratically, and the clock failed forever in the mid-1920s.[12] In the late 1940s the village still lacked electricity, running water, or a sewage system.[13] Although it was just over twenty miles to Taxco, one of the state's bigger towns, the trails that connected Ixcateopan to the outside world were in permanently dilapidated conditions, and men travelling by mule or pony took the best part of a day to reach either Taxco or the city of Iguala.[14] Had they a jeep, it would still take five or six hours to reach the state capital, Chilpancingo; but there were no jeeps in Ixcateopan. The governor had one, an ex–World War II Willys, but he had only visited the villagers once.[15] (They had, after all, complained that his election was rigged.)[16] As the tourist industry took off in Acapulco, the sole attraction that Ixcateopan held for visitors lay in the incongruity of its walls, paving, and larger houses, all fashioned from a locally quarried marble. It was an isolated village, in decline, or as one villager put it, "a hidden pueblo, which no one knew existed."[17]

Padre Salgado's sermon changed that.[18] The *presidente municipal* of Teloloapan, a town to the south, had happened to be in Ixcateopan that day to inaugurate the new telephone line and had gone to mass. He returned impressed and related the story to Bernardo Salgado, a Teloloapan landowner who worked as a stringer for the national newspapers. Bernardo Salgado wired *El Universal* the news and then went to Ixcateopan himself to find out more. Meanwhile, as the story made its tortuous way toward publication, the Ixcateopan village council had gone straight from the sermon to examine the evidence on which it was based and shortly thereafter informed the state government of the discovery.[19] The news caused uproar: by the end of the month journalists were roaming the village, a stream of visitors had begun to arrive and light candles in front of the church, and in the main square a banner read "Welcome to the Cradle of Cuauhtémoc."[20] Ixcateopan had been noticed.

Underlying the village's sudden prominence was a cloth-wrapped bundle of papers that Salvador Rodríguez Juárez found in his house, hidden, by one account, behind a shrine to the Virgen de la Asunción.[21] Salvador Rodríguez Juárez was one of the most knowledgeable men in the village: literate, inventive, possessor of a comparatively extensive library, and a completely unfounded reputation as a qualified doctor.[22] When he came across the seemingly sixteenth-century manuscripts and attached papers, however, he was unsure of their significance, and so he sought the priest's opinion.[23] He showed Padre Salgado a parish file entitled "Títulos del pueblo de Ixcateopan," which contained thirty-three pages relating to a land dispute between Ixcateopan and the hacienda of Zacatlán at the beginning of the nineteenth century, and an icon of the Virgin of the Assumption supposedly brought to Mexico in the early sixteenth century by the Franciscan missionary Motolinía. These were the kinds of local treasures to be found in every other village in the country. But he also showed the priest a book, *Destierro de Ignorancias y Amigo de Penitentes*, the pages of which were scattered with less-than-cryptic marginalia linking Cuauhtémoc and Ixcateopan. "His palace," ran one of the faded annotations, "is here. . . . King Cuauhtémoc native of Ychicatecpan has in these lands his Family and descendents."[24] Most arresting of all was a first-person account of the burial of Cuauhtémoc. On a sheaf of seven pages sewn into a hide cover, amid dark ink arabesques and authentically erratic spelling, the author claimed to have buried the last emperor beneath the Ixcateopan parish church and signed himself Motolinía.[25]

Ixcateopan lay well over a thousand miles from the place in the southern jungles where the Spanish hanged Cuauhtémoc, and there was no previously known link between village and emperor. In another epoch the scant indication of an improbable tomb might well have passed without comment. But it was the 1940s in Mexico, a period of intense nationalist promotion by the governing elites. Between 1947 and 1949 the ruling Partido Revolucionario Institucional (PRI) issued nearly a million free biographies of Mexico's national heroes.[26] Interior Minister Hector Pérez Martínez, the second most powerful man in

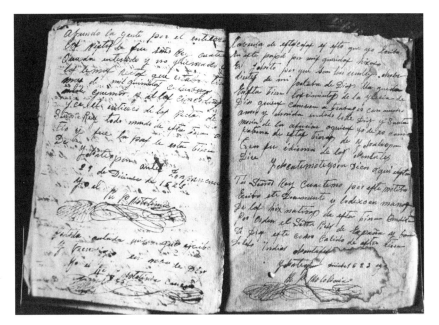

Figure 10. The Motolinía manuscript in the hide cover; courtesy of the Instituto Nacional de Antropología e Historia, Mexico City.

Mexico, wrote a popular biography of Cuauhtémoc in 1948; the historian Salvador Toscano was preparing another one in 1949.[27] Biography was not the only genre promoted by the state party: the cultural managers of the early PRI were also keen on history. In 1949 they launched a competition for the best history of the revolution, whose winner was Alberto Morales Jimenez's *Historia de la Revolución Mexicana*. Morales's book taught readers that the revolutionaries had made a clean break with the dictatorship; forged a popular, democratic movement; and successfully realised their followers' demands for social reform, refounding the Mexican nation-state.[28] Such nationalist discourse attained an everyday ubiquity, cropping up anywhere and everywhere, penetrating even the unlikely corners of the bullfight reports. The critic "Ojo," for example, attributed to Mexican bullfighters "the manliness and the patriotism . . . to make the public forget the existence of toreros of another nationality."[29]

Mexican cultural nationalism was not just wide ranging; it also bordered on the necrophiliac. In the three years before the emergence of the Ixcateopan documents, archaeologists had sedulously recovered supposed remains of Cortés and the Niños Héroes, the six cadets who had died defending Chapultepec Castle against the invading U.S. Army of 1847.[30] The head of the PRI proposed digging up the three main heroes of the revolution to rebury them beneath the Monument to the Revolution.[31] There would be attempts, it was rumoured, to bring back the bones of the creole historian Francisco Xavier Clavijero from Italy.[32] Even Porfirio Díaz's remains were reevaluated: Senator Joaquín Fagoaga petitioned the senate to bring the dictator's bones back from Paris, where they lay, *La Prensa* complained, "in a rubbish dump."[33] State governments busied themselves forming museums and departments of anthropology.[34] That this cultural nationalism met with a receptive audience was made clear by the sheer volume of Mexican tourists visiting the ruins of a picturesque past: in 1949 nearly half a million people visited the pyramids and colonial buildings that were the state's official historical sites.[35] In such a context the Ixcateopan tradition was not just the stuff of legend but also the stuff of high politics.

The revelations certainly could not have been more timely for General Baltasar Leyva Mancilla, the governor of Guerrero. The year 1949 was the centenary of the state's foundation, so he had prepared various routine commemorative gestures, such as a series of history seminars in January and a series of literary competitions in October, but he was not all that interested; he planned to spend all of 1.5 percent of the 1949 education budget on the celebrations.[36] To successfully locate and excavate the tomb of the last Mexica emperor would, however, be more than mere performance of the rites of power.[37] It would be a personal coup of the highest order. He needed one: his violent mismanagement of the 1948 municipal elections had discredited him with ordinary *guerrerenses* and, more importantly, with the president. (The Ixcateopan region, where peasant activists formed numerous dissident town councils in January 1949, had been moreover the most troublesome in those elections.)[38] The governor's principal backer, state labour leader Alfredo Córdoba Lara, was being widely accused of the murder of rival union boss "Pillo" Rosales; President Alemán heard the charges firsthand from Rosales's widow, who cornered him in Acapulco in early March.[39] When the president went on to tour the coast north of Acapulco, peasant protesters stopped his motorcade in Tecpan. Their leader was a schoolteacher who—in front of president, press, furious governor, and military zone commander—delivered an impassioned denunciation of local caciquismo, boss rule, and military violence.[40] The governor had overspent significantly on the presidential reception, to the tune of one hundred thousand pesos, and had reaped in exchange serious, consecutive embarrassments. Meanwhile the

Federal Security Directorate's man in Chilpancingo was filing critical reports; there were even rumours that Leyva Mancilla was to be pushed to take an indefinite leave of absence, the gubernatorial euphemism for being fired.[41] In the quest to finish his term, move upward, and shoehorn in a malleable successor, the discovery of Cuauhtémoc's tomb could provide bread and circuses and political leverage in the capital. What, he asked Bernardo Salgado rhetorically, could be more beautiful? There was, consequently, a certain urgency to the state government's reaction, and within weeks the governor personally visited Ixcateopan, inspected the documents, and named a commission of inquiry.[42]

The commission was originally formed by three guerrerenses, Dr. Alejandro Sánchez Castro, Mauro Huerta Molina, and Anselmo Marino Flores. They were chosen more for availability and loyalty than for any burden of specialisation: Sánchez Castro had been President Obregón's doctor and a federal deputy; Huerta Molina was a judge; and while Marino Flores was said to be an anthropologist, the Escuela Nacional de Antropología e Historia had expelled him degree-less for drunk and disorderly behaviour.[43] They would need more expertise, so the director of the Instituto Nacional de Antropología e Historia (INAH) was asked if he could assign the head of the Archivo Histórico, Eulalia Guzmán, to take charge of the investigation.[44] The governor chose her as the scholar most likely to come up with the right result; it was a loaded choice, for Eulalia Guzmán was a nationalist, a feminist, and a revolutionary indigenista, one dedicated to the preservation and the political promotion of indigenous culture and society.[45] Unlike most scholars of the time, she came from a provincial background in southern Zacatecas. Her political career began early when she joined the Admirers of Juárez, a club dedicated to promoting women's suffrage under the dictatorship; cofounded a school for women in Mexico City; and at twenty years old, backed the revolution of Francisco Madero in 1910. Guzmán was an active backer: when the counterrevolution of Victoriano Huerta broke out she went to the palace to plead for Madero's life and then accompanied his widow to collect the murdered president's body from Lecumberri Prison. She went on to form a group that smuggled ammunition (up their skirts) to the Zapatista revolutionaries and to organise a model school for indigenous education in Sonora. When the fighting ended, she became director of the national literacy campaign and deputy head of primary education in the Secretaría de Educación Pública (SEP, the Ministry of Public Education). Competent, committed, and close to several of the new national elite, she was a rising star in the emerging state's bureaucracy.[46]

Yet Guzmán subsequently turned away from education, administration, and the power it brought to enter the study of pre-Colombian cultures. Her 1932 work "Essential Characteristics of Ancient Mexican Art," the culmination of three years' research with the great archaeologist Alfonso Caso at Monte Albán and in the Mixteca Alta, argued forcefully and influentially for a discrete and coherent set of indigenous aesthetic values.[47] The National Museum immediately made her head of its archaeology department, and three years later the Secretaría de Educación Pública gave her the prize job of cataloguing prehispanic manuscripts in the libraries and museums of Europe. In 1940 she began what would become a lifelong attempt to rewrite history with a critical edition of Cortés's letters to Charles V: its thesis was that Cortés's account of Mexica culture and society was bogus, inventing despotism, militarism, and human sacrifice to morally and politically justify conquest. The broad thrust of her argument—the profound unreliability of conquistador accounts, rooted in their authors' political expediency and adherence to strong narrative conventions—was ahead of its time.[48] But the INAH refused to publish it and was rumoured to have warned off outside publishers, sparking an internecine feud that would endure.[49] When the remains of Cortés were discovered in 1947 Guzmán coauthored a dissident report that concluded, in opposition to the INAH's official findings, that the Spaniard had died of congenital syphilis.[50] Her revisionism and the abrasiveness with which she promoted it made her many enemies; but Eulalia Guzmán was one of very few women to succeed in an overwhelmingly patriarchal academic environment, and by 1949 even her opponents would concede her some "scientific credibility."[51]

On February 17 she went to Ixcateopan and examined the papers, concluding at first glance that they were false.[52] The signature that was supposedly that of Motolinía bore no relation to the real thing, and the marginalia in what was purportedly his book could not possibly have been written in his hand. *Destierro de Ignorancias y Amigo de Penitentes*, the work of the Jesuit Juan Antonio de Oviedo, had not been printed until 1769, more than two centuries after Motolinía's death. This anachronism was, however, explained away in a pastoral letter of His Excellency the Archbishop of Mexico Don Alonso Núñez de Haro y Peralta, which only now emerged. The letter was annotated, in an ink faded to the point of illegibility, with the date 1777 and the fragmentary line "This date I copied the ancient . . . as they were . . . dust."[53] The hypothesis that the papers were imperfect eighteenth-century copies of older, lost documents was enough to keep Eulalia Guzmán interested and in the village, where preliminary work seemed to reveal a complex folk tradition encoding the whereabouts of Cuauhtémoc's tomb.

The villagers had at first been suspicious of the snooping outsider, and bar a single interview she had come across little to corroborate the story of the documents. Guzmán had been on the point of returning to Mexico City when the secretary of the ayuntamiento urged her to address the village elders. He assembled about two hundred of them in the town hall, where she delivered an impromptu peroration on the glory of the last emperor.[54] Coming from another scholar, it might not have worked; but Guzmán originally came from a place quite like Ixcateopan, the dry mountain village of San Pedro Piedra Gorda, and her understanding of her audience may just have helped her move them. Whatever the case, when the speech ended twelve old men came forward to volunteer their versions of the legend. Their accounts, relayed to them during distant childhood, rearranged the same basic elements: that Ixcateopan had been the capital of a kingdom, that Cuauhtémoc had been born there, and that he had died far away but had been carried back and buried beneath the church.[55]

In light of these interviews, Guzmán postponed her departure and collected further reports of songs, dances, and other village rituals that suddenly acquired fresh relevance. The clues ranged from minor details, such as the villagers' obligatory practise of removing their hats while passing the church, to the structure of complex social performances.[56] In the course of the Carnival celebrations, some informants said, it had once been customary to simulate, against a backdrop of tolling church bells, the hanging of a man from a cedar tree in the plaza. This was performed in the midafternoon on Sunday, Monday, and Tuesday of Carnival; in the aftermath of each mock execution an escort of dancers called *ahuileros* would accompany the hanged man to the eastern end of the church, where they would tearfully bid him farewell.[57] Their song, *ahuiles*, had been literally unintelligible to most villagers for years, worded as it was in the Nahuatl that few still spoke.[58] It was, according to Rodríguez Juárez, readily deconstructed as an homage to Cuauhtémoc, thinly disguised to avoid the priest's interference. There was even one report of people praying and lighting candles in the road outside the presbytery to honour the soul of the king who was buried there.[59] Between interviews and folklore, Eulalia Guzmán would leave the village convinced that there might be substance to the Ixcateopan tradition.

She was also convinced that in terms of evidence she had merely scratched the surface. Apart from showing her the papers, the villagers had taken her to an elevated stone platform on the southern edge of the village that they called the *momoxtli*, the Nahuatl word for altar. There she made a superficial reconnaissance and found pottery fragments that she identified as Aztec. The building's function was unclear; but from its size, approximately sixty yards square, it had evidently been of some significance, and Guzmán would later come to believe it was Cuauhtémoc's palace.[60] Most suggestive of all, Rodríguez Juárez had, in sworn secrecy, shown her a letter that his grandfather had written as a crude will during the revolution.[61] It was not, however, lands or livestock that the will provided for but secrets and documents.

The author described the papers that had already emerged and begged anyone into whose possession they might fall to preserve them, as they concerned "a long-talked of living letter which a missionary father left among the Indians." He also went on to list several other documents that had not been revealed in February: court records of a dispute between the village and its priest in the last days of the colony, the journals that contained his own "understanding of these secrets," and an envelope sewn shut that gave "the facts of everything."[62] Under pressure from the village council, Rodríguez Juárez admitted in early March that he had all these documents.[63] In May, finally able to return to the village, Eulalia Guzmán examined them.[64] The envelope contained two apparently blank sheets of a coarse paper made from cotton fibre coated with egg white.[65] These, when gently heated, revealed themselves as penned in invisible ink: one, a faded and incomplete Motolinía letter, related (under a sketched crucifix) that he had buried a king, while the second, yet more fragmentary, yielded a reference to "this Holy tomb of. . . ."[66] Exotic and improbable as pulp fiction, these disparate pointers to a grave were given some sort of coherence by the accompanying master narrative of the Florentino Juárez journals.

Florentino Juárez, a rancher and small-town politician, was the late maternal grandfather of Salvador Rodríguez Juárez. In the five volumes of his journals, written in the late nineteenth and early twentieth centuries, he claimed to be the heir to a secret village tradition that stretched back to the sixteenth century to record the fate of Cuauhtémoc's bones. His account held that the emperor's body had been cut down from the silk-cotton tree and smuggled out of the southeast by a group of Indian deserters from the Hibueras expedition. Walking by little-known paths, evading the pursuing Spanish, they made it to central Mexico, where, after weathering an unnamed plague, they returned the body to Ixcateopan.[67] There he would be kept because, as journals, parchment folder, and marginalia in *Destierro de Ignorancias y Amigo de Penitentes*

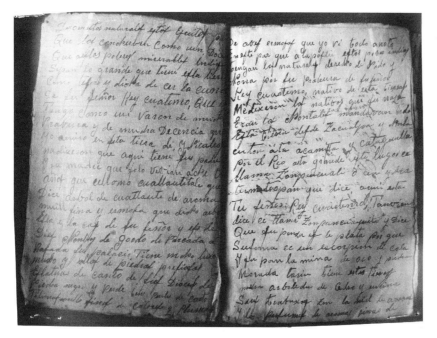

Figure 11. Pages from the Florentino Juárez journals; courtesy of the Instituto Nacional de Antropología e Historia, Mexico City.

all related, Cuauhtémoc, hitherto believed to be Mexica from Tenochtitlán, had in fact been born in Ixcateopan and was by birthright king of the Chontals.[68] That he should end up beneath a church, on the face of it an unlikely end for an indigenous high priest, was due to a missionary, a man who "was very poor and a young man with great sympathy for the poor Indians."[69] This was the famous Toribio de Benaventes, one of the twelve Franciscans who landed in Mexico in 1524, whom the Indians nicknamed Motolinía, "the poor man." He gained the confidence of the Indians; they revealed their secret to him; and he, on December 29, 1529, reburied Cuauhtémoc.[70]

The mystery that Motolinía constructed around the tomb, swearing the people of Ixcateopan to secrecy and writing in invisible ink, stemmed, he explained, from fear of his own people, the Spanish. He was not afraid for himself but for his flock, whom the parchment folder described as "these miserable Chontal Indians"; and consequently, he wrote, "No one may note this because I have it forbidden to write the life of this Lord King for the mere love of my sons and by God I am not afraid of the henchmen of the Inquisition."[71] In order to commemorate and to conceal the emperor the church of Nuestra Señora Santa María de la Ascensión was built over his grave. Juárez included a series of purported colonial court records in the journals, which attested how the village elders had for centuries resisted attempts to renovate the church that might have revealed or desecrated the grave.[72] Meanwhile the legend of Cuauhtémoc's tomb in Ixcateopan was handed down successive generations of what became the Juárez family.[73] These were stories, wrote Florentino Juárez, "which the elders used to tell me," "which they told me they knew as one knows a prayer."[74] The long chain of what his notebooks called the "living letters," the carriers of the tradition and the guardians of the papers, passed from Florentino Juárez to his daughter Jovita, on her death to her sister María Inés, and thence to her nephew, Salvador Rodríguez Juárez, who broke with the family's four centuries of silence and revealed the tradition.[75]

To accept that this might be true, and that there might actually be a body beneath the altar place, would require revision of the consensus on basic events in prehispanic and early colonial history. In this, however, the guerrerenses had chosen their academic well, because if there was one member of the INAH hierarchy who sought to recast that narrative as profoundly as possible it was Eulalia Guzmán. The Ixcateopan tradition was an overtly indigenista text: a political (and literal) version of "idols behind altars" that posited not only an epic quest to give the last emperor the burial that he, custom, and posterity deserved but also the paradoxical preservation of that quest, encoded in popular culture, across four centuries. It was a persuasively emotive myth; and while Guzmán was not without doubts, she kept them private and let herself be persuaded.[76]

Her belief must have been encouraged by the enthusiasm of the villagers, for whom the possibility of unearthing Cuauhtémoc was a moving one. Later investigations revealed that some had only the vaguest idea of who he was, but the central component of his symbolic identity, that of resistance in overwhelmingly unfavourable conditions, was something that the marginalised (then as now) had no difficulty whatsoever in grasping.[77] The Ixcateopan legend had a straightforward poetry. It departed from a romantic quest, the ancient villagers' dedicated, difficulty-strewn, at times dangerous journey bringing Cuauhtémoc's body back from the southern jungles to the homeland. It then changed into a story of clan loyalty and its survival against the odds, a subtle, unproclaimed victory of the closest human ties over the cold power of the outside world. Between them, these added up to a statement of the centrality of forgotten villagers to whatever Mexico really was. It gave the people of

Ixcateopan a special dignity that everyday life too often denied. It was natural that the last emperor became almost overnight an affectively powerful symbol that the villagers longed to materialise. "Would," a group of elders told one journalist, "that we knew where our King was."[78] It was "the only hope they had of immortalising their village," and when it became known that the church would be excavated there were, according to the schoolteacher Obaldina Barrera, people who went every day with candles to pray that Cuauhtémoc be discovered. "We have to," she remembered one woman say, "ask our [patron] saint to enlighten them . . . to enlighten these people who come to work in order that something might be found."[79]

There was also a prosaic side to all this. The Cuauhtémoc investigation was the village's only visible hope for improved roads, services, and tourist income; some villagers later tried to make the best of the state government's unaccustomed attention by renewing their petition for an *ejido*, which had been steadfastly ignored since 1936.[80] Individuals such as Salvador Rodríguez Juárez were quick to grasp the potential material benefits of the find, and in the formal record of the documents' discovery that the village council drew up (in quintuplicate), he made sure that his ownership of the papers was reaffirmed and inserted an early plea for some form of reward.[81] He went on to amplify this plea in a petition to the president in which, amid requests for drinking water, electricity, roads, a vault for the remains, and a monument to their glory, he also asked that the government grant him the Juárez family house, which had been sold off some years beforehand.[82] Ixcateopan was a village where even Carnival celebrations proclaimed that life was harsh and ephemeral. The *canto del ahuile* ran:

Why do you look so sad?
Why shouldn't we be sad
If we're coming to Lent?
Who will God pardon?
Who will celebrate this Carnival?
Perhaps us again?
Perhaps others?
Who celebrates this Carnival?[83]

No one was naive enough not to realise that on the fate of the investigation hung much of the future of Ixcateopan itself, and as a consequence the community exerted pressure on both members and outsiders to believe in the grave's existence. "We are," the village secretary wrote to Guzmán at the start of the investigation, "fighting to get people to cooperate."[84]

On top of this local pressure to find Cuauhtémoc, there was a considerable degree of interference from the state government. They were, after all, funding the investigation: INAH's director, Ignacio Marquina, had been indifferent, limiting himself to paying Guzmán's second-class bus fare.[85] The governor of Guerrero, however, was an ambitious man. That he took the affair in deadly earnest was obvious from the start, when he posted detachments of the 72nd Regiment of the Reserva Rural in Ixcateopan to guard the documents and sent Huerta Molina to be his representative in the village.[86] It was, according to the sycophantic state congress, only due to the "more than usual patriotism" and "unlimited aid" of General Leyva Mancilla that the investigation was undertaken at all.[87] Once the commission informed him that they believed that Cuauhtémoc's remains were in fact under the altar, he obtained the relevant permit from the Ministry of National Properties and demanded that they be exhumed immediately. To the varied objections of academics from state and federal bodies he applied a ruthless logic: "If they tell me that there's a treasure right here beneath my feet, I don't have to go around to ask my neighbour, look, what do I do? I go and dig and bring out the treasure, and if I don't bring it out that's because there's nothing there."[88]

Eulalia Guzmán was panicked by this urgency. She had been commissioned to examine the documents; she was not an archaeologist, and she was unqualified to dig. The general, however, threatened to excavate the church with or without technical assistance, and she finally agreed to coordinate the dig, starting in November or December 1949. To begin before the rainy season ended would, she explained, be unscientific. But the governor and Guzmán were working to different timetables. The centenary of the state's foundation, he told her explicitly, was to be celebrated on October 27. He wanted to know before then if there was a body in Ixcateopan or not. Finally, unable to deny him, she found herself opening the dig early in the morning on September 20.[89]

It began both badly and publicly. The little church at the western end of the plaza was packed with villagers, local government officials, and journalists when Eulalia Guzmán announced that her team would begin by destroying the altar. They had tried tunnelling beneath it only to be thwarted by the lack of solid foundations.[90] The altar was clearly indicated as the site of the tomb in the so-called 1810 documents; it would have to go.[91] The excavators, however,

Figure 12.
The altar of Santa
María de la Asunción.
Photograph by
Armando Salmerón
Moctezuma; by
permission of the
Salmerón family.

Altar mayor de la Iglesia de Santa María de la Asunción.

including Guzmán, an old teaching colleague of hers called Gudelia Guerra, the anthropologist Anselmo Marino Flores, and a group of eight labourers, had no idea of how to dismantle the relatively large altar.[92] It was a man casually recruited from the crowd gathered outside the church who, claiming experience as a civil engineer, prepared to direct operations.[93] But the altar, vile neoclassical wedding cake that it might have been to an outsider's eye, was still more than a mere technical obstacle.[94]

To Eulalia Guzmán both altar and church were meaningless, architecturally unremarkable containers for the object of her search.[95] To at least some of the villagers, however, they were tangible community possessions that were being violated with crowbars, and by one o'clock they had organised a protest in the main square that threatened to turn violent.

Before work could continue it was consequently necessary to fetch the governor and quell what one journalist painted as an incipient riot.[96] General Leyva Mancilla gave a crowd-pleasing speech promising full reconstruction of the church interior and an improved road to Iguala, a quid pro quo that the villagers accepted.[97] But Guzmán was clearly unhappy with the confusion enveloping her dig, and the next day she wrote urgently to Marquina, the director of INAH. She had been waiting for an archaeologist, Carlos Margaín, to arrive; he was apparently still in New York. It would be, she wrote, "impossible to halt work until señor Margaín arrives, as the Governor, who will be here at any moment, wishes that it continue with all possible speed." She asked INAH to send a substitute for Margaín as soon as possible, claiming that the dig was too important for her to take sole responsibility.[98] Marquina did nothing. The governor's representative had unequivocal orders not to suspend operations for any reason, and so they dug on, without even a pause for Sunday.[99]

Guzmán would make two more attempts to slow the pace of excavations, requesting a second engineer on September 23 and suggesting a more cautious approach to the supposed grave site two days later.[100] In both cases she was turned down by the state government commission. Disorder had become the defining characteristic of the dig. No string grid was laid out to mark the site and provide accurate reference points to locate anything they might find; as the men hacked through the church floor nobody was keeping a field diary or drawing or photographing the excavation's progress.[101] When they uncovered an ossuary three yards from the altar, containing a large quantity of jumbled bones, and then the more recent burials of three priests, separated by planks, at the northern end of the altar, both sets of remains were casually left aside as the search for a more important grave went on.[102] It was not even Guzmán who directed where the men worked. She and the military doctor Alejandro Sánchez Castro quarrelled over where to extend the diggings, after which it was Sánchez Castro, according to several witnesses, who traced a cross on the church floor and instructed the peons to cut trenches along the intersecting lines.[103] Accounts of the dig tend toward the confused, the contradictory, and the clearly self-aggrandizing, and despite the quantity of material left behind it is often difficult to reconstruct the progress of the excavation. Some conclusions, though, are unavoidable: that Eulalia Guzmán had little or no control over events and that the dig was chaos.

By September 26 the workers had carved a trench nearly five feet deep, running east–west under the vanished altar; they had gone through three different

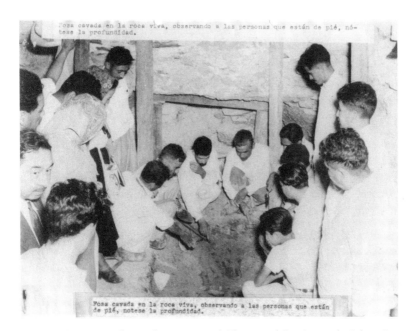

Figure 13. The tomb is uncovered. Photograph by Armando Salmerón Moctezuma; by permission of the Salmerón family.

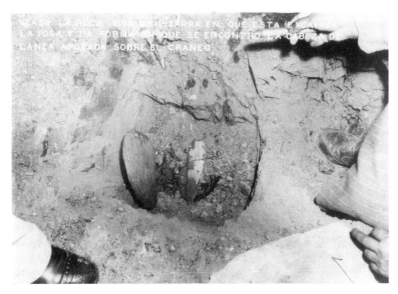

Figure 14. First view of the tomb. Photograph by Armando Salmerón Moctezuma; by permission of the Salmerón family.

floors and removed a large pile of boulders; and they had hit rock. A further trench one and a half feet deep had been dug traversing most of the exposed rock, and the team had yet to unearth anything that would back up the story of the Juárez papers.[104] The journalists had lost their initial enthusiasm, and the members of the state commission had taken off that morning to swim in a nearby waterfall.[105] Guzmán herself seemed to have concluded that there was nothing there; evidently disheartened, she was not even inside the church early that afternoon.[106] The villagers, however, continued to dig. It was Salvador Rodríguez Juárez's brother Abel who, extending the trench to the east of the vanished altar, came across a small gap in the rock, filled with mud. With the next blow he felt his pick break through into open space and immediately smelled what was described as a stench of copper oxide. He stopped momentarily and shouted to the others. Then Sánchez Castro came over and began to pick as well, and within a short time they uncovered a cavity that measured slightly less than a foot a side, covered by two flat stone slabs.[107]

While Leobarda Rivera went to fetch Eulalia Guzmán, and the church began to fill with people, they lifted the slabs out. Underneath they found a roughly shaped copper plaque and a copper spearhead, propped up on a broken skull.[108] The diggers paused, the *Excélsior* photographer took the picture, and then the foreman passed the plaque up to Guzmán. She brushed the dirt off, examined it briefly, and announced with tears in her eyes that they had found the tomb. Crudely scored into the copper was a swallow-tailed cross and the legend: "1525–1529. Rey e S. Coatemo."[109]

Memory twists times like these toward the mythical. Decades later, Salvador Rodríguez Juárez remembered how, as the grave was opened, an onlooker began to chant hymns in Nahuatl. The governor's son remembered a crowd of ten thousand Indians gathering, seemingly out of nowhere, to watch in perfect silence in front of the church. Bernardo Salgado remembered the greatest thunderstorm in living memory, an echo of the storm that closed the last day of Tenochtitlán, lashing the village with biblical rain that night.[110] None of that happened. But the afternoon of September 26, 1949, was an extraordinarily poignant time for the people of Ixcateopan.[111] As soon as the council heard the news they ordered that the church bells be rung, and men and women poured from the fields and houses toward the plaza, the men abandoning their work and the women leaving tortillas to burn on the griddle.[112] The platoon guarding the entrance to the church was mobbed, and the four reservists were pushed out of the way by the swelling crowd; when the bell ringer came down from the belfry he could not

Figure 15. The copper plaque; courtesy of the Instituto Nacional de Antropología e Historia, Mexico City.

glimpse the grave through the mass of villagers.[113] Inside the church journalists gathered, labourers and onlookers sobbed manfully, and the crush grew denser until, some two hours after the initial discovery, Eulalia Guzmán took a national flag, picked up the plaque and the spearhead, and walked out to the churchyard. There she stood on a table; flanked herself carefully with Rodríguez Juárez and three of the village elders; ceremoniously revolved in a full circle to display the relics to the four cardinal points; and, competing with church bells and fire-works, announced the discovery.[114] The semiotically perfect photograph was taken; the crowd sang the national anthem.[115] Telegrams were sent to the gover-nor and the president. Later, as Guzmán and the municipal president mounted the first guard of honour in the church, the village began to celebrate.[116]

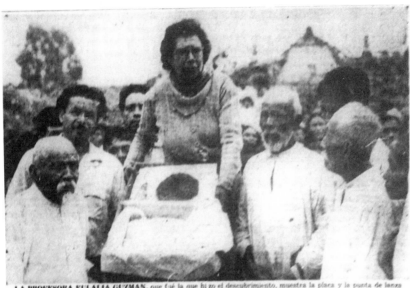

Figure 16. Eulalia Guzmán displays the relics; courtesy of *Excélsior.*

The next day the remaining contents of the grave were lifted out, wrapped in paper and rags, and put away in shoe boxes.[117] They made an esoteric collection:

a fragment of human skull (frontal and parietal regions); this fragment by way of a box contained in its interior the following jewels: 29 metallic beads of about half a centimetre in diameter, 8 small beads of the same metal, that is to say, of lesser size than the former; a jade bead of about three centimetres at its widest point, perforated, as are the previously described; a jade bead of about one centimetre in diameter, perforated, three half beads of amethyst, that is to say, three half spheres of amethyst of less than a centimetre in diameter; a crystal, apparently an uncut diamond of about three-quarters of a cubic centimetre; a thin metal ring; another ring, a band, of the same metal (rings as if for fingers); half-burnt human remains; that is, bones, in the main part fragmented, some burnt and some half-burnt, in contact with loose soil, whose classification will be made later. At the bottom of the above-described grave and as a base to the aforementioned deposit, a copper plaque was found, rectangular, of one hundred and thirty-five millimetres by one hundred and seventy-eight millimetres, in a horizontal position and with its long side pointed from southwest to northeast.[118]

The governor arrived in the late morning to pronounce his unshakable politician's verdict on the grave: "This," he said, referring to the bones' authenticity, "is perfectly clear." Then, having laid necklaces of white marigold flowers before the empty hole in the ground, he mounted a brief guard of honour with General Miguel Z. Martínez, the state's military commander.[119] Afterward he promised electricity, presidential visits, drinking water, museums, roads—for the expected avalanche of visitors—and ceremonies for the village that had kept the secret of Cuauhtémoc.[120] The ceremonies, at least, began immediately: the state congress created a new decoration, the Cuauhtémoc medal, and awarded it to General Leyva Mancilla and Eulalia Guzmán.[121] Against the odds, Guzmán seemed to have triumphed, as both archaeologist and nationalist. Fervour for Cuauhtémoc and the prehispanic past that the last emperor symbolised was about to swamp the country's politicians, press, and some of its ordinary people. The tomb find was being called "the most important historic event of our century."[122] Cuauhtémoc, wrote one commentator, was alive once more: "resurrected from oblivion."[123]

Chapter 3

Scandal

Should at some point the ill-intentioned [come] to judge our secrets, you should be warned that history is not made by the vanquished but by the victor; and this would unleash a fearful scandal.

—Florentino Juárez Journal 2, folio 13

ON THE SAME DAY THAT CUAUHTÉMOC'S GRAVE WAS OPENED IN Ixcateopan, a Compañia Mexicana de Aviación DC-3 burst into flames and crashed on the slopes of the volcano Popocatépetl. There were no survivors, and before the rescue teams could arrive, scavengers stripped the twenty-one dead passengers of their valuables. It was not this that kept the crash in the news, for planes went down with grim regularity at the time. It was, rather, the importance of those passengers: among the dead were Gabriel Ramos Millán, head of the Comisión Nacional del Maíz and one of the president's closest friends; Blanca Estela Pavón, a starlet; Paco Mayo, a gifted photojournalist; and Salvador Toscano, the young secretary of the Instituto Nacional de Antropología e Historia (INAH) and one of the preeminent historians of prehispanic Mexico.[1] His last and unfinished work was a biography of Cuauhtémoc. He had been one of the scholars best qualified to pronounce on the possibility of the Ixcateopan legend containing truth, and the week before the crash he had gone on record in *La Prensa* with his doubts concerning the tomb's existence.[2] Now, within two days of his death, a macabre report came in from the village. Someone was spreading the rumour that his death, far from being accidental, had been deliberate punishment for his disbelief. It was *brujería*, witchcraft: each of the tomb's eight small beads, the story went, represented an opponent of the last emperor who would die for his scepticism. An unpopular local priest had been the first to die; Toscano was the second victim. By 1951 four deaths were attributed to the curse.[3]

The aggression and resentment that underlay this ghoulish fiction were nothing new. Conflict—academic and popular, philosophical and political, local, regional, and metropolitan—was woven into the diverse threads of the Ixcateopan investigation from the beginning. In the village itself the atmosphere was frequently strained and sometimes menacing; caught between the promise of reward should the grave exist and the fear lest abstract erudition declare it nonexistent, the villagers felt themselves to be in a vital struggle against disbelievers, opportunist outsiders, and big-city snobs.[4] They tenaciously defended the documents and their authenticity against all comers. When the General Staff sent a colonel with orders to collect the Juárez papers, "for safekeeping," the municipal president refused and cabled a request for constitutional guarantees against military violence to President Alemán.[5] The village council formed a vigilance committee to guard the documents and church; villagers followed and suspiciously observed the visiting journalists and researchers; Rodríguez Juárez refused, point-blank, to let the documents out of his sight.[6] When his elderly uncle gave an interview disclaiming that the documents had been in the family for generations, he was quickly silenced and later retracted his story.[7] Such tensions, present from the start, only grew in the course of the investigation. During March rumours spread in north Guerrero that INAH and an unnamed journalist were busily pilfering Ixcateopan of its treasures for sale in the United States, sections of the metropolitan press launched wild attacks on the foreign nationals working in Mexican archaeological zones, and the *Excélsior* correspondent César Lizardi had a serious quarrel with Rodríguez Júarez and abandoned the story.[8] Such defensive hostility was not exclusively for outsiders. There was also a high degree of intravillage conflict, and well before the end of the affair its principal actors would be united as often by mutual dislike as by common interest.[9]

Yet those who wished to believe in the grave were pushed together, whatever their enmity, by the volume of criticism coming out of Mexico City. The Juárez documents were sufficiently dubious to be dismissed out of hand at an early stage as "crude forgeries," an opinion that assorted academics repeated at a meeting of the Asociación Alemana Mexicana in March.[10] The General Staff, having failed to get hold of the documents, claimed aloofly to be disinterested as they were apocryphal anyway.[11] Professors and students in the National University's history faculty agreed that Ixcateopan, although an excellent topic of conversation, was a bit of a joke.[12] As the excavation began the heavyweights in the ranks of Mexican archaeology and history had no scruples about talking to the press, and as a consequence readers of even the tabloids were kept informed of the argument. It was readily assimilated: with varying veneers of diplomacy, men such as Silvio Zavala, the deputy director of INAH, Daniel Rubín de la Borbolla, director of the Archaeological Museum, and Arturo Arnáiz y Freg at the Colegio de México all agreed with Gonzalo Obregón's blunt verdict: that to have taken Ixcateopan seriously was "another of Doña Eulalia's insanities."[13] José Vasconcelos, the former deacon of the revolution's cultural nationalism, wrote off the Ixcateopan papers as insignificant.[14] Even Ignacio Marquina, Guzmán's immediate superior, had no intention of backing her. Bidding her farewell as she left to begin excavations, he told her that she would find nothing, that it was all a fantasy, and that she was the only dupe. The day of the discovery he told reporters the same thing.[15]

It was consequently embarrassing when the unthinkable came to pass and Guzmán actually came up with a tomb. The antipathy between the excavation team and INAH was public knowledge: in the days leading to the discovery, the rumour had circulated that INAH was on the point of withdrawing recognition from the Ixcateopan dig.[16] Now, however, for reasons of both confirmation and etiquette, the department had to send representatives to the village. They were already suffering criticism as deskbound wastrels. "It is not the same," Sánchez Castro had observed, "to explore a budget as to come and explore the archaeological zone of Ixcateopan."[17] On September 28 Jorge Acosta, a senior archaeologist, arrived in the village, where he found Guzmán reenacting the discovery for photographers and film crews. He was joined the next day by Marquina and Alfonso Caso, who had been Guzmán's supervisor and who was perceived, in the words of the British ambassador, as "the most able and objective archaeologist in the country."[18] On September 30 they were shown the grave artefacts and then the human remains, kept by now in a sealed glass tank. The church interior was dark, and Caso wanted to carry the bones outside to examine in stronger light. But the villagers, some armed with old Mauser rifles, prevented him from touching them. Archaeologists and journalists would alike remember the crowd's hostility in those moments, until Caso, politically aware as ever, gave up on inspecting the bones and gave instead a speech.[19] It would not be necessary to examine the remains, which should be kept in Ixcateopan out of respect for the wishes of those who buried him. Eulalia Guzmán had made a discovery of the greatest importance, and her detractors should remind themselves of her recognised academic standing. Finally, briefly and coldly, Marquina spoke, confirming that the excavation had been found in good order.[20]

This, however, was all a sop to the press and manifestly untrue. Nothing about the dig was in order. When the visitors asked for an inventory they were told that no such thing existed; there were neither diagrams nor photographs of the excavation in progress, nor a field diary, nor a chart of the location of bones and artefacts within the grave, all "notable errors." The best record of the dig that Guzmán could offer them was a site map sketched from memory two days after the grave was opened and some photographs from *El Universal*, of which only two were of any use.[21] The fragment of skull, supposedly that of the last emperor, had been further broken by the peons as they hastily pulled it out of the grave.[22] The lance head, Acosta immediately noted, had not been forged but, rather, cut from a sheet of beaten copper.[23] It was politically impossible for Marquina and Caso to do much but mouth clubby platitudes on that tense first visit, but their encomia were mere window dressing to cover their underlying doubts. As Eulalia Guzmán delivered a further speech thanking villagers and government institutions for their support, Caso interrupted to brusquely call her aside.[24] Their exchange went unrecorded and largely unremarked. We can, however, guess its import with some confidence. Her old supervisor was warning her that INAH would have to examine the grave contents in more depth before confirming her find and that whatever she, the governor, or the press might say, nothing, as yet, was certain.

Caso, who had by this stage in his career become something of a referee to the perpetual skirmishing within Mexican academia, had gone to Ixcateopan without obvious preconceptions, inclined, if anything, to believe in the grave.[25] But the combination of slipshod dig and unprepossessing artefacts threw him off balance. Caso had himself excavated the landmark Tomb Seven in Monte Albán, where several Mixtec nobles lay surrounded by the status indicators that their rank required: rings, pectorals, weapons, a jade-plated skull, and an abundance of other items in gold, silver, jade, turquoise, obsidian, amber, coral, crystal, and bone.[26] He must have expected some analogous display of material power to accompany Cuauhtémoc's tomb in Ixcateopan.[27] When he was disappointed he began to question the identity of the man beneath the altar. Even in the harsh conditions of the late 1520s, to have bundled the last emperor into a narrow grave accompanied by little more than some indigenous costume jewellery was an act of extraordinary lèse-majesté. And so once back in Mexico City he moderated his previous support of Eulalia Guzmán and confined himself to masterfully ambiguous interviews.[28] Meanwhile Ignacio Marquina, after conferring with the secretary of education on October 3, announced that an INAH commission would be formed to verify the tomb's authenticity.[29]

Within days those skilled at the game of searching out subtexts in the media knew that their report would condemn the Ixcateopan find, because after two weeks of suitably purple nationalist prose the editorial line of *Excélsior* suddenly shifted. The bones, implicitly demoted, were now only "believed" to be those of Cuauhtémoc, and a leader urged readers to await the results of the INAH studies before drawing any conclusions.[30] Mexico City's chattering classes had been infected by an epidemic of rumour: that the tomb's artefacts were made of tin, that the bones were those of an old man or a woman, that the skeleton had two right kneecaps.[31] This last was uncomfortably close to the truth. The INAH commission had dispatched Eusebio Dávalos, an archaeologist, and Javier Romero, an anthropologist, to Ixcateopan to look at the grave and its contents. They later claimed, disingenuously, to have made the trip under the impression that their report was a mere formality.[32] But whatever their prior opinions, Ixcateopan would surprise them, initially with the lack of method in the excavation (Guzmán, while no archaeologist, was not ignorant of the basic principles of a dig, having previously excavated various tombs in the Mixteca) and then with the animosity of the villagers, who once again prevented the outsiders from removing the bones from the church.[33] So they began to sort through the bones inside the church, in "terrible conditions."[34] It was then, they later wrote, that their surprise turned to "genuine alarm." The skeleton had two left humeri, two right heel bones, and four femurs.[35]

The INAH report was completed by October 14; that it was handled as dynamite is evident. The archaeologist Carlos Margaín, despite damning the excavation, refused to sign the final draft, feebly citing insufficient data.[36] The governor of Guerrero telegrammed Secretary of Education Manuel Gual Vidal, telling him to suppress the report outright.[37] Gual Vidal did hold it back for nearly a week, but finally, having explicitly sought and obtained President Alemán's permission, and pressurised by leaks from senior archaeologists to the papers, he released it on October 19.[38] A certain quality of institutional panic seeps through accounts of the intervening five days, for after two weeks of national celebrations the INAH conclusions were unfavourable.

The commission's general summary was deliberately lacklustre, stating that "the scientific proofs that might allow the remains discovered to be identified as those of Cuauhtémoc do not exist."[39] Beneath that surface blandness, however, the individual reports were incendiary. Neither the writing nor the contents of the Juárez documents were sixteenth century. Nor was the copper plaque that identified the grave: the inscription was in a hand with suggestive similarities to the hand that had penned the Juárez documents. The dates on the plaque were written in the same anachronistic nineteenth-century form as those in the documents, with thousands separated from hundreds by a comma. The inference of a common author was unavoidable. As for the remains, Dávalos and Romero "could not believe that it could have been overlooked": they were not of one but of five different persons.[40] Cuauhtémoc's tomb had turned out to contain a young adult male, it was true, but accompanied by an adolescent, a young woman, and two small children. Fragments of their different skeletons had been pieced together to give a layman's idea of a complete corpse. It was Silvio Zavala who risked himself with the most clearly worded of conclusions. Florentino Juárez had never been the "living letter," a stoic guardian of four centuries' secrets; he had, rather, been an imaginative, cunning, grave-robbing peasant, and in the late nineteenth century he had concocted a spectacular fraud.[41]

Zavala's report was an impressive production despite the necessary haste with which it was written. The prose was lucid, the argument detached and persuasive; the verdict, however, was politically unacceptable. It met with widespread repudiation. Journalists and politicians who had enthusiastically embraced the cause of Cuauhtémoc, Eulalia Guzmán, and Ixcateopan were made to look fools, and they reacted bitterly. Protesters, ranging from the National Bloc of Revolutionary Women to a group of neighbours in Jojutla, Morelos, sent angry telegrams and letters to the president.[42] Both José López Bermúdez, the party secretary-general, and Adolfo López Mateos, a future president, publically condemned the report. *La Prensa*, citing anonymous sources within INAH, described the negative report as "untechnical, incomplete, partisan and weak."[43]

And this was comparatively moderate. For one commentator, the INAH officials were "demonically possessed."[44] General Leyva Mancilla called Zavala's work a "crime against the patria,"[45] while the great mural painter Diego Rivera, apoplectic, described the entire commission as "either perverse, anti-Mexican politicians, who know perfectly well that they will wound the people and the Government which employs them, or inept professionals who don't realise the national value of the cases and objects they're dealing with. What they've done is so disastrous that if tomorrow the peasants, sublime Indians who guard the tomb Mauser in hand, were to lay hold of the naysayers and, putting them against a wall in Ixcateopan, shoot them, they would have committed an act of absolute historical and patriotic justice."[46]

Such reactions may have been more demagogic than academic, but they were also physically intimidating; criticism in 1940s Mexico was often enough expressed with fists.[47] As "the curses of an outraged people rained down upon [the commission's] members," they came to realise just how poisonous a chalice they had been passed.[48] Soon the INAH commission was in retreat. On October 21 Zavala called for further investigation into the problems of Ixcateopan, distancing himself from the scandal but implicitly downgrading his own work as less than definitive.[49] The controversy ran untiring for another month, until the secretary of education went back to President Alemán for instructions. He was ordered to resolve the debate with a new investigation, and on December 12, 1949, the Secretaría de Educación Pública (SEP) announced a second multidisciplinary commission, the Comisión Investigadora de los Descubrimientos de Ixcateopan (the Investigatory Commission for the Ixcateopan Discoveries).[50]

The first act of the new body was to invite the press to a ceremony in which they placed a wreath and mounted a guard of honour at the base of the Cuauhtémoc monument in Mexico City. It was a revealing moment. The ten assembled specialists included historians, anthropologists, archaeologists, archivists, a geographer, and a chemist; they would later be joined by a sociologist. All the most relevant academic institutions in Mexico, bar INAH—now irrevocably cast as the villain of the piece—were represented.[51] Among the members of what would be nicknamed the Gran Comisión were some of the most influential Mexican scholars of the twentieth century. Alfonso Caso, who would emerge as the dominant personality of the group, had in addition to his long record of major digs produced the consensus correlation of prehispanic and Gregorian calendars; he had also been the first director of INAH, the rector of the National University, the founder of the Instituto Nacional Indigenista, and the minister of national properties.[52] Manuel Gamio, his elder colleague, was not just Mexico's first modern anthropologist; he had undertaken seminal research at Teotihuacán, but he was also known for his texts as a nationalist ideologue and for his numerous directorships of state anthropology and indigenista agencies. By 1949 he was recognised as the godfather of the entire anthropological establishment.[53] For all his standing, though, Gamio was to treat the proceedings of the committee with terse, barely concealed contempt, seeing much of the discussion as a waste of time.[54] He may have been missing the point: his presence on the commission, like the commission's presence at the statue of Cuauhtémoc, was eminently symbolic. The Gran Comisión's function, as much political as purely academic, would be to provide, in a hopefully far-off future, an unimpeachable verdict to close an increasingly embarrassing scandal. Meanwhile, in the strongly hierarchical world of the Mexican intelligentsia, its members' credentials and their political nous were supposed to calm what had become far more (and at the same time, less) than a scholarly debate.

There was, of course, a long history of bloody personal feud within INAH and its predecessor institutions, and Eulalia Guzmán had been on the worst of terms with most of her peers for nearly a decade before Ixcateopan.[55] Inside the professional politics of Mexican archaeology, however, this was nothing particularly unusual. The social organisation of archaeologists, like other Mexican intellectuals, into tight cliques known as camarillas combined with the windfall rewards that a major find brought to cause frequent and personalised hostilities.[56] "The rivalries between [archaeologists]," one insider wrote, "reach at times the intensity and malice of the quarrels between highly-strung artistes of the theatre or cinema."[57] Manuel Gamio regularly accused rivals of malpractice, under such unequivocal headlines as "Scandalous Archaeological Fraud" (and this in a peer-reviewed journal).[58] Caso himself had been accused of forging the Monte Albán jewels to burnish his reputation. Alfonso Toro, then director of the Prehispanic Monuments Agency, believed the accusations and temporarily blocked the archaeologist's funding. The two men never spoke again.[59] "Nothing," the British ambassador was told when he tried to make sense of Ixcateopan, ". . . can exceed the jealousies of [Mexican archaeologists]: They would rather be deceived by their wives then that others should make important discoveries in their stead."[60] Such representations were more generalised than isolated; in the 1939 Cantinflas film *The Sign of Death* the fictional Dr. Gallardo, an eminent archaeologist, is presented as initially temperamental and arrogant and eventually, evilly, deranged. "Archaeology," Gallardo himself observes, "is not a science for the good-natured."[61]

A certain quantity of mutual libel was, then, to be expected in the wake of many discoveries. With the release of INAH's negative report, however, the case of Ixcateopan became sui generis. Never before had such a public discovery been discarded as fraudulent, and never before had an archaeologist responded as aggressively as did Eulalia Guzmán to the questioning of her work. She herself had doubts regarding the tomb's identity. When Jorge Acosta first arrived in Ixcateopan he was told by Guzmán, "in great secrecy," that she did not believe that they had yet found Cuauhtémoc. She was, she said, undoubtedly close, but the remains she had so far discovered were probably those of sacrificed slaves, placed there as a signpost to the real tomb.[62] She would give a similar account to Dávalos, and while she later denied that the conversations had ever occurred, her own actions gave her the lie: in some secrecy, without ever reporting to INAH, she went on to make preliminary excavations within the chapel of San José in Ixcateopan and at the ,, the supposed site of Cuauhtémoc's palace.[63] Her story, carefully unpublicised, was that she was searching for the tombs of Cuauhtémoc's relatives. That the new dig was conceived two days after the bones were declared spurious is, however, no coincidence at all.[64] But whatever her true beliefs regarding the skeletons she had actually dug up, she would carry to her own grave two apparently unshakable convictions: that the Ixcateopan tradition was genuine and Cuauhtémoc was buried (somewhere) in the village; and that there was a wide-ranging conspiracy, coordinated from inside INAH, to deny that, to minimise the significance of the indigenous contribution to Mexican history, and to destroy her reputation.[65]

This was not quite as paranoid as it might seem. Guzmán's vision of the Ixcateopan controversy was informed by the two previous scandals that had pitted her against her colleagues: the alleged INAH blacklisting of her revisionist edition of the letters of Cortés to Charles V and her contradiction of the INAH report on Cortés's remains. Emperor and conquistador had always been inextricably linked in Mexican historiography, antagonistic halves of a distinctly labile myth. Guzmán fell firmly on the indigenista side of the debate; Cortés was, in her eyes, "a genius of the lie," a lascivious schemer who had treacherously undermined the pacifist federal meritocracy that was the Mexica Triple Alliance.[66] Having done so, he then preempted history's verdict by writing a considerable part of it himself. Determined to right this historiographical wrong, Eulalia Guzmán lost no opportunity to reinvent the life, deeds, and diseases of Cortés. In winter 1946 Javier Romero and Eusebio Dávalos had excavated Cortés's tomb inside the Hospital de Jesús in downtown Mexico City; an INAH commission on which Dávalos sat reported that the Spaniard had suffered from various chronic illnesses, including osteoporosis, and that the markings of his bones could indicate a range of infectious diseases but that he had not suffered from syphilis or tuberculosis. Guzmán disagreed and inverted their conclusions to find, in a report published in January 1947, that the "little man," the "physically and pathologically abnormal individual" in the grave, had lived with dwarfism and died from syphilis. (Her report can be found made mural in the upper gallery of the National Palace, where Cortés is transmuted by Rivera from the iconic warrior barbarian of his earlier work into a ghoulish syphilitic hunchback.)[67] Romero and Dávalos were both on the first INAH commission to study her find in Ixcateopan; when they declared it a fraud, she interpreted it as an ideologically based conclusion and, moreover, an act of personal revenge.

She had, however, been prepared for it. Before the dig had even begun Guzmán had gone to the coauthor of her Cortés report, Alfonso Quiroz Cuarón, for assistance. Quiroz Cuarón, an eminent criminologist, was head of the Department of Special Investigations of the Banco de México and a well-connected man.[68] In August 1949 he had provided her with a photographer and a chemical analyst to study the Ixcateopan papers; in the first days of October, hearing of the formation of the INAH commission and rightly presupposing that it would declare the tomb fraudulent, he had helped Guzmán to recruit a varied group of experts to defend her discovery.[69] Deriving from institutions as diverse as the National University, the Banco de México, and the Military Medical School, the group's qualifications ranged from the genuine to the dubious.[70] With the exception of Luis Chávez Orozco, none of them were notable as historians or archaeologists; they were all, however, convinced that the Ixcateopan tomb was authentic. Between them they would produce nine reports before the Gran Comisión released its own and a further eleven afterward.[71]

The reports were impressively diverse, in both content and quality, and covered all possible ground in arguing the tomb's authenticity. Alejandro von Wuthenau, a fashionable architect, traced the history of the church of Santa María de la Asunción back to the early sixteenth century and described several stylistic similarities to other churches, such as San Francisco de Tlaxcala, known to have been constructed by Motolinía.[72] José Cuevas, an engineer, stated that the building material of the deepest layers beneath the present-day church was early sixteenth century, that the floors covering those layers had been found intact during the excavation, and that the nineteenth-century altar's lack of foundations would have made any attempt to insert the grave after that altar's construction structurally impossible.[73] The writing on the plaque, despite appearances to the contrary, was held by the palaeographer Ana María Cortés Herrera to be sixteenth century.[74] As for the plaque itself, Enrique Bustamante used an x-ray analysis of the ratio of cuprous to cupric oxide on the plaque surface to lend it an age of 424 years.[75] Finally, a pathology team that included Quiroz Cuarón took the motley collection of human remains in the tomb and reconstructed the skeleton of a tall, athletic male, twenty-five to thirty years old at the time of his death, of the blood group O common to most of the indigenous population of Mexico, with deformities on the bones of the right foot suggestive of severe burns.[76] The Spanish had, as every Mexican knew, tortured Cuauhtémoc by burning his feet.

The sum of their arguments could be presented as a watertight case; it was welcomed by a crowd in Chilpancingo that blocked the streets while the church bells rang and the state band played patriotic music.[77] Some of the Banco de México group realised, however, that it was far from that. With the notable exceptions of von Wuthenau and Chávez Orozco, Guzmán's supporters produced reports that were not just partisan but profoundly flawed. Cuevas's entire case for the authenticity of the burial turned on the integrity of the ancient church's white earth floor, proving that the tomb had been laid before or during the construction of that church. There was, however, no record of the integrity or otherwise of that floor, which Guzmán's excavation had comprehensively destroyed, and Cuevas's conclusion rested on an unsupported assertion.[78] The palaeographer Cortés was faced with a plaque inscription that, with its joined-up scrawl, dates in Arabic numerals, and thousands separated from hundreds by commas, had no sixteenth-century equivalent. Evading the simplistic conclusion that it was not in fact sixteenth century, she declared it "*sui generis*, and as such independent of the canons established for headstone inscriptions," and finally found that "despite [its] disguise," it was of sixteenth-century provenance.[79] As for Bustamante's determination of the plaque's age, dated with uncanny precision to 1525, it was negated by the authors of the x-ray analysis on which he had based his calculation. "I have seen with great surprise," wrote Carlos Graef, director of the Universidad Nacional Autónoma de México Physics Institute, "that the results obtained by the Physics Institute have been presented as though they were a determination of the age of the copper plaque. . . . [N]o value whatsoever can be attached to the ages of 300 and 424 years which Dr Bustamante Llaca calculates for the age of the patina on the copper plaque which was studied."[80]

The Banco de México pathology report, prepared by Quiroz Cuarón, José Gómez Robleda, and Liborio Martínez, met with an even harsher fate: a four-part dissection in the pages of *Excélsior*.[81] In the acrid series the three authors were accused, in some detail, of unscrupulous manipulation and presentation of data and rhetorical techniques that amounted to logical contortionism. In their quest for a respectable antiquity for the Ixcateopan remains they had, for example, compared the bones' specific density with those of a skeleton from Monte Albán, arguing that the similar value implied a similar antiquity. Their calculation ignored the statistical insignificance of a data set of two, the effect of different ages at death on postmortem density, the effect of different burial conditions on rates of decay, and, most obvious of all, the fact that the bones from Ixcateopan had been burned while those from Monte Albán had not.[82] The critic, Joaquín Roncal, attacked their methods and conclusions at some length. An anonymous satirist in the same paper was more blunt: the Banco de México group was, he wrote, "pulling our legs."[83]

Such reactions were not sensationalism. Even within the (marginally) more diplomatic confines of the Comisión Investigadora's sessions, the pathology report, one of the centrepieces of the authenticity case, was met with incredulity. Liborio Martínez and José Gómez Robleda had presented it as the fruit of sixteen different field trips to study the bones in Ixcateopan and hence of intrinsically greater reliability than the Dávalos/Romero report, based on a single examination.[84] Yet despite their alleged empirical exhaustiveness, the most basic tasks of inventorying and then matching the bone fragments had been plagued with blunders: one fragment had been classified in the inventory as an ulna, only to be later recycled as a fibula. Another fibula had starred in one photograph as a "left radius" and in another as a "right radius." The vertebrae had been confidently arranged in a demonstrably mistaken order. These were just some of what Gómez Robleda himself, the one member of the Gran Comisión who was to remain a defender of the tomb's authenticity, was forced to acknowledge as myriad mistakes in the reconstruction of the skeleton. It had been, he concluded, "very badly done."[85]

It was, in fact, as were all bar two of the Banco de México reports, academically negligible. They were not, however, researched or written to convince an academic audience. The publication records are eloquent: von Wuthenau's report first appeared in the Partido Revolucionario Institucional's tame paper, El Nacional; Guzmán made extensive use of the columns and letters pages of, among others, Excélsior, El Universal, and La Prensa; and Cuevas, Guzmán, and Quiroz Cuarón all first released their reports in Cultura Soviética. None of them would see the light of day, save as the basis for rebuttal, in specialist publications.[86] This is not surprising, for the majority of the articles eschewed the conventions of scholarly prose, adopting instead a strange and contradictory style that blended nationalist kitsch, vituperation of the opposition, and constant invocation of authorial probity. Discussion was largely replaced with shrill assertion, typeset with a generous quantity of bold capitals; their findings, began more than one sentence of the pathology report, were "IRREFUTABLY proven."[87] Critical arguments were not so much engaged as dismissed: the palaeographer entitled her answer to the Gran Comisión's rebuttal of her work "A reply to the mistaken objections to the report entitled 'The inscription of the Ixcateopan tomb was etched in the sixteenth century.'"[88] Taking their lead from Guzmán and Quiroz Cuarón, most of the authors portrayed the Banco de México group as committed and objective scientists confronting insidious pro-Spanish prejudice within academia. Denying personal or ideological stakes in the outcome of the controversy, they would repeatedly claim that the authenticity of the tomb rested on scientific grounds. "In matters of experimental science," Guzmán wrote, "as is here the case, one doesn't launch polemics, argue, or pronounce judgement, but prove and accept the results." In the case of Cuauhtémoc's bones, she would frequently (and tautologically) state, "Science [had] been proven by science."[89]

Such positivist blustering would later prove toxic to her academic reputation; it was, at the time, politically invaluable. The jurisdictional lines between history and politics were (and would continue to be for some time) eminently blurred. For the majority of Mexicans, the final arbiter of the tomb's authenticity would be Manuel Gual Vidal, the secretary of education. It would be he who controlled which version of Cuauhtémoc's genealogy, life, and death went into the textbooks and he—with the president looking over his shoulder—who decided whether Ixcateopan should be consecrated as one of the symbolic centres of *historia patria*, official history.[90] And in that decision academic opinion could be bypassed in the interest of what was perceived to be nationalist expediency.

It would not be the first time: there was, as recent precedent, the case of the Niños Héroes. These were six military cadets who were supposed to have been the last defenders of Chapultepec Castle against the U.S. Army in 1847, who had fought with bayonets when the ammunition ran out, and who had died one by one, until the last remaining cadet wrapped himself in the flag and jumped to his death.[91] During the 1944 commemoration a general indicated that he knew where they were buried, and a military commission was immediately formed to disinter their remains. Within five days they had discovered the necessary six skeletons in the Bosque de Chapultepec.[92] There was, however, a problem:

the remains came from a mass grave, which contained bodies of the numerous dead from both sides. Positive identification of the cadets was out of the question: on request, however, INAH produced a report that concluded that the skeletons were of young males and might be those of the Niños Héroes.[93] The secretary of education—backed by a group of undistinguished but eminently "official" historians—then pronounced that they were the Niños Héroes, in time for the assorted remains to be deployed as ceremonial ammunition in rites marking the centenary of the U.S. invasion.[94] With like demonstrations of the power of wishful thinking in defining the course of "official" historiography, it is unsurprising that Guzmán and the Banco de México group should have tried to convince the politicians rather than the academy.

The informal leaders of the group, Eulalia Guzmán, Alfonso Quiroz Cuarón, and José Gómez Robleda, were well placed to exert backstage pressure. Guzmán and Gómez Robleda were, admittedly, members of the left-wing opposition that had coalesced in the Partido Popular; but while they were ideologically distant from the Alemán government, their connections remained sufficiently powerful to guarantee them some influence. Guzmán had been a close friend of Luis Cabrera, President Carranza's ideologue and finance minister, and a protégé of Vasconcelos during the latter's period as secretary of education.[95] Gómez Robleda had been a prominent classmate of Alemán at the Escuela Nacional Preparatoria, had held senior posts in the Ministry of Public Education during the 1940s, and would become subsecretary of education in 1952.[96] He exerted his influence in the sessions of the Gran Comisión, fighting a vigorous campaign of committee room politics to moderate, obfuscate, and delay their final report.[97] Guzmán went directly to the secretaries of the presidency and education. The day before the release of the INAH report she wrote to Gual Vidal, asking him not to arrive at any official conclusion before reading the Banco de México reports; he complied.[98] She went on to hold up the Gran Comisión for several months by asking him to instruct them not to begin work until they had received her account of the investigation, which she then adamantly refused to provide.[99] Quiroz Cuarón, meanwhile, wrote regularly to both Gual Vidal and Alemán with copies of the Banco de México reports.[100] The cumulative effect was to persuade the secretary of education, at least temporarily, that the tomb was genuine.[101] More than the gossip on the cocktail party circuit, it was Gual Vidal's actions that were eloquent. In November 1949 he led a "patriotic caravan" of history teachers, local deputies, and bureaucrats to the village; in early 1950 the SEP magazine *El Maestro* reported the tomb as Cuauhtémoc's real

Figure 17. Cuauhtémoc and Cortés on the cover of the 1950 history textbook, *La Nación Mexicana: Sus orígenes*. Photograph by Paul Gillingham.

resting place; and in August 1950 the secretary attended—and consequently, implicitly, endorsed—a pro-authenticity meeting.[102] He also permitted a new generation of primary school history textbooks, released in 1952, to instruct Mexican children that Cuauhtémoc was buried in Ixcateopan.[103]

It was not just high politics that swayed Gual Vidal. Teachers, bureaucrats, municipal presidents, and other low-level components of the government machine sent in copious plans for ceremonial production centred on Cuauhtémoc, for what were usually mixed motives. A certain—and difficult to quantify—proportion of the Mexican public reacted to news of the discovery in Ixcateopan with displays of genuine enthusiasm.[104] The complex question of the blend of coercion, opportunism, and voluntarism that motivated individual initiatives or massive attendance at ceremonies to commemorate Cuauhtémoc will be considered later. Some of the impressive quantity of ritual production in the aftermath of the Ixcateopan find must be seen, however, in Durkheimian terms: as generated by, and an expression of, already extant and widely experienced emotions. Eulalia Guzmán harnessed those emotions, in an effective campaign to exert public pressure on the secretary of education and the president. In addition to her constant presence in newspapers and on the radio she gave lectures across the country, in venues that included state legislatures, provincial cultural associations, the Instituto Politécnico Nacional, the Union of Newspaper Workers, and the Mexican Alpinists' Association.[105] (Other pro-authenticity figures also went on tour: Quiroz Cuarón, for example, gave a lecture in Veracruz in January 1950.)[106] Women's organisations gave Guzmán, a leading feminist, heavy backing. A 1949 petition for the remains to be recognised was headed by eleven groups including the Bloc of Revolutionary Women, the Society of Mothers, and Mexican Nurses and Midwives. Mexico City's Central Feminine League proposed Guzmán for a Medal of Civic Merit, while the Mexican Association of Women University Graduates asked the National University to grant her an honorary doctorate.[107] The consequent ubiquity of her message helped to define and maintain a marked degree of public sympathy for the Banco de México group, which found expression in appeals to Gual Vidal and Alemán to recognise the tomb's authenticity.

Some of these came from people or groups with evident personal interests in the affair, such as Salvador Rodríguez Juárez, Arnulfo Fuentes Jaimes— another member of the Ixcateopan elite—or the Ixcateopan village council itself.[108] Others, however, held more ideological motives; their letters move along unusual discursive routes and ask for nothing in return. Among the numerous letters of congratulations that President Alemán and Eulalia Guzmán received is one from a certain Jorge Hernández of Fresnillo. "We," he wrote, "who recognise la Gran Tenochtitlán as the only Motherland, are not disposed to accept the result of the [INAH] report, as to do so would reinforce the insults and humiliations of which we have always been the target."[109] For indigenistas such as Hernández, the verdict on the tomb's authenticity was inseparable from a wider ruling on the status of indigenous peoples in the Mexican past and present. A folk song summed up the perceived racism underlying the debate:

Viva Cuauhtémoc, patriots!
King of kings,
Still doubted by idiots,
Creoles and *gachupines*.[110]

Such overt politicisation kept the Ixcateopan controversy vigorously alive, in academic and political forums and the front pages of the newspapers, for over eighteen months. The Gran Comisión never fulfilled its principal function, that of calming the aggression of the initial debate. It served, if anything, as a focus for its intensification. Before their report was even published, its members were subject to increasingly venomous personal attacks in the press, many of them penned by Eulalia Guzmán.[111] By early 1951 the list of her victims was sufficiently long and distinguished that the historian Arturo Arnáiz y Freg would claim it an honour to be included.[112] In late 1951, well after the much-delayed release of the Gran Comisión report, the gossipy intellectual Salvador Novo found himself sitting near Guzmán at supper in the Centro Vasco. There, he ironised to his diary, "[she] let her soup go cold, savouring in its place the nourishment of an improvised conference on the respective bones of Cortés and Cuauhtémoc."[113] For even Novo, once a sympathiser, Eulalia Guzmán had become a bore.

She was, however, a successful bore. The Gran Comisión's report was finished on February 7, 1951, handed over to the secretary of education, and released two and a half weeks later.[114] Despite the last-minute pleas of José Gómez Robleda to water down their findings—to avoid using their "moral authority . . . to cause problems for the Government we serve, yet less to cause deeper divisions among Mexicans"—it was firmly negative.[115] The conclusions of the first commission were refined and repeated: the documents were apocryphal or fraudulent; the plaque inscription was modern, even down to the name—the last emperor had been known in the sixteenth century as Guatemuz or Quauhtémoc but never "Coatemo," which can be translated from Nahuatl as "the serpent that descended"; and the grave contained the jumbled remains of at least four incomplete skeletons.[116] The report was and remains a definitive work. After a final meeting with Guzmán, however, the secretary of education disowned it. It went unpublished until 1962, while Gómez Robleda's favourable report was promptly published by the SEP itself.[117] In light of the unresolved conflict of opinion between the Gran Comisión and the Banco de México group, the press release read, there was an evident need for further investigation: an open verdict.[118]

Chapter 4

The Usual Suspects

The Government of the Republic already holds a favourable opinion of
the remains' authenticity, before we've even handed in our reports.
                    —Manuel Toussaint, sessions of the Comisión Investigadora

THE TOMB OF CUAUHTÉMOC IN IXCATEOPAN IS QUITE CLEARLY A
forgery. It is in some ways a clumsy forgery: the grave artefacts are risible, the
skeleton is a botched assembly job, the skull is a woman's, and the grave marker,
the copper plaque, was manufactured with either extreme haste or censurable
carelessness.[1] In other aspects, however, the Ixcateopan fraud is sophisticated.
Whoever constructed it provided the tomb with a narrative that was to some
extent historiographically plausible; they invented and disseminated a complex,
yet strategically vague, oral tradition to back up that narrative; and conscious
of their own limitations, they explained away the obvious failings in the diplomatic of the Florentino Juárez documents with the ingenious excuse that these
were naive eighteenth-century copies of sixteenth-century originals.[2] Yet for all
their skill and occasional brilliance, the forgers had undertaken an extraordinarily difficult task, and they did not manage to convince the specialists. The
constituency of believers in the Ixcateopan tomb has been restricted, since the
early 1950s, to nonspecialists, with particular emphasis on guerrerenses, presidential candidates, and the most committed indigenistas (such as the groups of
ritual dancers called *concheros*) who make annual pilgrimage to the village.[3]

Lay faith in the tomb's authenticity was not completely absurd.[4] There were,
in addition to the copious quantities of misinformation produced by Guzmán

Figure 18. Dancers celebrate the birth of Cuauhtémoc in the church of Santa María de la Asunción, Ixcateopan, February 23, 2009. AP Photo/Eduardo Verdugo.

and her supporters, various intuitive difficulties in accepting the Instituto Nacional de Antropología e Historia (INAH) version of events. The grave had been found carved in the rock six feet beneath an altar that weighed several tons. The excavation team had found it impossible to tunnel under that altar; it lacked any semblance of the foundations that might have made tunnelling, without significant engineering, possible. The puzzle was self-evident: if eight men working publicly were unable to get into the grave without causing lengthy and noisy destruction, how could one or two men have inserted the bones in total secrecy? And yet more obscure than method was motivation: why would anyone have wanted to invest so much effort in trying to fool a country?

The INAH report gave no conclusive answers. Its authors had neither the time nor the evidence to argue in detail for their attribution of the fraud. They only knew that Florentino Juárez had possessed the forged sixteenth-century documents, which gave clear signs of late-nineteenth-century composition, and that in writing his journals he had laid claim to generations of oral tradition, recording a posthumous odyssey that ended with Cuauhtémoc's burial in

Ixcateopan. There was no other immediately obvious forger; there would be, in the foreseeable furore over the report, demands for an explanation of who-dunit. And so, while qualifying his version as a hypothesis and admitting the possibility of unidentified coauthors, Silvio Zavala ascribed the grave's invention to Juárez himself.[5] From a long-dead rancher's scant outlines and above all from the journals themselves, Zavala painted a "people's historian," proud of the indigenous past, resentful of Spanish dominance, and bent on righting history and its blind injustice. Juárez's contemporaries, many of them "humble field-hands . . . dressed in white, with sandals and big sombreros, [who] inherit[ed] unknowing the grandeur and sovereignty of the ancient Mexican nobility," had largely forgotten their last emperor; Juárez had aimed to remind them not just of Cuauhtémoc but of an entire culture balanced between concealment and extinction.[6] The rancher had been an "instinctive and poetic historian" or—in drier terms—an ideologically motivated organic intellectual.[7] It was a mytho-poeic and affectively powerful account of a man from nowhere, an authentic *don nadie*, struggling through fraud to defend, or re-create, or maybe even just create, a memory of his people's past.[8]

It was, equally well, a canny discursive strategy. While negating the tomb's authenticity, Zavala was countering the indigenista text of the secret burial of Cuauhtémoc with another, equally indigenista in content and rhetoric, of creative popular resistance to the hegemony of a hispanicised elite. This was a solid preemptive defence against the attacks of those who desperately wished to believe in the tomb. It was also a failure. Political and academic questions aside, two deep-seated, near-universal prejudices undermined Zavala's conclusions. One was the assumption (widespread until recently in both Mexico and academia) that provincial ranchers such as Juárez were incapable of knowing the ropes of their own histories and equally incapable of manipulating the symbols that those histories offer. The other was the *leyenda negra*, the "black legend," of the Porfiriato: the postrevolutionary representation of the late nineteenth century in Mexico as a period of ignorance, illiteracy, and generalised obscurantism.[9] It was unimaginable to many Mexicans that a countryman such as Florentino Juárez should have been as aware as a twentieth-century anthropologist of double unilineal descent among the central Mesoamerican peoples or that he should have known that his own village had once been Chontal, both of which were prerequisites for penning the journals. They would—irrespective of the contradiction inherent in believing peasants capable of remembering a secret tomb but not their ancestors' ethnic identity—perceive the fraud as beyond the abilities of a villager. That Florentino Juárez should have been the forger seemed, as Luis Chávez Orozco put it, "patently untrue."[10]

And so ever since 1949 people have sought, in the words of both Zavala and Olivera de Bonfil, "a mind of greater scope" behind the legend and tomb of Ixcateopan.[11] The earliest candidate, rumoured before the grave even came to light, was (with a certain inevitability, given the pervasiveness of what Alan Knight has called "statolatry" in contemporary Mexican culture) that shady and villainous abstraction, the state.[12] The thesis that members or associates of the federal government might have created a tomb to provide a focus for cultural nationalism, and as a distraction from shocks such as the peso devaluations of 1948 and 1949, may have been far-fetched. It was nevertheless common currency in the offices of at least one mainstream newspaper. When the tomb appeared, and appeared genuine, an editorial in *La Prensa* expressed repeated relief that it was not "a well-meaning trick, prepared in advance to raise the spirit of the nation during the social and political crisis of our times."[13] Echoes of such suspicions travelled as far as the Comisión Investigadora: as they discussed sending paper samples from the Juárez documents for chemical analysis to determine their age, Dr. Joaquín Izquierdo warned darkly of the possibility that the samples could be substituted for others of authentic sixteenth-century provenance.[14] Belief in the Machiavellian ambitions—if not always abilities— of the ruling elite was built into popular culture in twentieth-century Mexico, and an emotionally satisfying conspiracy theory could run for decades. This one did: when a third academic commission was formed in 1976 to revise the Ixcateopan case, several of its members began with the hypothesis that the tomb was the material creation of the Alemán administration.[15]

That government would, as will become apparent, try to capitalise on the discovery. But the politicians were opportunists rather than inventors. It would have been extraordinarily difficult to both construct and uncover the tomb in the same epoch, requiring complex local alliances and a leakproof network of villagers to stand the test of prolonged media attention. It would have been impossible to do so without some form of simultaneous and legitimate work in the church to cover the noise and entry of workmen; and the last substantial alterations to the church interior had been undertaken in 1921, when the cupola was given a cement covering and inset with late-nineteenth-century English porcelain plates.[16] The oral tradition that lent both credibility and legitimacy to the fragile story of the documents, and which must be considered a central component of the fraud (without its encouragement Guzmán would not have launched the excavation), was no overnight invention; it has been reliably traced back to the late nineteenth century.[17] Finally, and perhaps most convincingly, it would have been a particularly inept Machiavellian who engaged in high-risk archaeological fraud and did it so awkwardly. Both the numerous rough edges of the tomb and the confused responses of the government to the ensuing scandal suggest anything but a coldly planned elite conspiracy. It was, after all, the education secretary (accused of being a "strictly honest" man) who, amid the euphoria of the tomb's discovery, ordered INAH to investigate its authenticity. He could equally well have congratulated Eulalia Guzmán on her discovery; organised an immediate, legitimizing, presidential visit to Ixcateopan; and launched a triumphalist rewrite of textbook history. Gual Vidal did none of this, and President Alemán turned down invitations to go to the village.[18] None of the education secretary's behaviour indicates anything more than confusion, irritation, and concern over the controversy that accompanied the bones from the grave. He was a technocrat and a law professor and a friend of the president's; he was not, one diplomat observed in a double-edged compliment, much of a politician, and he was certainly not a bureaucratic master forger.[19] That some should have considered him or his colleagues as responsible for the Ixcateopan tomb is, in short, more revealing of Mexican expectations of their ruling class than anything else.

If the canard of contemporary governmental responsibility was easily shot down, the assumptions that lent it wings—that the tomb must be the work of either an elite member or a contemporary or both in the same person—were nonetheless enduring. When these assumptions were combined with suggestive evidence pointing to forgers other than Florentino Juárez, academic attention put two other men in the dock. One was the nineteenth-century soldier, politician, diplomat, and writer Vicente Riva Palacio y Guerrero. The other was a village politician, a phony doctor, the original discoverer of the documents, "the last living letter," and a direct descendant—he would end up claiming—of the Mexica royal family: Salvador Rodríguez Juárez.[20]

The case against Riva Palacio hung, initially, on little more than a road sign—if indeed there was one—naming the main square in Ixcateopan in his honour.[21] Even by the standards of the tangled and often empirically challenged speculation surrounding the tomb, this was not much of a smoking gun. But Riva Palacio had also used forged documents in writing about Cuauhtémoc in his landmark popular history, *México a través de los siglos*; and the combination was enough to make Zavala include the hypothesis of Riva Palacio's involvement in the INAH report and to make Manuel Toussaint, a specialist on Riva Palacio, and Arturo Arnáiz y Freg propound that hypothesis during the early meetings of the Gran Comisión.[22] It would be considered once more in 1956, when for a brief moment Antonio Pompa y Pompa seemed on the point of discovering Cuauhtémoc's real tomb in Chiapas.[23] And it would finally be researched in some depth in the course of the 1976 Bonfil investigation. Significant sectors of academic opinion, in other words, found the idea of Riva Palacio's implication in the forgery attractive. And this is unsurprising, for possible prejudices in favour of well-educated upper-class forgers aside, to delve into Riva Palacio's biography is to find copious circumstantial evidence for his authorship of the tomb.[24]

Vicente Riva Palacio y Guerrero was born in Mexico City on October 16, 1832, to a family that was, in terms of the postindependence political elite, of markedly blue blood. His father, Mariano Riva Palacio, was a prominent liberal politician who had been governor of the department of Mexico on several occasions and who defended the Hapsburg emperor Maximilian in front of the kangaroo court that condemned him to death.[25] His maternal grandfather was Vicente Guerrero, scion to one of the larger property holdings in the state, which would take his name, and one of the foremost caudillos of the south during the wars of independence. Guerrero had been civil and military commander of the region in the aftermath of independence, a fleeting holder of the presidency, and a figurehead to the 1830 southern rebellion against the centralist government. Riva Palacio never knew his grandfather; in the winter of early 1831 Vicente Guerrero was invited aboard an Italian ship lying in Acapulco, kidnapped (at the behest of the government he opposed), and murdered.[26] Guerrero bequeathed his grandson a powerful name and apparently influential regional contacts. When, in 1880, the state of Guerrero was undergoing a typically divisive race for the governorship, both sides wrote to Riva Palacio seeking his support.[27]

It was more than inherited symbolic capital that underlay this political clout. Riva Palacio was from an early age a political animal: by the age of twenty-three, a law degree already behind him, he had become an alderman in Mexico City, and by 1861 he was a federal deputy.[28] When the French invaded in 1862 he recruited a troop of irregular cavalry and turned out to be more than a *tintorerillo*, a pen-pusher, in successfully leading them through the prolonged guerrilla campaigns that ended Maximilian's regime. In 1865 he became governor of Michoacán and commander of the Army of the Centre, and in 1868 he became a member of the Supreme Court.[29] When General Porfirio Díaz

Figure 19.
General Vicente Riva
Palacio y Guerrero;
courtesy of Benson
Latin American
Collection, University
of Texas, Austin.

rebelled against the government in 1876, Riva Palacio joined him; it is possible that he drafted the rebellion's manifesto, the Plan de Tuxtepec, before he was again given the Army of the Centre. Once Díaz's seizure of power was complete, Riva Palacio was rewarded with the cabinet post of minister of development and was later made president of the Chamber of Deputies. By 1880, at the peak of his career, he was fancied as a presidential contender, and Daniel Cosío Villegas has argued that he progressed so far as to write a manifesto. But he seems to have fallen between two stools, too powerful to meet Díaz's criteria for a puppet successor and, yet, once sidelined, too weak—without the manpower afforded by a traditional rural fiefdom—to do much about it. Riva

Palacio ended up, ironically, "managing" the 1880 federal election in favour of Díaz's astutely chosen stand-in, the pliable and corrupt Manuel González. Despite this service he was excluded from the cabinet, imprisoned for most of 1884, warned off participation in the elections of that year (which brought Díaz back to the presidency), and finally dispatched to a golden exile as ambassador in Madrid.[30] There *el general* wrote short stories, womanised, wooed society, and died.

His literary bent was not a late-found consolation in the political twilight. Riva Palacio was a lifelong and compulsive writer: a poet, historian, and playwright but, as much as a *littérateur*, a journalist and an author of historical bodice rippers. These novels, labyrinthine productions with lurid titles such as *A Married Nun, a Virgin Martyr*; *Memories of an Impostor*; and *The Pirates of the Gulf*, were written in the comparative calm of the late 1860s and early 1870s and published in weekly installments of thirty-two quarto pages.[31] They were both didactic and readable, drawing heavily on the archives of the Inquisition, which Riva Palacio had "privatised" in 1861, to combine ideologically charged histories of colonial Mexico with the frenetic action that pulp fiction demands.[32] (Riva Palacio would have appreciated Raymond Chandler's dictum: "When in doubt have a man come through a door with a gun in his hand.")[33] In the first few pages of *Calvario y Tabor*, to give an example of Riva Palacio's usual pace, readers are taken to the coast of Guerrero, meet the beautiful *morena* Alejandra, find out about a hidden treasure and a family tragedy, and end up watching as Alejandra is kidnapped and her virtue is (inevitably) imperilled. Such operatic plots, exotic, improbable, pervaded by violence and pressing sexual tension, came wrapped in language that tacked between the high romantic and the earthily ranchero—one Riva Palacio character is, memorably, "more in love than a cock"—and were massively popular, the *telenovelas* of their day. Print runs of six thousand copies, priced at a *real* apiece in Mexico City and one and a half *reales* in the provinces, sold out immediately and had to be supplemented by urgently produced second editions.[34] The clergy detested the novels: in the village of San Felipe del Obraje the parish priest confiscated and burned all the copies he could, while a colleague of the cloth denounced one book as a "web of the most repugnant coquetry and lubriciousness."[35] Readers, however, honoured them by transcribing some of their more memorable characters and lines into everyday speech; some sixty years after its publication, the politician and gunman Gonzalo N. Santos would self-consciously quote *Martín Garatuza* as he groped for a parting line.[36]

For all their qualities, however, one of the unavoidable impressions left by the novels is that of a talented man enjoying himself and paying the bills. He wrote three, none of them under six hundred pages, in just over a year, 1868, while simultaneously practising as a lawyer, holding down a seat on the Supreme Court, and editing the Republican daily *La Orquesta*.[37] It took his definitive political failure of 1880 to make Riva Palacio focus his extensive research, literary flair, and remaining governmental leverage in the production of what became the urtext of Mexican popular history, the monumental *México a través de los siglos*.[38] It started as a consolation prize: the incoming President González commissioned a History of the War against the Intervention and the Empire from the politically unemployed Riva Palacio. It ended up, eight years, five volumes, and a jail sentence later, as a complete history of Mexico from the fourteenth century to the liberalism triumphant of the 1850s. Riva Palacio organised the work and its publication, recruited historians such as Alfredo Chavero and Francisco del Paso y Troncoso, and himself wrote the volume that covered the colonial period. The book was produced, as José Ortiz Monasterio notes, on an almost industrial scale: each volume was written by a leading specialist, supported by teams of archivists, researchers, and army personnel.[39] The result was an overview comprehensive to the point of exhaustiveness, at times inspired, at times frankly unreadable, and enduringly influential. When the revolutionary leader and enthusiastic spiritualist Francisco I. Madero was considering a career in politics, José, one of his two significant early "spirit voices," chided him for his paltry knowledge of national history and recommended that he read *México a través de los siglos*.[40]

The distinction between those aspects of Riva Palacio's life that historians tend to take seriously, such as his politico-military career and *México a través de los siglos*, and the more frivolous, such as his sketches and his fiction, largely misses the point. The liberal elites of the mid–nineteenth century looked back on the traumatic instability of postindependence Mexico, a vista of endemic rebellion, transitory presidents and their constitutions of convenience, foreign invasions, massive debt, and more than one comic-opera dictator, and were inspired by the rational fear that their political community was all too imaginary. To this they added a distinct pessimism concerning their prospects of constructing a stable nation-state from the ruins of recent history and the considerable regional and ethnic diversity of the present. "Let us lift," suggested Ignacio Ramírez in 1856, "the thin veil of the mixed race which is drawn across the country and we will find a hundred nations which today, vainly, we struggle to blend into one."[41] In this struggle, waged with a wholly new intensity from the 1850s onward, popular culture became a central battleground. School classes, street names, public monuments, civic ceremonies, and village bands were all enlisted in a cohesive hegemonic campaign aimed at synthesizing and disseminating an affectively viable Mexican identity. *México a través de los siglos*, with its recasting of more than four centuries of Mexican history into a single uphill march toward the high ground of Juarez's victory over the conservatives, was part of that schema. As Riva Palacio wrote in the book's prospectus, one of his intentions was "[to bring together] in a single book an account of the different developments of a society which, amidst great difficulties, carries out the evolution that brings it to take up a worthy place alongside the most enlightened peoples." The reader of *México a través de los siglos* was to be left in no doubt that this end point, the citizenry of triumphant liberal Mexico, was the product of both conquest and colony, "a people that was neither the conquered nor the conqueror, but whom from each inherited virtues and vices, glories and traditions, characters and temperaments, and within which, without denying patriotic duties or fraternal bonds, nor provoking family quarrels, some could pride themselves on having the blood of the victors of Lepanto and San Quintin, and others of numbering among their grandfathers the sons of Moctezuma and Cuauhtémoc, and who would come to unite beneath a single flag, forming a single nation."[42]

While Riva Palacio never stated the nationalist purpose of his novels with such clarity, they were nevertheless, and as much as his more formal historical writing, a response to one intellectual's call to "make *belles lettres* into a defensive weapon."[43] The overriding theme of all seven novels parallels that of *México a través de los siglos*: a deterministic journey, through secular processes of cultural exchange, resistance, and rebellion, toward an independent mestizo Mexico. As José Ortiz Monasterio has argued, to disaggregate Riva Palacio the novelist from Riva Palacio the historian and Riva Palacio the politician is to ignore the common purpose that drew together the diverse threads of his life, namely, what he called his "savage idea of Patriotism."[44] El general was first, foremost, and self-consciously a nation builder.

This, however, barely differentiates Vicente Riva Palacio from other literary liberals of his generation and is in itself insufficient to warrant an accusation of tomb forgery. Public engagement with the perceived problem of a fragile national identity was more a rule than an exception for writers of the time, and the work of Mexican contemporaries such as Ignacio Altamirano,

Manuel Payno, Guillermo Prieto, Ignacio Ramírez, and Manuel Rivera Cambas was shot through with similarly purposive nationalist themes and imaging.[45] Across nineteenth-century Latin America, similar politician-novelists saw their fictions as bridges between their territories' different social classes and ethnic groups, tools for engineering national unity.[46] A specific interest in Cuauhtémoc is hardly a distinguishing feature either: the late 1880s and 1890s saw something of a literary boom in plays, odes, and essays dealing with the last emperor's life, and the multiple references to Cuauhtémoc that punctuate the Riva Palacio canon also pervade the production of other authors. Where Riva Palacio does stand out from his contemporaries as a possible creator of the Ixcateopan tomb is in the earliness and intensity of his interest in Cuauhtémoc and in the conflu-ence of that interest with an equally early and radical reappraisal of the value of Mexico's (hitherto largely ignored) archaeological heritage. He was, addition-ally, profoundly interested in popular traditions—the myths, legends, and odes that invested corners of Mexico, and specifically Mexico City, with magic realist pasts.[47] And he was, finally, profoundly conscious of the problems of evidence and verifiability inherent in any attempt to write histories of the preconquest or early colonial periods. If Riva Palacio never committed major archaeological fraud, it was not through any lack of the necessary intellectual baggage.

Riva Palacio had in fact played a central role in the governmental iconi-sation of Cuauhtémoc of the late nineteenth century. The symbol of the last emperor had not gone wholly unexploited before then: creole writers such as Carlos Sigüenza y Góngora had used him as a referent for resistance; Morelos had invoked him as one of the fathers of independent Mexico in opening the Congress of Chilpancingo; and another priestly rebel, Fray Servando Teresa de Mier, had even claimed direct biological descent from Cuauhtémoc.[48] (This was not as far from the discursive mainstream as historians have made out; Benito Juárez too spoke rhetorically of his "progenitor, Cuatimoctizin.")[49] Cuauhtémoc was also represented outside Mexico as an archetype of American autonomy. In 1827 the Colombian José Fernández Madrid composed a five-act tragedy, *Guatimoc*, in which the last emperor calls for Americans to be "free, or dead; slaves, never!" An 1844 Independence Day speaker in Guatemala rhetorically asked his audience if they recalled "how the ill-starred Cuauhtémoc expired amid pain and torments."[50] But these were passing, ill-defined, and predomi-nantly abstract references, lacking even the common ground of a standardised name. The Jesuit historian Clavijero's *Historia antigua de Mexico*, published simultaneously in 1826 in London, Mexico, Colombia, Buenos Aires, Chile,

Peru, and Guatemala, stopped at 1519 and contained no information about Cuauhtémoc at all. Writing in 1841, the usually observant and well-informed Scotswoman Fanny Calderón de la Barca seemed to ignore Cuauhtémoc and believe Moctezuma to have been the last emperor.[51] It was not that great an exaggeration when, in the 1852 *Diccionario Universal de Historia y Geografía*, José Fernández Ramírez described Cuauhtémoc as "forgotten"; even twenty years later, in Rivera Cambas's influential popular history, *Los gobernantes de Mexico*, Cuauhtémoc received a mere five mentions compared to Moctezuma's twenty-four.[52] Such asymmetry only reproduced that of the sixteenth-century chronicles, in which Moctezuma is the lead indigenous actor and Cuauhtémoc is little more than a deus ex machina who appears, fleetingly, at the end, in time to lose nobly and be martyred. But the resolutely unheroic raw material of Moctezuma's biography resisted refashioning into much more than the tale of a victim, and in their search for an indigenous origin figure the shapers of *historia patria* found themselves in a symbolic power vacuum. Had Cuauhtémoc not existed, it would have been eminently necessary to invent him, which is what, with varying degrees of empirical nicety, the cultural nationalists of the liberal era and the Porfiriato did.

Riva Palacio's principal contributions to this creative process were a novel, a history, and a statue. The novel, *Martín Garatuza*, was published in 1868 and tells the intertwined stories of a 1624 creole independence conspiracy and the fictional Carbajal dynasty. These ill-fated descendants of the last Mexica emperor serve as a device to retell, under the guise of family tradition, the history of the fall of Tenochtitlán and to introduce Cuauhtémoc. They also function as the purveyors of an unlikely semiotic twist. Cuauhtémoc is already deployed to symbolise (and legitimise) Mexican independence: both historically, through his resistance to Cortés, and fictionally, as ancestor of the priest Alfonso de Salazar, ringleader of the planned rebellion.[53] The challenge was to dissociate the emperor from indigenous revanchism, which Riva Palacio saw as "the source of historic mistakes and misled philosophical debates," and to connect him instead to the book's other central nationalist theme, *mestizaje*.[54] The solution was to give Cuauhtémoc a Spanish lover, Isabel Carbajal, and to make him the progenitor of a family, which becomes shorthand for an idealised Mexican polity. "The shadow of the eagle," he prophesies during their fertile last night together, "covered the dove, and a hope was born for my line and for my people; man of a new race, perhaps his descendants will break the chains of his brothers. . . . [I]f my name dies, my blood will make this earth fertile, because from my blood and your blood, Isabel, heroes could be born."[55] The single postcoital sentence encapsulates the ideological subtext of *Martín Garatuza*: Mexico was foredestined to be an independent mestizo republic, heir to the double legitimacy of the prehispanic kingdoms and the creole uprisings against a distant Spain. The message is evidently the same as that of *México a través de los siglos*, and so too is the character allotted to Cuauhtémoc, *simpático* (albeit in a slightly messianic way) and partially reconciled (most improbably) to the fact of conquest.

This reconciliation, achieved in *Martín Garatuza* through his relationship with Isabel, recurs in *México a través de los siglos* through his baptism—taking the name of Don Fernando Cortés Cuauhtémoc—and through the voluntary assistance that he and his son lend the Spanish in the "pacification" of the former Mexica territories. Readers opened volume 1 of *México a través de los siglos* to find on the first folio page a painting of Cuauhtémoc's baptism. Riva Palacio based his account of this damascene conversion, which goes squarely against the consensus of sixteenth-century sources, on two alleged royal letters of instruction filed in the Mexico City general archive.[56] Both are forgeries—clearly not his own forgeries—and Riva Palacio's arguments promoting their authenticity are unusually illogical.[57] Yet, while historically improbable, the mythical Cuauhtémoc whom Riva Palacio distilled from these forgeries made sound sense in terms of nationalist ideology. Cuauhtémoc, to work as an origin figure for nineteenth-century Mexicans, had to represent more than indigenous resistance to foreign invasion. He also had to signify, semiotically testing though this was, unification. Riva Palacio's originality lay not only in selecting Cuauhtémoc as the indigenous hero par excellence, promoting him over the heads of such contenders as Nezahualcóyotl, Xicoténcatl, Cuitláhuac, and Cacamatzin.[58] It lay also in finessing the figure of the last emperor into simultaneously standing for these opposed ideals, in making Cuauhtémoc, in terms of Mexican nationalism, good to think.

That Cuauhtémoc became good (and politically modish) to think is clear from the wave of cultural production inspired by his story in the 1880s and 1890s. He had previously been sporadically commemorated in isolated works such as de Madrid's play *Guatimoc o Guatimocin* (1835), the inconspicuous 1869 Cuauhtémoc monument on Mexico City's Paseo de la Viga, and Ireneo Paz's 1873 novel *Amor y Suplicio*.[59] From patchwork evidence, it seems that the story of the last emperor had primordial appeal to Mexican audiences: in 1790, for example, a play about the torture and death of Cuauhtémoc was smuggled past an unwary substitute censor to the stage of the New Coliseum, where it drew full and politically vociferous houses before being banned.[60] In general, however, Riva Palacio's bitter reflection that "Cuauhtémoc has never made it on the Mexican stage" applied well beyond the doors of the theatre.[61] By the late 1880s this was no longer the case. A short list of Mexican and Latin American authors who wrote about Cuauhtémoc between 1880 and 1910 would include Ignacio Altamirano, Alfredo Chavero, Ruben Darió, Manuel Orozco y Berra, Francisco Pí y Margall, Manuel G. Prieto, Justo Sierra, Francisco Sosa, and Eduardo del Valle.[62] There are numerous less recognisable names from the period with a work on Cuauhtémoc to their credit. José María Rodríguez, for example, wrote the libretto of an opera about the last emperor, apologizing in an appendix for its poor quality.[63] More ubiquitous than any of the above was the entrepreneur Isaac Garza's tribute: in 1890 he founded a brewery in Monterrey, the Cervecería Cuauhtémoc Moctezuma, and began producing fifteen hundred bottles of beer a day bearing the last emperor's name and likeness.

The idea that Cuauhtémoc was, as one historian phrased it, "the first and most illustrious of the defenders of the nationality founded by Tenoch in 1327" was one whose time had come, part of a new interest in connecting prehispanic and Porfirian Mexico.[64] The experience of successful but costly resistance to the French Intervention may have helped fuel the new cult: thus in 1878 the barrio of Ometepec in Puebla, a place that suffered heavily in the wars of the 1860s, became the new municipio of Ometepec de Cuauhtémoc, the comparison between Mexica emperor and everyday Mexican soldiers made explicit in the naming ceremony.[65] But there was a more concrete reason for writing about Cuauhtémoc to become almost de rigueur in the Porfiriato. The majority of the texts—including the labels on the beer bottles—were inspired by a single event: the construction of the Paseo de la Reforma monument to Cuauhtémoc.[66]

This was inaugurated on August 21, 1887, although Riva Palacio was not there to see it; he had been packed off to Madrid a year earlier. A crowd of the sort of people who attend ceremonies to unveil monuments—political and military leaders, bureaucrats, students, representatives of workers' societies, gente decente, "decent folk"—gathered. President Díaz arrived, a twenty-one-gun salute was fired, the national anthem was sung, a speech was given, and the monument was unveiled; another twenty-one-gun salute was fired; another speech was given, this time in Nahuatl; assorted worthies read patriotic prose and poetry; the anthem was sung once more; and a third twenty-one-gun salute rounded off the busy afternoon.[67] None of the dignitaries present, however, was

Figure 20.
Message in a bottle.
Since 1890 the beers
of the Cervecería
Cuauhtémoc Moctezuma
have featured stylised
Cuauhtémocs/Indians on
the labels, here overlaid,
revealingly, with two
Xs to hail the dawn of
the twentieth century.
Photograph by
Paul Gillingham.

as responsible for the statue they were inaugurating as the absent Riva Palacio. It had been his idea, ten years earlier, while minister of development, to plant statues of selected Mexican leaders the length of the Paseo de la Reforma, converting Mexico City's answer to the Champs Élysées into an allegory of the acceptable face of national history.[68] He had organised the competition to find a sculptor worthy of depicting Cuauhtémoc and negotiated a budget of 152,000 pesos for the winning proposal, a twelve-foot-high bronze Cuauhtémoc, flanked by nine-foot figures of Cacamatzin and Cuitláhuac. (This would eventually be cut by more than fifty thousand pesos, causing the latter two leaders' deletion.)[69] The size of the budget was an indication of Riva Palacio's belief in the monument's ability to influence cultural politics: it was equivalent to circa 20 percent of the city's tax revenues that year, or six hundred thousand rural labourers' daily wages.[70] He was right. Noreña's statue of Cuauhtémoc (grasping a short spear and looking suspiciously Grecian in profile and toga) was critically acclaimed, influenced a generation of architects to experiment with neo-indigenista designs, defined a locus for annual commemorations of the fall of Tenochtitlán, and provided

VISTAS, MEXICANAS.   163
MEXICO   MEXICO
ESTATUA DE QUAHUTEMOC   STATUE OF QUAHUTEMOC

Figure 21. Postcard of the monument to Cuauhtémoc on the Paseo de la Reforma, Mexico City, 1883–95. Photograph by Abel Briquet; courtesy of the Research Library, the Getty Research Institute, Los Angeles.

a daily and central reminder to *capitalinos* of the antiquity, and hence legitimacy and inevitability, of a Mexican nation that was still only half invented.[71]

Riva Palacio's instrumentalist approach to Cuauhtémoc's historical image, his search for the contemporary political utility of the past, was also evinced in his concept of archaeology. The discipline was in its infancy in his time, and not just in Mexico: Heinrich Schliemann only launched the Troy and Mycenae digs in the 1870s, and his work was initially rubbished.[72] Early archaeology in Mexico had consisted as much of chance finds, tourism, and pseudo-colonial pillage as of considered scholarly work.[73] (John Lloyd Stephens proposed buying the Maya sites he visited and transporting their buildings wholesale to New York.)[74] While a certain colonial romanticism pushed more people into archaeological expeditions in the later nineteenth century, a rigorous and systematic methodology was relatively slow in emerging. The key tool of stratigraphic analysis went unused in Mexico or the rest of the Americas until Manuel Gamio's dig at San Miguel Amantla, Azcapotzalco, in 1912.[75] Riva Palacio deplored the shortage of archaeologists in Mexico and as minister of development encouraged projects such as the conservation of Teotihuacán.[76] But more revealing—and influential—was his 1880 speech on Mexican ownership of archaeological material. Claude-Joséph Désiré Charnay had proposed exploring Teotihuacán in exchange for the right to export any pieces discovered. This was put to Congress, where Justo Sierra spoke in favour of the deal. Riva Palacio gave a firebrand reply. "Gentlemen," he ironised,

> I confess to being deeply moved. I love Science, but I hold, if you will, a savage idea of Patriotism, because I prefer fire to foreign domination. (Applause). I do not come to attack these great civilisations who shall bring us light in Mexico. . . . But that they should come to us saying that as these are hidden treasures, we should hand them over; that they should compare us to Egypt in her decadence and with India in barbarism; that they should come to us to say that all this can benefit European science, and as such we should permit them to just ship away all our treasures. . . .
> Sir, I cannot agree to this.[77]

That Charnay was French and disdainful of the cultures he studied ("one must not," he wrote, "labour under any illusion as to the beauty or the real merit of the American monuments") can hardly have helped. The deputies' eventual decision to refuse him permission was nevertheless unprecedented.[78] Riva Palacio's speech, and the decision it provoked, marked a watershed in the revalorisation of prehispanic culture, a process that led to archaeology and its material output forming a central component of state nationalism in the twentieth century.

The new interest in prehispanic history and culture was accompanied by a paternalist interest in improving the lot of (at least some) present-day Indians. Government-forged links of education, transport, and commerce were to bind Indians into close economic and cultural contact with the rest of Mexico. This schizoid combination—the exaltation of (parts of) indigenous culture accompanied by deliberate attempts to trade it in for modern homogeneity—is usually termed *indigenismo*. For some indigenismo dates only to the 1910s, for three reasons: the greater intensity with which revolutionary politicians and intellectuals

Figure 22. The colonial romance of archaeology: Alice Dixon
Le Plongeon with rifle, Chichén Itzá, 1873; courtesy of the
Research Library, the Getty Research Institute, Los Angeles.

reclaimed the indigenous past, the lesser racism with which they approached
the indigenous present, and the novelty of government policies that aimed to
modernise indigenous communities.[79] Yet such periodisation obscures some
important continuities. Riva Palacio and other Porfirian nation builders laid
vigorous claim to the distinguished, independent ancestry of the indigenous
past (metaphorically and biologically: Riva Palacio coveted the superior teeth,
hairlessness, and muscularity of the Indian).[80] Overt racism may have diminished slightly among revolutionary elites, but it stubbornly endured in many
of the teachers and bureaucrats who actually worked with Indian communities. Three interwoven habits of thought recur in their official writings from the
1930s and 1940s: the civilisation/barbarism dichotomy; the social Darwinism
that labelled societies "backward," less evolved, or racially inferior; and the old
opposition of white/mestizo *gente de razón* to "irrational," by clear linguistic

= Le Chichan-Chob ou la Prison à Chichen-Itza . Iucatan.

Figure 23. Attraction and disdain: Claude-Joséph Désiré Charnay's photograph of Chichén Itzá. From Claude-Joséph Désiré Charnay, *Ruines du Mexique et types mexicains,* 1862–63; courtesy of the Kislak Collection of the Rare Book Division of the Library of Congress.

implication childlike, *indios*.[81] The final point is more telling: the array of the revolutionary state's developmentalist agencies for Indians was unparalleled, and their heavy reliance on social scientists was innovative.

Even this, however, was not wholly unprecedented. Well before the Porfiriato politicians proposed what we would class as indigenista policies, such as bilingual education, which remained proposals because of state fragility.[82] Porfirians, imbued with their time's fierce concern for "progress," could hardly avoid considering the practical as well as ideological consequences of a large indigenous population. By crude linguistic criteria, one in five Mexicans were Indian; by cultural criteria, Gamio later estimated, as many as three-quarters of Mexicans were indigenous.[83] Porfirio Díaz's presidential report for 1896 claimed that a "practical project to disseminate elementary education among the indigenous class" was under consideration.[84] The powerful technocrat José Limantour closed his 1901 speech to the *concurso científico nacional* with a peroration that recognised Mexico's double ancestry, condemned the "barbarity" of European beliefs in racial superiority, and concluded that indigenous communities' problems were uniquely environmental, there to be vanquished with education, hygiene, and public morals.[85] The First Indigenista Congress aimed to bring similar technocrats and intellectuals together to discuss ways to improve indigenous populations' living standards.[86] Ethnographers also made their appearance: in 1895 the Congress of Americanists met in Mexico City.[87] Admittedly not much happened, barring some general public health policies whose principal benefits were to indigenous peoples. In the 1880s, for example, governors in both rich and poor states targeted smallpox (which remained particularly lethal for Indians) through mass vaccination.[88]

Yet if indigenismo was an ideology only partially realised by the Porfirians, its developmentalist aspects far more conceptual than concrete, this does not negate its existence: communism, for example, is not generally understood to originate in 1917. The ideas of redemption through progress were there—they were eminently Porfirian—even if the will or ability to materialise them was not. It was not just Indians who went without state education in the nineteenth century; so did all of Mexico's marginalised, as proposals for mandatory public education came and were defeated. Yet the federal government did persuade state governments to accept the principle (if not the obligation) of free mandatory primary education, stressing its application to Indian as well as white and mestizo populations.[89] When to this is added the emic usage of indigenismo (at least immediately) before the revolution, the ideology's prior existence seems undeniable. The change from Porfirian to revolutionary indigenismo was quantitative as well as qualitative, a reflection not just of new political priorities but also of enhanced state capacities, a bigger bureaucracy with greater technocratic reach to deal with long-standing ambitions. Prerevolutionary indigenismo was, as Alan Knight has posited, "more rhetorical than real"; but it was a rhetoric spouted with some vigour and a reality present even if embryonic.[90]

Riva Palacio was central to Porfirian indigenismo, and the later scholars who suspected his hand in the Ixcateopan tomb knew that he had combined intense interests in Cuauhtémoc and contemporary archaeology, that he had wittingly used unreliable evidence in constructing a politically convenient history of Cuauhtémoc, and that he had family ties linking him to the state of Guerrero. He held, furthermore, what was in a positivist age an unconventional philosophy of history. His novels were, he claimed, history and not fiction.[91] "History," he wrote in a short story based on popular tradition, "doesn't tell everything thus: but I find legend more satisfying. . . . [Legends] have a freshness that is a joy and an interest which grips; and then, studied under the light of history, they get covered with the dust of the archives, tamed with the *bons mots* of the literati and they lose [their] magic."[92] Riva Palacio was clearly pulled in different directions by what Pierre Nora dubbed the "sacred context" of memory and the "prose" of history.[93] He knew very well what existed (and equally important, what did not exist) in the national archives, having drawn up an index of their contents while secretary of the *ayuntamiento*. He had, additionally, held onto the archives of the Inquisition for at least eight years. Finally, the sense of humour that informed another forgery—the verses of a provincial poetess called Rosa Espino, incontestably Riva Palacio's work—should not be discounted.[94] Riva Palacio might have felt the Ixcateopan tomb to be necessary, patriotic, and a bit of a laugh.

But the history of Riva Palacio's involvement in the Ixcateopan fraud was not so much joke as shaggy dog story. The hypothesis was sound, and the fit of character to crime was reasonable, in terms of ability if not morality: among eminent Porfirians, Riva Palacio was the best man for the job of forging Cuauhtémoc's tomb. The a priori argument that such a sophisticated forger would not have created a grave with such rough edges is inconclusive. Had Riva Palacio been behind the Ixcateopan legend, he would have necessarily recruited local help in physically making the tomb. Such local help could well have botched the implementation of el general's plan: burying too many femurs, disregarding instructions on falsifying the plaque and tomb contents. Yet any vision of Riva Palacio as an architect whose dreams were sabotaged by witless builders is undermined by a return to the blueprints of the fraud, the Motolinía documents. These he surely would have fabricated himself, particularly the marginalia in *Destierro de Ignorancias* and the hide folder manuscript; they contained what were supposed to be copies of Motolinía's signature and as such were technically demanding works. It is impossible to believe that a man who in *México a través de los siglos* had reproduced facsimile signatures of many of the great and good of sixteenth-century New Spain should have got that of Motolinía as completely wrong as did the author of these two documents.[95] The language of the journals does not read like even a disguised Riva Palacio: a man whose opinion of the conquistadors lay between ambiguous and conciliatory, whose coauthor had called Cortés "the bravest captain of the century" in *El libro rojo*, was unlikely to then describe that same captain, in the words of the first Juárez journal, as "petty and evil."[96] Finally the tomb is, as we shall see below, dated by several indicators to the early 1890s. Aside from a brief return to bury his wife, Riva Palacio left Mexico—forever as it turned out—in 1886.[97]

Conspiracies, even in nineteenth-century Guerrero, could be run by re-mote control. Juan Álvarez, the caudillo who ruled much of the region from independence until his death in 1867, used to organise periodic rebellions against noncompliant central governments by post.[98] With such a possibility in mind, the 1976 commission sent José Ortiz Monasterio to review the Riva Palacio archive in Austin, where he searched the files on Riva Palacio's his-torical writing, the files of unspecified content, and, most important of all, the collected correspondence from 1850 to 1886. He found no trace of any contact between Riva Palacio and Ixcateopan; he did find that el general had surpris-ingly few dealings in the state of Guerrero. From his correspondence there is only one allusion to a visit, or rather a retreat from the French, which took him through the state in the mid-1860s. With the exception of 1880, when his work as González's election fixer gave him cause to exchange letters with local and regional political bosses, his communications with Guerrero and its elites were cursory: between 1881 and 1886 he received all of seven letters from the state. Riva Palacio's knowledge of guerrerense politics and his networks of influence were, even from the peak of national power, surprisingly ropy. His attempt to install his brother Carlos in a deputyship in the state was ignored by Juan Álvarez's son, who placed his own client in the seat.[99] This is hardly the profile of a cacique who could tracelessly direct the creation of a fraudulent prehis-panic tomb from several thousand miles away.

As for the naming of the Ixcateopan square in his honour, it may have been a heartfelt tribute to Riva Palacio's career, increasingly eulogised once it was safely terminated, or it may have been the mere vagaries of fashion. Nearby towns did much the same: Coyuca de Catalán named an "Instituto"—of what we are unsure—for him in 1890; Teloloapan, a street in 1898.[100] A single place-name remains the only evidence linking Riva Palacio to Ixcateopan. Vicente Riva Palacio would have been an engaging forger, an escapee from one of his own novels—perhaps *The Impostor*—and a boon to scholars who deal in top-down nationalist social engineering. Yet such an interpretation would be overly cynical. Riva Palacio was both a fabulist and a serious historian. And evidence is the other problem in believing in Riva Palacio's involvement, evidence that would connect him to Ixcateopan: there isn't any. The life of Mexico's greatest romantic nationalist gives us a window onto the world of ideas where someone forged Cuauhtémoc's bones, but it does not give us their forger.

Chapter 5

Forgers

And then there's the terrible difficulty of proving fraud: who did it? What
were they after? And why? And how did they dig under the church?
—José Gómez Robleda, sessions of the Comisión Investigadora

ALTHOUGH HE DID NOT DO IT, WE CAN IMAGINE VICENTE RIVA PALACIO
as an almost lighthearted forger. For Salvador Rodríguez Juárez, in contrast, the
tomb in Ixcateopan was anything but a joke. That the bones were genuinely
all that remained of Cuauhtémoc and that the Juárez family was a dynasty of
nationalist saints became for him the tenets of an odd crusade that stretched
from 1949 up until his death. Like most crusades worthy of the name, his drew
a curtain of idealism over an essentially materialist goal: the restoration of his
family's decayed economic and political preeminence in the village.

Salvador Rodríguez Juárez was born in Ixcateopan in the rainy season of
1906, the fourth of Primitivo Rodríguez and Alberta Juárez's six children.[1] His
parents had made a politically astute marriage, allying the cacical power of the
Juárez family with the upwardly mobile Rodríguez brothers, migrants from
Guadalajara.[2] Severo Rodríguez, the eldest, was parish priest between 1891
and 1894; Primitivo had been the sacristan and a member of the town council in 1896.[3] This did not make him a model citizen—model citizens were by
no means the backbone of Porfirian local government—and village archives
and oral histories make him out as violent and quick to challenge authority.
In 1904, for example, he was denounced to the village council for refusing to
give up his gun at a bullfight, an incident that, together with a series of charges

brought against other members of the Juárez family, charts a marked waning of their factional power in the early 1900s.[4] Rodríguez was even, according to the regional historian Román Parra Terán, imprisoned in Chilpancingo around the turn of the century.[5] When the revolution began Rodríguez and his eldest sons, Amador and Manuel, armed themselves and helped found the *defensa social*, the village self-defence unit, in vague alliance with the *zapatista* revolutionaries who headquartered in Ixcateopan for much of the period.[6] By the end of the fighting Manuel was the local commander, Uncle Florencio was mayor, and Primitivo was dead.[7]

The Rodríguez Juárez family should have been as well placed to weather the war as anyone in Ixcateopan, linked as they were to both established and emerging elites. The revolution was not as severe for the civilian population of northern Guerrero as it was across the border in Morelos, where six bitterly hostile campaigns, the burning or reconcentration of entire villages, and the Spanish influenza epidemic of 1918 reduced the population by some 40 percent between 1910 and 1921.[8] Ixcateopan, in contrast, underwent minimal demographic change, its population declining less than 2 percent across the revolutionary years.[9] The village was nevertheless in a conflict zone: Ixcapuzalco, a neighbouring and rival village, was destroyed, its population dispersed.[10] From the day when Modesto Beltrán rode into town, declared for the revolution, burned the local archive, and rode out again until the final settlement of 1920 Ixcateopan saw the comings and goings of various armed bands—*maderistas, federales, constitucionalistas*, and zapatistas—who brought insecurity, forced loans, violence, and dearth. "For three seasons," remembered one villager, "we ate agave, banana stems, weeds and things, whatever, there wasn't any corn. This place really suffered, there wasn't any corn because of all the revolutionaries."[11] For Salvador Rodríguez Juárez the revolution meant the loss of his father, his grandfather, much of the family wealth including their shop, and a considerable part of his education.[12] Both church and government schools operated sporadically between 1911 and 1919, by which point he should have been finished with primary school and attending, perhaps, a school in Toluca or Chilpancingo.[13] Rodríguez Juárez was instead, like the majority of his generation in the village, left with the scraps of a mainly informal education, and he stayed in Ixcateopan through the revolution.[14]

His life in the 1920s is obscure, in part because he later gave several different versions of it.[15] By the age of eighteen it seems that he had moved to Mexico City, encouraged, perhaps, by his brother Manuel's backing of Rómulo

Figueroa—a conservative would-be warlord and the wrong horse—in the national rebellion of late 1923.[16] Around twenty-five villagers rebelled, and although they were amnestied in exchange for surrendering their weapons, the ensuing intravillage political divisions forced some to leave town.[17] Whether Rodríguez Juárez's migration was forced or entrepreneurial, it proved a route to accelerated social mobility. Exactly what he did in Mexico City is unclear: some say he worked behind the counter in an ironmonger's shop, while others hold that he was a hospital porter.[18] When he returned to the village in 1928, however, he claimed to be a doctor and produced qualifications to prove it. He had, he later told a historian, personally fabricated his medical diploma, as "regrettably the villagers need to see papers to believe."[19] Disbelieved by outsiders, the diploma ("well made, with signatures, seals and all") was enough—combined with his family prestige, his notably Caucasian phenotype, and the symbolic capital afforded by residence in Mexico City—to establish Rodríguez Juárez as Ixcateopan's local doctor.[20] (He was qualified, according to his letterhead, in "Minor Surgery," "Naturist Methods," and "Hypodermic Medicine.")[21] His rhetoric, a dissonant blend of metropolitan and familiar village voices, leavened by name-dropping (President Obregón, he said, had made him a doctor, Alfonso Caso had made him a bureaucrat) and arcane gobbets of abstruse information, was a further weapon in his advancement, and from the late 1920s his position among the village elite seemed secured.[22] In 1929 he bolstered it with an honorary appointment as a deputy inspector of Artistic and Historical Monuments; meanwhile his brothers Manuel, Abel, and Amador Rodríguez and his uncle Leopoldo Juárez had taken the astute decision to back, and initially monopolise, the local section of the Partido Nacional Revolucionario, the state party.[23] In 1932 Salvador became municipal president, and in 1936 he was reelected.[24] During the 1940s he occupied assorted small-town administrative and prestige posts—sanitary agent; official orator for the *fiestas patrias*, the nationalist celebrations of independence; treasurer of the school construction committee; chairman of the Sociedad de Padres de Familia, a powerful lay Catholic organisation—ratifying and reinforcing his networks of influence.[25] He was not wealthy, powerful, or violent enough to be a cacique. He was, however, an established member of the municipal ruling class, profiting as what Eric Wolf terms a "broker," one of the few men in Ixcateopan who understood the workings of both village and, to some extent, national communities.[26]

There he might well have stayed were it not for the discovery of his grandfather's documents and the tomb to which they led. As it was, the events of 1949 changed Rodríguez Juárez forever. None of his brothers had known anything about the secret of Cuauhtémoc in Ixcateopan, and although he later retold his youth as a heroic quest for the tomb, all available evidence suggests that Salvador Rodríguez Juárez was just as much in the dark.[27] He was at first reluctant to show the Juárez documents to either the sacristan or to the academics and journalists who came to the village in February and March, hardly the behaviour of a man whose life's existential mission is on the verge of completion.[28] It was not that he knew nothing about Cuauhtémoc. The story of the last emperor was schematically taught in the second or third year of primary school from at least the late 1880s, when Rivera Cambas's history textbook became a curriculum standard, and villagers more than a decade older than Rodríguez Juárez remembered learning about Cuauhtémoc.[29] Even in the chaos of Salvador Rodríguez Juárez's education, it is likely that he learned the same lessons: Alfonso Treviño Rivera, born the same year as Rodríguez Juárez, recalled being taught about Cortés's torture of Cuauhtémoc in the village school immediately after the revolution.[30] He undoubtedly came across the pottery and statuettes from the prehispanic era that children such as Eliseo Solis and Alicia Miranda dug out of the ruins on the southern edge of Ixcateopan, the momoxtli, and collected or sold.[31] He would also have picked up echoes of the rising interest surrounding indigenous history in the 1920s and 1930s. At some stage, probably after the death of his aunt María Inés Juárez in 1936, he inherited his grandfather's collection of books, a library of over three hundred tomes including specialist history texts and regional rarities such as the *Album de Arce*.[32] He was even a lowly member of the national bureaucracy that administered archaeological zones. And yet for all that before 1949 he left no signs of any interest whatsoever in the last emperor.

The uproar that villagers and outsiders made out of the discovery of the documents led him to reconsider Cuauhtémoc, his family, and the importance of being Indian, and by May 1949 he was inventing a new persona. Late that month Eulalia Guzmán made her second visit to Ixcateopan and met a newly confident and garrulous Salvador Rodríguez Juárez.[33] The slightly bewildered, closemouthed informant of her first trip was gone; in his new incarnation he was self-consciously the last living letter, coached since the age of twelve by his aunt Jovita to be the guardian of the village's secret. That secret tradition now wove together the Florentino Juárez narrative with an involved and sentimentalistic biography of Cuauhtémoc, precise to the point of reporting his parents' speech when they first met in the 1450s.[34] This was just the beginning of a new expertise. In August Rodríguez Juárez went on to provide an exegesis of yet another Motolinía manuscript that he had stumbled across, hidden, this time, in a reliquary. "Juan" and "Cruz," named in the letter as natives of Ixcateopan, were, he explained to Guzmán, the two men who had accompanied the Franciscan to Puebla.[35] By October he was "constantly giving talks to whoever cares to listen on the genealogy and career, in life and death, of Cuauhtémoc."[36] Across the ensuing years the more he read, and the more he lectured visiting politicians and tourists, the more elaborate his personal historiography became. By 1973 he was claiming that his "studies stretched back to the beginning of the History of Mexico and that [he was] in possession of authentic chronicles of Fray Bernardino de Sahagún."[37] His relatives paid to have his diatribes about the conquest published; the ghost of Motolinía was held to have visited his family.[38] Cuauhtémoc's tomb and legend became, in the end, inseparable from Rodríguez Juárez's life.

His fascination with Cuauhtémoc was not in the least the fruit of the quixotic battiness that some visitors to Ixcateopan identified.[39] It was an opportunistic, rent-seeking response to the discovery, in a geographical area without notable natural resources, of the entirely new resource of history. Salvador Rodríguez Juárez pieced together a profoundly individualistic claim to the benefits of this resource on the basis of both privileged knowledge—his identity as the last living letter—and ancestry—as a descendant not just of the tomb guardians but also of prehispanic royalty. The earliest and most fundamental of those benefits was regular access to regional and national political elites. Visitors to Ixcateopan between February 1949 and March 1952 included the local federal deputy, the governor of Guerrero, the secretary-general of the Partido Revolucionario Institucional, the revered left-wing general Francisco Múgica, the revolutionary artist Diego Rivera, the labour organiser and presidential candidate Vicente Lombardo Toledano, and Adolfo Ruiz Cortines, Alemán's eventual successor in the presidency. All of them met Salvador Rodríguez Juárez for a handshake at the very least.[40] Secretary of Education Gual Vidal granted him a private audience on the same day as he released (and rejected) the Gran Comisión's negative report.[41] On April 7, 1950, ex-president Lázaro Cárdenas, the most affectively powerful of the surviving revolutionary leaders, dropped by Rodríguez Juárez's house with his son Cuauhtémoc, leaving a note to communicate their "homage and admiration" for him and the other villagers.[42] By the end of his life Rodríguez Juárez had met most of the presidents of postwar Mexico.[43]

These fleeting contacts, presumably meaningless for most politicians concerned, were highly significant for Rodríguez Juárez's career as a village politician. Contemporary Mexico was a society with its own, revolutionary version of the royal touch; observed proximity to the powerful served to counteract not scrofula but powerlessness.[44] Every major politician attracted an entourage of those whom one journalist mocked as "the eternal and sticky politicians who follow [them] everywhere . . . with the illusory hope of receiving even one of their glances or, at very best, a handshake."[45] Such strategic sycophancy was neither as ridiculous nor as fruitless as the journalist made out, as the personalism endemic in postrevolutionary politics meant that the most minor contact with the great and good could translate into major local power. Jorge Ibargüengoitía has described the case of a Chamula who achieved lifelong authority in his community by dint of giving Cárdenas an *abrazo* in Mexico City on the day of the oil expropriation.[46] Something similar happened to Salvador Rodríguez Juárez: being seen hobnobbing with the metropolitan elite served to authenticate his new identity and to give him access to a whole new level of authority in Ixcateopan. This was expressed in part through personalist, in Weberian terms charismatic, domination of many of his fellow villagers. But Rodríguez Juárez's authority was also channelled, in an outré tribute to the bureaucratisation of power in the 1940s, into a formal institution of his own devising, the Comité Pro-Autenticidad de los Restos de Cuauhtémoc. Rodríguez Juárez founded this pressure group in a town hall meeting on June 11, 1950, installing himself as president and "Secretario de Prensa y Propaganda"; official business was conducted from the committee's headquarters at No. 1 Calle Independencia, also known as Rodríguez Juárez's house.

A cynic might see this front for Rodríguez Juárez as a matter of stationery, self-importance, and little else. The Comité Pro-Autenticidad was more than that, though, and its members ambitiously pursued their proclaimed goals of obtaining governmental recognition of the bones' authenticity and encouraging ceremonies to honour their emperor. Their first successes came in August, when Ixcateopan's name was changed to Ixcateopan de Cuauhtémoc, Cárdenas agreed to act as the Comité's honorary president, and the metropolitan press covered the Comité's launch in Ixcateopan.[47] Over the next three months Rodríguez Juárez circulated letters to strategic organisations in the worlds of education and the media, such as the National Union of Press Editors, the National Union of Education Workers, and the Ministry of Public Education; to other municipalities in Guerrero; and to state congresses across Mexico. He asked this sizable cross section of bureaucrats and state politicians that they extend his organisation by founding subcommittees, that they encourage a letter-writing campaign petitioning President Alemán to decree the tomb authentic, that they organise patriotic tourism (in "caravans") to view the Juárez documents and Ixcateopan, that they invite him to lecture on the Juárez family and the tomb, and that they cough up some money to help allay "the enormous costs of this Campaign." A certain scent of scam clung to those last three points, and the brush-off replies from Veracruz and Chihuahua are probably typical of legislators' responses. Rodríguez Juárez met with slightly more luck in Guerrero, where subcommittees were formed in the municipality of Tlacoapa and the hamlet of Metlapilapa.[48]

The Comité's real success, however, lay in Ixcateopan and in its backstage purpose as a vehicle for controlling local politics. It brought together Rodríguez Juárez's allies among the officeholding village elite, such as Julio Cuestas and Sidronio Parra, fortifying their faction in local politics. The Comité lent that faction a paranoid yet persuasive ideology, namely, the defence of the intertwined interests of village and nation against ill-defined conspirators. It gave members the prestige of contacts with state- and national-level elites, and it encouraged a popular perception that the development programmes that followed the tomb find—the provision of electricity, running water, a telephone line to Pachivia—were in reality its members' achievement. It also lent them new and impressive titles in a historically title-mad culture. The Comité was functionally a political party and one that installed at least two municipal presidents (Julio Cuestas in 1952, Delfino Sales in 1954) in succession.[49] Its very structure and name mirrored the ephemeral committees that ambitious men formed every six years to promote presidential candidacies, thus clambering from obscure localities onto a national gravy train. The Comité Pro-Autenticidad served, additionally, as a site of local power that paralleled and often overshadowed the village council. It could even be used toward the ambitious end of enforcing a party line regarding the tomb. When Rodríguez Juárez learned that dissident villagers were publicly rubbishing the Ixcateopan tradition he denounced them to the municipal president in Orwellian terms as "disturbers of social order." There was more than bluff to this stab at cultural hegemony: at least two dissidents, the schoolteacher Modesto Jaimes and the cobbler Dario Alvarez, were arrested.[50] Across the 1950s Rodríguez Juárez's ascendancy in the village was sufficient to allow him a lengthy campaign against the local priest, José Landa, over the usufruct of church buildings, funds, and other assets, and when Landa refused to hand them over, to arrest him as well.[51]

The would-be doctor also profited economically from the tomb find. The Juárez's large townhouse on the Plaza Vicente Riva de Palacio had been sold in 1946 to the village council for use as a schoolhouse.[52] As soon as the documents were publicised (and before the tomb was even discovered) Rodríguez Juárez asked for its return. In the formal record of the documents' discovery, drawn up on February 4, 1949, he petitioned the president of Mexico that the house and the family's "other assets" be restituted, "in light of the fact that Dr. Rodríguez had the great glory to receive from his ancestors this Precious Treasure of Mexican History and as the heir of the family Rodríguez Juárez."[53] On reflection he euphemised this demand with a more diplomatic request for the use of the house as a family museum and tried to co-opt Eulalia Guzmán in support. She refused, but the state legislature acceded and instructed the village council to give Rodríguez Juárez the property. They were not, according to one account, overly enthusiastic; the recently inaugurated schoolhouse represented more than a quarter of the *municipio*'s public property; but in January 1952 they handed it over.[54] Given that the house had never been his in the first place—it had belonged to his uncle Florencio, who was still alive in Cuernavaca and who had fallen out with the rest of the Juárez family—this was a double triumph (although an ephemeral one, as the house did not remain long in his possession).[55] It was not his only attempt to realise the economic possibilities of the tomb. In early 1950 he tried to sell his account of the legend and the discovery in Mexico City as a radio drama.[56] His involvement in the church scandal, which stretched to physically seizing the building and channelling the alms collected for the Santo Niño to himself, was only possible given the logic of the tomb find, within which Rodríguez Juárez's successful transmission of the secret gave him a claim to jurisdiction over the church itself.[57] (The claim was endorsed by the state government, which appointed him official guardian of the remains.)[58] Such demands on the various economic spoils were sufficiently ambitious to embarrass even his fellow pro-authenticity campaigners. As Leopoldo Carranco Cardoso put it, "Le importaba el dinerito": he cared about the loot.[59]

Salvador Rodríguez Juárez, in short, did not have to read French sociologists to know that "symbolic capital . . . in the form of the prestige and renown attached to a family and a name is readily convertible back into economic capital."[60] The equation was simple. The Ixcateopan legend generated a sizable quantity of symbolic capital: the "living letters" of the Juárez family were, in one paper's words, "worthy successors of their dead emperor."[61] Such repute could be exchanged for political and economic capital. But Rodríguez Juárez was not particularly skilled at making these transactions, and the clumsy eagerness with which he pursued the benefits of Cuauhtémoc's bones aroused suspicion. The profits that he might and to some extent did reap provided an obvious motive, in hindsight, for creating the fraud in the first place. In the course of the 1976 investigation the historian Luis Reyes García visited Rodríguez Juárez in Ixcateopan to interview him and to photograph the Florentino Juárez documents. Rodríguez Juárez then surprised him with a further twelve allegedly antique manuscripts, which attempted to fill in gaps in the tomb's history and to rebut some of the criticisms of earlier academics. They were all lamentably badly forged contemporary productions. They did cause Reyes García to revise his opinion of the tomb's origins. Far from increasing its credibility, however, the new documents merely persuaded Reyes García that the entire Ixcateopan tradition, including the original Florentino Juárez papers, was actually Rodríguez Juárez's work. "It may be said," he concluded, "that the author of 'the secret of Ixcateopan,' as it is now known, is Señor Salvador Rodríguez Juárez, although in no way can it be thought that he began from nothing."[62]

The detail of Reyes García's argument is complex, synthesizing his own research with that of the two previous commissions. The argument's underlying structure is, however, simple. The documents that Rodríguez Juárez produced in 1976 were bogus. They included falsified signatures similar to one in the Florentino Juárez journals, texts that could, on careful rereading, be interpreted on the grounds of content as post-1915 in origin. They were therefore not produced by Florentino Juárez, who died in 1915, but by Rodríguez Juárez himself. Some of the linguistic and orthographic tics of these journals cropped up in the original bundle of documents—the hide folder and the book *Destierro de Ignorancias*—and in the inscription on the copper plaque covering the tomb cavity. They were all consequently products of the same hand. The entire fraud, from 1976 "codex" to 1949 tomb, was the nationalist fantasy of one man: Salvador Rodríguez Juárez.

To conclude that the 1976 documents were fraudulent was no interpretive leap in the dark. They were a gaudy collection of improbabilities, errors, and romantic conceits. The codex came on two sheets of rough-edged yellowed paper, across which a trail of footprints meandered before heading straight up the steps of a pyramid, drawn in elevation, and into a building on top. From there they continued across a plan of the Ixcateopan church to end in a pile of boulders beneath the altar. Advanced semiotics were never going to be necessary to work that one out: the trail of footprints represented the wanderings of Cuauhtémoc's body, ending at rest in Ixcateopan. The iconography, however, was all wrong. Trails of footprints were commonly used in indigenous pictograms to mark journeys or routes, but the footprints usually alternated right with left in an accurate representation of a walking man's tracks. The Ixcateopan footprints came in parallel sets, like a barefoot man in a sack race. The brushwork, in place of the firm and economical lines that characterise genuine codices, was a wavering mess. Most damning of all, the plan of the churchyard contained a wall that, from evidence in the parish archives, did not exist until the late nineteenth century.[63]

The written manuscripts were equally blunder-filled. Two sets of purportedly Spanish colonial papers were designed to corroborate a sixteenth-century origin for the tomb. One was a set of parchment fragments, promiscuously littered with Motolinía signatures, which Rodríguez Juárez claimed were the only remains of the original sixteenth-century testament to Cuauhtémoc's burial. The parchment, however, was a collection of fragments of the parish registers, one of which was compromisingly dated "February Seventeen Hundred and...." The other was a certified copy dated 1892 of a 1532 Franciscan manuscript from the Church of San Hipólito in Mexico City. In it Sahagún, Motolinía, and three other Franciscan monks witness the legal complaint of fifty-three nobles from Tlatelolco concerning Cortés's torture and execution of Cuauhtémoc. In the course of their statement they let slip that the last emperor is buried in "Ichicateimotiopan." Such record is made, runs the text, "that it may be written in the books which Fray Bernardino [Sahagún] has been ordered to write." There are two immediate problems. One is that Sahagún was not ordered to write his history until 1547 at the earliest. The other is that the paper on which the "1892" copy is made is dated 1900.[64]

The final class of documents in the 1976 collection aimed to fill in the four centuries of silence between Cuauhtémoc's death and the appearance of the Ixcateopan tomb. They included a handwritten copy of what was supposed to be a 1577 manuscript, brought from Rome by Rodríguez Juárez's uncle Severo, which contained an indigenous grammarian's instructions to paint of (but not to relate or write of) his ancestors' graves. There were the testaments of two other seventeenth-century "living letters," Mariano Moctezuma Chimalpopoca and José Amado Amador, counselling their descendants to guard the documents and the secret of Cuauhtémoc's tomb. From the eighteenth century came a book, *Trabajos de los Apóstoles*, with an undated and anonymous note concerning "the tombs of the old kings"; and from the nineteenth, semiliterate marginalia in an undated catechism signed by a nonexistent Ixcateopan parish priest, which highly commended the inhabitants of the village and their secret. There were, finally, what were supposed to be two hitherto-undiscovered Florentino Juárez journals. As a collection the documents were marked by grievous linguistic, palaeographic, and historiographical errors, which Reyes García catalogued with the pointed irritation of an academic who feels that he is being taken for a fool.[65] Salvador Rodríguez Juárez had tried to defend the tomb on two fronts, hurling as much detail and as many famous names as he could muster at readers of the Cuauhtémoc narrative while simultaneously chronicling the legend's transmission mechanisms. It was an entrepreneurial but foolhardy approach, and it did not work.

Once he had solidly established Rodríguez Juárez as a forger, Reyes García tried to establish connections between these 1976 forgeries and the original Juárez journals. One of the spurious 1976 journals, notebook 6, contained a "Florentino Juárez" signature that had been executed in pencil and clumsily inked over. In Reyes García's eyes this was the hesitant technique of an unconfident forger imitating a preexisting model. Such a signature, pencilled then inked, also graced one of the original journals, the first Florentino Juárez notebook. This too was consequently forged; and as all five original notebooks were in the same hand, all five had in reality been written by Salvador Rodríguez Juárez. There was more than palaeography to this argument. Reyes García had also reread the original journals and highlighted some of their apparent anachronisms. In notebook 5, called "The Prophecy of the Three Toribios," the author links Toribio de Astorga, Toribio de Benaventes (Motolinía), and Toribio de Arrieta (the parish priest between 1902 and 1917) with the fate of Ixcateopan and the tomb. Each is described in the past tense as having completed his mission. It was, Reyes García argued, impossible that Juárez should have written this; he had died in 1915, two years before Arrieta's period as parish priest came to an end.[66] Notebook 4, "General Neri's Great Interest in Discovering the Secrets of Ixcateopan," seemingly referred to two eminent Porfirians, the local warlord Canuto Neri and the president's personal doctor, Dr. Aureliano Urrutia, as engaged simultaneously in discussions concerning the tomb. This was unlikely: Neri had died in 1896 (victim, rumour held, of a poisoned sombrero that the president sent him), while Urrutia only became the presidential doctor in 1909.[67] Had Florentino Juárez written the journal he surely would not have committed such glaring chronological mistakes. Finally, and most disturbingly, both notebooks 2 and 4 confidently predicted that the tomb would be discovered in "the year 50."[68] This was so close to the actual date of the tomb's discovery, 1949, as to allow Reyes García only two conclusions. Either Florentino Juárez had been psychic, or else Salvador Rodríguez Juárez had written it in the foreknowledge that he would "find" the tomb between 1949 and 1951.[69]

It was here, however, that Reyes García's argument began to falter. The inking-in of the Florentino Juárez signature in notebook 1 was not in the slightest conclusive proof of Rodríguez Juárez's authorship. It was a cretinous piece of document tampering that did much to dispel the aura of relative antiquity—fading pencil, old paper, erratic orthography—that the notebook's author had created. Whoever was responsible had completely failed to grasp the basic mechanisms for representing antiquity and its corollary, authenticity. One might argue that Rodríguez Juárez went to some length to imitate aging processes only to destroy their effect by tracing over faded pencil with fresh ink. It is more coherent to posit that he was responsible for the overwriting of the signature and nothing else. There is, moreover, evidence to support that hypothesis in Eulalia Guzmán's correspondence with Rodríguez Juárez. On August 26, 1949, she wrote to him in Ixcateopan concerning the conservation of the documents. "Take special care," she admonished him, "of the Motolinía document and its envelopes; don't tear or throw anything away, however useless it might seem, nor change nor alter anything, albeit with the best intentions, such as, for example, going over the words which are already fading in pencil. There will be time for doing all of these things; but not now."[70] At one point during her August 1949 visit to the village Guzmán actually confiscated the key papers from Rodríguez Juárez.[71] That she had caught him in flagrante is the inevitable conclusion.

As for the contents of the original Juárez notebooks, their anachronisms are less real than apparent. The parish priest Toribio Arrieta was etched into the village's historic consciousness because of his role in the early days of the revolution, when a federal general had ordered the villagers to leave Ixcateopan before he razed it to deny the zapatistas its use. Arrieta, who was already practised in sheltering villagers from the depredations of both sides, went to see the general and persuaded him to revoke the order.[72] This made him very much a village hero, the man who had saved Ixcateopan; at least one ballad was written in his honour, and villagers remembered him warmly over sixty years later.[73] When notebook 5 refers to Arrieta as having completed his mission and later specifies that the priest "will fulfil [his duty of] charity in the decisive era of revolution and plague," it seems evident that it is this defining moment, and not his career as a whole, that is being described.[74] Precise dating of the planned resettlement is difficult; it occurred, however, before the zapatista commander Adrián Castrejón established his headquarters in Ixcateopan in 1914, and the most probable date is February 1912, when the government ordered a statewide policy of reconcentration.[75] As Juárez was still writing about the tomb in his testament of 1914 and alive until 1915, there is no reason why he should not have described Arrieta as having "completed his charge."

The controversial passage of notebook 4 runs as follows:

> General Don Canuto Neri told me that it was necessary to consult General Don Porfirio Díaz in relation with the agreements which we had with Don Beltrán Perfecto of Teloloapa and the señores Flores of Tasco, Don Mateo said that he was taking care of meeting with Dr. Urrutia, entrusted with explaining the matter to Don Porfirio as agreed.... Don Perfecto told me that the secret should be kept for more time because General Neri was not well and might perish, although Dr. Urrutia wholeheartedly took charge of everything, given that he was Don Porfirio's personal doctor.[76]

This can be read, as Reyes García argued, as a naive juxtaposition of two temporally separate people. But Florentino Juárez did in fact have connections to both men. He corresponded with Neri in the mid-1890s; in a letter of August 1893 Neri promised to intercede for him with Porfirio Díaz over an unspecified problem.[77] As for Urrutia—later notorious as interior minister under the Victoriano Huerta dictatorship—he was a major in the Chilpancingo garrison from 1895 to 1899 and director of the state's Antonio Mercenario Hospital from 1897 to 1898. In 1950 he admitted that villagers from Ixcateopan had tried to contact him—toward, José Aviles Solares estimated, 1899—for his assistance in uncovering the tomb.[78] In the light of such known contacts notebook 4 is better interpreted, particularly in light of its confused and syntactically impoverished prose, as a deliberately semiarticulate summary of Florentino Juárez's attempts to reveal the tomb to the national elite.

The most convincing piece of evidence for Reyes García's linking of the 1976 forgeries to the original Juárez journals was the uncanny accuracy with which notebooks 2 and 4 predicted the tomb find. "They told me," the author of notebook 2 wrote, "that it is foretold by the sages of that time that at the beginning of the year 50 . . . the secret will be discovered."[79] To identify "the year 50" with 1949 and find it an extraordinarily suspicious coincidence was a natural progression. It ignored, however, the context of these predictions. They came in the midst of passages that owe heavily to Florentino Juárez's interest in spiritualism, the belief that the dead could communicate with the living. In another spiritualist passage he dated the "generation" of the three Toribios to the year 447.[80] Given that the "first Toribio," Motolinía, was born at the end of the fifteenth century, it seems that Juárez did not use the Gregorian calendar when in spiritualist mode. Furthermore, Juárez explicitly linked "the year 50" to the reapparition of the comet of 1857. "There is a time," he wrote, "to reveal these things; and it is said by the elders that that will be at the end of the year 50, and there will be plentiful signs in this area; the signs of truth, the signs so they told, that a comet that came in 1857 will appear; it will come to herald the beginning of the year 50; if you know not what to make of this and God still grants life, be it to me or to my nephew José Jaimes, consult him and he will answer."[81]

Decoding this gnomic bunkum is impossible, as is consulting José Jaimes; he died in 1926.[82] But it is extremely unlikely that even such an empirically casual forger as Salvador Rodríguez should have made an unfulfillable astronomical prediction. The first brilliant comet to be visible in the Northern Hemisphere in his adult life was Arend-Roland, which came in 1957, and no major comet or meteor shower was predicted for the period 1949 to 1951.[83] Florentino Juárez, on the other hand, lived in an era when apocalyptic obsession with comets was a global phenomenon, fuelled in part by the extraordinary frequency of their passing. On April 3, 1843, fifty thousand members of William Miller's sect awaited doom in New England, their faith confirmed by a comet with a fifty-degree tail that appeared in broad daylight. In 1857 two ancient comets were wrongly conflated by a German philosopher into a single astronomical monster that he held would strike Earth on June 13, a prediction that spread panic across Europe. The comet, which never came, was commemorated in Paris by miscarriages, churches doing unaccustomedly brisk business, and one entrepreneurial type's marketing of "a comet-proof suit." In England, the politician and novelist Benjamin Disraeli wrote a typically sardonic letter, attesting that "the world is very much frightened about the Comet . . . in 4 & 20 hours we may be shrivelled or drowned. In the meantime, if the catastrophe do not occur, we hope to be at Torquay by the end of next month."[84] In San José de Gracía, Michoacán, it was held that a comet heralded the end of the world on December 31, 1900, causing a newly rich heir to spend the lot in three days' partying; and in Sayula, Veracruz, the 1910 Halley's Comet return and its aura of doom formed the most memorable event of the future president Miguel Alemán's childhood.[85]

At the same time as comets horrified people—the end of the Mexica world was supposedly foretold by a comet, the 1789 meteor shower sent people fleeing to the Virgin of Guadalupe's shrine in Tepeyac—they permeated popular culture.[86] "El Cometa de 1843" was one of the most commonplace cantina names.[87] Florentino Juárez had exceptional opportunities to observe major comets with the naked eye, for 1860 to 1890 was a period of exceptionally intense cometary activity. Dramatic comets were visible in the Northern Hemisphere in 1860, 1861, 1874, 1880, 1881, and 1882. The Great September Comet of 1882 was the brightest comet in over a thousand years; an engraving from José Guadalupe

Figure 24.
Detail from José Guadalupe Posada, "Great Comet and Fiery Blaze," ca. 1899; courtesy of the Art Institute of Chicago.

Posada's "End of the World" series shows a public square filled with terrified ad hoc astronomers (over a text proclaiming, "We're toast!").[88] There were at least two astronomical events, the Leonid meteor shower of 1899 and the Halley's Comet return, that were very publicly awaited in the years when we know that villagers were trying to reveal the tomb.[89] The Mexico City pamphleteer Antonio Vanegas Arroyo even produced a six-centavo booklet that predicted the annihilation of Earth by a (particularly punctual) comet at nine minutes past three on the afternoon of Monday, November 13, 1899.[90] Salvador Rodríguez Juárez was hardly a likely author of precise predictions involving comets; it is distinctly more credible to attribute the year 50 passages, together with the notebooks in which it occurs, to Florentino Juárez.[91]

For Luis Reyes García, however, a neat and revisionist solution to the problem of Ixcateopan was in sight. Having connected the Florentino Juárez journals to Salvador Rodríguez Juárez, the last requirement to complete his thesis was a missing link among the 1976 documents, the Juárez journals, and the initial bundle of Motolinía documents that signposted the tomb. He found this link in spelling mistakes. All three groups of documents contained attempts to feign antiquity and indigenous origins through erratic orthography. The hide folder and the marginalia in *Destierro de Ignorancias* both contained deliberately distorted Spanish: their author wrote *ache* in place of *hace*, *chombres* in place of *hombres*, and *chorcado* instead of *horcado*. Similar confusions between the use of *c*, *h*, and *ch* ran through the Florentino Juárez journals and at least one of the 1976 documents, the "Manuscrito de José Francisco." Although such practise was commonplace among forgers of land titles in the colonial period, Reyes García considered it a stylistic fingerprint proving that all the documents had been written by Rodríguez Juárez.[92] Finally, three of the 1976 documents contained the phrase "Rey e Señor Coatemo," which had first appeared on the copper plaque that sealed the tomb. The handwriting, Reyes García argued, was the same on this plaque as in the 1976 documents. It was consequently evident, he concluded, that at some point in 1947 or 1948 Salvador Rodríguez Juárez had forged not only all of the Ixcateopan documents but also the tomb itself.[93]

The specific criticism could be made that palaeographic comparisons of writing scored in copper with a cold chisel to writing with a pen on paper are somewhat adventurous. There is, however, a more general flaw in this last phase of the Reyes García attribution. It relies on a backward chain of reasoning by which any stylistic or linguistic similarities between a known forgery and an older document are taken to prove that both are products of the same hand. Yet any forger who was aware of the style and contents of earlier documents would logically imitate them to preserve coherence within the fraud narrative, irrespective of whether he or she had fabricated those earlier documents. Salvador Rodríguez Juárez had ample time to study the original Ixcateopan papers and would quite naturally mimic them as closely as possible in producing his additions to the legend. To take such mimesis as evidence that he composed the original documents is logically unacceptable.

Yet there is assorted evidence to implicate Salvador Rodríguez Juárez as a forger in 1949 and beyond, and it is abundantly clear that the creation of his medical diploma was merely an overture to his later work.[94] Even Eulalia Guzmán, who from the start wanted the tomb to exist, was quick to mistrust Rodríguez Juárez; after just two brief visits to Ixcateopan she requested a sample of his handwriting.[95] In mid-August 1949 she wrote to the editor of *El Universal* telling him that she "still harboured doubts."[96] Guzmán explained just what those doubts were to Leopoldo Carranco Cardoso, a guerrerense politician and historian who was an intimate of the governor and a key mover in the tomb find. She felt, she told him, that Rodríguez Juárez might be making it all up and that further association with him might damage her career.[97] At the beginning of September Guzmán's worries were reinforced when Rodríguez Juárez showed her the Motolinía letter that he had found hidden in a reliquary. The reliquary was no antique and would later be identified as the legacy of one Trinidad Lagunas de Arroyo to Rodríguez Juárez.[98] As for the Motolinía letter contained within, it was obvious to Guzmán that it was a forgery.[99] She continued to believe it possible that Cuauhtémoc was interred in the village, but she was also convinced that Rodríguez Juárez and other villagers were trying to salt the mine of sixteenth-century artefacts. She was not alone in this belief: as the village secretary helped to examine and transcribe the documents he noticed that Rodríguez Juárez "added the odd word." (This may be the origin of the incongruous concluding pages of both notebooks 4 and 5, which break sharply with the preceding style and content to make specific and flattering references to Rodríguez Juárez himself.)[100] "I believe," Guzmán wrote to Marquina on September 5, "that the excavations should not be delayed any further, taking into account the state of mind of certain of the inhabitants of Ixcateopan."[101] The clear implication was that Rodríguez Juárez might, in his ham-fisted attempts to "authenticate" the Ixcateopan tradition, prevent the discovery of a genuine tomb.

The ambiguity that the discovery generated only functioned as an incentive to further forgery. Had the tomb been either authenticated or rejected out of hand Rodríguez Juárez might have rested easy; as it was, the debate that began in September 1949 drove him to continue his creative history making in a series of attempts to shore up the legend's shaky credibility. This was predictable: as Hugh Trevor-Roper puts it,

> The successful forger soon becomes the prisoner of his forgery. Once the experts begin to suspect him, he loses the initiative. Then
> The same arts that gain
> A power must it maintain,
> and new forgeries must be invented to counter circumstances discovered. New documents must be forged, or imagined, and back-dated.[102]

In October 1949 Rodríguez Juárez sent a telegram to Mexico City summoning Guzmán to the village, where he revealed part of what would later emerge as the "Manuscrito de José Francisco"; in October 1950 he showed the 1976 Ixcateopan "codex" to a reporter.[103] And it was not just manuscripts that were being manufactured by this stage. There was also a date, 1539, that appeared on the lintel of the church entrance and a coat of arms of Charles V, the Spanish emperor at the time of the conquest, that manifested itself flanking the window over the main door. Neither had been remarked prior to the discovery.[104] Both were new additions to the church's decor.[105] Guzmán had warned the municipal president to keep an eye on the building in August 1949, telling him with (unaccustomed) delicacy that "although there is no need to recommend extreme vigilance to ensure that there be no material change in the floor or the walls inside or outside the church, or in the matter of the documents, it is always good to bear it in mind." She had, she revealingly continued, "already written to Dr Salvador Rodríguez in this respect."[106] Complete certainty regarding the identity of the freelance church restorers is impossible. But whatever the source of the church renovations, it was evident to several actors in 1949 that while the outside world was investigating their history, someone in the village was busily forging it.[107] It was not, self-evidently, that Salvador Rodríguez Juárez was innocent; he was a forger, and he was active in 1949. But he was neither the sole nor the master forger that Reyes García depicted.

There are, for a start, striking differences between Rodríguez Juárez's known writings and the bulk of the 1949 documents. The author of the Florentino Juárez journals (notebooks 1–5) followed one of the central tenets of the skilled liar:

that vagueness can be an asset. Excessive detail is both improbable and contestable. The contents and discourse of the journals are shot through with a healthy respect for the abilities of the scholars whom the author aimed to take in. Rather than display privileged knowledge and generate suspicions, he presented himself as the metropolitan stereotype of a quintessentially uneducated peasant, at times barely literate, who was a mere conduit for the blurred remnants of his elders' memories. In projecting such a persona he largely suppressed his own opinions, knowledge, and importance. The journals contain no references to any text sources on the conquest, and only four historical figures of national significance are named: Porfirio Díaz, Motolinía, Cortés, and Cuauhtémoc himself. The journals do contain multiple professions of ignorance: describing the transmission of the legend from the village elders, the diarist admits that "they told me many things which I do not remember any more."[108] As for his own role in the legend, it is described in a minor key. His father had bequeathed him the documents, but the tradition did not stem exclusively from his family. The knowledge of Cuauhtémoc's tomb was a village, communal possession, which he had "the good fortune to know from the mouths of the elders."[109] Such pronounced caution runs through the diplomatic strategy of the fraud; with the puzzling exception of the letter in invisible ink, none of the other documents are presented as sixteenth-century originals. They are advertised, rather, as flawed copies of originals that have crumbled to dust, a classic forgers' rhetorical device much used in ancient Egypt.[110] Such a farsighted detail was typical of the production as a whole; not just shrewd but marked by a quality that, were the forgery not quite so audacious, we would call conservatism.

Rodríguez Juárez was anything but conservative, and where his predecessor played the peasant, he played the professor. His writings were packed full of what he envisioned as legitimizing references to the mainstream historical narrative. In his 1973 statement of the Ixcateopan tradition he cited a mixture of chroniclers and historians that included Bernal Díaz, Gómara, Sahagún, Tezozómoc, Riva Palacio, and Alfonso Caso.[111] The 1976 documents were spiked with the names that he extracted from such readings: Ahuitzótl, Juan de Tecto, Martín Jacobita, Moctezuma Ilhuicamina, Doña Marina, Tilzilacatzin, and Emperor Maximilian. Where the first forger insinuated by omission, Rodríguez Juárez aimed to name-drop his way to persuasion. The author of notebook 1 related "that on Shrove Tuesday the 26th of February 1525 the king died hanged in a place which I do not know by name"; Rodríguez Juárez, in contrast, knew that the place was Izankanac and said so.[112] Having a venomously low opinion of the historical trade, whose members he described as "cowards, low-lifes, unstudious, unscientific, pseudo-researchers," he also had no qualms about trying his hand in the fabrication of sixteenth-century documents.[113] The reliquary letter, the Ixcateopan "codex," and the remains of the Motolinía testament were all his work. There were, finally, key differences between the discourse of the 1976 documents and that of the Florentino Juárez papers. Where the 1949 documents spoke of Ixcateopan's present and the prehispanic past with a mixture of fear and sorrow, Rodríguez Juárez was verbally violent about the Spanish, the academy, and the clergy.[114] He adopted some of the tropes of twentieth-century nationalism, such as *la mexicanidad*; most notably of all, he rewrote the tradition to convert it into the exclusive property of the Juárez family, who were now a "dynasty" with links to Mexica royalty.[115] (He passed himself off, in contemporary press interviews, as a direct descendant of Cuauhtémoc.)[116] And he carefully wrote himself in, explicitly bequeathing himself the "legacy" of the family in the final pages of notebook 6.[117] Such differences in the discourse, content, and diplomatic of the Ixcateopan documents all serve to draw a line between what are in reality two bodies of work.[118] One, composed of the 1976 documents and the manuscript of the reliquary, is Rodríguez Juárez's work; the other, comprising the remaining Motolinía documents and the Florentino Juárez journals, is quite clearly not.[119] If prose, to paraphrase Hemingway, is architecture, then the original documents are classical; the Rodríguez Juárez additions are baroque, and a particularly decadent late baroque at that.[120]

So much for the documents. As for the tomb, it is unthinkable that Rodríguez Juárez should have constructed it. This is not for mere psychological reasons, although it should by now be clear that the primary forger was far more gifted than the hubristic would-be doctor and Aztec nobleman. It was impossible for Rodríguez Juárez to make the tomb between 1947 and 1948 for the simple physical reason that several tons of neoclassical altar stood in his way. The altar was formed of a core of stone and rubble, faced up, and plastered; its base measured approximately five feet by four, and it had no foundations whatsoever.[121] When Guzmán's team dug a preliminary trench in front of the structure they found it resting on compacted stony earth. They judged successful tunnelling to be out of the question; the altar would collapse on anyone who attempted it.[122] The latest possible date for the insertion of the tomb is consequently that of the construction of the last altar. The fragmentary parish archives fail to record when that altar was built. Its predecessor, however, was built in 1869, as a foundation stone used as filling in the last altar attests; and it is not a twentieth-century production, as none of the villagers interviewed in 1976, many born in the 1890s, could remember such a major event as a change of altars.[123] Its construction can consequently be placed with some confidence in the late nineteenth century, before Salvador Rodríguez Juárez was even born.

Who, then, was the primary forger, and when did he create the tomb? The chronology of modifications to the church, adroitly traced by Sonia Lombardo, rules out anyone from the twentieth century. There were only two brief periods of substantial work inside the church during which the altar could have been built and the grave could have been inserted: the early 1870s and the early 1890s. One large-scale remodelling came in 1874, when the side chapel of the Santo Niño was added.[124] This, however, came close on the heels of the previous altar's construction in 1869; and as Alfonso Caso remarked, one doesn't build an altar every other year.[125] The *ciprés*, the small dome that topped the altar, is moreover characteristic of a much later period, namely, the 1890s. Such minor ecclesiastical follies were then fashionable: Lombardo discovered a similar domed altar in Acamixtla dating to 1891, while the diocesan archive in Chilapa records at least one other, installed in the parish church of Apaxtla, about thirty miles to the south of Ixcateopan, in 1894. (This one was evidently more popular with the priest than with his parishioners, who wrote to the bishop asking if they really had to contribute to its construction.)[126] It was during the early 1890s that the second series of major alterations to the church was carried out: the construction of a clock tower and a new sacristy in 1890, extensive repairs to the cupula following a lightning strike in 1891, the installation of a clock in 1893, and some unspecified "material works" reported by Severo Rodríguez in April 1894.[127] It was during one of these major works projects that the altar was constructed, and with it the tomb.[128]

A tomb created in the early 1890s and a man creating its history in his diaries; these alone are enough to identify the diarist, Florentino Juárez, as the primary forger of Ixcateopan. When the same man is remembered as inventing the village traditions that locate and commemorate the tomb, his responsibility becomes certain. Villagers recalled how Juárez and a small group of clients and allies spread the legend and inculcated its principal behavioural marker, the custom of removing one's hat in passing the church to honour the dead king within. The majority of Eulalia Guzmán's informants in 1949 had in fact been peons for either Juárez or José Jaimes.[129] Such efforts stretched well beyond the village: Juárez also tried to persuade two consecutive *jefes políticos* of his district, Aldama, of the tomb's existence and made various attempts to contact the president himself.[130] According to the headmaster of the village school, he even walled up the leftovers of tomb building inside the family house, a mere seventy yards from the church. This became the schoolhouse in 1946.[131] When the building was renovated the labourers broke into two sealed rooms, one at the west end of the main corridor and the other in the north of the house. They contained, according to the contemporary headmaster Pedro Román Gómez, partially burnt bones, old books, and papers.[132] Within the gallery of hearsay, gossip, and deliberate deceit that constitutes much of our evidence surrounding the tomb, such numerous pointers lead to a single picture. Whether Florentino Juárez had knowing collaborators inside the village or not, there can be no doubt that he was the primary forger of the Ixcateopan legend and the tomb it announced. Whether that is a satisfactory solution or not is a different problem; for it begs the further, equally twisted question of why on earth he did it.

Figure 25.
A visitor ceremonially doffs his hat outside the church. Photograph by Lyman Johnson.

Chapter 6

Of Villagers and Bones

Everyone used to say: Don Florentino didn't belong to Ichcateopan;
Ichcateopan belonged to him.

—Salvador Rodríguez Juárez

IT WOULD HAVE BEEN EASIER HAD FLORENTINO JUÁREZ BEEN AN
inveterate letter writer or an obsessive diarist. As it was, bar the journals he left
little paperwork to flesh out the man who made Cuauhtémoc's tomb. His name
recurs across seventy years of the village archives; but those archives, although
more complete than many in Guerrero, are still fragmentary. They were burned
twice in 1876, when rebels took the plaza and destroyed what they could of the
municipal government's files.[1] They were burned again in March 1911, when
the revolutionary Modesto Beltrán "came to the town hall . . . threw the whole
ayuntamiento's archive outside . . . and down below the soldiers were setting
fire to it, the flames springing up from the papers as they burnt."[2] They were
burned once more by Catholic counterrevolutionaries in 1929 and then left in
mouldering bundles in the basement and attic of the town hall, periodically
picked over by historians.[3] Setting fire to the archives was, one villager rightly
commented, "a pantomime": a moment of polysemic theatricality when the
literacy that aided repression was neutralised, the legitimacy of government
was publically denied, and the carnival of misrule was consummated.[4] (It was
also a good practical way to eliminate embarrassing police or land records,
throwing material as well as symbolic spanners in the works of domination.)
It paralleled an enduring government penchant for amnesia by bonfire; more

than one historian has been cheerfully told by guerrerense authorities that certain records, such as state treasury files, are ritually burned.[5] This is more than a regional phenomenon; as Luis González has observed, "Destroying archives is an old Mexican custom" (a very old one: the warrior Itzcóatl is supposed to have burned all the Mexica's early records when founding the empire in 1430).[6] Such continual attempts to destroy accountability, cognitive capacity, and memory itself are themselves part of Guerrero's history, a history that is fragile, powerful, and readily manipulable.

The chasms between competing representations of regional history are clearly evinced in Ixcateopan. Outsiders visiting the village in the twentieth century tended to find the exotica they came to find: a hilltop lost world, remote, poor, and above all Indian. This was not just the version of an ideologue and dreamer like Diego Rivera, who called the villagers "sublime Indians," but, rather, a generalised representation disseminated by scholars, journalists, and politicians. Eulalia Guzmán described her workmen as "indigenous diggers"; the correspondents of *Excélsior*, *El Universal*, *La Prensa*, and *El Nacional* all described the villagers collectively as *indígenas* or *indios*; a long line of *políticos* paid tribute to the impeccably indigenous inhabitants of the village.[7] "Indian" was, in their metropolitan discourse, moulded in a lengthening tradition of state indigenismo, a positive, Rousseauian attribute. Such outsiders also drew on the civilisation/barbarism dichotomies of the nineteenth century, which—together with their subjective blurring of ethnic and economic categories—made most peasants indiscriminately "Indian" in urban eyes.[8] Guzmán's diggers, however—several of them members of the municipal officeholding elite, drawn by the cash salary of four pesos a day in a cash-poor place—did not see themselves as noble savages.[9] Before Cuauhtémoc's bones muddied the waters, emic representations of ethnic identity went largely unromanticised in Ixcateopan. Villagers knew full well that to be "Indian," once the visiting *chilangos* had left, was to be at the bottom of society, and they persistently identified themselves as "pure creole."[10] It was a claim, rooted in secular racialist hierarchies and enduring socioeconomic realities, to intrinsically higher status for Ixcateopan as a mestizo cabecera village, politically dominating neighbouring, more "Indian" villages and hamlets. In Ixcateopan in 1940 only six people would admit to census officials that they spoke Nahuatl; a majority told census takers that they ate wheat bread and wore shoes, both key status markers; they insulted men from nearby Pachivia by calling them "Indians . . . pure broken down snotnoses, dirty from here to the chest, and, well, Indian people."[11]

Ixcateopan was, however, an ancient settlement and as such had once been ethnically Chontal, a part of the province of Tepequacuilco. It was conquered by Moctezuma I in the mid–fifteenth century, becoming a border town in the front line of a war that continued up until the conquest.[12] In the first administrative division of New Spain Ixcateopan was not granted to any individual but became instead Crown lands, paying taxes directly to the colonial government.[13] It was also a *corregimiento*, the provincial seat of government, ruling ten other cabeceras including the future municipios of Ixcapuzalco, Cuetzala, Apaxtla, and Teloloapan. Yet despite this distinction the initial influx of Spanish was slow, and in 1579 the only Spaniard for several leagues in any direction was Captain Lucas Pinto, the *corregidor* or lieutenant-governor. In that year he followed King Philip II's order for a general survey of Spain's lands in the Indies, responding to fifty standard questions to create a useful overview of the territory. Pinto's answers sketched a place in tension between the endemic poverty of its land and the emerging opportunities afforded by Taxco's booming silver mines, which bought Ixcateopan's maize, cattle, and dairy produce and paid good money—four reales a week—for Indians willing to work in the cramped, twisting tunnels digging out ore.[14] In the seventeenth and eighteenth centuries such opportunities attracted steady in-migration—Doña Rosa María Martínez Orejón, for example, founded the livestock Hacienda Santa María Magdalena in 1766—and with it mestizaje: the 1768 census of the village counted 262 Indians, thirty-four mestizos, and eight Spaniards.[15] In the 1830s, however, the mining sector went into vertiginous decline—by 1872 only sixteen of Taxco's listed 144 mines were being worked—and Ixcateopan became the periphery of a periphery.[16]

When Florentino Juárez was born in 1842, then, the village was economically stagnant, increasingly isolated, and on the brink of notable shifts in long-established social structures. Despite their proximity, as the crow flies, to Mexico City, the village and its region were more akin to the frontiers of the remote south than to the more prosperous altiplano. Most of Guerrero's territory is filled by the Sierra Madre and the Sierra de Taxco, whose peaks rise to well over two thousand metres and stretch from the northern borders to a thin coastal strip of patchily fertile plain. What forest, swamp, and river were to the south, these mountains were to Guerrero, a formidable natural obstacle to commercial agriculture, extractive industries, and viable communications. With the exception of certain coastal areas, a single major river valley, and scattered pockets of irrigated land, most of the state's surface was covered by unforgiving uplands and forest, exploited for subsistence purposes by slash-and-burn smallholders. The railways that inserted other regions of Mexico into national and international markets barely grazed the north of Guerrero, reaching Iguala in 1892 and the Río Balsas in 1900.[17] As late as the mid-1920s the journey across the state from Acapulco to Mexico City involved fifteen days on muleback, without benefit of road; the sole river freight service likewise took fifteen days to cover the short distance from Coyuca de Catalán to the Balsas railhead.[18] Freight costs from the interior to the Pacific or to the capital remained ruinously high, as assorted infrastructure schemes—highways and railroads, shipping on the Balsas—successively foundered.[19] In Aldama, the village's district, even muleteers were (by the admittedly disreputable 1895 census) extremely scarce: there were only three listed, compared to the sixty-four working coastal Galeana.[20] For Florentino Juárez's lifetime, and for a long time after his death, Ixcateopan was an island in an archipelago of rural settlements, whose small populations were largely isolated from the world outside the immediate, locally meaningful places of their *terruños*.[21]

Isolation did not mean autonomy, and key governmental decisions did eventually percolate down from a distant capital to the village administration. In 1827 Ixcateopan was shuffled from the jurisdiction of Zacualpan to that of Teloloapan; in 1849, from the state of Mexico to the newborn state of Guerrero.[22] At relatively regular intervals news of wars, rebellions, coups, and their associated proclamations arrived. None of these had the impact of the mid-century liberal government's land reform. Under the terms of the Ley Lerdo, passed in 1856, "The ownership of all urban and rural properties of civil and ecclesiastical corporations in the Republic will be assigned to those persons who are renting them, for an amount corresponding to the rent at present paid, calculating this as to be equal to a 6% annual interest."[23] In Ixcateopan the principal documented forms of tenure were community lands, village endowments, and *cofradías*, the religious confraternities.[24] All were corporate holdings, liable to the dissolution prescribed by the Ley Lerdo; all would have to go.

Traditional analyses of the effects of liberal land reform paint it as an example of unintended consequences run riot: aiming (at least formally) to engineer a Jeffersonian democracy of prosperous smallholders, the liberals instead succeeded in providing ideal conditions for monopolistic aggrandisement by a few well-situated individuals and immiseration for the rest. Revisionist regional studies argue, in contrast, that the legislation could be slow and incomplete in implementation, frequently leaving communities that resisted in possession of communal lands, and that the sudden influx of land onto the open market did stimulate, in some regions, the formation of a new and dynamic class of capitalist smallholders. Such are Ian Jacobs's conclusions for northern Guerrero: in the districts of Alarcón and Hidalgo, to the east of Ixcateopan, Jacobs found eighteen out of thirty-four communities maintaining some corporate holdings up until the revolution. Meanwhile, in their midst, there emerged a "new village elite," formed by precisely those "small productive tendencies" that liberals aimed to encourage.[25]

In Ixcateopan results are less clear-cut than either traditionalists or revisionists might wish. Land reform began earlier than in neighbouring Hidalgo: when Governor Arce surveyed its effects in 1886 he found sixty-two new property titles in the Aldama district and six properties classed as haciendas in the municipio of Ixcateopan itself.[26] By 1901 there were 156 ranches, 17 haciendas, and 67 pueblos listed for Aldama and Hidalgo, compared to 79 ranches, 13 haciendas, and 103 pueblos in 1877. The emergence of a local rancher elite is evident: about a third of all ranches in Guerrero were located in these two districts.[27] It was a dynamic class: in Ixcateopan the new ranchers set up shops and cantinas, produced soaps and alcohol, and complemented subsistence with cash crops such as sugar and cotton. On this economic basis they successfully established local hegemony, displacing an older generation: in Ixcateopan none of the families who signed the 1849 petition for the foundation of Guerrero remained among the officeholding municipal elite in the 1880s and 1890s, a single generation later.[28] So far, so revisionist. But while local rather than absentee, the new landowners shared the same aggressive approach to aggrandisement as any stereotyped Morelos *hacendado*, deploying usury, water deprivation, and a tenacious hold on local political office to obtain further lands by tactics at best illegitimate and frequently illegal. While central government circulated effete exegeses of *desamortización* legislation, urging state authorities not to dispossess long-term occupants, local communities were being evicted: in 1887, for example, the farmers of Tilapa, a cofradía holding outside Tenanguillo, had their lands auctioned from under them.[29] The new concentration of landholding is clear: only six of the municipio's sixteen communities preserved any communal lands, and by the turn of the century only forty-nine men in the entire municipio described themselves as ranchers. Cadastral surveys, even those taken long after the revolution, give a detailed depiction of the Ixcateopan new village elite as a narrow and locally wealthy group, firmly entrenched in power, holding down an extensive new village poor. If we take Miller's estimate of five hectares as the minimum plot size for an average family's subsistence needs, 48 percent of Ixcateopan landowners in 1939 still fell below subsistence level; ranchers owned nearly 60 percent of the municipio's cultivated land while constituting less than 10 percent of the landholding population.[30] (This, according to both oral histories and census data, was a lesser concentration of landholding than that of the Porfiriato.)[31] In Ixcateopan the land reforms of the liberals met, to some extent, their economic purpose. Socially, politically, and in the proclaimed terms of the reformers themselves—"[its] principal purpose is to favour the most disadvantaged classes"—they failed.[32]

By the 1890s Ixcateopan's new economy was firmly established. It was characterised, above all, by that peculiar overlapping of subsistence and surplus-trading livelihoods that typifies peasant societies in transition to capitalism. The base was still overwhelmingly agricultural: of the economically active population, 1,687 were peons and a mere thirty-eight were traders, bakers, teachers, or servants.[33] Most men still grew most of their food; their year was determined by the life cycle of the maize plant. From March onward the majority whose land was neither irrigated nor overly fertile began to clear the scrub of their *tlacolol* plots, traditionally planted every two, eight, ten, or even twelve years, depending on the soil quality. It was a simple slash-and-burn system, with some intercropping (typically of *chile*, beans, and squash) but no crop rotation; it required lengthy fallow periods, when farmers allowed the scrub to return and slowly replenish the thin soil. By the end of May the fields were prepared, and farmers waited for the first rains in order to sow the seed held over from the previous year. The rainy season was an anxious time. Food stocks ran low or out; death rates rose as the cold and the damp aggravated the two principal killers, malaria and pneumonia; meanwhile subsistence, dependent on rains being neither too light nor too heavy, hung in the balance for many villagers. In October or November came the harvest and with it the end of uncertainty. If there was a good harvest, then a smallholder such as Miguel Treviño might end up with a small surplus: one or two *cargas*, the locally varied measure of maize that ranged from one hundred litres in the Ixcateopan region to nearly three hundred in parts of la Montaña.[34] This could be sold—depending on the vagaries of others' yields—for anything from two to five pesos a carga.[35] If it was a bad year, then a smallholder such as Ignacio Santana would have to sell his lands to one of the village wealthy for a single carga of maize.[36]

Faced with structural insecurity, villagers resorted to various coping strategies. There was, for a start, the growing cash economy, in which most villagers had a toehold. Some worked as field hands, *jornaleros*, exchanging their labour from sunrise to sunset for the peseta, the standard twenty-five-centavo wage. Most had a skill, whether agricultural, artisanal, or political, that could be exchanged for money: Jesús Barrera used to shape roof beams for a peso to a peso fifty a time, Cleto Parra was a part-time muleteer, Refugio Bustamante made shoes at fifty centavos a pair, Jesús Álvarez trained fighting cocks, Jesús Ribera was a slaughter man, and Jesús Morelos made and sold adobe bricks.[37] For the landless there was always the option of sharecropping, in which family labour transformed marginal land into some sort of productive plot. The land-lord generally provided seed on credit and took a portion of the crop as rent, a system that enabled subsistence while removing much chance of social mobil-ity (children of sharecroppers often minimised school attendance in favour of necessary fieldwork).[38] It would be interesting to know the precise sharecrop rent, a useful measure of tenant bargaining power. All we have, regrettably, are imprecise references in oral histories that suggest that it was not as onerous as, say, the 50 percent of harvest that Tomás Bustamante has found operating among sesame-cultivating sharecroppers in Tierra Caliente in the same period: the Hernández family, for example, never paid more than a carga and a half for their rent.[39] When these fleeting indicators are combined with the pronounced labour surplus—evinced in oral accounts, the complete lack of coercive labour mechanisms such as *tiendas de raya*, and high levels of out-migration—we can hypothesise that the poor in Ixcateopan had a certain level of infrapolitical "pull" over the new village elite.[40] (Although lower rents than in other regions may also have been influenced by the paltry sustainable surplus that could be extracted from the municipio's rocky slopes.) It was a pull illustrated in the uncertain status of some of those rents, in evolution from a supposedly voluntary con-tribution from former communal owners to their deed-holding representative toward the harder-edged obligation of a rent.[41] Such rents could not always be mechanically charged; the gift of foodstuffs and other minor acts of charity, on the other hand, seem to have been widely practised by the new village elite both in Ixcateopan and across entire regions such as the Costa Chica, the coast south of Acapulco. They were probably more tactical necessity than optional altru-ism.[42] Many landholdings were of recent origins and questionable legitimacy: in 1895 the governor complained to Mexico City that "individuals' requests relating to the nullification of land titles granted by the *prefectos políticos* of the state's districts under the desamortización law are frequently received by this Government."[43] Illegitimacy of tenure imposed a certain hegemonic delicacy on the principal landholders in relations with tenants, who were usually "friends" or *compadres*. Without such delicacy and its associated symbolic cleansing of wealth, landlords such as Juárez, remembered (at least by his clients) as "good with the peasantry, with *los de abajo*," could not have survived.[44]

Florentino Juárez's lands, shops, and wealth were of both recent and questionable origin. In charting his youth the only documents we have are his and his first daughter's birth certificates: they show, however, that José Florentino Juárez was born on October 14, 1842, to Amado Juárez and Petra Gal and that these were not among the contemporary village elite; the socially strategic godparents, Hilario de la Cruz and Francisca Ricarda, seem both, from their names, to have been indigenous. Twenty-six years later, at the birth of his first daughter, Gilberta Jovita Juárez, comes another snapshot: Juárez is married to Juana Sales and is working as a labourer.[45] From then onward Juárez's wealth and social standing and our records of the same grow in tandem. In 1875 he built the large townhouse across the square from the church, one of only three houses in Ixcateopan with a private well and one of the few that employed servants, and by 1879 he had entered municipal politics as the *síndico*, the village treasurer.[46] He had quickly become the rancher whom villagers remembered a century later for his wealth and power: the man who had the finest horses and his own roulette wheel; who cached, it was rumoured, money and silver in the mountains; who took his family to Mexico to have their clothes tailored; and who had "lands all over the place."[47]

For any member of the new village elite there were two phases to getting rich: the first social leap from anonymity to sufficient capital holdings to obtain political office and contacts and the ensuing use of that political clout to maintain and expand those holdings. We are, concerning the first phase in Juárez's rise, next door to ignorant. He was at his peak a cattle rancher, and enterprising cattle trading was a classic route to social mobility. Another of his generation, Pedro Mójica, started as a herdsman, bought land, and then began raising and trading cattle, ending as a well-established rancher; José María Salgado followed a similar path.[48] (Cattle, a literally mobile form of capital, could bypass the commercialisation problems posed by poor communications.) Assorted vague and dark hints from village gossip, on the other hand, attribute Juárez's initial wealth to violence. "You should look," said Josefina Jaimes, "at his background, and then you'd realise a lot. . . . [H]e was always on the run." "I don't say that he was a bandit," said Ninfo Ibarra, ". . . I don't know why he was always fleeing the government." "He was," according to Santiago Alvarez, "a wrong'un for a long time."[49] Gossip, as James Scott emphasises, is one of the principal weapons of the weak in the subterranean class conflicts that underlie facades of clientelist calm and as such is, particularly at a century or so's distance, slippery evidence.[50] These accounts are often, moreover, chronologically confused, conflating the nineteenth century with the revolution. A central image of several villagers' accounts of Juárez was, all the same, that of a man on a white horse on the run. He and his family were, certainly, violent operators: Juárez was variously described as beating a man to death in Romita, pulling a pistol on fellow landowner and ally José Jaimes in a land dispute, and trying to violently fix elections.[51] The village archives are well stocked with reports of violence by Juárez and his sons, while the *Periódico Oficial* lists diverse charges against them, such as Odilón's regrettable attempt to kill the local police chief in 1903.[52] Perhaps, then, he began accumulating power at the intersection of violence and stock farming that is *abigeo*, cattle rustling, a comparatively common way of getting rich in nineteenth-century Guerrero.

But if he did indulge in other people's cattle, Florentino Juárez was never caught (historically) napping—unlike his son Florencio, who later tried to sell cattle with forged stock certificates, a classic indicator of rustling.[53] Alongside enterprise and violence, the other key to social mobility was literacy, and here we have more evidence. As late as 1900, only 156 people in the municipio—a whole 2.3 percent of the population—were literate.[54] Anyone in that literate minority was virtually guaranteed municipal office: as one villager remembered, "In those days those who knew how to read, well, they became president."[55] Those who were literate in turn taught the ambitious: José Jaimes was taught to read by the town secretary; Juárez, probably, by the parish priest when he served as a sacristan in the church.[56] Once inside the small circle of municipal officeholders, Juárez moved from position to position for over twenty years, the formality of annual public elections euphemizing the underlying reality of (sometimes consensual and sometimes conflictual) *caciquismo* by the "señores," the village elite. "In those days," another villager explained, "they did it on the basis of friendship, right? Like friends they'd say let's name so-and-so president, let's invite the friends. . . . [T]here were [elections,] but all the same they'd already made their minds up."[57] Village politics, in short, bore out the anthropologist Claude Lévi-Strauss's dictum: "Writing . . . seems to favour men's exploitation more than their enlightenment."[58]

Juárez began his career in a village faction that was led by Vidal Ybarra and included José Jaimes. He made village treasurer in 1879, with Ybarra as *presidente municipal*, and he returned (under Ybarra again) in 1885 as village judge; he was deputy justice of the peace in 1890 and judge of the civil registry from 1894 to 1897. In 1898 he became presidente municipal; as late as 1911 he came back, after a decade in the local political wilderness, as treasurer once more.[59] For many of these years, whether in office or not, he seems to have been determinant in municipal politics. It was Juárez, for example, who kept the *papeles del pueblo*, the essential village papers, from the colony. Juárez corresponded with *jefes políticos*, bishops, and other state-level players such as the rebellious General Neri; he was, even when he fell from grace in the 1900s, untouchable enough to ignore local officials for the eloquently simple reason that he was "Don Florentino."[60]

Literacy gave Juárez wealth that gave him political power that led to more wealth. Instability of land tenure was nothing new in the Mexican countryside, and each village's history was interwoven with land conflicts with haciendas, neighbouring communities, and the state. Between 1713 and 1808, for example, San Martín Pachivia and Santo Tomás Tenanguillo engaged in a secular war of legal attrition against the family of "el español Torres," the owners of three haciendas bordering (and encroaching upon) the villages' lands. The postindependence division of the hacienda of Oculistlahuacán between Teucizapan and other hamlets led to periodic and violent boundary disputes in the planting season, in which the only clear winners were the local officials called in to adjudicate.[61] Whole settlements could be founded to contain others' territorial ambitions: Pipincatla was founded by the villagers of Ixcateopan as just such a bulwark against the scorned hordes of Pachivia.[62] State attempts to disentail villages' communal holdings began substantially before 1856. An 1825 Estado de México law assigned the administration of village lands to the municipios, a measure that theoretically enabled the small-town politicians of the cabeceras to dispose of their subject villages' communal lands; an 1827 Michoacán law similarly decreed the distribution of communal lands to increase production. Such legislation was, however, generally unenforceable. In 1840, for example, Teloloapan's prefect reported that "resistance of the 'commons' had prevented the agents of the state from administering village lands."[63] In such struggles, literacy enabled access to the metropolitan codes of the referee state: villagers who could read and write could defend themselves in the colonial courts against the aggrandisement of others or, in turn, engage in erudite aggrandisement themselves. In such struggles perjury and fraud were old friends. As one testy viceregal court decision from the Pachivia papeles del pueblo complained,

"Some with just the story of having been dispossessed of lands waters and other things obtain Royal Orders for their restitution . . . [and the justices] . . . award the restitution demanded without the necessary procedure, frequently dispossessing others who quietly, pacifically and legitimately are in possession."[64]

Those who made spectacular gains were generally elites rather than peasants, and desamortización, as much as a rupture, was a further biasing of the tenure system in favour of literate, well-connected predators. A string of general officers used the new legislation to establish vast estates across Guerrero: General Cáceres took part of the northern municipios of Cuetzala and Apaxtla; General Carrera stitched together lands across the eastern highlands into the hacienda "Anáhuac de la Sierra Madre"; General Jiménez enveloped the town of Quechultenango in his central hacienda; and General Martínez occupied much of the municipios of Copala, Cuautepec, San Luis Acatlán, Tlacoapa, and Metlatónoc. In the Acapulco region General Diego Alvarez aggressively extended his father Juan Alvarez's Hacienda La Providencia, getting the local prefecto político killed in the process.[65] Even the more progressive of the Porfirian functionaries helped themselves to others' lands. Governor Francisco Arce seized large estates in the districts of Bravos, Allende, Guerrero, Alvarez, and Tabares; Perfecto Beltrán, the efficient longtime jefe político of Ixcateopan's district, took the hacienda of Tilapa thanks to a rent agreement he found in the local archives and added to it, in time, forty-eight mining plots in Arcelia; Cipriano Salgado, his predecessor, took extensive common lands from the villages of Santo Tomás, Ahuatepec, and Totoltepec.[66]

Florentino Juárez did not lag behind. The mechanisms of forming a large estate were varied and covered a wide spectrum of fraud and legitimacy, and Juárez, along with many other villagers, did obtain some lands in an apparently inclusive redistribution of communal property. His grant, however, consisted of scarce irrigated land on the banks of the Río San Miguel and of what one traveller described as the "exceptionally productive lands" to the south of Ixcapuzalco, Ixcateopan's rival village to the west.[67] This was not coincidental, but rather obeyed a strict correlation between social class and quality of land grant; as Ezequiel Colín remembered, "The poorest who couldn't speak weren't given anything. . . . [For the poor] there are no irrigated lands."[68] Other lands Juárez obtained through violence, as when he threatened Jaimes with a pistol over a land sale, or through abuse of authority. When presidente municipal, for example, he seized part of the schoolyard adjoining his townhouse; he later had his eldest son, Odilón, then in local government, sell him more of the same plot.[69] By the end of his life he had pieced together a string of ranches across the municipio, which stretched from the woodland and hilly pastures of the Cerro de En Medio and the Cerro Grande down to the fields of Ojo de Agua, a small—"at best two hundred paces wide by two musket shots long"—flatlands watered by a large spring.[70]

This blend of strategies—legitimate purchase, rigged redistribution, usury, violence, and peculation—was common to the new village elite. José Jaimes, for example, obtained the cofradía's sixty hectares of prime land by persuading the tenants to trust him, when the law forced its privatisation, with the individual title as a mere cover for their traditional collective occupancy. Across the indigenous communities of la Montaña such legal artifices were generally respected; in Ixcateopan, however, the de facto tenure was ignored, and the lands ended up in the Jaimes estate. The church proved more than once a fertile resource: while in the *ayuntamiento* of 1876 he granted himself part of the churchyard and some ten years later obtained part of the former ecclesiastical living of the Hacienda la Magdalena. He went on to buy out the smallholders bordering his sugar ranch, San Miguel; when his neighbour Santiago Ibarra refused to sell, Jaimes, who lived upstream, cut his water supply. Ibarra then sold Jaimes his ranch, El Aguacate, for two hundred pesos. The rancher was, finally, a prolific extender of credit, in the form of both cash and medical services. When Taxco and Teloloapan had one doctor between them, when traditional cures could quite literally involve boiling black cocks, and when the *Periódico Oficial* endorsed remedies such as coffee and lemon juice for headaches or wearing sweet-smelling linden flowers on the nose against cholera, José Jaimes's apparently effective work as an amateur doctor gave him access to further land titles, deposited against future cash payment. Many such loans were eventually foreclosed. Epidemics, such as the typhoid of 1920, were particularly profitable periods.[71]

Jaimes's success was no mystery to his *peon de confianza*, his right-hand man: the landowner was, he maintained, in league with the devil.[72] This was an isolated glimpse of a transcript that remained hidden even in the 1970s, when the Instituto Nacional de Antropología e Historia Ixcateopan interviews were conducted—for the presidente municipal then was a Juárez, and one of the principal landlords was a Jaimes.[73] Michael Taussig has convincingly analysed such beliefs as a widespread folk critique of capitalism: men at the collision points of (predominantly) moral and capitalist economies often attribute success in the new arts of capital reproduction to practise in the older arts of devil worship. The muleteer Sidronio Parra was likewise supposed to be in Faustian bond, as were the monopolizing ranchers of the Costa Chica; the principal usurer of Acapulco, el "Gato Capón"; the San Luis Potosí cacique Gonzalo N. Santos; and the indigenous coffee growers of Juquil, Oaxaca.[74] It must have been a satisfying story to tell; it was also a powerful reflection of the incomprehensibility, and perceived immorality, of a shift in land tenure that saw a handful of families take over the majority of the municipio's lands. Among those five families—the Teráns, the Sales, and the Zaragozas, along with the Juárez and Jaimes clans—the latter two were the most landed and the most enduring. The Jaimes estate ended up summing over six hundred hectares; Florentino Juárez, even after losing his Ixcapuzalco holdings, still owned lands totalling 643 hectares. Even in decline, the two families between them owned around a quarter of the entire municipio.[75]

Juárez and Jaimes were, in economic terms, model Porfirians, for on this enterprisingly acquired landed base they built small but diverse business empires. Both were leading members of the village's narrow commercial class—twenty-three registered merchants in 1900, most of whom were probably itinerant or market traders like Ignacio Hernández—with shops on the *camino real* to Taxco and on the village's main square, selling maize, beans, rice, chile, coffee, cane liquor, and paraffin. They exported foodstuffs in considerable quantity: a surviving telephone message from 1906 shows Juárez selling fifty cargas of maize—about five tons—to Mateo Flores, a member of Taxco's principal merchant family.[76] Both set up small industries: Jaimes grew sugar cane in the narrow but fertile river valley to the south of the village and brewed it into the alcohol called *aguardiente*, while Florentino Juárez owned the area's only soap factory.[77] Holding such concentrations of land, local industry, and trade, Juárez and Jaimes controlled much of the village's employment, rents, food supplies, credit, and external contacts. Their resulting social networks began in Ixcateopan with their peons, tenants, sharecroppers, customers, and debtors and ended at the highest level of state politics. They had, in the classic fictive kinship euphemisms for clients, "*compadres* and friends all over the place."[78]

Juárez and Jaimes were also, perhaps inevitably, the village's cultural leaders. They impressed locals with their knowledge of herbalism, medicine, and science: Juárez had formulas to make cows give more milk and to cure rabies, while Jaimes "tried to discover some useful advances for humanity, one of them was to do an experiment so that teeth should grow back and he was doing some experiments it was just that the economics of it, perhaps, he wasn't able to achieve that, but I think he did manage it in an animal."[79] Both dabbled in the voguish spiritualism of the period, "magnetizing" tables so that spirits might answer questions about present and future, such as where one villager's stolen animals might be found (for sale at midday in Sultepec, the table rightly answered).[80] Both joined the Masons, among whose national leaders was longtime governor Francisco Arce. Both sent children on to higher education (Odilón Juárez went to the Instituto Literario in Chilpancingo, Camerino Jaimes became a doctor, another Jaimes became a *licenciado*).[81] Both amassed considerable private libraries; the municipal library after the revolution was named in Juárez's honour.[82] It is unsurprising that they should have been called "don," that villagers should have greeted them respectfully, doffing their hats and in some cases kissing their hands, for Juárez and Jaimes were the José Arcadio Buendías of their time and place: the village patriarchs.[83]

Yet they were the patriarchs of a village in decline. Ixcateopan was no closed corporate community, a group of cultivators of common land who redistributed wealth internally, fiercely united against a hostile world; the municipio was, rather, a divided place.[84] Villagers in the cabecera itself identified themselves as belonging to either the barrio de arriba or the barrio de abajo, identities so deeply ingrained and so deeply opposed that they were believed to be rival ethnic groups. The barrio de arriba, it was said, had been Aztec; the barrio de abajo, Chontal.[85] Their mutual antagonism found everyday expression in everything from politics (the barrio de arriba was dominant) to people's places in church (the two barrios sat separately on big occasions, at least) to feast days, when the young men of the two groups would wrestle and wage phony war with fragments of clay or pumpkin.[86] Such long-running status divisions overlapped with the increased class divisions of the new economy. The village was, moreover, distanced from the other main settlements in the municipio, Ixcapuzalco and Pachivia, and was increasingly left behind economically by the strong growth of Teloloapan, the market town to the immediate south.[87] As a result Ixcateopan's elites were not particularly powerful in the region, and their weakness translated across the 1880s and 1890s into the shrinking of their territory. In 1883, 1885, and 1888 several southern hamlets—Tonalapa del Sur, Rincón Chiquito, Rincón Grande, Coatles, and Yierba Buena—were taken by Teloloapan. In April 1890 the western village of Ixcapuzalco petitioned the state congress for permission to form its own municipio. The jefe político backed it, so on November 29, 1890, the state congress passed the relevant law, and on January 1, 1891, Ixcapuzalco became cabecera of the new municipality of Pedro Ascencio Alquisiras.[88] At the beginning of the nineteenth century the municipio of Ixcateopan had covered some 585 square kilometres; once Ixcapuzalco was gone, a mere rump of 225 square kilometres remained. For the people of Ixcapuzalco 1891 was something of a revolutionary Year Zero: they seized various church properties to set up offices and a school, ceased paying taxes to their local rivals, and set off to see if they could worship outside of the parish of Ixcateopan.[89] For Ixcateopan it was the local equivalent of the 1848 U.S. landgrab: the village lost over half of its territory, and the richest half at that.

There were powerful, *longue durée* cultural reasons for this municipal divorce. Neighbouring villages, whether rival cabeceras or rivals for the privileges of being cabecera, tend strongly to enmity. Manuel Gamio's study of the Valle de Teotihuacán describes a series of such dyadic relationships between the valley's communities and claims it as a peculiarly Mexican pattern.[90] Luis González y González goes further, claiming that every village in the Hispanic American world was a bitter rival to its closest neighbour.[91] To Eric Van Young, village bids for independence from their cabeceras are local expressions of Mexico's "long history of centrifugal struggle."[92] Such bids became endemic in many regions of Mexico during the wars of independence: between 1812 and 1821 the number of municipios rose steeply to 630.[93] This fragmentation continued across the nineteenth century. As Michael Ducey notes, the conflicts between cabeceras and subject villages over land use and taxes formed a "structure of discontent" in village life, "one of the central themes of Mexican rural history." These intervillage struggles found expression at all levels of politics, from village secessionist movements to choosing different sides in national conflicts.[94]

Ixcateopan and Ixcapuzalco enjoyed a secular rivalry, stretching back, villagers knew, to the prehispanic world and expressed—once more—in fundamentally ethnic terms. Ixcapuzalco, it was believed, had been Mazahua, while Ixcateopan had been Chontal.[95] The two villages had warred even before the Spanish arrived in the New World, and the same dyadic pattern continued through their modern histories; as Florentino Juárez wrote, Ixcapuzalco was "the bitter enemy of the sons of Ixcateopan."[96] In the mid-nineteenth-century wars of the Reforma liberal Ixcateopan was the target of raids from conservative Ixcapuzalco, raids led by the shadowy Colonel Agustín Trujillo, who "came at night killing men" and who, in one gory memory, dragged a rival behind his horse through the streets of Ixcateopan, "smearing fragments of brain behind him."[97] In the early 1910s the villages fell into rival camps again, and Ixcateopan, nominally zapatista, was again raided by pro-government forces from Ixcapuzalco, which at one point tried to destroy the village by ordering the people's "reconcentration" to Ixcapuzalco.[98] Intercommunity violence did not end after the armed revolution: as late as the 1930s, Román Parra Terán remembered, armed villagers from Ixcapuzalco used to ride into town, capture women, and, once or twice, kill villagers. The hangover of violence persisted into the postrevolutionary period, when villagers did not play basketball together or even visit each other.[99] Such rivalry was clearly well established long before Ixcapuzalco's secession, which only reinforced it.

Yet there was more than the violent rivalries of provincial political culture behind the split with Ixcapuzalco; that village's political economy likewise favoured secession. Located in the northwest of the municipio, Ixcapuzalco was surrounded by the area's prime lands, described by a contemporary traveller as "a large expanse of productive lands excellent for maize, wheat, beans and chickpeas." There were even gold mines, albeit unexploited; the contrast with the rocky slopes surrounding Ixcateopan was marked.[100] By the late nineteenth century Ixcapuzalco had, on several key indicators, surpassed Ixcateopan: while the villages had similar numbers of merchants, Ixcapuzalco had considerably more ranchers and a population three times as literate as that of Ixcateopan.[101] Ixcateopan, on the other hand, was in economic decline, shadowing the long decay of its main market, Taxco. By the 1890s the state's silver production was worth all of double that of its cheese production, and Taxco's handful of surviving mines were worked exclusively by *buscones*, individual miners scratching a living from tired veins of silver.[102] A municipio was, as Peter Guardino observes, more than a political or symbolic unit; it was also "the strategic high ground in struggles over local resources."[103] Everybody knew that: children picked up this basic truth in school, where one later guerrerense textbook told them that "progress is more difficult in the pueblos which are not *cabeceras municipales*, because all the public revenues go to the *cabecera municipal*, the capital of the state and the capital of the Republic."[104] Ixcateopan, as cabecera, collected local taxes and was consequently the only village in the municipio to have any money in the public purse. Her elites also enjoyed the considerable advantages of controlling justice and education.[105] Yet, as the village's economic power waned and that of Ixcapuzalco grew, the justification for their lopsided political relationship came to an end.

Ixcapuzalco's secession shocked the villagers of Ixcateopan in more ways than one. It translated into an instant loss of revenues: deprived of, for example, 25 percent of the value of all alcohol sold in Ixcapuzalco and its eighteen

Figure 26.
Cuauhtémoc's
tomb today.
Photograph by
Lyman Johnson.

hamlets, the municipal treasurer henceforth struggled to balance his books.[106] It spelled a clear loss of prestige: the municipio became one of the smallest in Guerrero and lost its status as a vicariate.[107] It bitterly divided the new village elite. Félix Sales, presidente municipal at the time, was rumoured to have been bought off, and Florentino Juárez in particular never forgave him.[108] Juárez had particularly strong reasons to resent the loss of Ixcapuzalco, for it spelled not just political decline but also the surrender of jurisdiction over an area that contained some of his prime lands. He had been awarded former communal lands in Acatlipa, to the southwest of the village of Ixcapuzalco, and he had put together a substantial cattle ranch to the south of Ixcapuzalco.[109] Where evidence exists it is clear that such lands were obtained by a mixture of illegitimate and sometimes downright illegal methods.[110] In such a context he did not have to read Machiavelli (although he may well have, *The Prince* being an eagerly read guide to everyday politics in other villages) to understand that the loss of political control would, in the end, mean the loss of his Ixcapuzalco landholdings.[111] Small-scale absentee landowners had poor prospects in the nineteenth century, it being difficult for smallholders or ranchers to work across administrative boundaries. At best, they met resentment; at worst, they could be forced to sell up or lose their lands.[112] Such was Juárez's fate. His son Florencio had married a girl from Ixcapuzalco and gone to work the family lands; but once the village seceded they sold up and moved away.[113]

So Juárez, the local judge at the time, led his faction in vigorous resistance to municipal amputation. He asked the northern caudillo, General Canuto Neri, to intercede with the state government in December 1890 and petitioned the bishop of Chilapa that the parish, which still encompassed Ixcapuzalco, might stay in one piece "in accordance with General Neri's recommendation."[114] (General Neri, according to some in Guerrero, did try to draw President Díaz's attention to the tomb.)[115] In 1895 he was part of the ayuntamiento that petitioned the state congress, asking that Ixcapuzalco be returned to Ixcateopan's administration, hopeful, perhaps, that the new governor (a Neri ally) might be more amenable to Ixcateopan than the old one.[116] And while Juárez pursued his case through conventional channels, writing pleading letters to generals, bishops, and congressmen, he was also following a less conventional strategy, namely, the painstaking creation of a politically loaded work of art: Cuauhtémoc's tomb.

Chapter 7

Forging the *Patria*

Three requisites for a work of art: validity of the myth, vigour of belief, intensity of vocation.
— Cyril Connolly, *The Unquiet Grave: A Word Cycle by Palinurus*

AT SOME STAGE BETWEEN 1890 AND THE END OF 1893 THE VILLAGERS built a new altar, and Florentino Juárez dug down through the chalky rock under the church floor to bury a body's worth of burnt bones.[1] It may have been 1890, when the villagers were busy installing a clock in the church tower and building a new sacristy. It seems more likely that it was 1891, when lightning struck the church dome and caused it to partially collapse onto the altar below.[2] The tomb was in place by the end of 1893, as Juárez told the jefe político Cipriano Salgado of its existence, and Cipriano Salgado ceased being jefe político late that year.[3] Whether the rancher had help within Ixcateopan is a question open to speculation. Juárez was a solitary man and could well have worked alone.[4] José Jaimes, on the other hand, would have been a natural ally. He belonged to Juárez's faction and opposed Ixcapuzalco's secession; he was a well-read small-town nationalist; and he later knew all about the tomb, telling his family and clients about it and writing an epic poem about Cuauhtémoc and the mystery of his final resting place.[5] The Rodríguez brothers—Severo, the village priest between 1891 and 1894, and Primitivo, the sacristan—likewise might well have helped by allowing Juárez access to the church (a much more probable, if more prosaic, way in than the secret tunnels of village gossip).[6] They were certainly close to Don Florentino, who married his daughter Alberta to Primitivo and petitioned the bishop of Chilapa to keep Severo in the village in 1894.[7] Yet, even if he did have collaborators, the fraud was overwhelmingly Juárez's creation: for it was Juárez who pieced together its origin myth, encoded in an exotic collection of peasant journals and would-be colonial documents, and Juárez who began to tantalise fellow villagers with cryptic stories of a treasure, or a king, or Cuauhtémoc, long hidden beneath the parish church.[8]

A primordialist interpretation of this process, seeking out long-standing cultural bonds between people and their age-old nations, might propose that in the rancher an ancient, organic commitment to the indigenous past met with the intense modishness of Cuauhtémoc in the 1890s and drove him to *forjar patria*—to forge the fatherland—in an extraordinary act of creation. It is undeniable that villagers in Ixcateopan, as elsewhere, felt intense, earthy, emotional bonds of place to their locality, their *patria chica*. Sometimes the *chica* was even dropped: thus the monthly reports from Ixcateopan to the *jefatura política* in the late 1880s called the various villages and hamlets *patrias* plain and simple.[9] Antonio Díaz Calderón, born in the late nineteenth century, clearly communicated this passionate attachment to Ixcateopan, stressing to his anthropologist interlocutors that "I was born here, this is my land, this is my home, here in Ixcateopan, I'm not from anywhere else, I'm from here."[10] Florentino Juárez's journals communicate glimpses of similar passion, when he refers to Ixcateopan as a republic, lists the "beautiful" things the indigenous people there made and their "delicious" food, or lays out how he "came to believe that the most pernicious and evil person is he who has neither God nor Fatherland."[11] To relocate Cuauhtémoc to his village would satisfy these affective bonds to Ixcateopan by inserting the place deep into the national historical narrative, a common enough goal, as recent work by Trevor Stack, Samuel Brunk, and Claudio Lomnitz demonstrates, in provincial Mexico.[12]

Yet to accept such an explanation is difficult for several reasons. Florentino Juárez was clearly mestizo: both by phenotype—villagers described him as "wheat-faced," and his grandson's pale face surprised metropolitan visitors— and by culture.[13] Ixcateopan in his time was a strongly, self-consciously mestizo society, where only nineteen people still owned up to using "the dialect" Nahuatl. (To speak it, more than one villager said, was shameful.) Yet fewer acted in the village's central Indian tradition, the dance of the ahuiles, whose words were being forgotten and substituted with Spanish.[14] The voice of Florentino Juárez in his journals, when not playing the "living letter," carries an almost orientalist, museumising fascination with a vanishing Indian past, a past to which he is more interested outsider than heir.[15] Finally, and most suggestive of all, it would be an extraordinary coincidence that had Juárez forging the tomb at the same time as the Ixcateopan elite faced the political crisis of their generation, the secession of half the municipio. The journals themselves connect the two epoch-making events. In their pages Ixcateopan—"the republic of the Lord King"—is given sweeping prehispanic boundaries, stretching "from the place of Acamixtla, Chotalcuatlan, Zaculapan, Acapetlahuaya, all of the Río Grande, Cuexala, the Río Balsas, the plains of Iguala, the Río of Camposano Acerrar bridge to Camixtla." Yet "the villages belonging to the Republic of our king [have] come to secede; we have already seen that; all [the villages] seceded and all that remains to us is the mere municipality, greatly reduced; and they said that all this is due to the fact that very close to the village, that is to say in this province, very large treasures are hidden."[16] Thus Ixcateopan has been unjustly punished—territorially mutilated—precisely for its centuries of dogged silence, its loyalty to Cuauhtémoc, the village's native son and the symbolic father figure of modern Mexico. Yet the journals offer hope, for "there is a time to reveal these things."[17] And once revealed, what benevolent, gesture-drunk dictator could deny Ixcateopan the restoration of its historic boundaries? The justice is clear; the nationalist logic, impeccable; the inference of an instrumentalist motive, as Salvador Rueda suggested, inescapable.[18]

It is, of course, a broadly acknowledged fallacy to assume that all human behaviour is dictated by rational-choice considerations, and Juárez's decision to forge Cuauhtémoc's tomb may not have been wholly materialist.[19] Lightning struck and damaged the church in late evening on August 13, 1891.[20] This was the most probable opportunity for Juárez to insert the tomb. This was also the anniversary of Tenochtitlán's fall to the Spanish, a day marked in 1521 by heavy electrical storms, and the date that the first Franciscans arrived in 1523.[21] It may be that the rancher had been reading about Cuauhtémoc the week before, as the state gazette customarily published articles about the last emperor to coincide with the anniversary of his empire's end. A spiritualist like Juárez might, on the other hand, have read the coincidence of dates and weather as a sign. He might even have received direct, otherworldly encouragement from Motolinía, the Franciscan at the centre of his legend making, or from the last emperor himself: Cuauhtémoc, along with Pancho Villa, is the most common shade invoked by Mexico's spirit healers.[22] Life-changing directions from beyond the grave were far from unheard of at this time. The figurehead of Mexico's revolution, Francisco Madero, was told to brush up his national history by one spirit, "José," and to rebel against Porfirio Díaz by another, "Benito Juárez."[23] This was not the first time that the undead had taken against Don Porfirio: in 1896 another spirit forecast a revolutionary end for the dictator.[24] Strange to our eyes, such logic would not have been that strange in turn-of-the-century Mexico or anywhere else in the contemporary Atlantic world for that matter. Spiritualism had originated in New York in 1848 and rapidly spread across America and across the sea, recruiting eminent English scientists, politicians, and poets. Belief in a quite garrulous, interventionist spirit world was not incompatible with what Marshall Sahlins has called "common bourgeois realism": thus Sir Arthur Conan Doyle, who through Sherlock Holmes became one of the nineteenth century's great rationalists, was simultaneously a committed spiritualist. (Holmes himself, in "The Adventure of the Veiled Lodger," flirted with spiritualism.)[25] There may also have been an elective affinity between occultists and early archaeologists, something in the fairy-tale quality of both pursuits that bound them together. The American archaeologist William Gates was inspired by Madame Blatavsky's *Secret Doctrine* to studies of the preconquest Maya, while the anthropologist Manuel Gamio argued that indigenous *brujos*, witch doctors, were deploying the same "unknown energies" as contemporary practitioners of psychic phenomena, magnetism, and hypnotism.[26] Yet this can only be speculation, as evidence-free assumptions concerning dead people's mental processes make for poor history. This chapter cannot claim to know Juárez's mind or the precise paths by which he arrived at a superbly ambitious tomb fraud. What can be done, on the other hand, is to explore just how doable that fraud was, by dint of examining the multiple cultural materials on which Juárez could draw in his creation.

Whether spiritualism played a part in the tomb's genesis or not, it is clear that the forgery owed heavily to the interplay of Florentino Juárez's pragmatic entrepreneurship with his very specific cultural context, a potent blend of provincial and metropolitan knowledge and practices. The scheme to take back Ixcapuzalco via archaeological fraud was innovative but not eccentric; it was a rational and viable (if mythopoeic) solution to a thorny problem in local politics. The building blocks of the fraud lay all around the rancher in Mexico's political, popular, and dominant cultures. From prevailing political culture came the pronounced mutability of internal borders, the power of cultural nationalism as a tool for individual self-promotion, and the strongly necrophiliac cast of that nationalism, revelling in the paraphernalia of death and its commemoration. This latter may well have stemmed from the baroque Catholicism of popular culture, which also contributed long-standing village appreciations of not just the spiritual but also the material and tactical importance of magical relics. Popular culture also provided Juárez with many examples of fraud, most notably long traditions of forging colonial land grants for use in land disputes, with both large landowners and rival communities. Elite culture, finally, was in the late nineteenth century enchanted by the romance of the new scientific discipline of archaeology. The everyday experiences and the hungry reading of a local worthy like Juárez gave him easy access to all of these influences. All it took was a particularly gifted *bricoleur*—man as Claude Lévi-Strauss theorised him, an incorrigible improviser, cobbling together ideas and acts from the limited available flotsam of existing cultures—to piece them together.[27]

The starting point for the fraud was Juárez's foreknowledge that the loss of Ixcapuzalco was reversible. Municipal borders were not cast in stone, and there was no reason why, if its elite could outcompete that of Ixcapuzalco, the village should not recuperate its old lands. It would not be the first case of successful municipal revanchism: the village of Mochitlán, for example, had won and lost its municipal independence from the market town of Tixtla three times in some thirty years. There had once been another municipio called Ixcateopan, a small, heavily indigenous settlement in the highlands bordering Oaxaca; but in 1887 the cabecera was shifted from Ixcateopan de San Lucas to Alpoyeca, and in short order the municipio itself was renamed Alpoyeca. On the Costa Grande the municipio of La Unión absorbed Zacotula in 1868, lost Petatlán in 1870, and then reabsorbed it in 1871.[28] In the experience of someone like Juárez, borders had always been mutable. Guerrero had not existed when he was born, and Mexico itself was a creation of his parents' generation (an unstable creation, at that, its borders threatened by neighbours and secession movements, its first map as much a hopeful attempt to fix a timeless, consecrated national space as anything else).[29] The territory that would become Guerrero was subdivided into seventy-one different municipios between July 1820 and January 1821. Most of them disappeared in 1835, when centralists legislated that municipios could only exist in towns of eight thousand people or ports of four thousand.[30] The state itself was created in 1849, carved from the states of Mexico, Michoacán, and Puebla; the first century or so of Guerrero's history saw the creation of ninety-seven municipios and the suppression of a further twenty-two, while another ten had their names changed.[31] Thus municipal borders were in reality quite fluid. In the nineteenth century they were as much a scoreboard in regional politics, monitoring the influence of regional and village políticos, as they were immutable, culturally consecrated administrative divisions. When the tough villagers of Xochiapulco in the Sierra Norte de Puebla fought well against the French, central government rewarded them with their own municipality and lands from haciendas.[32] Ixcateopan's shrinking borders reflected the fact that village elites had not distinguished themselves in the game of regional politics, failing to keep up with the rising economic and political power of their neighbours. Yet those borders—were the village leaders to improve their game—could well expand once more.

The tool Juárez chose to increase his and his village's regional sway was cultural nationalism: he would make his village faction the owners of a central symbol of Mexican independence. This was a sound rational-choice calculation, for a bold nationalist gesture was an ideal way of currying favour with key decision makers. People who lived in Mexico enjoyed an unusually rich store of foundation myths in the prehispanic past, and writers and politicians had long tapped those myths. Pride in the prehispanic past lay at the centre of early nationalist discourse. When Morelos declared Mexico independent in 1813 he invoked the "spirits of Moctezuma, Cacamatzin, Cuauhtémoc, Xicotencatl and Catzonzin" to witness that the rebels were "about to re-establish the Mexican Empire, improving its government." The congress he addressed was named Anáhuac; and while the constituents did not name the new country after the old Aztec Empire, they did state in the Act of Independence that Mexico had "recovered the exercise of her usurped sovereignty."[33] The independence leaders were described as the children of Moctezuma by orators across the 1820s and 1830s; while, Rebecca Earle argues, this "Indianesque nationalism" waned thereafter, it remained something of a rhetorical norm to invoke Cuauhtémoc in Independence Day speeches across Mexico from the 1840s through the 1870s.[34] (Even Emperor Maximilian, imposed during the 1860s in a failed French colonial adventure, adopted such discourse: during his first Independence Day speech he called Mexico "Anáhuac" and condemned "the slavery and despotism" of colonialism.)[35] Mexicans' support for Hidalgo and Morelos, said one 1846 orator, "proved that they were descendents of the intrepid Cuauhtémoc; that they were of the race who fought at Otumba, who drove the conquistadors from Mexico in the famous *noche triste*."[36]

Yet, for all the wealth of primary material, Mexican identity was initially fragile, a fragility increased by the chaotic early years of independence. Between 1821 and 1848 Mexico swung between the regimes of Emperor Agustín Iturbide, various short-lived presidencies, and a dictator, Santa Anna, who gave his amputated leg a state funeral. (The leg was dug up and fed to street dogs when he fell.)[37] Three foreign powers—the Spanish, the French, and the Americans—invaded on different occasions (and to very different extents). Between 1830 and 1850 more than 80 percent of the budget went to servicing debt and to paying off a predatory military.[38] Amid this turbulence it was difficult to detect signs of a functioning national identity; in many regions, on the contrary, people strived to opt out of being Mexican. In 1835 Zacatecas seceded temporarily; in 1836 Texas separated more permanently; in 1839 Tabasco considered following, while Yucatán actually did in 1841.[39] The American invasion of 1846, far from uniting Mexicans in resistance, provided the occasion for several score-settling regional wars, and by 1848 the government was deploying more troops against other Mexicans than it ever had against the U.S. Army. These internecine wars were the "longest and most important" of the period, pitting creole elites against the politically and economically marginalised.[40] In their aftermath Mexico's political elites began a cohesive effort to refound their country, beginning with a new constitution and a wide-reaching set of liberal reform laws. Their debates on Mexico's future were marked by a shocked sense that Mexico was intrinsically divided by geography, culture, and race. Mexico was not, conservative linguist Francisco Pimentel argued, "a nation, properly speaking"; it was "two different peoples in the same territory, and what is worse, two peoples to a certain extent enemies."[41]

The reaction of the elites, from the mid-century on, was to invest heavily in nationalist symbols, civic rituals, and standardised education to inculcate a sense of patriotism in these diverse populations. In 1854 they introduced a National Anthem (written by a Catalan); in 1856, a monument of the *madre patria* grieving for "the brave and illustrious Mexicans who gave up their lives" in the war; in 1858, a national map, in whose borders an emerging and uncertain nation-state was portrayed as natural, inevitable, and long-standing; in 1869, a monument to Cuauhtémoc; and in 1871, the first ceremony to commemorate the cadets who had defended Chapultepec Castle against the gringos, the Niños Héroes.[42] In 1887 another monument to Cuauhtémoc was unveiled, and Juárez Day was instigated; in 1892 the Día de la Raza, a commemoration of the arrival of Columbus, was invented; across the 1890s Avenida Reforma, the new main thoroughfare in Mexico City, was lined with the statues of liberal heroes, two from each state.[43] The state founded schools and teacher-training colleges to disseminate the nationalist stories behind these inventions and in the late 1880s made children's primary school attendance a legal obligation in Mexico

City.[44] National projects had regional counterparts. In Guerrero the great developmentalist governor Francisco Arce, whose three terms spanned from the late 1860s to the 1890s, was "the first who raised up monuments in honour and remembrance of the caudillos of our national independence, sons of our soil; a humble one, as befitted the circumstances of his first administration, in Tixtla, the birthplace of the unconquered General Don Vicente Guerrero, and another, now more sumptuous, in his second, in this city of Chilpancingo, to the magnanimous General Don Nicolás Bravo. . . . [H]is veneration for our heroes did not end there, as at his instigation their glorious names have been given to perpetuate them to Districts, Cities, towns and villages."[45] None of this was offhand; it was, rather, an intensive campaign to flesh out the abstraction of being Mexican, and it became markedly more intensive in the last twenty years of the nineteenth century.

The main ingredients of this nationalism were a population that, for all its diversity, had undergone considerably more religious acculturation than those of the Andes or Central America; a near-century of violent, popular struggles against outsiders—the Spanish during independence, the Americans in the 1840s, and the French in the 1860s; and the mythic and material remains of complex and urbanised prehispanic societies.[46] While scholars have questioned the weight of Indian themes within Porfirian nationalism, the use of the Aztec past was seen at the time as more powerful and more ubiquitous than ever before.[47] Indigenous themes and motifs permeated much contemporary literature, particularly with reference to Cuauhtémoc. From 1887 onward, August 21, the anniversary of the unveiling of the monument to Cuauhtémoc, became a focus for meetings, parades, literary salons, and children's magazines to remember (or to fantasise about) the indigenous past. In 1893 the "Sociedad Literaria Cuauhtémoc," whose members included the minister of development and the president of the Supreme Court, organised a lengthy evening of speeches and poetry readings in the tlatoani's honour. In 1894 Manuel Prieto watched as "flowers, guilds and thronging crowds, horses and carriages hurl[ed] themselves towards the calzada de la Reforma" to celebrate the indigenous past; in 1895 Cuauhtémoc joined Hidalgo as one of the faces of Mexico's postage stamps.[48] Cuauhtémoc's was not the only indigenista monument unveiled in these years: on September 16, 1891, the statues of two other Aztec emperors, Ahuizótl and Izcóatl, were placed on black marble plinths at the entrance to Reforma.[49] Indigenismo influenced far more than monumental art. By 1895 indigenista paintings including *The Torture of Cuauhtémoc* and *Cuauhtémoc's*

Prison were on permanent exhibition in the Museum of Fine Arts.[50] Proposals for "neo-Aztec" architecture became modish: Luis Salazar called for a "national modern architecture.... inspired in the monumental archaeological buildings," and some entrepreneurial builders formed a construction company specifically to produce neo-Aztec buildings.[51] By 1900 there had been attempts at "Aztec letters" and a "Zapotec piano"; all that was missing, scoffed one critic, was an Aztec tram.[52]

Such satire reflected just how commonplace indigenous themes had become in Mexico City's dominant culture and how controversial they could yet prove. Some opponents took aesthetic aim at indigenismo: the statues of Ahuizótl and Izcóatl, dubbed the *indios verdes*, the "Green Indians," were savaged by the press and quickly exiled from Reforma to the more peripheral Paseo de la Viga.[53] Neo-Aztec architecture was demolished by Francisco Rodríguez as based on "mutilating, copying first an Aztec, then a Zapotec and now a Maya fragment ... sticking these elements together ... until a motley blend is obtained and applied to a building whose form, proportions and location is modern."[54] Other critics took straightforwardly political aim: the lithographer Alfredo Zalce etched a mixed procession of Aztec and Porfirian notables passing alongside a flattened peasant, above the title "The Porfirian dictatorship demagogically promotes the Indian."[55] In 1894 Francisco Cosmes commemorated Independence Day by publishing an article that ridiculed indigenistas, called Cortés the "true father" of Mexico, and deemed Cuauhtémoc about as Mexican as Socrates.[56] Yet, while indigenismo was a paradoxical rather than consensual ideology, it was at the centre of energetic Porfirian attempts to materialise a national identity.

Mexican elites purposively synthesised these attempts when they designed pavilions to represent the nation at the world's fairs, pavilions in which representations of the glorious indigenous past jostled uneasily with compilations of statistics and photographs of railways and bridges.[57] Such displays were designed at the very top of the Mexican state: the committee for the world fair in Paris in 1889 consulted President Díaz on all aspects of the pavilion. They attempted to mobilise large numbers of Mexicans: the Development Ministry called for artisans across the country to send in their local products for the Chicago World's Fair.[58] And they were very expensive, revealing their importance in the governmental scheme of things: Paris, for example, ended up costing over six hundred thousand pesos, some 1.6 percent of that year's budget.[59]

Such intensive investment bought a mishmash of representations of Mexico, one of which was profoundly indigenista. The Paris pavilion was a (heavily criticised) pastiche, which tried to synthesise details from Palenque, Chichén Itzá, Itzalá, Xochicalco, Uxmal, Tenango, Teotihuacán, and Mitla, all the while, revealingly, "distanc[ing] itself from the dimensions of ancient monuments that opposed modern necessities and tastes."[60] At the Mexican pavilion in Madrid in 1892 visitors moved through rooms decorated with murals of Mexica history, browsing among feather art, pottery, jewellery, skulls, reproductions of codices, copies of a rain god, and a sacrificial altar, while statues of Cuauhtémoc and Xicoténcatl loomed above them.[61] Porfirian nationalism was not cohesive. It was riven by nineteenth-century culture wars between liberals and conservatives over the significance of the colonial and prehispanic pasts and by the contradictions inherent in attributing high value to the indigenous past and low value to the indigenous present—the degeneracy, "relative inferiority," "perverse instincts," and proximity to "bestiality" that the first bulletin of the Sociedad Indigenista Mexicana explored.[62] The Paris pavilion materialised those contradictions, simultaneously displaying a statue to Cuauhtémoc and the pickled head of an Apache leader, Juan Antonio.[63] The Cuauhtémoc festivities of the 1890s acted out those contradictions: in 1890 a commission of Indians had to ask a general to intercede so they might obtain permission to dance in the commemoration of the last emperor.[64] Yet Porfirian nationalism was ubiquitous as well as illogical, and Porfirian nation builders gave Cuauhtémoc a leading role.

Pavilions in Paris or Madrid, poetry readings in the National Music Conservatory, and statues on Reforma were a long way from the mountain village of Ixcateopan. Yet village politicians knew all about them, because the *Periódico Oficial del Gobierno del Estado de Guerrero*—Guerrero's state gazette—clearly communicated the national political elites' interest in purposive nation building. The weekly newspaper, founded in 1877, was part of a late-nineteenth-century explosion of such official newspapers: that of Morelos dates to 1869; Michoacán, 1871; Nayarit, 1878. It was required reading for local worthies: its pages ranged freely across new legislation, "lost and found" adverts for stray animals, court proceedings, commodity prices, tax breaks, and almanacs of noteworthy happenings across the state. Alongside this wealth of practical information, the gazette also coordinated the rhetorics and ritual practices of nationalism, which steadily intensified in Guerrero's towns and villages across the 1880s and 1890s. An August 1893 edition, for example, reminded readers that August 20 would be the anniversary of the defence of Churubusco against the gringos, while on August 21 ayuntamientos should fly their flags at half-mast in memory of Juan Álvarez, the great caudillo of Guerrero.[65] On May 5, 1894, readers were told what to think and do about the Cinco de Mayo, the anniversary of Mexico's defeat of the French in the Battle of Puebla, and were instructed and entertained by a feature on the National Anthem.[66] The gazette was demanding: during one month at the turn of the century guerre-renses were ordered to observe no fewer than nine days of public ceremony.[67] Yet while it was heavily promoted by elites, the carnivalesque experience of nationalist ritual was also popular with the ruled. By 1886 villagers had formed a brass band to serenade the *fiestas patrias*; in 1891 the roof of an Ixcateopan house collapsed under the weight of families who had climbed up to see the Independence Day parade.[68]

In these flurries of nationalist ceremony the newfound significance of Cuauhtémoc stood out. Florentino Juárez owned a library of over three hundred books, including some specialist history texts.[69] He would have been well aware of Cuauhtémoc's biography; of its important lacunae, including a tomb site; and of the boom of cultural production surrounding the last emperor after the inauguration of the Mexico City monument. He might well have read the influential Justo Sierra's *México social y político* (1889), with its impassioned tributes to Cuauhtémoc; he might well have heard of, or even gone to see, the painter Leandro Izaguirre's "immensely popular" painting *The Torture of Cuauhtémoc*, first exhibited in 1892.[70] Yet even had he been less well read, the *Periódico Oficial* alone could have led him to Cuauhtémoc. Articles between 1887 and 1893 described the ceremonies, statues, and pavilions of the nation-building elites, all of which repeatedly signalled Cuauhtémoc's central impor-tance to Mexican national identity.[71] Imagination was useful but not essential to the villagers who were to take up and further disseminate the cult, for the gazette both summarised the exemplary lessons of Cuauhtémoc's life and pro-vided large tracts of prefabricated language with which to pass them on. The result was a cohesive campaign that stretched from Mexico City down through the state capitals and out to the remotest cabeceras. On August 21, 1887, for example, the Mexico City monument to Cuauhtémoc was unveiled with con-siderable ceremony and speechifying. In Chilpancingo, Guerrero's capital, the occasion was marked by a "Cuauhtémoc parade"; and in Ixcateopan, the fol-lowing month, that parade's highlight was transmitted with a blow-by-blow account of the keynote address by Luis Guillén, a scholar of the state's Literary Institute. Cuauhtémoc, villagers might thereby learn, was not dead; Guillén was, in fact, addressing him:

You have not died, your life is our memory. . . . Star of the first magnitude who sears the vast sky of patriotic history, and whose most pure twinkling lights up the furthest reaches of the American continent; come out of the fog that has hidden you for more than three centuries; look at the beautiful picture proffered by a grateful people, remembering with pride your sublime patriotism; and from the heavens of your immortality, where your name is carved in letters that burn, receive the enthusiastic ovation which here, on this unforgettable day, the free sons of Guerrero offer you.[72]

Elite efforts to promote Cuauhtémoc as a national father figure translated into a regular flow of such articles, centring particularly on the August anniversary of the fall of Tenochtitlán. "Mexico," wrote the editors in August 1890, "is the *patria* of Cuauhtémoc. . . . [H]e alone synthesises our past, that distant yesterday that is the most legitimate robe for our national pride, with its grandeurs and its glories, with its disasters and its vicissitudes, with its joys and its bitter sorrows. Mexico without Cuauhtémoc is inconceivable."[73] Such rhetoric held out three very specific messages: that honouring Cuauhtémoc was central to being Mexican; that the last tlatoani was, as such, effectively immortal; and, finally, that his body was missing. To provide that body, completing the story, providing an "altar to the *patria*," was, in such an environment, a self-evident project, an overliteral response to nation builders such as Ignacio Ramírez, who had called for Mexicans "to reconstruct the independent and conquering Indian with the skeleton of the subjugated or wandering Indian."[74]

Such metaphysical ramblings could well be interpreted in material terms, as an implicit call for a body, because governments across the Porfiriato were profligate with dead bodies. Politically significant corpses constitute, as anthropologists have noted, "a kind of charismatic stockpile," and the fetishisation of dead leaders' bodies is a near-universal phenomenon that substantially predates the age of nationalism.[75] Herodotus, for example, describes the quest of the Spartiates to recover the bones of Orestes, convinced by the oracle that this was a prerequisite for victory over the Tegeans.[76] The body of Theseus was likewise tracked down, exhumed, and returned in pomp to Athens some four centuries after his death (bringing the amateur archaeologist, Cimon, great popularity).[77] Intensive periods of nation building only intensify such "dead-body politics": thus dead composers and other cultural heroes were brought home by the planeload across Eastern Europe in the immediate aftermath of the end of communism.[78] In 1991 the Serbian leadership prepared for war by circulating a travelling exhibit of the bones of Saint Lazar—the defeated hero of the Battle of Kosovo, the Serb origin figure—around a disintegrating Yugoslavia.[79] Porfirian politicians likewise invested heavily in the complex rites of state funerals that became masques, playing out lessons in citizenship on a massive scale on a regular basis: Matt Esposito has catalogued no fewer than 102 state funerals across the period 1876–1911. The early 1890s, he finds, were the heyday of this somewhat necrophiliac nationalism. There were more state funerals between 1890 and 1893 than during the entire preceding decade.[80]

It was at this stage that the style and substance of Porfirian state funerals was established, through events such as the 1891 funeral of Carlos Pacheco, former minister of development. Pacheco's body was brought by train to the capital, where he was exhibited in the Palacio de Minería, the headquarters of the Development Ministry. The space was festooned with symbols of successful war and development—cannon, rifles, models of a locomotive and a bridge, a map of Mexico, and a monocle. The following Saturday President Díaz led the funeral procession to a special cemetery reserved for the great and good, a large crowd guaranteed by the day, the spectacle, and the reduced streetcar fares.[81] Porfirians' enthusiasm for the didactic possibilities of death ritual was so great that illustrious corpses, when not available, were recycled via exhumation, translation, and reburial. Thus Nicolás Bravo, a guerrerense leader in the War of Independence, was reburied three times. In 1886 his remains were dug up and reburied in the Pantheon in Chilpancingo; in 1903 they were moved once more, this time to Mexico City, in memory of the general's defence of Chapultepec Castle against the Americans in 1847; in 1921 they were relocated to the Column of Independence on Avenida Reforma.[82] Such journeys were slow and ritually dense. In 1903 state and federal employees, schoolchildren, and soldiers were drafted in to watch as, to the sound of funeral music and cannon fire, Bravo's bones were exhumed and removed to the town hall. In the evening the governor led the bones on a second parade, from the town hall to a public site where a mass, nationalist wake might be held. The Chilpancingo rituals over, the remains were sent with a guard of honour on a procession through various pueblos, all of which might organise their own local ceremonies, to Iguala, where after a further round of ceremony they caught the train to Mexico City. Once more the state gazette formed a transmission belt between national and village elites, reporting the ceremonies in detail and providing its readers with the clear-cut templates of appropriate affective responses.[83] Through such intense coverage readers like Florentino Juárez were continuously reminded of the political utility of the physical remains of the great and dead. In this context Juárez's wager—that anyone producing the bones of Cuauhtémoc would be rewarded—was straightforward.

It was a bet made by more than one regional politician in the late nineteenth and early twentieth century. Sometimes the subjects of such symbolic claim staking were not even dead: thus in 1888 one Señor Aguilar laid claim to President Díaz himself, on behalf of another remote guerrerense village, Xochistlahuaca. Don Porfirio had, Señor Aguilar said, been born and baptised there, not across the border in Oaxaca; but the perfidious Oaxacan government had stolen his birth certificate to keep hold of the symbolic capital inherent in remaining the president's birthplace.[84] At other times the bones, like those of Cuauhtémoc, were initially mute. Thus Tlaxcala's agrarian leader Manuel Montes bolstered his political power in 1922 by "discovering" and adopting the remains of local hero Domingo Arenas, a zapatista general, remains so successfully lost during the revolution that few now believed them genuine.[85] Arenas's *jefe*, Zapata himself, was similarly subject to competition for possession of his body once dead: Chinameca, Cuautla, and Tlatlizapán fought it out for the honour and benefits of being the revolutionary's last resting place.[86]

The use of Cuauhtémoc's bones as nationalist relics was, moreover, heavily favoured by the cultural templates of Catholicism, templates that across Latin America shaped hero cults in thought and word and deed.[87] The language of intercessive Catholicism was from the start borrowed to paint nationalist cults as parallels (and hoped for displacements) of the cults of saints.[88] The bones of Nicolás Bravo, for example, were "sacred relics" of an "immortal" and "blessed" man; when they were moved to Mexico City they travelled to "the altar of the *patria*."[89] Colonial villages had adopted saints to assert identity and autonomy and to raise money. To possess the relics of a patron saint that could be publicly brought out on All Saints' Day was a major expression of community and corporate power, and so colonial villages stole relics, fought over them, and even imported them from Spain.[90] Saints travelled across Guerrero, defecting heartlessly from village to village: San Nicolás de Tolentino, for example, a thirteenth-century Italian Augustine, first appeared in two coastal villages but later moved uphill to the mountain community of Zitlala.[91] Such cults weathered liberal anticlericalism well: when the rains failed in turn-of-the-century Teloloapan, the patron saint, San Francisco, was brought out and paraded around town, returning to the church in a downpour.[92] In adopting Cuauhtémoc and moving him to Ixcateopan, Juárez aimed to provide an updated, secular counterpart to such long-lasting, politico-magical resources.[93]

Juárez's strategy, major archaeological fraud, was no leap in the dark either. Mexican archaeology had begun a century or so earlier: in 1773 the priest Ramón Ordoñez organised the first expedition to the great Maya city of Palenque, and in 1777 José Antonio Alzate explored the central Mexican hilltop city of Xochicalco.[94] It was from the start a self-consciously political discipline. Alzate, for example, wrote of how "indiscriminate zeal . . . greed and ignorance" had destroyed the Mexican monuments, which "would have made it clear that this was one of the most powerful nations in the world."[95] His writings were initially censored, but in 1786 Emperor Charles III lifted the ban on the study of prehispanic antiquity and ordered various expeditions that were quickly memorialised in print. In 1788 Alzate published his account of the explorations of Tajín, a major ceremonial site in southern Veracruz. Two years later the astronomer Antonio León y Gama dug up the Piedra del Sol, a massive Aztec calendar and sacrificial stone, next to the cathedral in Mexico City, disseminating his discovery in a finely illustrated book. In 1805 Charles IV ordered Guillermo Dupaix and the artist Luciano Castañeda to draw up a catalogue of the antiquities of New Spain; in 1808, on the very brink of collapse, the colonial state set up an Antiquities Junta to regulate future excavations.[96] Formally, the newfound interest continued after independence: in 1822 the Antiquities Junta was reconstituted, and in 1827 congress prohibited the export of prehispanic artefacts.[97]

Yet there were relatively few digs over the next seventy or so years, as the poverty and instability of early independent Mexico restricted archaeology to a handful of adventurers, travellers, and the French colonial invaders of the Comission Scientifique du Mexique. In the 1880s, however, a second wave of excavations and publications revitalised and popularised the indigenous past. This was in part exogenous: museums and scholars from around the world came to Mexico to dig and to collect and in so doing drove up demand for the fragments of the Mesoamerican past. It was also in part endogenous, as Mexican researchers and politicians together revalorised those fragments. In 1870 the government instructed jefes políticos to exercise "devoted and continued diligence" in collecting antiquities.[98] In 1877 the National Museum began publishing a scholarly journal; in 1885 the government created a new agency to conserve archaeological sites, the Inspección General de Monumentos Arqueológicos de la República, and a museum of anthropology; in 1895 the government hosted an international anthropology conference, the Congreso

Figure 27. Illustration of the Piedra del Sol, an early printed demonstration of the sophistication of Mexica culture. From Antonio de León y Gama, *Descripción histórica y cronológica de las dos piedras que con ocasión del nuevo empedrado que se está formando en la plaza principal de México, se hallaron en ella el año de 1790* (Mexico City, 1792); courtesy of the Kislak Collection of the Rare Book Division of the Library of Congress.

de Americanistas; and in 1897 a law made archaeological monuments national property.[99] The elites' new appreciation of prehispanic artefacts was revealed as they began policing archaeological sites and the export trade: posting guards at major discoveries, confiscating a Chac-Mool statue from Auguste Le Plongeon in 1878, and stopping Charnay from exporting Teotihuacán artefacts in 1880.[100]

Such interest stretched beyond metropolitan elites. Provincial politicians established museums and filled them with artefacts or shipped their prehispanic treasures off to the capital in search of favour. Everyday countrymen, meanwhile, demonstrated their own appreciation of prehispanic artwork by vigorously resisting some collectors. By the 1880s interest in archaeology and its products was shared across Mexico's classes and regions.[101]

These were the years of the explorations (and botched reconstructions) of Teotihuacán and Mitla and the beginnings of archaeological tourism. In 1885 Leopoldo Batres, the most public if not the most able archaeologist of his time, drew up a state-by-state guide for visitors to Mexico's archaeological

Figure 28. Auguste Le Plongeon (with beard) and Chac-Mool. Photograph by Alice Dixon Le Plongeon; courtesy of the Research Library, the Getty Research Institute, Los Angeles.

161

sites, complete with handy itinerary suggestions.[102] In institutional and cultural terms the Porfirians made a great leap forward, effectively inventing modern Mexican archaeology. Yet the combination of a new field with low technology and low funding kept Porfirian archaeologists at odds with each other and far from a consensus, or even a chronology, on the cultures they dug. As a consequence, one astute observer found, Mexican archaeology as late as the 1930s "consisted largely of question marks."[103]

This combination—the growing value of material from the prehispanic past and uncertainty regarding the actual contours of that past—constituted an invitation to fraud. Here, too, Juárez worked well within the boundaries of his culture, for fraud was a commonplace strategy across Mexico. Land tenure since the conquest had been fluid, property rights uncertain; land disputes in both the growing towns and the countryside revolved around *titulos primordiales*, early colonial land grants that took precedence over subsequent titles. Such metropolitan documents were sources of economic, political, and symbolic power, and they were, as such, regularly faked. James Lockhart found a "factory . . . for false titles" in the environs of colonial Mexico City, a production line of forgery where villagers in land disputes went to have their pictogram-laden titles made—part to order, part from standard templates—on indigenous *amate* paper, age-yellowed by a quick smoking. Between 1685 and 1703 nearly fifty of these Techialoyan codices were produced, combining maps of communal lands with title claims founded on the grants of the prehispanic great and good.[104] (Similar circumstances—political instability, property rights in flux, and low literacy levels—tend to produce similar waves of fraud anywhere. English monasteries took up forging Anglo-Saxon royal writs in the century after the Norman conquest with such enthusiasm that over half the surviving charters of Edward the Confessor are suspected fakes.)[105] The villagers of Axapusco in Veracruz, for example, deployed a land grant from Hernán Cortés, dated May 1519, in their land claims, an impossible document, given that it predates the foundation of Veracruz that would lend it legal meaning. In the eighteenth century petitioners avowing descent from Cuauhtémoc claimed extensive lands in the Mexico City barrio of Tlatelolco, citing a 1523 grant from Philip II that ceded the family land in recognition of the last tlatoani's services to the Spanish. The lawyers of the Real Audiencia had little trouble recognizing that fraud; all other considerations aside, Cuauhtémoc was alive and Philip II was not even conceived in 1523.[106] In Juárez's time the villagers of San Francisco Mazapan, near Teotihuacán, were transferred to the jurisdiction of their hated rivals, San Martín, with the connivance of a village judge who—duly paid off—forged a document giving their consent.[107] Closer to Juárez's home, colonial papers from neighbouring Pachivia recorded how aggressors from Coatepec had invaded Pachivia's traditional lands and managed to disappear the relevant titles—or so Pachivia claimed—"maliciously hiding [the documents] . . . claiming that the governor to whom they had delivered them died and they don't know where he put them." However, Pachivia's representatives smugly testified, "they did not realise that my people were sharp and had the [forethought] to make copies of the many and aforementioned documents (perhaps for curiosity, or perhaps because they feared exactly what has happened)."[108] Juárez's position as judge and trustee of the Ixcateopan papers gave him access to this ambiguous collection. They would have provided an education in the long traditions of destruction and forging of colonial documents, as well as key materials such as formats to be mimicked, colonial bureaucrats' names to be adopted, possibly even paper to be recycled. They may just have been inspirational.

This long tradition of both subaltern and elite fraud fused, in Juárez's time, with the new value of archaeology to foster the systematic mass production of forged prehispanic relics.[109] Edward B. Tylor, an early social anthropologist, found the manufacture of sham antiquities to be "a regular thing" when he travelled through Mexico in the 1850s.[110] Tylor's colleagues fuelled the business, falling victim "so often . . . [to] money-making tricksters."[111] By the 1890s mistrust was so generalised that one archaeologist's report explained how his discoveries could not be forgeries, a necessary precaution as "many persons, especially in the Capital, busy themselves in the fabrication of ancient objects, and for this reason I place no trust in any one but myself."[112] Demand for archaeological objects was not just professional. As the American journalist John Finerty noted in 1879, "Visiting 'gringos,' in general, make much ado about Aztec idols, and, of course, an 'industry' in that line has been developed, with the result that 'false idols' are as numerous in and around the City of Mexico as round bullet 'relics' on the field of Waterloo. A stout idol, with big ears, a pug nose and cross eyes, can be had very cheap indeed."[113] Archaeological fraud became so widespread in the late nineteenth century that the 1878 World's Fair devoted a special section to examples of notable forgeries; the National Museum dedicated an exhibit space to fake prehispanic pottery; and the government's principal archaeologist, Leopoldo Batres, wrote a book on the subject. Shenanigans with the archaeological record were, he argued, inevitable,

Figure 29. The Barrios brothers of San Juan Teotihuacán display moulds for forging "Aztec black pottery." From Leopoldo Batres, *Antigüedades Mejicanas Falsificadas: Falsificación y Falsificadores* (Mexico City, 1910); courtesy of the Randall Library Special Collection, University of North Carolina, Wilmington.

for "one of the industries which has been most developed since long ago has been the falsification of antiques."[114]

Yet in Mexico, Batres elaborated, the industry of forgery was better developed than anywhere else in the Americas.[115] (Although it seems to have been rivalled or even surpassed by that of Egypt, and the period was one of a global boom in archaeological fraud.)[116] Its roots stretched back to the late sixteenth century, he claimed, when the fad in Spain for souvenirs of conquest became so intense that natural supplies in Mexico City failed, leading enterprising sons of conquistadores to recruit indigenous potters in the barrio of Tlatelolco to churn out black "Aztec pottery" suitable for European tastes.[117] By the Porfiriato archaeological fraud had become more than a niche in Mexico City's artisan trades. Different regions of Mexico now specialised in different fraudulent production. The villagers of Teotihuacán made black pottery, gold- and bronze work came from Mexico and Oaxaca, silverwork from Puebla, obsidian masks from the Mixteca.[118] This "very subdivided," specialised industry was carefully catalogued by Batres, who should have known what he was talking about: he owned eighty moulds for fake pottery, knew leading producers, and was, according to one antiquities dealer, himself involved in a failed attempt to sell a fake crystal skull (in reality made of glass) to Mexico's National Museum.[119] Mexican antiquity fraud was even big enough business to attract producers outside Mexico. Batres describes the manufacture of stone arrowheads, knives, and lance heads near Amiens in France, where extensive flint deposits provided necessary raw materials.[120] Jane Walsh has convincingly proposed a nineteenth-century German origin for those most iconic of prehispanic artefacts, the life-size rock crystal skulls owned by the Smithsonian, the British Museum, and the French Musée de l'Homme.[121] Archaeological fraud, in short, was lucrative enough by the late nineteenth century to be a transnational business, not just in consumption but also in production.

While it is difficult to quantify just how lucrative archaeological fraud was, isolated cases give some idea of the incentives that brought forgers—"above all creatures of the market"—into production in such numbers in this museumising time.[122] At the high end of the market, Walsh has traced French dealer

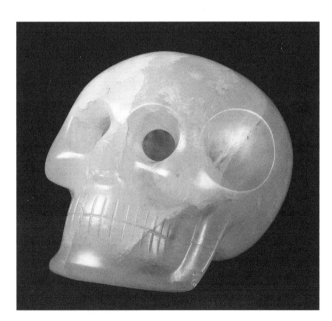

Figure 30.
"Aztec" crystal skull, Smithsonian Institution, Washington, D.C.; by permission of James DiLoreto, Smithsonian Institution.

Eugène Boban's repeated attempts to sell rock crystal skulls in Mexico, France, and New York. One first appears—not among the pre-Colombian artefacts—in Boban's 1881 sale catalogue, valued at thirty-five hundred francs. The glass skull he fraudulently offered to the National Museum in 1886 (in partnership with Batres) was priced at $3,000; the crystal skull he did sell to Tiffany's of New York, which peregrinated to the British Museum, went for $950.[123] These were large sums for their time. Toward the other end of the market, William Henry Holmes of the Smithsonian found elaborate "modern-antique" black pottery vases for sale, complete with exciting provenances, at five dollars apiece at the railway station in Teotihuacán.[124] In nearby Atzcaputzalco Scottish prospector and antiquities dealer William Niven seems to have subsidised villagers by renting their fields and paying cash wages year after year as his workers dug up tablets they themselves created and buried, artefacts that he read as the remains of a forgotten culture.[125] The producers at the bottom of the commodity chain of archaeological fraud did not, generally, realise huge profits. In a cash-poor economy, however, even the promise of regular salaried employment was significant, and historians need to think in terms of purchasing power parity when considering the benefits of forgery. The five dollars Holmes was asked for his vase was the rough equivalent of twenty days of a miner's wages, or a month's pay for a domestic servant, or up to a ton or so of maize.[126] Holmes, moreover, was a tough customer. A "charming old fellow" whom William Spratling met in northwestern Guerrero in the 1920s asked five thousand pesos for a "few crude sculptures," an optimism quite possibly founded on profitable encounters with earlier, gullible outsiders.[127] Much relic creation was industrial: forgers used high-speed rotary wheels for cutting and polishing, petrol baths to make obsidian more workable, and solder to piece together filigree goldwork. The copper moulds for mass producing pottery were made by galvanizing waxwork dummies.[128] In an economy that remained essentially extractive and agricultural, archaeological fraud may have been Mexico's most successful industrial export sector.

Did it extend as far as 1890s Guerrero? Some of Juárez's contemporaries clearly realised the marketability of foreign-friendly fantasies of the prehispanic past. In 1897, for example, guerrerense guides led the hapless William Niven to what they sold him as "the lost city of Quechmietoplican," forty miles from the state capital of Chilpancingo. Hot on Niven's heels followed the first secretary of the French embassy. At this stage Guerrero's embarrassed elites weighed in through the state gazette:

Figure 31.
"Aztec" black pottery
vase purchased by
William Henry Holmes
in Teotihuacán in
the 1880s; reprinted
by permission of the
American Association
for the Advancement
of Science from *Science* 7,
no. 159 (February 19,
1886).

EXAMPLE OF MODERN-ANTIQUE MEXICAN VASE (HEIGHT, 11 IN.).

We have followed the story of this discovery, at first with indiffer-
ence, then with curiosity, ending up in astonishment at the imaginative power of Señor Niven to reconstruct on the basis of insignificant
ruined foundations, possibly mineworkings . . . a magnificent city
full of temples. . . . We are the first to recognise Señor Niven's right
to see more or less marvellous cities wherever he best pleases, and if
we dare to contradict him in regards to Quechmietoplican it is due
to the fact that eight days ago the honourable Monsieur Boulard de
Pouqueville . . . came, map in hand, to find it, without joy, despite having taken the same individuals as guides . . . and [we wish to] avoid
that excursions of this type should recur.[129]

Yet they did not succeed, and a willingness to satisfy foreigners' archaeological curiosity by hook or by crook remained. Some thirty years later an ancient farmer named Don Carmen lured Spratling to disappointing ruins in the mountains just north of Ixcateopan: "*Hombre*, I [said] to him along toward the evening of the third day, you promised me that we would come across all sorts of decorations, stone masks, of the most-ancient-ones-who-have-gone-before, and there is hardly a single one to be seen!"[130]

Conclusive evidence for archaeological fraud in 1890s Guerrero is lacking. Yet, when intense demand for artefacts emerges, demand of the sort evinced by Niven or Boulard de Pouqueville or Spratling, then forgeries are rarely far behind. As Mark Jones concludes, "The commodification of culture—the global tendency to treat art and antiquity as market commodities—augments the value of originals, thereby encouraging their faking. [Forgers] move quickly to take advantage of the high prices produced by a new fashion."[131] It is suggestive, moreover, that postrevolutionary Guerrero was recognised for its illicit trade in real artefacts and for its intensive production of fraudulent ones. Frederick Peterson estimated that some five thousand fake artefacts had been sold in the state between 1930 and the early 1950s and describes a sophisticated production process for Olmec stone masks and figures, in which carvers copied from journal illustrations and asked dealers and collectors for feedback on their authenticity.[132] Iguala was by then a long-standing centre of artefact recovery, an entire world of shady archaeological dealing populated by characters such as "el Mudo," "the Mute," "la Pioja," "the flea," and the forest warden who was believed to have made his fortune "requisitioning" real artefacts from the gullible. Taxco was a centre of forgery, whose production was commercialised by Spratling, now its handicrafts impresario (responsible, Michael Coe argues, for the introduction of many of those fake Olmec masks into the world of North American collectors).[133] Ixcateopan lay between towns that were, by the first half of the twentieth century at least, centres of archaeological salvage and forgery. In such a context it is unlikely that Juárez was the first entrepreneurial faker in northern Guerrero.

The rancher's creation was, finally, favoured by his metropolitan audience's perceptions of a cultural chasm separating them from their provinces, an attitude tersely summed up by the colonial beauty La Güera Rodríguez: "Outside Mexico City it's all Cuautitlán."[134] Such types had trouble conceiving that fluent, instrumentalist manipulation of the past could come from a place they saw as godforsaken. Ixcateopan was, one Mexico City newspaper said in 1899, "a place hidden from civilisation"; the village was, a bureaucrat reported thirty years later, "without life of its own, drowning in poverty."[135] The plaque on the wall of the village museum, created in 1976, deems the entire region "extensive, little known . . . accessible only by the Mexico–Acapulco highway, which is like an enormous bridge that crosses the dark currents of cultures and peoples still isolated." The secular construction of villagers as near-illiterate, doomed to exist on the wrong side of the civilisation/barbarism dichotomy, proved enduringly influential. Consequently, as we have seen above, more than one generation of scholars looked hard for forgers outside the village. Yet in reality Juárez was by most sociological standards an intellectual. Weber, who defined intellectuals as those "who by virtue of their peculiarity have special access to certain achievements considered to be 'culture values,' and who therefore usurp the leadership of a 'culture community,'" would have seen the rancher in those terms; Gramsci would certainly have agreed.[136] He was, moreover, an intellectual ideally situated among dominant, popular, and political cultures to create an archaeological fraud with a patina of popular authenticity. A self-made man, a village cacique, and an avid reader, Juárez had a power to imperceptibly yet dramatically alter village and national narratives that no outsider could match.

He even had a clear-cut template for his fraud, in Manuel Payno's classic novel Los bandidos de Río Frío. This rambling nineteenth-century Mexican epic came out in installments between 1888 and 1891, at the peak of Ixcateopan's secession crisis. In its pages Payno describes the novel, tongue in cheek, as "famous and historic." He was right: the book was one of the very few best sellers of its time, and it is extremely unlikely that Juárez missed it.[137] In its opening paragraph readers learn how "in a ranch located behind the Cuesta de Barrientos that, according to what we have been told, is called Santa María de la Ladrillera . . . lives a family of the indigenous race. . . . The people of Tlalnepantla say that this family is a descendent of the great emperor Moctezuma II and that they have many other lands that the government has taken from them, as well as the inheritance, which is worth more than one hundred thousand pesos."[138] Continuing that first installment, Juárez might read the family's reaction to this dispossession: "To further the case of Moctezuma's heir against the government they had retained a little shark of a lawyer, just qualified, who was looking for business and cases and who was called Lamparilla."[139] Lamparilla has particular talents "for complicating businesses and imitating any handwriting"; he is also

related to the general archivist don Ignacio Cubas, a clerk well-known for his knowledge of antiquity and his dealings with old papers, charters and books from the earliest times of Spanish domination. Cubas, who was an enthusiast of Moctezuma, Cuauhtémoc and of everything that belonged to the *raza* and to the history of the Aztecs, gave Lamparilla the means to copy [*compulsar*] the royal and pragmatic charters of Charles V and the Queen, Doña Juana, and they ended up unravelling the history of the descendents of the emperor of Mexico and holding the key to strange things secret to the rest of the world. With these weapons, the baptism certificate of Pascualito and an account from Ameca, from whence the family came, Lamparilla went to the government, claiming something like half a million pesos in back payments, six thousand pesos a year for the current pension, and the title of the whole volcano of Popocatepétl with its woods, waters, gorges, sands, snows, sulphur and inner fire, or in exchange for this a fabulous sum of money.[140]

Things begin well: the Secretaría de Hacienda, the Treasury, pays up regularly to the tune of a few hundred pesos, and Moctezuma III mortgages the ranch to buy lands and livestock. But the final settlement drags, their lawyer's faction in Mexico City launches a coup d'état that fails, and the ranch is devastated by a press gang from the army who conscript Moctezuma III.[141] In the hundreds of ensuing pages the would-be emperor becomes something of a bit player. Yet persistence pays off for both character and reader. By the end of what Payno called his "neverending novel," Lamparilla's political machinations have won vital presidential recognition of the family's claim, and Moctezuma III's gifts for fighting have lent him the military power to enforce it.[142] Historical fraud, self-belief, and entrepreneurial talent combine in a twistedly meritocratic way to give a petty rancher vast estates.

Payno took pains to point out that this was less improbable than it seemed. "Every day," he wrote, "various people turn up who claim to be very close relatives to the emperor of Mexico, and the government has to proceed with great circumspection, as otherwise the entire Mexican treasure would not be enough to pay the pensions of so many heirs. . . . [Lamparilla was] no more than an agent of one of the many relatives of Moctezuma."[143] Early anthropologists' fieldwork and records from the Treasury archives show that Payno was not stretching the truth. Unrecognised direct descendants of prehispanic royalty were indeed to be discovered in the modern Valley of Mexico. In 1917 Manuel Gamio's team read through the parish archives of San Juan Teotihuacán and turned up the successors of the Texcocan poet-king Nezahualcóyotl, who were living as impoverished smallholders with no idea of their illustrious stock.[144] Those more aware of their ancestry could and did sue the government for stipends promised by the colonial administration. In the 1880s and 1890s the Secretaría de Hacienda faced several demands from descendants of Moctezuma for unpaid pensions owed to them as Mexica royalty, some of which dated back to the 1830s. Most of the claims were paid, ranging from $692.82 for Amalia Maldonado to $19,761.61 for Vicente Carvajal Tellez Girón, Marqués de Aguilafuente.[145] With such huge sums at stake, it is unsurprising that these pensions were the target of feuding between relatives; for all the complications, though, Hacienda continued to pay them until 1932.[146]

It is not, perhaps, how Cuauhtémoc's tomb came into existence so much as how it could fail that remains Ixcateopan's central mystery. Juárez did an extraordinary job of bricolage, turning to "an already existent set made up of tools and materials, to consider or reconsider what it contain[ed] and, finally and above all, engag[ing] in a sort of dialogue with it and, before choosing between them, index[ing] the possible answers which the whole set [could] offer to his problem."[147] Yet across the last twenty years of his life Juárez struggled fruitlessly to have his mythical Cuauhtémoc unearthed. He told the priest, Severo Rodríguez; he told powerful regional merchants, like the Flores family of Taxco, and business contacts in Zacualpan, across the border in the Estado de México; he told two consecutive jefes políticos; it seems likely that he told General Canuto Neri and that he tried to tell President Díaz.[148] By the end of the Porfiriato Juárez's village allies were, it seems, telling any outsider who might listen; thus a shopkeeper told a travelling medicine salesman in 1907 that "there was a secret about Cuauhtémoc which no one could reveal until an earthquake should destroy Ixcateopan."[149] But it proved strangely easier to bury bones than it was to dig them up, and the closest Florentino Juárez came to success was a brief allusion in the metropolitan press in 1899, when he was mayor.[150] It may be that Juárez's credibility had suffered too much from his political decline. Perhaps, on the other hand, Mexico City politicians were loath to unearth a symbol of resistance in an unruly frontier zone. Cuauhtémoc was not just used by the Porfirian state: he was also used against the state, as when the "Hijas de Cuauhtémoc," an early feminist group, launched a petition protesting against the dictator.[151] General Neri, caudillo of the Ixcateopan region and seemingly an ally of Florentino Juárez, rebelled against Mexico City in 1870 and again in 1893.[152] Whatever the reasons, the tomb failed to change anything in Juárez's lifetime. The bones remained hidden. Ixcapuzalco's secession endured. Ixcateopan's other patriarch, José Jaimes, moved up in the world, spending increasing amounts of time in Teloloapan, the booming market town where his son became doctor and later mayor.[153] Juárez, in contrast, railed for a decade against the villagers, the state government, and his sons. In 1915 he died up in the hills, hiding from the revolutionaries who had shattered his world.[154]

Chapter 8

Using Cuauhtémoc I

> Rituals may make a show of power, but they run the same risk as other shows: they may fail.
>
> —Peter Metcalf and Richard Huntingdon,
> *Celebrations of Death: The Anthropology of Mortuary Ritual*

JOSÉ VASCONCELOS DID NOT THINK MUCH OF THE INDIGENOUS PAST OR its contribution to the Mexican present. The revolutionary education secretary (1920–24) publicly eulogised Cortés, called the conquistadores "a race of demi-gods," and proposed that the day of their arrival be made a national holiday; in the terms of his day he was a *hispanista*, a person who opposed indigenista narratives of the national past with a renewed emphasis on the Spanish roots of modern Mexico. Prehispanic art, an incontrovertibly mainstream taste by the 1920s, left him cold. He described the Monte Albán treasure as "cheap jades and suspect jewels." The Mayan city of Uxmal was, he noted after a visit, "uniformly barbarous, cruel and grotesque. No sense of beauty in the decoration, mere palaeographic work." Cuauhtémoc, he wrote, was a fiction, a subversive invention of Anglo-Saxon historians.[1] There was consequently some irony in the decision to send him to the 1923 centenary celebrations of Latin American independence in Brazil, taking as Mexico's gift a statue of Cuauhtémoc. Vasconcelos was left in Rio de Janeiro with an expensive statue—a reproduction of the Reforma monument, cast in the United States—to a hero in whom he did not believe. "Look, *che*," the Argentine delegate told him, "I think this [Cuauhtémoc statue] is a gaffe because nobody around here knows who that

Indian is, and, on the other hand, there aren't any Indians in Argentina, neither are there any here in Brazil, just blacks; it's a mistake for your government to represent Mexico with a symbol that has no resonance in the rest of America." Vasconcelos himself knew nothing about Cuauhtémoc, he later confessed, but he was outraged. The Argentine's disdain inspired him to a long-winded, impassioned speech, in which the last emperor became a symbol of Latin American political and cultural renaissance, an end to the "lengthy colonising of our spirits," and a sign for resistance, this time to the United States. That Vasconcelos's Cuauhtémoc was mainly fictional did not bother him. When accused of conflating several different indigenous leaders in his speech, he replied, "I am not making history; I am trying to create a myth."[2]

Vasconcelos was not the first cultural caudillo to try this: the rhetorical deployment of prehispanic histories by Mexican elites, sometimes against the ideological grain, stretched far back into colonial times. In 1680 the creole intellectual Carlos de Sigüenza y Góngora welcomed the incoming viceroy of New Spain with a series of triumphal arches that eschewed the usual sycophantic comparisons with heroes of classical antiquity and provided, rather, Aztec rulers as archetypes of the political virtues. Cuauhtémoc was painted with the mottoes "He will not submit" and "His mind remains unwavering." In the accompanying play Sigüenza y Góngora elaborated further: "Mexicans need no longer envy Cato, as they have in their last emperor someone of whom it might be said, as Seneca said of him, 'Despite the many times that the Republic changed, nevertheless no one saw Cato change.'"[3] As a referent for resistance, constancy, and courageous self-sacrifice Cuauhtémoc was a recurring fixture in speeches and texts commemorating independence across the nineteenth century, even as the intensely Indianesque rhetoric of the first generation of postindependence politicians faded. "Cuauhtémoc's blood," schoolchildren read in the *Biblioteca del niño mexicano*, "had borne fruit at the end of three hundred years."[4]

The figure of Cuauhtémoc was emblematic of the potential and the pitfalls of indigenismo as nationalist resource. He was, on the one hand, a Great Man and as such encoded a simple, universal heroic narrative rather than the messy complexities of a culture. On the other hand, he presented cultural nationalists with some clear challenges: an absence of reliable detail concerning his life and an established symbolic identity that ran counter to narratives of unification through mestizaje, the idea that, as one history textbook had it, Mexicans formed "a single great family."[5] Yet the combination of primordial appeal with the vigorous Porfirian promotion of the last emperor made him a ubiquitous, if semiotically strange, presence in Mexicans' imaginations by the early twentieth century (and not just Mexican imaginations; one children's history told its *lectorcitos* that the "whole world" admired Cuauhtémoc).[6] Porfirian filmmakers commemorated the centenary of independence with a short production, *The Torment of Cuauhtémoc.*[7] Cantinas were named for the presumably teetotal tlatoani; sycophants invoked him as the gold standard of compliment.[8] The French traveller Charles Etienne Brasseur compared Porfirio Díaz to the last emperor; a governor in Mariano Azuela's revolutionary novel *The Flies* is called "the very image of our Father Cuauhtémoc."[9] (The counterrevolutionary government of Victoriano Huerta, on the other hand, was memorably described by Álvaro Obregón as "a pack with bloodstained jowls that howls in every key and threatens to dig up the remains of Cuauhtémoc, Hidalgo, and Juárez.")[10] Such commonplace usage, and the ineffable contradictions it carried, came through strikingly in a 1919 history textbook, which called Cuauhtémoc "the whitest man of pre-Colombian Mexico."[11] The poet Ramón López Velarde came up with a happier formula to sum up the centrality yet the inescapable distance of Cuauhtémoc as an origin figure, coining the description *joven abuelo*, "the young grandfather," in his classic nationalist poem "La Suave Patria."

The revolutionaries of the 1910s and 1920s brought new impetus to such imaginative uses of Mexico's indigenous past and intensified a practical focus on its indigenous present. Their reasons for doing so spanned the political and the socioeconomic, the immediate and the long range. Mestizo leaders used indigenismo as a recruiting tool, in terms both literal, as when Obregón recruited Yaqui troops to launch his military career, and metaphorical, as when later políticos delivered speeches in indigenous languages, a "pseudo-revolutionary fashion" in the 1920s and beyond.[12] Particularly in plantation zones like Yucatán, revolutionary governors also used indigenismo as a weapon to break the power of the old, conservative landholders who constituted their main opponents. Indigenista programmes designed to foster cultural links between Indian and national communities were believed to bring clear material payoffs, incorporating Indians into the modern economy as both producers and consumers.[13] In more strategic terms, cultural nationalists such as the anthropologist Manuel Gamio saw indigenismo, ideological and above all practical, as critical to building a viable, powerful nation-state, forging "a new *patria* made from iron and bronze intermingled." This, he went on, demanded the work of "friendly hearts" (especially anthropologists) who might "Indianise themselves a little bit," to "awaken" indigenous peoples and, retooling their "anachronistic and inappropriate" cultures, "make the national race coherent and homogeneous, unified in language and convergent in culture."[14] While billed as "Indianisation," it was a change more in method than in aim, a shift, as Knight puts it, from coercive to enlightened integration, in which the "virtual crusade" that Porfirian Mexico launched to exterminate the Yaqui was succeeded by the "modern missionaries" of revolutionary education.[15]

Both approaches rested on a racialist interpretation of the Mexican world, and both agreed on the desirability of reengineering that world to remove the undesirable components of Indian cultures. Diversity was deemed difficult, pluralism problematic: thus President Calles promoted whites-only immigration in the later 1920s, arguing that "[coloured immigration] weakens [the race], thereby complicating our ethnic problem, serious in itself," and President Cárdenas famously called for the "Mexicanisation" of the Indian.[16] What exactly this meant was clearly spelled out by the Secretaría de Educación Pública's magazine for teachers. "Integration," its first editorial proclaimed, meant "a common language, identical ambitions, the same necessities and the same means of satisfying them."[17] The explicit drive to acculturate and homogenise was criticised by the Marxist anthropologists of the 1960s and by the foreign scholars who followed them as ethnocidal. As Guillermo Bonfil Batalla puts it, "The goal of indigenismo, put brutally, consisted in achieving the disappearance of the Indian."[18] Revolutionary indigenismo—much like its Porfirian ancestor, disreputable, disowned, yet inscribed in its genes—was not all that coherent, and behind its liberating rhetoric it promoted at best a patriarchal dependence.

Yet incoherence was in part a product of complexity. Indigenista intellectuals cannot be understood in a purely regional context but, rather, need examination inside the global market of ideas in which they moved. The most influential of all, Manuel Gamio, was, on the one hand, strongly influenced by the social Darwinism of his Porfirian forebears, whose tropes—"groups vegetating in the lowest stages of evolution"—riddle both his ideological and his anthropological writings.[19] His training at Columbia with the great anthropologist Franz Boas had, on the other hand, made him something of a cultural relativist, who opposed the traditions of foreigners such as Alexander von Humboldt and Mexican sceptics to argue that prehispanic art was neither ugly nor barbaric and should be assessed by its makers' aesthetics alone.[20] In weighing up the perceived costs of diversity, Mexico's new cultural managers wrestled with the same questions as intellectuals across the global periphery, trying to square the circle that was non-European nationalism. Successful nation-states needed to promote the unique distinction of their own cultures, but they also needed to acquire some of the raw material power of Western culture. "Homogeneity" was among other things code for a culture, a set of social structures, and an economy that could articulate with and compete with the industrial West. This appeared a particularly urgent task when Gamio wrote in the 1910s, a decade that saw the United States encourage a coup in Mexico, occupy the country's main port, cut off sovereign credit, and send ten thousand soldiers trekking fruitlessly across the north in search of Pancho Villa. Brute considerations of realpolitik underlay Gamio's admiration for the most successful model from the periphery, Japan, which he defined as an archetypal, European-style patria: a territory that enjoyed ethnic unity; a common language; common cultural outlines; similar and authentic religious, political, and moral concepts; and the shared memory of a common past.[21] This, Gamio well knew, was not a given but a recent creation. The Japanese were, he wrote, a "precocious" people whose "inexhaustible energy" led them to great achievements.[22] A generation earlier, facing what the intellectual Fukuzawa Yukichi described as "the futility of trying to prevent the onslaught of Western civilisation," their elites had consciously bid Asia good-bye, forging an original, top-down synthesis of their own culture and that of the West.[23] The meteoric success of their new nation-state was self-evident; a whole fleet of Russian battleships attested to it from their watery graves. Gamio, Vasconcelos, Sáenz, and their successors aimed for a similarly successful fusion, a triangulation between what might be preserved of indigenous (and Hispanic) culture and the overwhelming outside force that was their "common threat."[24]

The tools they designed to achieve this were both technocratic and cultural. Education was fundamental and well funded—absorbing 17 percent of the total budget in 1923, compared to 7 percent in 1910—reaching out to indigenous communities through the dramatic expansion of rural schooling and through specialised institutions such as indigenous boarding schools.[25] Alongside the educators, and all other development agencies, came the anthropologists; "it is axiomatic," wrote Gamio, "that anthropology in the true, broad meaning of the term, should be the basic knowledge for conducting good government."[26] The government agreed, backing him as the first head of the Dirección de Antropología. Gamio's career exemplified the strong overlaps between cultural and technocratic indigenismo: between 1915 and 1925 he wrote one of the key nationalist texts, *Forging the Patria*; founded the Dirección de Antropología; served as second in command at the Secretaría de Educación Pública; and judged the 1921 "India Bonita" beauty contest.[27] For all the attention that the cultural productions of indigenismo attracted subsequently, it was the technocratic side that received the most attention at the time. President Obregón gave the Ministry of Public Education more money than it actually requested; he described the great Rivera murals, on the other hand, as a cheap way of decorating government buildings.[28] While the state built schoolhouses on an unprecedented scale, the history textbooks used inside them remained much the same as those of the Porfiriato, and while Vasconcelos commandeered state resources to print massive runs of schoolbooks, they were editions of the European classics.[29] Although the "India Bonita" competition celebrated indigenous women, it was organised by a newspaper in a circulation battle and yielded equivocal results.[30] A more cohesive cultural indigenismo only emerged in the 1930s, with its fresh textbooks, its films, and even its Boy Scouts, whose troops were named after indigenous peoples and whose hierarchies were named after Mexica ranks.[31] Both types of indigenismo were shot through with contradictions, hypocrisies, and failure: even in the key area of indigenous education the state failed to fulfil its goals of enduring indigenous schools and the local cadres to man them.[32] Yet they brought an intensified appreciation of indigenous culture past and, more significantly, present. For all its ad hoc ambivalence, the "India Bonita" competition signified a different world from that of the Porfiriato, where one popular street show, captured by the photographer Casasola, billed itself as "Indians and Poisonous Animals."[33]

Revolutionary indigenismo maintained if not promoted the prominence of Cuauhtémoc in Mexican high, popular, and political culture. Cuauhtémocs populated the cultural production of the revolutionaries from the beginning: the 1918 film *Cuauhtémoc* instructed cinema audiences—while outside the cities the civil wars ground on—in the cardinal virtue of unity.[34] An early trade union called itself the "Cuauhtémoc of Workers."[35] Poets continued the Porfirian fashion for all things Cuauhtémoc. In 1924 Carlos Pellicer published a stirring ode—

Oh sweet ferocious Cuauhtémoc!
Your life is an arrow
that has pierced the eyes of the Sun and
still goes on flying through the sky!

—while the same year in the Ministry of Public Education Diego Rivera painted an austere mural of Cuauhtémoc, whose simple robe, straightforward gaze, and slingshot, a reference to his putative role in stoning Moctezuma, all signed his quintessentially revolutionary identity.[36] Alfonso Reyes described Cuauhtémoc's story as an epic comparable to the Aeneid.[37] B. Traven, a hugely popular novelist of adventure and revolution, even claimed to have found the tomb in 1931. He was living with the Lacandones, an indigenous people in the southern state of Chiapas, researching the books that would be the "jungle cycle," and they—he said—showed him the grave.[38] But he kept the alleged discovery secret and was a terrible source anyway; "B. Traven" was a front for a writer who kept his real identity secret "through mythmaking and using multiple pseudonyms, the inventive lie, the bluff, and the double bluff."[39] Meanwhile, less mysteriously, major politicians—President Lázaro Cárdenas, Colima would-be strongman General Miguel Santa Ana—named their sons Cuauhtémoc.[40] They salted their speeches with references to Cuauhtémoc—one manifesto of agrarian rebellion, the guerrerense Vidales brothers' Plan del Veladero, referred to Cuauhtémoc as inspiration—and they organised conferences for teachers to learn about the last emperor.[41]

Such invocations continued across the 1940s. Cuauhtémoc and the Niños Héroes were "the paradigm of Mexican heroism," one journalist wrote, "the only figures in our history that are clean of stains."[42] The communist painter David

Figure 32. Cuauhtémoc turns the tools of the imperialist against him. José David Alfaro Siqueiros, *Cuauhtémoc redivivo*; courtesy of the Sala de Arte Pública Siqueiros; permission from the Instituto Nacional de Bellas Artes and the Artists Rights Society.

Alfaro Siqueiros made four murals and some dozen paintings of Cuauhtémoc over the decade, complex ideological productions encompassing nationalism, Popular Front-ism, and anti-imperialism and which assert both the extraordinary material advantages of the capitalist world and the possibility of the weak overturning it.[43]

For all the artist's intentions, none of his pieces achieved the sway of the illustrator Jesús Helguera's work: two iconic, deeply kitsch images of the last emperor that remain all-pervasive in Mexican popular culture.[44] Such mass-produced, brightly coloured pictures became ubiquitous, cropping up in unlikely places such as the homes of conservative Catholic ranchers in Jalisco.[45] Even the bullfight, a deeply Hispanic cultural arena, housed representations of Cuauhtémoc: the matador Mauro Liceaga paraded with a ceremonial cape richly embroidered with the last emperor's image.[46] In 1947 the national mint stamped his image on the new five peso coin, and a rural schoolteacher wrote to the president asking that the day of Cuauhtémoc's death be declared a national holiday.[47]

Besides romanticism, besides elective affinity, there were two forms of instrumentalism at work in such gestures. One was collective/hegemonic. As the Partido Revolucionario Institucional's 1950 "Action Programme" put it, "The development of programmes of civic education and political training will help to stimulate the fulfilment of duties towards the *Patria*, the State, society and the home, through the divulgation of apposite examples, biographies of great men, national and foreign, as well as by the celebration of heroic acts and transcendental historical events."[48] The state used the rapid spread of modern communications technology—the growing numbers of cinemas, printing presses, gramophones, radios, and the first televisions—to dramatically up the volume of those divulgations and celebrations. Government gazettes, traditionally used to coordinate civic ritual by listing key dates, detailing ceremonies, and providing models of rhetoric and affective response, were now supplemented by multiple official and semiofficial periodicals. Cinemas expanded across small-town Mexico, showing newsreels of ceremonies such as the anniversary of the oil expropriation.[49] In 1951 the Secretaría de Educación Pública distributed twenty-five thousand records of the National Anthem to bolster the gravitas of school ceremonies.[50] Perhaps the most important mass medium for nation building, though, was the ubiquitous radio. By the 1950s there were ten factories making radios—including the General Electric Azteca M-578, Zapoteca MF-417, Otomí M-251, Mixteca M-135-M, and Huasteca M-123—and some 1.2 million radio receivers in Mexico.[51] It was commonplace, a traveller reported, "to hear

Figure 33.
Reproduction of
Jesús Helguera's
Cuauhtémoc
from beside
Cuauhtémoc's
tomb in
Ixcateopan.
Photograph by
Lyman Johnson.

a wireless blaring forth from the door of a humble adobe hut in some quite remote village," while in one Mexico City tenement four out of five families owned a set.[52] The network owners were close allies of the party elites, and broadcasting was from the outset a propaganda tool, mixing mariachis and radio dramas with party speeches, reports of nationalist ritual, "programmes of a cultural nature, on the occasions of historical commemorations, to fortify the civic spirit," a "military cultural hour," and even birthday serenades for the Virgen de Guadalupe.[53] For the critical ceremonial of presidential reports and transfers of power, the Secretaría de Gobernación went beyond faith in radio's intrinsic popularity and ordered local governments to place loudspeakers in markets, public squares, and official buildings. All stations carried the live transmissions, and the bureaucrats of the Dirección de Información encouraged businesses to put speakers outside their premises and tune in.[54] This saturation coverage continued into the age of television, which began with the transmission of Alemán's fourth presidential report.[55] Nationalist practice and key state rituals could, quite suddenly, be experienced secondhand with strikingly little effort. The cultural managers of the early authoritarian state collectively grasped the instrumentalist potential of the newfound, countrywide leverage and made it one of their key "weapons of the strong" in stabilizing an inequitable society.

The other form of instrumentalism was individual/careerist. In a rapidly shifting political world, where policy initiatives could prove treacherous and allegiances could prove ephemeral, organizing nationalist ceremonial was a safe bet for personal advancement. Alberto Pani, for example, resigned from government in 1920 when President Venustiano Carranza was overthrown by Álvaro Obregón; politically in decline, Pani invented a commission to celebrate the centenary of Mexican independence and used the ensuing lavish festivities as a path back to the very heart of power, winning appointment to the Secretaría de Hacienda.[56] Given such double incentive for political actors to busy themselves with the mechanics of cultural nationalism, it was predictable that revolutionary políticos would try to find Cuauhtémoc. At least one did: Urbano Lavín, a regional politician down on his luck, came to Ixcateopan to find Cuauhtémoc in the late 1920s or early 1930s. Lavín recruited local worthies and spent a week looking for traces of Cuauhtémoc before leaving disappointed, defeated by the secrecy with which Juárez had invested the tomb.[57] It was consequently predictable that once the tomb was unearthed politicians would react enthusiastically.

Yet the controversy that preceded the discovery made federal politicians wary of promoting Cuauhtémoc's remains or his symbol, and they made little response to the discovery for the first ten days. The discoverers and the press, however, made Cuauhtémoc omnipresent in this period and eventually prompted national elites into action. On October 4 the former secretary-general of the party, Teófilo Borunda, proposed a bill to congress "moving that the heroic figure of Cuauhtémoc . . . is the symbol of our nationality." As soon as the remains were verified, he continued, congress would join in the "national homage."[58] The mayor of Mexico City, Fernando Casas Alemán, took the same line: he was considering building a monument in the main square and renaming a central avenue for Cuauhtémoc once the Instituto Nacional de Antropología e Historia (INAH) authenticated the Ixcateopan bones.[59] In the senate three key Partido

Revolucionario Institucional (PRI) power brokers—Carlos Serrano, Fernando Moctezuma, and Gustavo Uruchurtu—presented a bill calling for a monument to Cuauhtémoc, part of which would be funded by civic subscription to include all of Mexico.[60] The secretary-general of the PRI, José López Bermudez, penned an (execrable) ode to Cuauhtémoc; Mexico's best-known poet, Alfonso Reyes, praised it lavishly.[61] A wave of public ritual spread across Mexico City and the provinces in autumn 1949. Nineteen fifty was declared the "Year of Cuauhtémoc," and daily ceremonies were announced. On October 8, 1949, forty thousand students and schoolchildren paraded to the Reforma statue of Cuauhtémoc; the October 12 Día de la Raza (a commemoration of Columbus) was hijacked to focus on the last emperor. Even the anniversary of the revolution on November 20 was colonised, with the day's ceremonial centrepiece constituting five hundred people spelling out Cuauhtémoc's name, surrounded by some six thousand dancers.[62] Buildings, streets, dams, and towns, including Eulalia Guzmán's birthplace and Ixcateopan, were renamed in memory of the last emperor.[63] For one of many hyperbolic commentators the Ixcateopan find was, above two world wars, the discovery of penicillin, or the invention of the atomic bomb, "the most important historic event of our century."[64]

Such ceremonial and speechifying promoted a radically simplified Cuauhtémoc. Those shaping the events and language that Mexicans might use to imagine the last emperor sidelined the most obvious meaning of his legend: resistance. Indigenismo was likewise played down at the highest level, with only a couple of senators calling for Cuauhtémoc to be commemorated with concrete assistance to contemporary indigenous communities.[65] Speakers such as Borunda instead emphasised Cuauhtémoc as Mexico's main origin figure; Cuauhtémoc was, he said, "not just a decorative figure in the gallery of our historic portraits, but rather represents the wellspring of our nationality and the strongest root which feeds the trunk of our Mexican spirit." The trope was adopted in the majority of other PRIísta tributes, which variously called Cuauhtémoc "the symbol of our nationality," "the spirit of the race," "the spirit of authentic *mexicanidad*," "the true Father of the Mexican Nationality," and "the root of the *Patria* itself."[66] It was a simultaneous, self-contradictory claim to extraordinary affective power and absolute symbolic vacuity. The result was a Cuauhtémoc stripped of historical specificity and its divisive power. This anodyne outcome was well phrased in an editorial in *La Prensa*, which called Cuauhtémoc a "constructive myth without negative angles . . . a perennial lesson for youth."[67] The rhetoricians of the early PRI focused on a couple of

Figure 34.
Imagining the
monumental, the
statue that went
unbuilt. José David
Alfaro Siqueiros,
*Homenaje a
Cuauhtémoc redívivo*,
1950; courtesy
of the Museo de
Arte Moderno;
by permission of
the Artists Rights
Society.

abstract nouns in promoting a cult to the last emperor: *purity*, in the education secretary's eyes, and *nobility*, in the party secretary's ode—after which, López Bermúdez wrote, at his epic poem's climax, Cuauhtémoc should be praised for his smile.[68]

"Normal," nonelite Mexicans had problems getting excited about such anodyne nonmeanings. As Jorge Ibargüengoitía put it, "The history that they have taught us is frankly extremely boring. It's full of monolithic great men who spend eternity saying the same sentence: 'peace is respect for others' rights,' 'we're off to kill *gachupines*,' 'do you think, perhaps, that I am on a bed of roses?' etc etc." Deliberate, schematic banality was part and parcel of politicians' attempts to depoliticise national identity. As Ibargüengoitía concluded, "If the History of Mexico that is taught is boring, it's not the fault of the events, which are varied and very interesting, but because those who fabricated it were not as interested in presenting the past as in justifying the present."[69]

In speeches, textbooks, rituals, and other "officialist" productions, the authors of mid-century nationalism systematically gutted Mexico's myths of divisive or factional meanings while striving to keep their mobilizing power intact. Thus the 1950 commemoration of agrarian revolutionary Emiliano Zapata was marked by presidential declarations that the agrarian problem had been solved and that Zapata, had he survived, would have been busy supporting the government's plans for infrastructure development.[70] In Oaxaca's Región Mixe, the indigenous cacique Luis Rodríguez retired his earlier fierce ethnic nationalism to make room for the timid civics classes of regional music, dance, basketball, and the odd military parade.[71] As politicians watered down the revolutionary past they invented new traditions characterised by a consensual blandness. This process sought to dehistoricise and depoliticise Mexican national identity in favour of a fuzzy national narrative that imposed obligations of unity, discipline, and mexicanidad while surrendering as few ideological hostages to fortune as possible. This is typical of myth, in Barthes's definition "constituted by the loss of the historical qualities of things."[72] It is also characteristic of what Eric Hobsbawm finds to be the "marked difference between old and invented practices. . . . The former were specific and strongly binding social practices, the latter tended to be quite unspecific and vague as to the nature of the values, rights and obligations of the group membership they inculcate."[73]

Yet exercises in doublethink carry universal flaws: a lack of affective power, a tendency to satire, sometimes self-inflicted, and a heavy reliance on tight mass media control. As Florencia Mallon notes, "The very ambiguity of discursive frontiers" can elicit "dramatic political and cultural creativity" by the ruled.[74] The official Cuauhtémoc shared all of these and added to them a very specific treble problem. There was, first of all, an academic problem: the cult's vulnerability to ridicule were the bones declared phony. There was furthermore a cultural problem: the promotion of Cuauhtémoc as a national origin figure rekindled long-standing debates between hispanistas and indigenistas over the relative contributions of autochthonous and Spanish cultures to the Mexican nation and over the history of that nation. And there was, finally, a high political problem. While president and cabinet were tentative in claiming Cuauhtémoc, other politicians from across the ideological spectrum moved quickly to identify the last emperor as their own political ancestor. The ensuing symbolic competition further undermined any meaning Cuauhtémoc might have had and any collective utility the government might have drawn from it.

The academic problem—how to locate Mexico's very origin in a forged tomb?—predated the discovery and was the most serious of the three. Both press and politicians linked Cuauhtémoc's symbolic fate—a new place in the nationalist pantheon as überhero, clearly ranked above independence or revolutionary leaders—to the authenticity of the Ixcateopan tomb. This was not particularly logical, but it is deeply understandable, as the suspicion prevailed among journalists, at least, that much nationalist ritual was founded on cynical prestidigitation, the polar opposite of what nations were supposed to be all about: "authentic," "organic," "telluric" communities.[75] When the INAH released its negative report, after nearly a month of celebrations of Cuauhtémoc and Ixcateopan, federal politicians moved into reverse and tried to decouple the last emperor from his fraudulent bones: as one headline announced, "The Official Report Will Go against the Ixcateopan Discovery. All the Same the Homage Will Be Made." This came straight from the president: at the press conference where the reports were released so, too, was Alemán's promise to continue with commemorations, including a monumental statue. The senate, likewise, passed the bill for a Cuauhtémoc monument on the same day that the leaked INAH report condemned the last emperor's remains. It was, *Excélsior* noted ambiguously, a moment of "magic realism." Bernardo Ponce, a conservative commentator, made the Cuauhtémoc scandal part of a critique of decades of invented nationalist tradition. Popular enthusiasm for Cuauhtémoc, he observed, was rooted in "the desire of the Mexican people for authentic heroes, symbols of purity, with stainless causes, very different from soldiers of fortune, political adventurers, serially glorified in a rush to industrially manufacture heroes."[76] The Ixcateopan discovery was, moreover, dangerously susceptible to the laughter that kills nationalist sentiment stone dead. By 1950 satire of Cuauhtémoc, his discoverers, and other cult promoters was widespread enough to move out of cartoons and editorials and into advertising. "Cuauhtémoc's treasures do exist . . . and they can be yours!" tabloids told their readers—at the Cuauhtémoc Furniture Factory.[77]

A second threat to Cuauhtémoc's affective power and any governmental use of it lay in the bickering between hispanistas and indigenistas. This, too, predated the actual discovery. In *Excélsior* Mariano Cuevas wrote off the documents from "some pueblo in Guerrero (I don't remember its complicated Aztec name, nor do I have any interest in remembering it)" as "child's play" aimed only at providing indigenistas with a new site of memory.[78] Arnaíz y Freg agreed: "These chapters [of our history] written by grave robbers and tomb raiders will permit future Mexicans to observe the curious fact that their compatriots from 1947 to 1949 . . . dedicated themselves with exemplary passion to opposing one tomb with another."[79] The discovery was, the party newspaper crowed, a blow to "so-called *hispanista* historians, who want at all costs to deliver themselves to the historical theory of Francisco Franco, the dictator of Spain, and negate everything that represents the essence of our authentic national identity. These wrongly-named 'historians' glorify the figure of Cortés in order to deny the pure life of the great patriot, Cuauhtémoc."[80]

El *Nacional*'s indigenismo was tinged with xenophobia; it was opposed by commentators in *Excélsior*, whose columnists at times verged on straightforward racism. Even there, however, there were voices claiming the tomb find as a boost to indigenous revanchism. An Arias Bernal cartoon, for example, sketches an archetypal "Indian" pedicurist brandishing a knife between the legs of an archetypal Spanish client, cheerily remarking, "By the way, Don Venancio, have you heard that they found Cuauhtémoc's tomb?" His client's reaction is horror; the castration metaphor is obvious.[81] Lengthy press attacks from commentators on each side of the cultural divide intensified as the authenticity scandal grew; they continued throughout the period; and they ran directly counter to the intended purpose of the cult, namely—as union sources put it— "the unification of the Mexican family."[82]

Finally, Mexico's other political actors threatened any state benefits from a Cuauhtémoc cult by competing vigorously for rights to his symbol, which, for all its weak points, was still seen as worth fighting over. By late 1949 Cuauhtémoc had become, in the U.S. embassy's words, "Mexico's most sought-after political asset."[83] Significant sectors of the ruling party had initially tried to enjoy the rents of that asset, laying claim to Cuauhtémoc's symbolic capital. But the "official" Cuauhtémoc, wrapped in abstract proclamations of purity, stoicism, and mexicanidad, was significantly less effective than the Mexican Left's Cuauhtémoc. There was a powerful elective affinity between leftists, from *cardenistas* to communists, and advocates of the Ixcateopan bones. Ex-president Lázaro Cárdenas visited Ixcateopan and became honorary president of the village's Comité Pro-Autenticidad de los Restos de Cuauhtémoc. Impressed by the villagers' "deep sense of patriotism," he then met President Alemán and urged him to recognise the remains as genuine and to provide the village with development projects.[84]

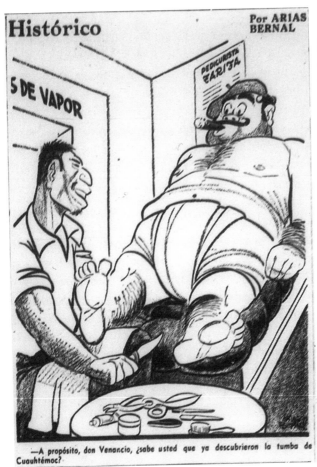

Figure 35.
Arias Bernal,
Excélsior, October 6,
1949; courtesy of
Excélsior.

Union leader Lombardo Toledano, who had just formed the Partido Popular, a dissident leftist party, spoke out for the bones' authenticity. Key pro-authenticity academics such as José Gómez Robledo and Luis Chávez Orozco were believed to be communists by the intelligence service; the dig's anthropologist, Anselmo Marino Flores, was the target of an investigation into communist infiltration of the bureaucracy; and one of the main promoters of the cult in Guerrero, the schoolteacher Juan Campuzano, was also a member of the Communist Party.[85]

Together such widely varying people formed a loose yet broad left-wing coalition that used Cuauhtémoc to oppose the administration in two ways.

One was a pragmatic critique of the government's incompetence in allowing the Ixcateopan discovery to become a scandal. One of the great national problems, Lombardo said, alongside the soaring cost of living, enduring *caciquismo*, rigged elections, and subservience to Washington, was "the campaign of hate against the purest traditions of our people and the values of our national identity . . . trying to deny the discovery of the great Cuauhtémoc's remains."[86] It was a fiasco, *La Prensa* told readers, attributable to "the incomprehensible muteness of those who could have stopped a lot of the speculation in good time."[87] The second (and considerably more powerful) critique was ideological. Leftist advocates for the tomb used their access to the press and public ceremonies to construct an alternative, "dissident" Cuauhtémoc, whose central characteristics were specific and politically loaded: incorruptibility and anti-imperialism.[88] Such imaging was immediate, almost reflexive: at the graveside Marino Flores told journalists that the discovery meant a halt to the cultural imperialism—literally *pochismo*, which Vasconcelos defined as "a borderlands *mestizaje* of the mediocre from both cultures"—that was sweeping Mexico.[89] It was developed, over the eighteen months that Cuauhtémoc regularly visited the front pages, by assorted writers and speakers. The Chilean poet Pablo Neruda used *Cultura Soviética* to publish verses that promoted the last tlatoani from the "young grandfather" to the "young brother."[90] Luis Córdova, in the same issue, made Cuauhtémoc a "soldier of liberty" who, allied with miners, peasants, artists, artisans, Red Army generals, and guerrillas from around the world, brought

His message of struggle for Mexicans,
Today when the insolent *gachupines* of this century
Want to immolate us in a "flowery war"
Without justice, filthy, without gods or ideals.[91]

The U.S. embassy judged that there was a "systematic campaign" to disseminate this reading and thus monopolise "the deep and aggressive pride of Mexicans in their Indian heritage. This pride was stimulated anew by the purported discovery of Cuauhtémoc's remains, and the Communists have been quick and clever to play on this emotion as a popular rallying point and as a useful means of furthering their nationalist and anti-foreigner line."[92] In November 1949 the Soviet embassy sponsored a commemoration of the Russian Revolution in which Cuauhtémoc was heavily invoked.[93] In February 1950 an unscheduled speaker violently seized the microphone at a state-endorsed commemoration of Cuauhtémoc's death to deliver an "anti-Spanish," "anti-government," and "extreme left" diatribe.[94] In March Eulalia Guzmán lectured on women, anti-imperialism, and Cuauhtémoc in the Iris Theatre as part of the Soviet-inspired "peace campaign."[95] By 1951 the muralist David Alfaro Siqueiros was comparing the last emperor to Arab nationalists, the Vietminh, and Mao Tse-tung.[96]

To further increase the government's embarrassment, such symbolic competition was not confined to the Left. The Christian Democrat Partido de Acción Nacional's magazine swung between a modulated scepticism concerning the tomb's authenticity and the promotion of a Catholic, hierarchically disciplined Cuauhtémoc. "In his heart," readers learned, the last emperor had "the ideas of Christianity"; they might consider, moreover, the difference between Cuauhtémoc and the timeservers and opportunists of the ruling party, with their demagogic celebrations of a symbol whose principled behaviour was so foreign to them.[97] The Unión Nacional Sinarquista, radical Catholics, had previously opposed the government's choice of symbols in favour of an alternative set of Catholic national heroes; but their criticism of Benito Juárez and the revolution's great men had only won them banning as an electoral party, and this time they announced a parallel claim on Cuauhtémoc. The last emperor, it seemed, was a *sinarquista* into the bargain.[98] A right-wing group in the army, formed to oppose left-leaning General Miguel Henríquez Guzmán and his presidential ambitions, took the name "The Cuauhtémoc Military Group."[99] Even the fascist Acción Revolucionaria Mexicana joined the festivities, organizing anti-communist commemorations of its own.[100] President Alemán received a New Year's card that carried on one side a picture of and an ode to Cuauhtémoc and on the obverse a call to consummate "the Independence of Mexico, kicking out the GACHUPINES and the JEWS."[101] Such radically opposed interpretations of Cuauhtémoc made him an extraordinarily elastic symbol, capable of encoding anything from Stalinist foreign policy to anti-Semitism.

The government had little immediate control over these different uses of Cuauhtémoc. Gobernación's bureaucrats could, to be sure, ban the neo-fascist Dorados from marching for Cuauhtémoc the anti-Communist; they could deny the communist Peace Congress use of the Palacio de Bellas Artes, relegating the delegates to a rundown boxing arena in a poor part of town.[102] But their control over the newspapers and the public sphere was not authoritarian enough to stop the vigorous academic, cultural, and political controversy surrounding

Figure 36.
José David
Alfaro Siqueiros,
*Cuauhtémoc against
the Myth;* courtesy
of the Sala de Arte
Público Siqueiros;
by permission of
Instituto Nacional
de Bellas Artes
and the Artists
Rights Society.

the last emperor. "Myth and ritual," observed Edmund Leach, "is a language of argument, not a chorus of harmony"; the clamour of that argument meant that the putative benefits to the government of developing a cult to Cuauhtémoc were quickly outweighed by the evident costs.[103] And so the Rio de Janeiro–like monument ("on a mountain," "of grandiose lines and, above all . . . massive") was never built.[104] The ceremonies were rapidly allowed to trail off in neglect. There were no major rituals for Cuauhtémoc in Mexico City in 1950 ("The Year of Cuauhtémoc"). In Ixcateopan the first anniversary of the discovery brought forth plans for major celebrations from governor and ayuntamiento; their invitations to the great and good, however—among them three presidents and every federal and state congressman—elicited a sad range of excuses.[105] The secretary-general of the PRI regretted his inability et cetera; President Alemán was not in Mexico City; the presidente municipal of Coyuca de Catalán claimed that it was raining too hard.[106] There had been talk of bringing ambassadors from indigenous groups across the Americas, but it never went beyond talk.[107] The second anniversary was sadder still: the new governor, Alejandro Gómez Maganda, said that his invitation had arrived too late, and only one of the two state deputies who were supposed to come actually showed up.[108] By the Día de la Raza of 1950 the only outside visitor Ixcateopan could attract was the radical comedian Jesús Martínez "Palillo."[109] The final piece in the controversy, the Gran Comisión's negative report, was convincingly buried. It was left unpublished for over a decade; a copy in Mexico's Escuela Nacional de Antropología e Historia remained with its pages uncut, the book never opened, until the late 1990s.[110]

Over the next two decades villagers, indigenistas, and guerrerense authorities continued to honour the Ixcateopan bones, and the national elites continued to ignore them. Foreign tourists did likewise, advised dismissively by *Terry's Guide to Mexico* that "the whereabouts of [Cuauhtémoc's] remains has ... remained a lively point of contention between Mexican savants who, year after year, keep coming up with new locations and new bones."[111] During President Luis Echeverría's *sexenio* (1970–76), however, regional and national interests intersected to favour the last emperor's resurrection. In Guerrero two long-running insurrections were tying down an estimated twenty-four thousand Mexican troops in an unpopular counterinsurgency campaign.[112] (The governor, meanwhile, was trying to promote regional tourism via the coach company he owned.)[113] At a national level, moreover, President Echeverría found Cuauhtémoc a useful vehicle for two arguments. He largely adopted the Left's anti-imperialist Cuauhtémoc as a figurehead for his *tercermundista* rhetoric: "Cuauhtémoc," he pronounced, "is the wellspring of organised resistance against dependency and colonial exploitation."[114] At the same time, and in an act of notable semiotic contortionism, Echeverría used Cuauhtémoc to try to lay to rest the ghosts of the students killed at Tlatelolco. In 1968, as Mexico prepared to host the Olympic Games, the government used the army to crush a long-running strike at the National University, firing repeatedly into a crowd of students in the Plaza of the Three Cultures at Tlatelolco. Echeverría had been interior minister, responsible for law, order, and—in the minds of most Mexicans—the massacre. His campaign speech in Ixcateopan contained an implicit equation: outgoing leader Díaz Ordaz, who presided over the student shootings and disappearances, was Moctezuma; the incoming Echeverría, "assum[ing] political power when political power, far from being attractive, was a challenge," was the self-sacrificing and symbolically opposed Cuauhtémoc. The last emperor, finally, was an object lesson to Mexican youth "to manifest our rebellions based on reason. . . . In his statesmanlike figure the youth of our century should find the paths of inspiration and the courage for their acts, not for absurd violence that shakes the creative order of our era, but rather to channel themselves. . . . in defence of the Republic's highest ideals."[115] Abroad, Cuauhtémoc was to represent tireless rebellion; at home, self-sacrificing self-discipline.

It was consequently unsurprising that the guerrerense call for a fresh investigation should be welcomed in Mexico City. In January 1976 the government convened a Ministry of Public Education commission, and the set-piece struggle of 1949–51 was reprised.[116] The commission was never going to produce the politically correct verdict. Once again it drew upon the brightest and best of Mexican academia, including the anthropologist Guillermo Bonfil Batalla, the archaeologist Eduardo Matos Moctezuma, and the historians Salvador Rueda and Sonia Lombardo; their main political contact was the undersecretary for education, influential anthropologist Gonzalo Aguirre Beltrán. Once again the state was unable to exercise the cultural control of, for example, Stalinist Russia (where archaeologists who did not toe the nationalist party line were shot).[117] Eulalia Guzmán recycled her earlier press and publishing campaigns, reinforced by some evidence newly forged by Salvador Rodríguez Juárez.[118] The members of the commission did come under pressure in Ixcateopan to say the right thing: Matos and Juan Yadeum hid from a crowd in the village while the local deputy announced that "they were just waiting for the archaeologists from the INAH so that once and for all they can say that Cuauhtémoc's bones are here." Later, over lunch, Governor Rubén Figueroa half-jokingly threatened to decapitate commission members who did not authenticate the bones. Back in Mexico City, however, the academics merely added to earlier condemnations of the tomb. Echeverría received them, heard their conclusions, and thanked them; Governor Figueroa ignored them completely and used the occasion to ask Echeverría to inaugurate a road and some waterworks. The government quietly dropped both grave and cult.[119]

Some state agencies continued to claim the tlatoani. In 1985 the Mexico City town hall published a substantial book mixing biography with defence of the Ixcateopan grave, part of its "National Civic Conscience" series; in 1986 the "Month of Cuauhtémoc in Ixcateopan" was pushed in a full-page advert in *Excélsior*, courtesy of the Tourism Ministry and the Instituto Nacional Indigenista.[120] However, 1976 was the state's last major attempt to derive benefits from this particular symbol. The commission members' reports, published individually after the collective report was withheld, were the final nails in Cuauhtémoc's nonexistent coffin.

The nationalist cult of Cuauhtémoc, assessed across the twentieth century, garnered at best mixed results. In instrumentalist terms, it was sometimes successful at the individual/careerist level. The governor, Baltasar Leyva Mancilla, had been in real political trouble in early 1949; his dogged promotion of Cuauhtémoc seems to have been critical in salvaging his career, and he ended up a brigadier-general, the third-ranking administrator in the Defence Ministry, and an enduring power broker in Guerrero. José Gómez Robledo, the consistent opponent of the Gran Comisión's negative consensus, was rewarded in 1952—despite his reported communist links and his former position as secretary general of the opposition Partido Popular—with the plum job of undersecretary for education.[121] Even Eulalia Guzmán, her reputation in tatters inside the corridors of power (both political and academic), obtained some benefits from her dogged nationalism. Diego Rivera asked her to organise his museum, Anahuacalli—it was, ironically enough, packed with faked prehispanic artefacts—and the more populist presidents López Mateos and Echeverría returned her to official favour.[122]

At the collective/hegemonic level, however, the Cuauhtémoc cult clearly failed. Behind the smoke and mirrors of the periodic mobilisations of schools, bureaucrats, and unions, the affective power of the "official" last emperor proved ambiguous. In 1910 the government organised a public competition to choose a centenary hymn: while 75 percent of the entries mentioned Hidalgo, fewer than 10 percent mentioned Cuauhtémoc.[123] In 1950, the official "Year of Cuauhtémoc," a mere couple of hundred spectators turned out voluntarily to commemorate his death, and some half of these were passing American tourists (a crowd greatly outnumbered by the simultaneous parade, next door, of workers honouring union boss Fidel Velázquez and by the three thousand who turned out the previous year to commemorate the 1938 oil expropriation).[124] The government made valiant attempts to incorporate the public in its commemorations. The monument was to be built by public subscription, its design drawn up by public competition, and its site chosen by referendum.[125] But controversy, press ridicule, and government abandonment seem to have damped down popular enthusiasm for Cuauhtémoc. "The pueblo," *Excélsior* thought one month after the find, had come to its "verdict: Doña Eulalia Guzmán turned out to be a fanatic. . . . [N]ow we don't talk about tissue of Cuauhtémoc, but rather tissue of lies. . . . Why doesn't Doña Eulalia go off and find Noah's Ark?"[126] The presidential in-tray offers some evidence for the rise and fall of Cuauhtémoc's popularity, with a surge of letters and telegrams from September and October 1949 giving way to a trickle of correspondence across the remaining year and a half of scandal.[127] A similar rhythm comes through even in the pages of the Ixcateopan church visitors' book, where thirty-seven pages of comments in the first three weeks shrink to a mere five pages by June 1950.[128] This lack of resonance had been prefigured by sceptics such as José Vasconcelos, who claimed that the public had no understanding of Cuauhtémoc, and the novelist Carlos Fuentes, one of whose characters is incapable of identifying the emperor from his monument.[129] It was further demonstrated by later attitudinal surveys: schoolchildren polled by sociologist Rafael Segovia in the mid-1970s did not rank Cuauhtémoc among the top three national heroes, while a 2001 study did not place him in the top ten.[130]

This does not mean that Cuauhtémoc lacked primordial significance for many Mexicans. The endurance of "dissident" Cuauhtémocs reveals the contrary. While the Mexican government largely abandoned its rights to the last emperor, his symbol was included in the wave of privatisations of the 1990s and was adopted by the opposition. Members of the Partido de la Revolución Democrática sporadically referred to the last emperor—it was, after all, led for a long time by Cuauhtémoc Cárdenas—and used an "Aztec sun" as their emblem. The party's losing candidate from the 2006 presidential elections visited Ixcateopan to lay a wreath on the grave, part of an extensive postelectoral campaign tour of Mexico.[131] Supporters of Chiapas's Ejército Zapatista de Liberación Nacional quoted Cuauhtémoc during the 1997 Mexico City demonstrations and periodically use the Reforma monument as a meeting place. (Highly aware of the importance of symbolism, these neo-zapatistas explicitly denied the late PRI's "rights" to Mexico's national heroes.)[132] One faction of the Ejército Popular Revolucionario, a Maoist guerrilla group that operated in Guerrero in the late 1990s, had a biography of Cuauhtémoc on its Web page and a leader whose nom de guerre was Colonel Cuauhtémoc; its insurgency was explicitly linked, by one Ixcateopan informant, to the last emperor's struggle against the Spanish.[133] Regional intellectuals in Campeche staked a claim to their own Cuauhtémoc, executed and possibly buried in the municipio of Candelaria in their state.[134] Cuauhtémoc also endured as a symbol in Mexican Americans' imagining of a new identity of the transnationally stoic and self-made. Some Chicano community museums reject conquest and colony as a source of periodisation, preferring instead to divide their histories into "preCuauhtemic" and "postCuauhtemic" times; the great farmworkers' leader César Chávez stressed Chicanos' need for good schools with the line "We must know who burned Cuauhtémoc's feet!"[135]

The "dissident" Cuauhtémoc was no more historically coherent than the official version. As Lyman Johnson notes, "The repackaging of the bloody-handed Aztec aristocracy with their passions for military conquest and human sacrifice as a Mexican pre-proletariat" is at best implausible.[136] But it is at least internally coherent. The "official" Cuauhtémoc, on the other hand, was not only sapped by the authenticity scandal and the accompanying suspicions of state complicity in fraud. It was, from the nineteenth century onward, systematically undermined by nonsensical attempts to straitjacket Cuauhtémoc into the dominant scheme of mestizaje. The images of Cuauhtémoc promoted by Riva Palacio, Vasconcelos, and a host of 1940s PRIístas were simultaneously icons of resistance and conciliatory origin figures who accepted the conquest and fathered the new mestizo nation. The semiotic tension was self-evident, and the result—wholly unbelievable, affectively impotent—was repeatedly caricatured as "a phony aztecism."[137] The effect, when combined with communist and Catholic and fraudulent Cuauhtémocs, was to create a last emperor who stood for everything and hence nothing. Mexicans responded accordingly.

Chapter 9

Using Cuauhtémoc II

The shameless will be humbled and the humble will rise up as lords and masters of their Mexican *patria*.

—Salvador Rodríguez Juárez, Florentino Juárez Journal 7

PERHAPS THE MOST INTERESTING CONCLUSION TO BE DRAWN FROM THE modern cult of Cuauhtémoc concerns the role of groups other than national elites in constructions of nationalism. That nationalist traditions and histories were inventions was commonplace in Mexico well before Hobsbawm and Ranger's influential work of the early 1980s.[1] In the 1950s the historian Edmundo O'Gorman dubbed America itself "an invention . . . not, certainly, . . . the sudden revelation of a discovery which might have displayed all at once an alleged entity mysteriously located, always and forever, in the lands found by Columbus, but rather . . . the result of a complex ideological process."[2] The mid-century playwright Rodolfo Usigli played repeatedly with the idea, calling the revolution "a factory of heroes" and Mexico "a country in which tradition seems a daily invention"; his greatest work, *El Gesticulador*, is the story of a humble academic who invents a past as a famous revolutionary to get ahead in life. Usigli was expressing an idea whose time had come. The opening night in 1947 was met by a twenty-minute ovation and chants of "U-si-gli"; the president ordered the cabinet to see the play and met with them to discuss the reaction.[3] Mexicans ranging from leading politicians to commentators in the newspapers discussed the verifiability and the political use of the past quite regularly. In 1949 Manuel Gómez Morín, leader of the Catholic opposition, condemned the state's "constant repetition of the false image of Acción Nacional . . . [blaming] the Party for the conquest, the crowning of Iturbide and Maximilian's empire."[4] In 1950 the tabloid *La Prensa* ran a long series in which Mateo Podan mulled over "one of the greatest vices of 'History' . . . that it has always attempted, through the political passion of those who write it, to dictate to us whom we should love, whom we should respect and whom we should venerate and obey. Thus History is an instrument of mystification, fraud and domination, part of religious education, that opium of the people."[5]

The Cuauhtémoc scandal stimulated many columnists to muse along similar lines, as their newspapers argued among themselves over the propriety of "official history." Before the scandal even broke *Excélsior* was using Cuauhtémoc as an opportunity to observe how "the Mexican Revolution has invented a crowd of heroes who are not heroes." This, the party newspaper replied (in a regular space for "orienting" its readers regarding the past, "Fichas para la Historia"), "only show[ed] that the writer [was] recalcitrant, reactionary and an enemy of all the advances which have been made by the popular movement and which manifest themselves, among other ways, in the liberty with which he himself [wrote]."[6] Such exchanges punctuated the course of the Cuauhtémoc scandal. They reflected a generalised, positively postmodern belief in the lability of any representation of the past.

If nations are inventions, who does the inventing? That nationalist stories are predominantly (or even purely) elite creations was (and remains) a powerful theoretical assumption, made by both lay and academic writers, reinforced by methodological limitations: evidence for nonelite manipulation of nationalist phenomena is often hard to find. Resulting analyses, reinforced by prevalent and schematic elite/subaltern dichotomies, paint sharp divisions between Machiavellian producers and passive, sheeplike consumers of national memory. This is the genre of social science whose vision, satirised by Antonio Gramsci, is of a world divided into "on the one hand, those with the genie in the lamp who know everything, and on the other those who are fooled by their own leaders but are so incurably thick that they refuse to believe it."[7]

Mexican elites did conduct an instrumentalist campaign from the 1880s to the 1970s to consolidate and to manipulate an affectively convincing Cuauhtémoc. The peak of this campaign has conventionally been assumed to be the text and ritual production surrounding the tomb find in 1949, a clear demonstration of a cohesive, massive, and top-down exercise in reengineering culture. Yet the most important politicians, the executives of both Mexico City and Mexico itself, were in reality chary of any involvement whatsoever with the Cuauhtémoc cult. (The president's correspondence strongly suggests that he took pains to avoid meeting Eulalia Guzmán.)[8] There were five major national rituals involving Cuauhtémoc between 1949 and 1951. None of them was ordered or organised at the highest level of government. The first Mexico City commemoration on October 8, with its tens of thousands of marchers, was initiated by the Escuela Nacional de Maestros; primary schoolchildren constituted its readily available parade fodder.[9] The Día de la Raza homage at the Cuauhtémoc monument four days later was the work of Acción Social, a subdepartment of town hall.[10] The incorporation of Cuauhtémoc into the Día de la Revolución was again the work of the Escuela Nacional de Maestros.[11] The only countrywide commemoration—a critical requisite were Cuauhtémoc to genuinely resonate with the Mexican "imagined community"— was proposed by the out-of-favour peasant union, the Confederación Nacional Campesina. The ceremony, a simultaneous meeting of peasant representatives in every state capital, at which peasant leaders would lay the foundation stones of monuments to Cuauhtémoc, seems never to have materialised.[12] The last major celebration in the capital, the February 26, 1950, commemoration of his death, was given a semiofficial gloss by representatives from three government agencies; but it was the work of a fringe group, "Restauradores de la Mexicanidad," who operated out of their founders' flat on the Calle Doncelles and believed themselves persecuted by "the Spanish power complex."[13] The classic instrumentalist model of nationalism does not in reality fit the Cuauhtémoc cult of the late 1940s all that well. The bulk of the rituals and the recovered memories were, rather, produced by regional politicians, bureaucrats, and peasants, men and women who shared the realisation that history is a natural resource and resolved to exploit it.

Guerrero's politicians were critical in sustaining belief in the tomb, and a raft of associated ceremonies, against the cold showers of metropolitan criticism and later neglect. Vox populi realised this from the start; one of the popular ballads called *corridos* recalled how during the dig

> General Leyva Mancilla
> Picked up all the bills
> And disdaining others' fears
> Never batted an eyelid.[14]

The governor was, as we have seen, determined to drive forward the dig over even Eulalia Guzmán's doubts; as soon as the documents surfaced he sent the head of the state's Acción Cívica, the department in charge of public ritual, to Ixcateopan.[15] At the graveside he declared the remains authentic and then ordered every municipio in the state to celebrate the discovery. On September 29 village politicians duly wielded the usual ceremonial tools of church bells, teachers, schoolchildren, bunting, and fireworks in memory of the last emperor.[16] The state legislature moved the state's powers to Ixcateopan in solemn ceremony on October 12, the Día de la Raza, and awarded medals to the governor and Guzmán.[17] When the Instituto Nacional de Antropología e Historia report turned out to be negative, Leyva Mancilla immediately told the national papers that Guerrero, his state, stood by the bones.[18] By 1950 the governor was busily reworking village popular culture to more efficiently reflect the new importance of Cuauhtémoc, ordering the Ixcateopan authorities to provide indigenous dancers with drums and red flags to perform the ahuiles on the anniversary of the discovery.[19] This initiative was not just confined to Ixcateopan: in villages such as Tlacoachistlahuaca and Xochistlahuaca on the distant southern coast, local authorities seem to have introduced a carefully crafted nationalist "indigenous dance" in the same years.[20] Leyva Mancilla's vigorous invention of tradition was seconded by other guerrerenses in strategic political posts. Nabor Ojeda, the long-standing peasant leader from the coast, was the first to bring Cuauhtémoc to congress, proposing that his name be engraved in gold alongside those of the revolutionary heroes on the chamber's wall.[21] Ruffo Figueroa, whose rancher family had led the revolution in northern Guerrero, was the president of the senate that introduced the main project to commemorate Cuauhtémoc, the monumental statue that was never built.[22] This regional promotion, temporarily uniting bitter political enemies, was—unlike the fractured, tepid federal response—a cohesive, top-down nationalist campaign.

It was articulated, outside of Guerrero, with the low- and mid-ranking public employees who tried to throw the weight of the state behind Cuauhtémoc. Such bureaucratic entrepreneurs were above all the teachers and functionaries of the Secretaría de Educación Pública (SEP). The minister, Manuel Gual Vidal, consulted Alemán before any major decision and followed the president's lead in maintaining public agnosticism toward the bones.[23] Beneath him, however, teachers and educational bureaucrats bombarded the ministry and other departments with suggestions for celebrating Cuauhtémoc. Many of their initiatives were implemented; the main Mexico City commemorations were, as we have seen, orchestrated and largely manned by the Escuela Nacional de Maestros. In Tlaxcala a teacher produced a primary school curriculum in which references to Cuauhtémoc colonised the teaching of all subjects ("Grammar: Cuauhtémoc's words as phrases or sentences: affirmative, interrogative, negative, admirational, imperative").[24] A Mexico City school inspector—"representing 200 school-teachers"—wrote dozens of letters suggesting medals, parades, school namings, presidential visits, and monuments and proudly reported the delivery of reliquaries containing earth from Ixcateopan to all the schools in his zone.[25] Guerrero's teachers hosted a meeting of their colleagues from across Mexico in Ixcateopan in April 1950; the village women greeted them with a banquet for which they dug eight roasting pits and shaped two thousand tortillas.[26] Other initiatives were beyond the reach of voluntarist and/or state capacities. Another teacher, Salvador Mateos Higuera, produced a ten-page plan for a new model city outside the capital, "Ciudad Cuauhtémoc," which was to be a lovingly crafted combination of Le Corbusier and neo-Aztec theme park.[27] And some teachers did not wait for other bureaucrats to move and took direct action instead. In the first weeks after the discovery groups of teachers from across Guerrero, from Mexico City, from Michoacán, and from the Instituto Politécnico Nacional made pilgrimages to the village.[28] The headmistress of one Mexico City school led pupils dressed in white to the offices of El Universal to lecture the assembled hacks on their patriotic duty to Cuauhtémoc, ending with a weird prayer to the last tlatoani.[29] A headmaster from Acapulco packed his pupils into fifteen cattle trucks and took them, along with unionised workers and dockers, to Ixcateopan.[30]

The energetic response of Mexico's teachers was in some ways overdetermined. A central part of their job was, after all, the promotion of "national integration" through a homogeneous national culture; they were the foot soldiers of the revolution's cultural nationalism.[31] Even at the end of the 1940s, moreover, the personnel of the SEP were significantly to the left of the rest of the state's operators, the heritage of the socialist education programmes of the 1930s and the Communist Party's successful recruitment drives inside the profession. They were, consequently, particularly susceptible to the Cuauhtémoc cult; as we have seen above, there was a distinct overlap between supporters of the Ixcateopan tomb and the Mexican Left. There was also almost certainly a clientelist explanation for some of the teachers' enthusiasm. Eulalia Guzmán had been a power in the Ministry of Public Education in its early years of the 1920s. As deputy head of primary education, which occupied an overwhelming majority of budget and personnel, she had been one of the most important everyday administrators in the SEP. Some of the numerous teachers who backed her work and spread the cult must have been her clients from that time.

Yet the bureaucratic entrepreneurs who pushed the cult of Cuauhtémoc were not just teachers. The director of the rural credit agency in Papantla, Veracruz—a town with a fierce tradition of indigenous rebellion—suggested that a free edition of Cuauhtémoc's biography be distributed among "peasants, bureaucrats, workers, etc."[32] At least one such idea contributed to the national campaign: the initiative to declare 1950 the "Year of Cuauhtémoc," which came from the veteran spy Raúl Cervantes Díaz. (He mooted it as part of a far larger scheme of economic nationalism, public health, public works, and "national unity"; eloquently, only the label was adopted.) Such bureaucrats may have taken their initiatives in part for genuinely affective reasons, but their care in registering them with central government suggests a complementary, careerist explanation. Cervantes Díaz was ambiguously described as "struggling with patriotic enthusiasm to carry out initiatives which ennoble him and the environment which inspires him."[33]

Finally, the president's in-tray shows that it was not even necessary to work within the state to realise the potential personal benefits of nationalist ceremonial. One Marcos Mena Gordoa wrote in twice with suggestions regarding the Cuauhtémoc monument, on which, having spent time in a foundry in the United States, he would be delighted to work (it would only cost twenty to thirty thousand pesos).[34] The would-be filmmakers of the Comité Coordinador de Unidad Proletaria wanted to make a short "that embodies in its graphic language a message of Mexican nationality" and asked for money and help.[35] A designer, Eduardo Cataño, suggested that a Cuauhtémoc medal be struck for distinguished military service and enclosed a sketch of the bronze bas-relief that he had made for that very purpose.[36] They were not the first to have like ideas: town halls across Mexico were plagued by unsolicited, privately produced nationalist materials—books, flags, periodical subscriptions—that salesmen pushed aggressively, unsubtly hinting that a refusal to buy might be politically damaging.[37] Ixcateopan, for example, was targeted not just by the sales departments of state media such as the *Diario de Guerrero* and *El Nacional* (though these, too, were annual supplicants for subscriptions, sycophantic adverts, local vendors, and the like).[38] The ayuntamiento was also subject to sales efforts from entrepreneurial types such as the president of the Lions Club in faraway Ameca, Jalisco, who wrote an impassioned pitch to the mayor offering his book *Father Hidalgo and His Men* (at a 50 percent discount, "as the business is not commercial but rather cultural and patriotic").[39] The Bloc of Revolutionary Journalists were pushier: they sent an unrequested five copies of their biography of the Niños Héroes (endorsed by the president and the education and defence ministries) and demanded the inflated price of ten pesos each.[40] Such activities—everyday people's self-conscious, half-cynical manipulation of nationalist symbols for political and material advantage—might well be called grassroots instrumentalism.

That grassroots instrumentalism was, of course, most strikingly revealed in the villagers' calculations of the benefits to be had from the cult to Cuauhtémoc in Ixcateopan. It was, after all, Florentino Juárez who provided the raw material for much of the ritual, forging the tomb in a doomed attempt to defend his local political and economic power. The rancher was neither peasant nor subaltern, and if his extensive lands had been of better quality, villagers might well have called him a hacendado. But in terms of metropolitan perceptions and politics, the politics that engage most analysts of nationalism, Florentino Juárez was an outsider, distinctly from the grassroots of society. He was a failing politician from an impoverished village in an impoverished state, whose children seemed bent on destroying his would-be dynasty before it had even taken root. The man who seems to have been his local patron, General Canuto Neri, was another national outsider, an also-ran in the fierce struggles for regional power. And some of Juárez's successors, as we have seen, were equally enterprising. Salvador Rodríguez Juárez, who claimed Cuauhtémoc as an ancestor, began producing additions to the forged documents before the tomb was even uncovered. In the aftermath of the discovery he built a "special shrine" in his house where visitors might kneel on three cushioned stools in front of an alcove containing oil paintings of Christ and the Santo Niño, two crosses, two plaster saints, four large candles, and the Juárez documents.[41] He aggressively insisted on his ownership of Ixcateopan's Cuauhtémoc: an entry in the church visitor's book that linked Eulalia Guzmán and Motolinía with Cuauhtémoc "at the spine of our nationality" was crudely amended to read "and all of them with Dr. Rodríguez."[42] When the state government gave him a certificate naming him "Custodian of the Remains of Cuauhtémoc and the Documents Relating to the Same," Rodríguez Juárez had it notarised in front of the mayor and told him that the new title did not reduce his "merit as Discoverer of the Tomb of the Emperor Cuauhtémoc."[43] By the time of the 1976 investigation he had made at least another twelve allegedly antique manuscripts, whose purpose was to paper over the cracks in the fraud narrative and to emphasise his own significance.

In this Rodríguez Juárez failed resoundingly: even sympathetic guests from the city found the village doctor a bit dodgy.[44] Neither was he all that successful in economic terms. The discovery triggered an initial flood of visitors who wanted to plumb Rodríguez Juárez for the legend of Ixcateopan; some fifteen hundred people signed the church's visitor's book between February 1949 and February 1950.[45] Their interest gave him significant amounts of social capital, which he hoped to convert into economic capital through at least three different projects: the recovery of the family house, public funding for his work promoting Cuauhtémoc and protecting the tomb, and a radio play. But none of these projects seems to have worked, and Rodríguez Juárez evidently did not make his fortune out of Cuauhtémoc.

Rodríguez Juárez did, however, successfully manipulate Cuauhtémoc's bones to restore his family's political fortunes in the village. Florentino Juárez had been a figure of substantial power in nineteenth-century Ixcateopan; after his death the family had gone into decline. Of the sons, Odilón and Leopoldo had bad reputations before the revolution and little reputation at all afterward. Florencio (himself "a man of the gun") had never got on with them; he seems to have moved to Taxco, where his son, Florentino Juárez Giles, "claimed to be a lawyer" and energetically tried to rig the 1948 local elections.[46] Unable to rely on his sons, Juárez took the unusual but not unheard of step of bypassing all bar Florencio and leaving half his estate to his daughter, María Inés.[47] Of those who remained in Ixcateopan, the grandson Manuel Rodríguez Juárez was the most successful, leading the village *defensa social*—the only effective local policing force—from the revolution onward. His brother Abel seems to have used violence in less socially acceptable ways, cropping up in the village archives as a brawler.[48] Salvador, finally, was a minor member of the elites: briefly mayor, a reliable speaker at village festivities, and the closest thing Ixcateopan had to a doctor. The brothers did not, however, necessarily support each other: Manuel and Salvador seem to have been on different sides in local elections on more than one occasion.[49] None of them had anything like the combined political and economic muscle of their grandfather. The story of the Juárez clan was, in short, a typical story of a family's rise and fall over three generations, fifty years or so of accumulation followed by dissipation.

Rodríguez Juárez used Cuauhtémoc's bones to reverse this decline in three ways. The would-be doctor used the Comité Pro-Autenticidad, as we have seen above, to capture the high ground of municipal politics, combining nationalism with a reminder of Rodríguez Juárez's new links to national politicians and to Lázaro Cárdenas in particular. The committee's Secretario de Actas, local schoolteacher Julio Cuestas, was a longtime village power broker and patron of

Rodríguez Juárez; he became mayor in 1952 in elections denounced as nonexistent by the incumbent mayor and the village opposition, gathered together in the rival "Frente Cuauhtémoc."[50] The result was a bitter power struggle and a rapid shuffling of mayors; nevertheless, it was another member of Rodríguez Juárez's committee, Delfino Sales Juárez, who won the next village election in 1954.[51] The Comité Pro-Autenticidad, remembered the schoolteacher Modesto Jaimes, dominated politics across the 1950s.[52] Ownership of Cuauhtémoc enabled more than the dominance of electoral politics. It also favoured Rodríguez Juárez's domination of local resource politics and above all the resources of development. Rodríguez Juárez was vice-president of the Comité Pro-Carretera, the campaign for a paved road to Taxco that was at the centre of the community's infrastructural needs, and he was also a key mover in the village's moves to ensure the supply of electricity.[53] And he may have also vetoed development initiatives that were not in his interest; it is worth noting that "difficulties which began to arise between the aforementioned professional and some important villagers" drove the Misión Cultural's doctor out of Ixcateopan in 1952. Rodríguez Juárez, formerly the only practising doctor in Ixcateopan, almost certainly felt threatened by metropolitan competition.[54] Finally, Rodríguez Juárez tried to monopolise the cultural politics of Ixcateopan by launching a lengthy campaign against the local priest for control not just of Cuauhtémoc's bones but also of the church buildings that housed them.[55]

This was a particularly far-reaching move, which tapped into decades of church/state conflict. The national struggles between anticlerical revolutionaries and traditionally powerful churchmen had their Ixcateopan equivalents. In the 1920s some villagers went to the hills as part of the Cristiada, the national Catholic counterrevolution, and the priest left town; in 1944 the governor reported that "the place's priest intervenes overly and dangerously in matters which are the people's to decide," and the ayuntamiento arrested Canuto Morales as a recruiting agent for the *sinarquistas*, the authoritarian Catholic underground; across the 1940s, authorities complained, the priest organised unconstitutional religious processions for the village saint's day in August. (They reacted with the odd exemplary arrest.)[56] The tomb find made the church an extraordinarily symbolically charged place, the centre of jostling, mutually incompatible religious and nationalist cults. Converting churches to the secular religion of nationalist education was nothing new: revolutionaries had often enough seized church buildings for schoolhouses, and letters to *La Prensa* in 1949 suggested that this be done in Mexico City to provide a resting place and another monument for Cuauhtémoc.[57] Such measures, both practical and possessed of a knowing symbolism, had been something of a national pattern in the 1920s and 1930s. Rodríguez Juárez followed it, leading village nationalists to seize the church and, according to the priest, some of the parish funds into the bargain. (He did install a collection box in the church to fund his maintenance of the grave.)[58] Removed from control over his own building—whose use was now organised by Rodríguez Juárez and other local power brokers—and tired of celebrating mass over a temporary altar, surrounded by the local reservists who guarded Cuauhtémoc, Father José Landa tried to build a new church. Even this was plagued by controversy, as Bernardo Salgado successfully intervened to stop any construction in the churchyard and to relocate the new, smaller church to the site of the rectory. Rodríguez Juárez was in the middle of the conflict; he even had Padre Landa arrested on one occasion. He had, the priest bitterly observed, become "the principal leader of the village."[59] He used that power, legitimised by the state government and by his own committee, to effectively take over Santa María de la Asunción.

The priest did not give up easily. He fought an intensive bureaucratic rearguard action against the kidnapping of his church; sent devout Catholics to remove the pews; got the state to provide cement, tiles, and masons for a new church; and in 1956 formally removed his ministry to the nearby hamlet of San Juan.[60] And José Landa was not the only villager to resist Rodríguez Juárez's cult. A group of local worthies—Modesto Jaimes (a teacher), Sara Torres (a local shopkeeper and landowner), Elodia López, and Modesto Rodarte—"far from collaborating with propaganda among the visitors to their shops and Restaurants, [busied] themselves in criticizing the lack of authenticity of the remains of our illustrious lord Cuauhtémoc."[61] Josefina Jaimes tried to counter Rodríguez Juárez's claim to the tomb's symbolic capital by planting alternative stories in a Mexico City magazine, *Entrevista*, deeming the village cobbler the real owner of the documents.[62] Outright denial of the cult's validity was the most direct means of subverting the new village regime; other stratagems included gossip regarding Rodríguez Juárez's sexuality and the theft of cult materials. In 1954 a malefactor broke the padlock on the cult's church collection box and made off with the money. At about the same time Rutilo Alvarez was accused of stealing and selling the crystal vases that the Rodríguez Juárez brothers had bought to adorn the tomb.[63] At one stage, an informant remembered, Salvador Rodríguez Juárez "was on the point of leaving Ixcateopan, they wanted to kill him."[64]

What did villagers who wanted to kill Rodríguez Juárez think of that master abstraction, Mexico? The question of how complex reactions to the Juárez clan's use of Cuauhtémoc articulated with preexisting village ideas of the nation is a difficult one, for—like some strange experiment in particle physics—the presence of observers after 1949 altered everything. We have scattered mentions from interviews of how everyday villagers in the 1970s said they had thought and felt about Mexico thirty years and more previously and a handful of quotes in contemporary newspapers. Yet it seems more reliable to go by what was done at the time rather than what was said substantially later, and in the memories and archival records of nationalist ritual from just before the tomb find there may be clues to reconstruct how villagers imagined the nation and the power and limits of that vision.

The last emperor appeared in a time and place where intense nationalist ritual had been the norm for some sixty years at least. State governments had followed federal example across the Porfiriato and imposed a busy ceremonial calendar, which the revolution had intensified to fever pitch in the 1930s. In mid-1930s Chiapas, for example, teachers were expected to organise celebrations for forty different state and national holidays during the school year; this was a selective version of the SEP's national ceremonial calendar, which in 1935 provided for fifty-four different holidays, including the Río Blanco massacre, Bastille Day, and the birthday of James Watt.[65] Schoolteachers and parents alike complained about the damage that teachers' many noneducational tasks did to the work of teaching, and in the early 1940s the SEP slimmed down its demands for ritual to a mere twenty-two national holidays a year.[66] The state government could always embellish such calendars—it called for sixteen ceremonies between September and December 1951—but it seems very unlikely that villagers played along.[67] The village band was instructed to serenade the flag on the official holidays when it was raised.[68] That aside, the municipal archive is revealingly silent about the organisation and performance of all but the most important national holidays: the Cinco de Mayo, the *fiestas patrias* for independence in September, and the newly invented Flag Day in February. (Villagers did not, revealingly, leave much record of celebrations for either the Día de la Revolución or the Día de la Raza.) A consideration of the greatest of those rituals, the several days spent celebrating independence, gives some idea of how local people construed Mexico and how much that construction mattered to them.

Preparation for the fiestas patrias began months in advance. In January the mayor recruited a handful of community leaders to form the *junta patriótica*, whose members in turn recruited their own commissions to organise raffles and dances.[69] Across the summer six or seven of these were organised, gatherings in the schoolhouse or town hall of twenty to thirty couples who danced to the music of the village band, which paused midway through each number to charge ten or even twenty centavos for the privilege. In the first days of September the pace heated up. Commissioners became talent scouts, divided into panels of three, each responsible for choosing and grooming a child to fill the festivities' starring roles: Generals Allende and Aldama, Miguel Hidalgo, La Malinche, the *corregidora*, and La América, a girl chosen to represent the entire hemisphere. Older villagers were chosen to form four groups of extras: *la indiada* (the Indian horde), *los españoles* (the Spanish), the *comerciantes/indios* (traders/Indians), and the *ladrones/criollos* (thieves/creoles).[70] For backstage duties the presidente municipal enthusiastically conscripted the able-bodied. In 1951, for example, he demanded fifteen people to clean up the Parque Hidalgo and another ten to decorate it with flags, crowns, and bouquets of flowers; ten to decorate the bandstand in the middle of the main square; and nineteen to build a set for the *actos cívicos*. (Realizing that this was all thirsty work, he also requisitioned 350 litres of the milky cactus alcohol pulque.)[71] Finally September 15 arrived, and at six in the morning the church bells woke villagers up for the rich social drama of the year's biggest party.

As dawn broke Ixcateopan's schoolchildren were marshalled to sing the anthem while the flag was raised, starting three days of symbolically charged festivities. At nine in the evening the actos cívicos continued with the three-act play, whose homegrown script varied but always centred on the discovery of the independence conspiracy in Querétaro and always ended with the Grito de Dolores, Padre Hidalgo's call to arms against Spain. Play over, the secretary read the Declaration of Independence, and the presidente municipal, wrapped in the flag, gave a second rendition of the Grito. The call to arms was not ignored, and the crowd answered the Grito by shouting, "¡Viva México!" and shooting their (largely illegal) pistols in the air. The ayuntamiento and the actors then led a parade through town followed by the band and the villagers. As they marched down to the cemetery they carried kerosene lanterns and set off fireworks, while behind them the church bells pealed and a small ceremonial cannon, dragged by another commission, thundered out a blank on each corner. The cemetery visited, the parade marched uphill to the Plazuela Cuauhtémoc.

Up to this point the festivities were fairly standard, recognisable anywhere in Mexico. Once in the Plazuela Cuauhtémoc, however, the villagers began to enact a revealing, locally particular set of rites. A mock castle was quickly set up, and the village rich took up their positions on top as the españoles. The indiada marched around the base and then tried to scale and capture it. Both sides were armed with wooden machetes (although allegedly the perfidious españoles sometimes smuggled in the odd real one), and there were sometimes injuries. Well after midnight the battle ended, and the villagers retired to recoup their energies for the next morning's parade. This one proceeded from the main square to the monument to Hidalgo and escorted three very different symbols—Padre Hidalgo himself, La América on horseback, and La Malinche dressed as a *china poblana*, the folkloric fast women who became nationalist icons of Mexican beauty. It was La América, though, who was the star, as the ladrones/criollos (thieves/creoles) sallied out of the side streets to capture her, and the comerciantes/indios (traders/Indians) fought them off. The Parque Hidalgo reached in safety, the fighting dissolved into speeches, poems, and a drink or two of specially flavoured pulque. Finally, the patriotic bacchanalia concluded the next day with a free dinner and dance.[72]

How did this make villagers feel, and what does it reflect of their beliefs in Mexico? The early parts of the fiestas patrias symbolised the interweaving of local and national communities, as local people acted out the fundamental national roles. When the mayor shouted, "Death to the bad government! Long live Mexico!" and the crowd thundered out the response, most concerned knew that they were doing the same thing at the same time as people like them across the country. The subsequent parade passed through spaces named for the national great and good—down Calle Vicente Guerrero, then up Calle Morelos to the Plazuela Cuauhtémoc—but took care to pass by the graveyard, linking their anonymous village dead to the mythical Mexican past. Yet the main content then swerved away from the nationalist master narrative, as villagers eschewed its happy ending in mestizaje and unification, stressing instead enduring resistance to enduring inequality. The Mexico that villagers chose to perform was strongly imagined in terms of ethnicised class conflict. In both the storming of the castle on September 15 and the parade of September 16, the village rich played the inseparable roles of ethnic and economic superiority, as first the Spanish and then the creoles. While the "Indians" of the village ruled were unequivocally the heroes, their victories in defending La América were annually ephemeral. The next year, all knew, they would be poor and under attack once more. In a further satirical twist, the wealthy ladrones/criollos got to dress richly, don swords and masks, and prance around on horseback; but the impoverished comerciantes/indios, under the guise of selling fruit, were licensed for a day to free comment. They took the opportunity to proffer carnivalesque put-downs of the local bourgeoisie and carnal slurs on their wives, offering to sell them, for example, herbal remedies "to keep your husband quiet." It was a time, Román Parra Terán remembered, "when everything could be said"; and in that liberty there was also an opportunity to give the abstraction of the nation real, local, meaning.[73] As with their ancestors, the carnivals of medieval Europe, the fiestas patrias juxtaposed order and anarchy in "a sort of comprehensive and poetic description of society . . . a satirical, lyrical, epic-learning experience for highly diversified groups."[74]

The lengths to which villagers went to make the independence commemorations worthy all evince that this ritual celebration of Mexico worked, that it entertained and moved people, that it was a source of pride as well as acid commentary, and that its larger themes were relevant to an immediate world. It may have been fundamentally conservative, keeping elites in check and giving the ruled a steam valve; it may equally have been a way of imagining social change. It clearly had an instrumentalist rationale. It afforded local politicians a cheap way to communicate an image of broadly consensual dominance, the basic qualification for remaining in government. For the ruled, meanwhile, enthusiastic participation bought them space to resist in other areas, covering up the solid evidence of unpaid taxes, unheeded literacy campaigns, and unanswered call-up papers with a veneer of obedience. For all concerned, acting out the nation was less complicated than acting for the state.

Revealingly, though, participation was also enforced by routine coercion. In the run-up to such ceremonies totalitarian-sounding "block inspectors" were entrusted with turning out all the families in their street for the festivities. Members of the junta patriótica who did not turn up to meetings were threatened with ten-peso fines—equivalent to a field hand's weekly wage—and pupils who did not attend the dawn flag ceremonies had their marks lowered.[75] Rituals that had not been locally scripted, such as Flag Day, often failed: peasants had little idea and less interest in performing them.[76] Even the more solid traditions of the Cinco de Mayo required judicious threats and bribes to be consummated.[77] In May 1947 the comisariado municipal for Pachivia wrote to Ixcateopan requesting a license for a raffle and fireworks display on May 5, explaining, "You know that it's necessary to do something to make things festive to get a crowd."[78] Entrepreneurial types, meanwhile, sometimes acted on the idea that patriotism is the last refuge of the scoundrel: in 1945, for example,

Filadelfo Rodarte used his position on the junta patriótica to rig the raffle and make off with twenty-five pesos.[79] Mexico, in short, seems to have had meaning and a powerful one at that: the majority of villagers in Ixcateopan's fiestas patrias identified their stories in what was presented as the national story. Yet theirs was not the official story in its entirety. It was, rather, a local and narrow variant; and beyond its terms of ethnically organised resistance to inequality, villagers seem to have been erratic nationalists.

This mixture of commitment to and cynicism regarding the nation, and that concept's central, deeply local meaning—an ethnically determined group of underdogs perpetually beset by the abuses of the powerful—underpinned both support for and opposition to Rodríguez Juárez's faction. The latter is wholly unsurprising. He and his allies had, after all, used Cuauhtémoc to monopolise the village's main sites of power, simultaneously alienating some of the ruled and some of the old elite. While detonating considerable political conflict, they had also initiated dramatic changes in Ixcateopan's popular culture. The village church had ceased to be a place of worship. The village patron saint, the *santo niño*, had been eclipsed by the last tlatoani. The main village dance, ahuiles, had been hijacked, its performance directed personally by the governor; the handful of remaining dancers were severely instructed to come out on September 26, not during Carnival, and "to duly organise themselves and not to just turn up on the day without any organisation as has previously happened."[80] What had been fun became a bore; and while cultists tried to make the ahuiles into evidence for the Cuauhtémoc tradition, the dancers simply stopped dancing. The ahuiles died out in the early 1950s, and with it, in 1955, went the entire cargo system that had sustained traditional village festivals.[81] Meanwhile Cuauhtémoc exercised a new labour demand on villagers, who were taxed one day a month of compulsory service guarding the tomb. Town hall fined those who failed to show up for duty.[82] Even Salvador Rodríguez Juárez was not wholly happy with the changes in the village, complaining bitterly at the end of his life that things were not as they had once been. Yet his family's record clearly reveals the usefulness of Cuauhtémoc to the Juárez clan. One of his sons, Jairo, inherited Salvador's job as "guardian of the tomb"; another, Rafael, became mayor and local deputy; his grandson, Rafael Barrera Rodríguez, was presidente municipal between 2002 and 2004.[83]

While Rodríguez Juárez was the most individualistic, he was by no means the only villager to attempt to barter the symbolic capital of Cuauhtémoc for more immediate gains. The days surrounding the discovery saw a string of people from Ixcateopan and northern Guerrero claim a whole new importance by dint of privileged historical information, such as the whereabouts of imaginary treasures or codices.[84] Somewhat later Canuto Nogueda Radilla, an anti-agrarian gunman from the coast, wrote a prolix defence of the tomb's authenticity in a national tabloid. The village as a collectivity repeatedly invoked the tomb in their petitions for state-sponsored development programmes such as electricity, drinking water, roads, and drainage, petitions that carefully repeated the catchphrases of metropolitan developmentalists such as "progress," "material and cultural improvements," and "the redemption of the Indian." The road, above all, was imagined as critical, linking the village to Taxco's lucrative tourist business.[85] The neighbouring villages of Ixcapuzalco and Pachivia clearly realised the comparative advantage that Cuauhtémoc could lend their rivals and fought back by denying that Ixcateopan contained the tomb and by claiming the last emperor as a native of their own *patrias chicas*.[86] Ixcateopan's municipal power already translated into an undue targeting of subject villages and hamlets for everything from corvée labour to conscription; in the zero-sum game of intervillage politics, any increase in Ixcateopan's power constituted a threat to its neighbours.[87] At the same time, however, Cuauhtémoc's bones were seen as a clear opportunity across the area. "Everybody," mused one villager, "tried to get something out of [Cuauhtémoc]."[88]

Public works, quickly promised, were slow to arrive. Eventually, however, Ixcateopan did get water and sewage works, a generator, a monument, a paved road to Taxco, and a truck service to Iguala. These were not unalloyed blessings: the trucks were owned by the village elites, reinforcing their grasp on local power, and they ran on roads partly built by local forced labour. They enabled, on the other hand, the carpenters trained in the Cultural Missions to set up workshops making *muebles rústicos*, rustic furniture, for the cities. As early as 1951 there were eight such shops, and for all the inroads of deforestation, they endured across the twentieth century.[89] Mass tourism never arrived, but at least once a year, during the February commemorations of Cuauhtémoc, the village hosted a throng of indigenista visitors who brought with them a brief surge of cash. Cuauhtémoc's bones generated intense competition and conflicts within the village. They led to major distortions of village culture. They did, however, also bring the village some of the elusive rural development promised by Alemán's Mexico.

The central significance of the cult that revolved around Ixcateopan lay in this paralleling of the elite mechanisms of nationalism, one by one, at a village

Figure 37.
Dancer and child
commemorate the
birth of Cuauhtémoc,
February 23, 2009.
AP Photo/Eduardo
Verdugo.

level. Some politicians and cultural power brokers in Mexico City engaged in an instrumentalist campaign to profit from the last emperor; so did their village equivalents. Education Secretary José Vasconcelos, distinctly not indigenous, deployed the symbol of Cuauhtémoc when it suited him; so, too, did villagers, for all the reality that "no Indians existed in Ixcateopan."[90] The figure of Cuauhtémoc was subject to intensive symbolic competition by national parties from across the political spectrum; in Ixcateopan both the dominant rancher/townsman group and the *agrarista* opposition formed political parties named after Cuauhtémoc.[91] There was, finally, something of a kulturkampf in metropolitan circles against dissident nonbelievers, focused on the tiresome academics who repeatedly denied the bones' authenticity.[92] This, too, had its village equivalent, and more than one sceptical villager found himself under arrest, accused of the Orwellian crime of "disturbing social order."[93] The cult to Cuauhtémoc was, in short, a cross-class construction, in which a certain amount of primordial material was quarried by elites, reshaped by peasants and bureaucrats, and built into a shaky do-it-yourself edifice. If any of this story's symbolic manipulators can be seen as successful, they were not the elite but these grassroots instrumentalists: everyday people who confronted material and political poverty with self-conscious, half-cynical manipulation of nationalist symbols, for both individual and group advantage. Both the Rodríguez Juárez family and the village did rather well out of Cuauhtémoc, receiving development programmes, monuments, and a newfound political prominence. They invented a vibrant tradition, the dancing for Cuauhtémoc's birth, that drew indigenistas and representatives of indigenous groups from far away every February 23. No amount of academic deconstruction can change that; and for the villagers, irrespective of what one guerrerense called "the quantity of foreign idiots who have written that [the tomb] is a fake," Cuauhtémoc was, is, and always will be buried in Ixcateopan.[94]

Conclusion

The Wealth of Nation Builders

[Nations are] dual phenomena, constructed essentially from above, but which cannot be understood unless also analysed from below, that is in terms of the assumptions, hopes, needs, longings and interests of ordinary people, which are not necessarily national and still less nationalist.

—Eric Hobsbawm, *Nations and Nationalism*

FOR MOST PEOPLE OUTSIDE THE VILLAGE, THE CULT OF CUAUHTÉMOC in Ixcateopan failed. It did not fail as resoundingly as some other nationalist productions, like presidential personality cults. After their power died few cared about Obregón, or Calles, or Alemán, who oversaw his own immortalisation in the names of streets, towns, dams, hagiographies, and an oil tanker (whose maiden voyage ended on Miguel Alemán Pier), who unveiled his own statue, and who lived to see it dragged from its plinth in 1968.[1] Like the emperor himself, the monument to Cuauhtémoc on Avenida Reforma survived the scandal and endured as an emotive, if less than central, symbol of Mexico.[2] Other monuments misfired. Cynics dubbed the unlovely Monument to the Revolution "the petrol station" and dismissed the statues of Ahuizótl and Izcóatl as "the Green Indians," pieces of metal so unwanted that they were moved five times in the last century.[3] Nicknames and jokes counted. They were one of the ways that ordinary Mexicans helped decide which nationalist cults would work and which would not, as the state reliably retired from rituals that did not draw a certain support. This is not surprising: as historians peer beneath the surface of the modern Mexican state they often enough find a popular veto, exercised on unacceptable teachers, bureaucrats, politicians, policies, cultural meddling, and, in this case, myths.[4]

Failure is interesting; most studies of nationalism focus on success stories or avoid the question altogether. Given the raw power of Cuauhtémoc's story, however, it is complicated to explain. He was a contradictory symbol for nation builders: his story meant resistance to most people and yet was also hawked as a morality tale of unification. After the tomb was discovered, intense symbolic competition heightened the contradictions. In campaigning to claim the last emperor as political ancestor, mainstream and fringe parties generated four very different Cuauhtémocs. There was the banal, pro-unity Cuauhtémoc of the state, the radical anti-imperialist Cuauhtémoc of the Left, the anticommunist Catholic/authoritarian of the Right, and the mystical Christ figure invoked by rhetoricians from all camps. Some historians argue that such flexibility makes a symbol stronger; the more meanings, the merrier.[5] Yet Appadurai is right in positing limits to the malleability of the past. For history to sway intellect and emotion four constraints need satisfying, namely, authority (some consensus as to what historical knowledge is), continuity (some consensus as to who interprets that knowledge credibly), depth (time for an interpretation to sink in), and interdependence (some correlation between differing views of the past).[6] All of these constraints were broken in the late 1940s by a historically dubious Cuauhtémoc of multiple meanings and glaring paradoxes. As a result the last emperor became a free-floating signifier, floating too freely to mean much at all. A minority interest, cherished in the main by guerrerenses, indigenistas, and leftists, he ended up more embarrassment than asset to the state. He was, consequently, sidelined by national governments that vigorously pushed safer myths of the long dead or the largely abstract: Hidalgo and Juárez, the Revolution, the Flag, the Soldier.

The fate of Cuauhtémoc's bones mirrored the rise and fall of indigenismo as a central strand of Mexico's official nationalism. As we have seen, indigenistas sought the contradictory goals of promoting Indian culture and history while incorporating Indians into a homogeneous mestizo Mexico. The extraordinary breadth of revolutionary indigenismo, encompassing public health, education, economic modernisation, arts and crafts, archaeology, anthropology, and the cult of ancient great men, was largely anticipated by its Porfirian predecessor, albeit more in word than deed.[7] By the 1890s indigenismo was clearly important enough to the powerful that a provincial rancher tried to recover lands and status by claiming the cult of Cuauhtémoc. Revolutionary politicians extended such claims to the Indian present, carefully speaking the same language as their indigenous recruits: Obregón was fluent in Mayo; Felipe Carrillo Puerto in Maya; Primo Tapia in P'urhépecha; and Gonzalo N. Santos in "Huasteca."[8] Federal and state governments quarrelled over control of the archaeological sites that Mexicans visited in large numbers.[9] Entrepreneurial types engaged in petty social engineering, imposing their idea of indigenous culture: in Hueyapan, Morelos, all seven Nahuatl "folksongs" were written by outsiders like school-teachers or Protestant missionaries.[10] The boss of Oaxaca's Región Mixe kid-napped a composer and jailed him until he produced appropriate indigenous music.[11] Between 1917 and 1950 the state invested heavily in a string of institu-tions—the Dirección de Antropología, the Secretaría de Educación Pública, the Departamento de Asuntos Indígenas, the Instituto Nacional de Antropología e Historia, the Escuela Nacional de Antropología e Historia, and the Instituto Nacional Indigenista—training social scientists and dispatching them to the countryside to promote development and national integration. They were, one anthropologist judged, manufacturing symbols of national distinction while "making the relationship of domination more satisfactory, less conflictive and more profitable"; indigenismo was "the vehicle of the expansion of industriali-sation," and the anthropologist was its driver.[12] Such critiques emerged in the 1970s, helping weaken state claims to legitimacy through indigenismo; by the 1990s political control of Indian symbols had been surrendered to parties like the Ejército Zapatista de Liberación Nacional that fought that state. The entire process, from adoption to quasi-abandonment, had taken about a century.[13]

Mexican indigenismo was admittedly for a long time the most innova-tive and influential in Latin America. Its promoters enjoyed a wealth of raw material, in the remains of highly sophisticated prehispanic cultures, rivalled only by the Andean countries. They invested considerable talent (and, initially at least, comparatively reasonable resources) in cultural and developmentalist programmes to make indigenous populations a central part of Mexico's past and present. Yet the indigenous past failed to move modern Mexicans the way the postcolonial past did. Sociologists in the second half of the twentieth cen-tury found Mexicans more awed by the great men of 1810 and the revolution than by Cuauhtémoc or Nezahualcóyotl.[14] Writers created a well-populated genre, the revolutionary novel, eschewing to some extent indigenous themes.[15] Rulers and ruled consistently collaborated to mount impressive performances of national identity for Cinco de Mayo, Independence Day, and the anniver-sary of the revolution; the indigenous past had no comparable ceremony. The results of the development programmes, moreover, were generally disappointing. The Instituto Nacional Indigenista enjoyed initial successes in its pilot programmes in Chiapas, but within a decade underfunding and local opposition had pushed its ambitious plans into terminal decline.[16] The teacher training offered through indigenous boarding schools was adjudged wholly inadequate, and indigenous teachers often did not want to return to their communities; literacy rates remained stubbornly low. Infant mortality and life expectancy in indigenous communities consistently and significantly lagged those of other Mexicans. Judged by both its potential and its noisy promotion, Mexican indigenismo yielded mediocre results.

Indigenismo was always a fragile plant. Mexico's nationalist projects were inherently centralizing, their promoters aspiring to cultural homogeneity; yet to promote Indian cultures seriously would be to promote a decentralised cultural patchwork encoded, as late as the mid–nineteenth century, in some 182 different languages and whose logical end points might perfectly well include the secession of the Yaqui or of Yucatán.[17] The result was extreme tension between elite aspirations to a Western, implicitly whitened, society and elite claims to a mestizaje with a substantial Indian component. Containing that tension required a nationalist doublethink that permeated official and popular culture in a series of strange juxtapositions. The curators of the Paris pavilion of 1889 mounted a statue of Cuauhtémoc and the pickled head of an Apache. In the 1910s Manuel Gamio described Indian cultures as less evolved than those of the West due to a lack of science and then stated that a lack of science did not connote racial inferiority. In the late 1940s newspapers advertised Belmont cigarettes with a pencil-skirted city girl who smoked one, seemingly unaware of the small Indian by her cocked hip or of the text running "Belmont is as genuinely ours as the costume of a 'Tzotzil' from Tenejapa, Chiapas."[18] Mexicans did not have to rely on such contorted messages of who they were. Most could follow an alternative story of mestizaje, a choice made easier as the census count of the indigenous population showed its steep relative decline, from 18 percent of the total in 1900 to 4 percent by 1960.[19] While indigenismo offered potent but problematic stories of identity, nation builders enjoyed an embarrassment of riches in alternative national symbols that they could, and eventually did, prefer.

It is very probable that Cuauhtémoc's bones contributed to the mid-century decline of indigenismo.[20] Intellectuals since the revolution had been forced to navigate between nationalist and universal criteria of quality; those whose course was adjudged insufficiently nationalist ran distinct risks. When the painter Manuel

Rodríguez Lozano opposed nation-building art in favour of "cosmopolitanism" he was denounced as an unpatriotic homosexual, his career destroyed.[21] Other self-identifying "cosmopolitans," the Contemporaneos group of writers, were admonished for the insufficiently nationalist nature of their work in the early 1930s; some were brought to trial for "outraging public decency" and were forced to resign their sinecures in the education bureaucracy.[22] The pro-authenticity campaigners' proposed tightening of state control of scholarship sparked a very public declaration of intellectual independence, when two hundred scholars signed an open letter defending freedom of speech, arguing that it was unpatriotic to deform scientific research to nationalist ends.[23] "Indigenista propaganda" was, Octavio Paz declared in 1950, "supported by fanatical *criollos* and mestizos, while the Indians have never paid it the slightest attention."[24] Collisions between nationalist would-be censors and scholars did not end overnight; in 1964, for example, Oscar Lewis's study of the Mexico City poor was condemned as "denigrating to the *patria*," its publishers sued, their director fired.[25] Yet the state's control of culture never became totalitarian, and an intellectual opening in the 1950s set up the enduring grasp of a "mafia" of cosmopolitan intellectuals on the high ground of elite culture. (And cosmopolitanism was not confined to high culture: these were also the years of the rise of *rocanrol*.)[26] Indigenista intellectuals like Eulalia Guzmán had little place in the world of Octavio Paz, Carlos Monsiváis, Elena Poniatowska, or Bill Haley, and she ended her life in comparative obscurity, her commemorative bust relegated to the dusty floor of the Ixcateopan ayuntamiento's basement.[27]

Yet, while fraud devalued the cult, it was completely unsurprising that the tomb should be fraudulent. When history is neither "good to think" nor generous with artefacts, cultural nationalists will reengineer it to provide the skeletons on which the flesh of national identity can hang. Forgetting, retelling, inventing, and forging are all key methods, and archaeology, for all its veneer of scientific dispassion—in part because of its veneer of scientific dispassion—is a central discipline. The famous archaeologist Leopoldo Batres, for example, used his expertise to expose prehispanic forgeries while simultaneously committing a monumental fraud himself, adding a fictional fourth floor to the Pyramid of the Sun in Teotihuacán for aesthetic and nationalist impact.[28] Archaeologists in the mid-1940s verified the official fraud of the Niños Héroes, whose alleged remains military diggers plucked at random from a mass grave in Chapultepec Forest.[29] While a nationalist fraud by accident not intention, the main relic of the cult to the Virgen de Guadalupe—Juan Diego's cloak, with its powerful image of an

American Mary—is also a fake of sorts: contemporaries believed it a painting, and the legend of its miraculous genesis is a later century's invention.[30] Major signs for three important icons of Mexican national identity—Cuauhtémoc, the Niños Héroes, and the Virgen de Guadalupe—are, in short, spurious.

Archaeological fraud for nationalist ends is, moreover, confined neither to Mexico nor to the distant past. In 1995 Liana Souvaltzi claimed to have discovered the tomb of Alexander the Great at the Siwa oasis in the western desert of Egypt, avowing that "the discovery of the tomb of Alexander the Great will contribute to our good image abroad. We must be proud to be Greeks." There were, however, no Macedonian elements to the tomb, no references to Alexander in the inscriptions, and the whole site was three hundred years too young.[31] In 2000 Shinichi Fujimura confessed to making dawn visits to his excavations to bury stoneware that lent ancient Japanese society a matchless sophistication.[32] In postwar Bosnia, Semir Osmanagic imagined a mountain near Visoko to be "the Pyramid of the Sun," a similar claim to the national legitimacy and prestige afforded by complex urban antiquity.[33] Such private initiatives are mirrored by some states' systematic distortions of the archaeological record for nationalist ends. The generously funded archaeology departments of Nazi universities, whose personnel doubled between 1933 and 1941, enthusiastically supplied proof of the wide distribution of the "Germanic tribes"; the SS Race and Settlement Office housed a Department of Prehistory, headed by the occultist Karl Wiligut. Their work prompted Soviet archaeologists to similarly imagine the Slavs as dominant in Europe; after the collapse of the Soviet Union, on the other hand, several radical nationalist leaders used their backgrounds in archaeology to oppose Russian dominance. As Neil Silberman observes, "All archaeological stories . . . can be read as narratives of the inevitability of certain lands to be conquered and the right of certain peoples to rule."[34] Forgery is an inevitable corollary of those stories. Fraud lies at the very heart of nationalism: one man's fraud is another man's invention of tradition and a third man's historia patria.

In making the last emperor's tomb, Florentino Juárez provided striking evidence for the idea that such nationalist invention may be a democratic pursuit, open to many.[35] While he started out in the poverty and anonymity of life as a field hand, he ended up a long way from his childhood friends. He became instead Don Florentino, one of the ranchers who ran Ixcateopan; had his lands been of better quality villagers might have called him a hacendado. But in terms of metropolitan politics or high culture, the politics and culture that engage many analysts of nationalism, he remained a *don nadie*, a man from the bottom of society.[36] Juárez was a failing small-town politician from a poor village in a poor state, whose children seemed destined to destroy his would-be dynasty before it took root. The man who seems to have been his patron, General Canuto Neri, was another outsider, an also-ran in the bitter struggles for regional power. And Juárez was not the only minor figure to manipulate Cuauhtémoc. In the history of the Ixcateopan tomb people from across society used the symbol of the last emperor and in doing so helped create and sustain the cult.

Such people are usually hard for historians to see, hiding in the minutiae of local records and the mechanics of minor museums or hinted at in the bureaucratese of routine administration. They seem nonetheless quite common in Mexico. The assumption of coherent, carefully planned and implemented elite instrumentalism, on the other hand, does not always withstand scrutiny. Nationalist products as disparate as 1920s history textbooks, the "India Bonita" competition, the first crop of Rivera murals, and the postrevolutionary cult to Zapata all involved as much messy improvisation as messianic vision.[37] While some famous politicians were enthusiasts for the cult of Cuauhtémoc, it is striking that the most powerful politicians of the day—first Porfirio Díaz, later Miguel Alemán—had remarkably little time for the last emperor. The real enthusiasts were political outcasts and the politically unknown. In similar fashion, the real enthusiasts for pouring over comic books to ensure suitably Mexican messages for the poor were not the state's cultural managers but, rather, the low-ranking, sometimes volunteer, bureaucrats who manned the censorship commission.[38] When the state government of Morelos declared Quetzalcóatl a *morelense* it was not their initiative but that of a village schoolteacher, who claimed the god-king as a native of his adopted home, Amatlán.[39] Claudio Lomnitz has repeatedly argued for the influence of local intellectuals, market vendors, bureaucrats, and the "popular classes" in self-consciously formulating and making tactical use of nationalism. Nationalism can be, Lomnitz notes, evoked and remade when textbooks remember the defiant suicide of a *niño hero*; but it can also be reimagined and used by peasants claiming land, or schools, or exemption from conscription; by market vendors making and hawking patriotic products; by provincial museum directors, whose exhibits demonstrate the centrality of their settlements to national history; or by an everyman with a hangover, pleading to his wife that the night before was Independence Day.[40] Knowing nationalist invention is not necessarily confined to the top of societies; a broad range of classes and status groups can and do use nationalism as a political instrument.

Such types, whom we might divide between grassroots instrumentalists and bureaucratic entrepreneurs, were vital players in this nationalist cult of Cuauhtémoc. Both types have been examined to the limits of the available sources above. Low-level bureaucratic entrepreneurs, in offices ranging from the Department of Primary Education to the Intelligence Service, used great initiative in creating and promoting projects to commemorate Cuauhtémoc. They clearly took such initiatives for aspirational as well as affective reasons. One of the unwritten rules of Mexican political or bureaucratic life was to distinguish oneself while avoiding media, mistakes, and responsibility. This led, in practise, to the popularity of projects that were quick, cheap, visible, and inoffensive.[41] Well-conceived nationalist ceremonial filled these criteria admirably. Grassroots instrumentalists are likewise commonplace in this story. Ixcateopan was notoriously poor in natural resources, a place of rapidly draining rocky soil on hills that blocked access to any significant markets. It was the inspiration of Juárez's family and faction to realise that history itself could be a natural resource and to use that realisation to turn an economic periphery into a symbolic centre. The resulting symbolic capital could be, as we have seen, turned into political position or money.[42]

This analysis has focused in particular on the Juárez family. They were, after all, the inventors and primary promoters of the tomb and its legend. They comprise an unusually well-documented group of grassroots instrumentalists, whose activities stretch across several generations from the 1890s to the present and who illustrate key characteristics of the type. The clan's success was based on acquiring a broader range of cultural tools than the immediate competition, starting with early literacy in an overwhelmingly illiterate village. Florentino Juárez collected an impressive library, some three hundred volumes; he joined the Masons, those carriers of Enlightenment power; and he learned the exotically powerful codes of spiritualism. The sources depict his son Odilón as a wastrel, but he was clearly academically gifted, going to university in Chilpancingo and becoming the village teacher. One grandson, Salvador, passed successfully as a doctor; another, Florentino, as a lawyer; at least one of the great-grandsons, Rafael, is a licenciado. All of the family understood that literacy means great leverage in rural communities; they saw, as a proverb much cited in Mexico holds, that "in the kingdom of the blind the one-eyed man is king." Reading and writing led the Juárez family to political power and wealth. This in turn reinforced family members' quests for comparative educational advantage and gave them all extraordinary access to metropolitan knowledge. They used it to forge professional careers and to adopt nationalist imaginaries, recasting village and national memories to their own, local, instrumental ends.

How can we know whether the creators and promoters of the tomb were straightforward cynics or—at least in part—primordialists, believing in their unbroken connection with the indigenous past and profoundly moved by it? It is impossible to weigh the exact balance of self-interest and sentimentalism underlying the nationalism of dead people who leave relatively paltry records. In the more heartfelt passages that Juárez and his grandson wrote we can glimpse two apparently primordial components. One is the rhetoric of local distinction: the authenticity and quality of regional culture and the overlooked claim of anonymous villagers to consecration in national textbooks. The other is a paean to secular, indigenous resistance to the wealthy, the white, and the foreign, ranging from conquistadors to creoles to modern historians.[43] This echoes the local version of the fiestas patrias, the independence celebrations that—in the mid–twentieth century, at least—allowed villagers to play out a morality tale of the struggle and endurance of los de abajo, the Indian underdogs, and to define that struggle as the main meaning of being Mexican. Stories, ideologies even, of ethnic resistance are common to village intellectuals in Mexico. It is superficial and reductionist to read such ideologies as nothing more than facades for self- or group advancement.[44] The degree of their primordialism, however, is questionable: across Latin America local historians tend to double as political activists, whose history is "not so much an uncompromised reflection upon the past, as a vehicle for changing the course of history."[45] As Brooke Larson has shown, Andean indigenous leaders were driven by political necessity to come up with their own, contestatory meanings of the past.[46] I believe that we should attribute some genuinely affective motives to Florentino Juárez: like better-known fabulists in this history, like Vicente Riva Palacio or B. Traven or Octavio Paz, he realised that the missing grave made Cuauhtémoc's story "a true poem in search of fulfilment."[47] Yet at the same time the predominantly instrumentalist quality of the rancher's behaviour seems clear.

The timing of the forgery is, for a start, deeply revealing. Like many of his elite counterparts, from nineteenth-century liberals to twentieth-century revolutionaries, Juárez only turned to forging the nation when in trouble, as Ixcapuzalco seceded in the early 1890s. His hold on the village, its neighbours, and his lands was gravely threatened by the secession crisis. Cuauhtémoc's tomb was his riposte. The collective and individual instrumentalism of his forgery was innovative but not exceptional. Similar instrumentalist use of history can be found across the Mexican countryside. It can reach heights of unabashed cynicism: in Xochistlahuaca, Guerrero, the plum role of Cuauhtémoc in the two-day "indigenous" Dance of the Conquest is traditionally claimed by men from the tiny mestizo minority. (The role, they explain, "calls for a more imposing individual, tall and with a strong voice.")[48] More common, perhaps, is the blend of self-interest and existential belief that characterises the local intellectuals of Tepoztlán, Morelos, who have for generations "played Indian" to live up to metropolitan expectations, claiming in return material benefits that range from communal lands to tourism to the cancellation of a golf course development.[49]

This strategy, the fusion of rich local detail with a fictitious, metropolitan idea of "the Indian," also underlay Cuauhtémoc's tomb. And that fiction is the most powerful argument against a primordial interpretation of that fraud. Primordial nationalism is at root the product of powerful cultural continuities. While ethnic identity is a continuum rather than a dichotomy (and one prone to marked conceptual slippage), it is difficult to argue that Juárez lived in an Indian village. While villagers still explained much conflict and resistance in ethnic terms—Aztec or Mazahua versus Chontal, Indians versus creoles and Spanish—Ixcateopan was a mestizo cabecera that dominated and economically exploited neighbouring, more "indigenous," subject villages.[50] Juárez had weak links to the Indian past and present: he did not appear indigenous in dress, phenotype, or practices; he did not speak Nahuatl every day and may not have been able to speak it at all; and his interest in regional indigenous culture was that of a sympathetic outsider, a collector of folklore on a modest scale. The rancher made a rational-choice calculation of the benefits of an "Indian" ethnic identity and—in the legend of Ixcateopan, at least—adopted one. Communities across the Americas faced similar choices: in late-nineteenth-century Bolivia, for example, local Aymara leaders claimed a new identity as Incas, the ethnicity glorified by their Liberal rulers.[51] Such cases are examples of what Pierre van den Berghe has called the individual choice model of ethnic identity, whereby that identity is

the result of individuals making more or less conscious decisions dictated by their perceptions of their self-interest. . . . In numerous situations, individuals are found consciously to manipulate ethnic boundaries to their advantage. The way they dress, talk and behave shifts abruptly and predictably depending on the context. Many people literally "commute" culturally between ethnies, presenting an assimilated front in one situation, but being "traditional" in another (Colby and van den Berghe, 1969; Philip Mayer, 1961). Sometimes this strategy is subtle and requires the precise opposite of assimilation. If the dominant group rewards "traditional" behaviour, this calls for "playing the native."[52]

This was Juárez's choice. He was ahead of his time, as this strategy was soon found across revolutionary society. Society women like Frida Kahlo pushed their Mexican credentials with elaborate neo-indigenous costumes; it became something of a formula for peasants petitioning the government to claim indigenous credentials.[53] Don Florentino was not the only grassroots instrumentalist in this history: after the tomb find the entire village followed his lead. Many were sceptical beforehand, as evinced by their initial silence with Eulalia Guzmán or by their near-riotous opposition to the destruction of the altar. Afterward, however, the rewards of being Indian were self-evident. Village elders moved from vague recollections of Don Florentino's words to a new precision. The sacristan remembered how after 1949, "when there was a change or, well, a revision [in the legend] that some of the older gentlemen came up with, they took it as something new, as something that drew their attention, and then they remembered and began to relate that [Cuauhtémoc's cortege] took so many days' march and that they walked at night and such-like."[54] The letters that villagers wrote to politicians asking for aid were filled with proclamations of Indian identity; when they pleaded for the president to recognise the tomb's authenticity they asked "that he take into account the clamorous petition of this indigenous village forgotten for centuries and centuries and do it justice."[55] Their would-be monopoly on the Indian past was meanwhile contested by neighbouring villages, the long-standing rivals of Ixcapuzalco and Pachivia, which both claimed Cuauhtémoc for themselves. People across the region set out to rewind history and to remake themselves—fleetingly, often on paper, usually just for the government—as Indian.

In this sense, of course, the tomb owed to Mexico's rulers: the grassroots instrumentalists who produced or promoted it were bidding for state favour, and official history, rhetoric and practices were both their ingredients and their specifications. Juárez needed to know what nationalist expectations his legend should live up to; the late-nineteenth-century texts flowing from Mexico City and Chilpancingo gave him answers. The novels and histories of Vicente

Riva Palacio told readers of the biography of Cuauhtémoc, the outlines of his culture, the mystery of his missing grave, and his central place in being Mexican. Manuel Payno's great novel, *Los bandidos de Río Frío*, may well have given Juárez a plot. The state government's weekly gazette, above all, must have been critical, blending practical information with political news and nationalist instruction. Its pages contained abundant stories, ideas, and words for local leaders to adopt.[56] Such gazettes transmitted the state's cultural nationalism from metropolis to village. But in those villages people like Florentino Juárez took up that nationalism and made it their own, blending high and political and popular culture to come up with something distinctive. His bricolage in turn influenced elite ideas of the nation.

This does not necessarily change the way we think of nation building. Different nationalisms take different courses, and the mechanisms analysed above may be of greater or lesser importance in Bosnia, or India, or the United States. It remains clear that elites start modern national identities, patching together tradition and invention into would-be useful myths. The extent to which the ruled consume those myths determines nationalism's success. Yet the ruled are more than mere consumers. In this case, at least, they were also the producers. Such grassroots instrumentalists may not always succeed: Florentino Juárez's creation brought him no benefit at all. But neither—unlike failed attempts to manipulate religion, or revolution—did it carry much risk or cost him that much. And when nationalism works, it can bring its makers advancement and wealth, no matter who they are, which encourages, in modern Mexico at least, a wealth of nation builders.

Appendix

The Florentino Juárez Journals

The content of these documents is strange and lends itself to lengthy study.
—Silvio Zavala, "Dictamen acerca del hallazgo de Ichcateopan"

I. Instructions of Don Florentino Juárez to his children on leaving in their care the documents referring to Cuauhtémoc

The living letter which our forebears bequeathed us with four pages which are in a leather cover and which speak, so they said, of Padre Motolinía; until the living letter could no more, he wrote in a prayer book and there are the notes; there remain the village's titles which I keep; the documents which they gave out in Mexico when they protested against the decisions of a padre are also copied there.

I copy these documents just as they are and I write down my understanding of these secrets in order that they might be preserved given the hazard of the revolution, and should these documents come to fall into the hands of the revolutionaries, whosoever they be, I beg them not to destroy them, to put them in the hands of the civil or military authorities, or in the hands of the priests; this is interesting and [concerns] a long-talked of living letter which a missionary father left among the Indians.

A blank sheet of paper closed with thread, of which I neither understand nor know anything, is the most interesting; by accord of the elders I guard [it] from that village which became the bitter enemy of the sons of Ixcateopan. My father Amado Juárez handed over these documents to me together with some older ones which told me of an empty page which is stuck together; this is interesting and gives the facts of everything.

II. The manuscript of the hide folder, attributed to the Franciscan Motolinía

f.1 I leave these writings with these natives that they might keep them as a record that these poor miserable Indians might know the great treasure and fortune that this land has to be the cradle of their lord king Cuatemo, whom I hold as a man of much courage and much decency; whom I admire in this land of Ychicateopan. They told me that his father and his mother who only lived here th . . . years are here that she was called Cuallautital which means *cuatlaute*, [a] tree of fine and beautiful scent that the said tree is in the house of their lord and is ten men wide . . . jewellery of precious stones carved statues of their gods in black and green stone . . . very fine cloths of colours and feathers

f.2 of beautiful birds which I saw I note all of this that these poor Indians might in coming years have their natural laws honoured and that they honour for his courage their lord king Cuactemo, native of this country. The natives told me that his race was the Chontals they ruled all this land from Zacaulpan and Chulacuton [?] to Acamista and Cataguatla [?] along the river up to the big [*sic*] this place is called Zonpancuali, that is Ychatecmoteopan which means, here is Your lord King Cuactemo, it is also said that it is called Zonpancuaguil and means that his *penza* is silver because its form is a scorpion from the tail and its bread the goldmine and purple stone; these lands also have much woodland of cedar and oak its products are bees' honey and the fine scents of . . .

f.3 Noone may write this down this because I have it forbidden to write the life of this Lord King for the mere love of my sons; and by God I am not afraid of the henchmen of the Santo Oficio; I leave in these miserable Chontal Indians I, the Reverend Father Motolinía. (signature)

f.4 Their emissaries told me that their lord king Cuactemo died hanged and afterwards for many days they walked with him on their backs wrapped in rich cloths of these lands his bones were kept for a long time in his palace until I ordered that the many bones which lay abandoned be burnt, I order and bury the remains of this lord king Cuatemo in this place that the natives might have respect for everything and that [their] faith in God might have foundations; having his holy church where the remains of this king and lord of the Chontals, brave and highly distinguished in all they do, lie buried; this country has everything beautiful and pleasing, rich in trees with fine wood, many brown and very fine people very charitable very pious in the charity of God

These days are of holy festivals and in their course everyone is baptised in church and if we were dividing we would not have the people of this land.

f.5 There were many people for the burial of the remains of their lord king Cuatemo. He was buried and not burnt like the other remains which were abandoned I ordered more than one thousand five hundred skulls burned and five days later I buried the remains of this lord king everyone from this country came and there was peace in this land of Ychcateopan formerly Zonpancuagli.

29 December 1523

I the Reverend Father Motolinía (signature)
Written entry the only one which I write and bless in the name of God
I the Reverend Father Motolinía

f.6 The truth of these things is this that I write on this paper for my beloved sons in Jesus Christ because they are so humble, obedient to my word of God; there lie in this land the foundations of the church of God which they begin to lay with great love and charity in all that God and Santa María de la Asuncíon who I leave as patron saint of these lands of Ychcateopan which in the Chontal language means Ychcatemoteopan which means here is your lord king Cuactemo; for this reason I write this document and I leave it in the hands of my native sons of this blessed land by command of the king of Spain and the bounty of God this favourite of this land of the Chontal Indians . . .

Ychcateopan December 1523 I
Reverend Father Motolinía (signature)

III. The fragmentary manuscript in invisible ink

Lord God in whom I place. . . . and all my hope . . . Santa de . . . Puebla de los . . . 1,537, By the bounty of. . . . to God. . . . time will tell what. . . . I bur. . . . King. . . . my Lord God. . . . this Holy tomb of. . . . your Servant in Jesus Christ our Lord

Amen.

Shower your grace on these sons and love for your holy m . . . amen a 15,37

IV. The letter of the reliquary

Lord Holy God in whom I place all my love and hope and salvation. Puebla de los Angeles 1,537 By the Holy grace of God I Leave to my sons that Remembrance and blessing to my beloved Sons in Jesus Christ which is the immortal Record that in 1529 Ychicatupan I buried Lord King Cuatemo 29 December 1,525 Time will tell what I saw and did love for these poor Indians may they return to their land blessed by God love to the people of Zonpancuaguitl.

Provincial Governor 1537

Father Toribio Motolinía	these my sons
Gobernador pal.	Juan y Cruz
(signature)	sons by Jesus Christ
of Zonpancuacuitl.	

V. Alleged court records from the late colony concerning a dispute between the villagers of Ixcateopan and their parish priest

The year 1809[1]

In this royal court the commissions of the native sons of Ixcateopan in the province of Santa María de la Asunción presented themselves and said they were native sons of that province where they have great respect and veneration for their church for which reason they beg that the parish priest be ordered not to destroy the main altar of that church.

The gentleman José Amado and José stated that they keep ashes very sacred to them; for which reason it is ordered that that altar not be destroyed, that everything that was burnt and destroyed in the fire be replaced, although the walls be covered with tiling and not *zacate* as before; but without digging in the place which the natives claim with much eagerness; they say that they do not present documents as they do not know their whereabouts, that they swear by God the truth of what they say and do not sign as they do not know [how], and the other due to diminished sight; I do so as does my attendant.

August 20 1810.
Manuel de la Concha
Diego de Ocampo.
Attendant,
Lucas de Aguado.

VI. Testament of Florentino Juárez

My children the greatest and most momentous concern of my soul, it is lamentable and painful that [of] my sons, Florencio should be bad-natured and envious; Odilón and Leopoldo are drinkers for which reason I leave [this legacy] to my daughters Jovita, Alberta and María Inés Juárez. I leave to the hands of Jovita the greatest treasures of Ixcateopan that they might keep them with the greatest respect and vigilance, zeal, daily light [candles], incense, the treasures of justification of our generation.

The male child who stains the good name of his father and takes from my daughters the treasure which I leave with them, and later may come to take away the legacy which I give to my daughters, of my belongings [with] which our Lord God has succoured me; should he do this, water and salt will turn on him and he will end up degenerate and I will not recognise him as my son before neither God nor the lords of the world.

January 7th 1914
Florentino Juárez (signature)

VII. The Florentino Juárez journals, volume 1 of 5

f.1 Notes which I make referring to the accounts which the elders of Ixcateopan gave me. I write them in the *capire comisaría* of Izcapuzalco, Odilón please put these notes into a notebook of clean paper for me and hand them over to Jovita in order that she might put them together with the papers which you know are the village's property.

your father
Florentino Juárez
(signature)

Send Federico Brito with paper, envelopes and a pencil; I don't have paper.

f.2 Notes of the conversations of the elders when they delivered me the papers.

The elders told me, when they delivered the secrets of the village, that they had these facts by custom.

They told me that a young king who was called Cuauhtémoc had from these parts ascended to the throne; that this young man was between 23 and 25 years of age and had been called to Méjico that he might give aid in the wars of the conquistadores and that he remained there many days fulfilling his duty. For a while after he went, he bore his responsibility; he was intrepid, valiant, very brave and they told me that he was a young man at the outset of life, who was never married to any lady; he kept his youth and was from these parts; that after a certain time he was de—

f.3 -feated by the forces of don Fernando Cortés and that he was [defeated] that they had him tortured and went as far as to burn his feet making him walk in the company of other lords; after several days march they wanted to baptise him and he did not consent; he was unconquerable, he had the gift of being very pure, in speech he never used bad words, and [while] travelling as a prisoner they denounced him, and [said] to don Fernando Cortés that this young king was going to rebel against his rule and then the petty and evil man Cortés hanged him in the company of other mexican lords, and he hanged the young king and he stayed hanging hanging [sic] for more than thirteen days and that between 25 and 30 deserters stole him [his body] and wrapped him in blankets, and they f.4   brought him walking by little known paths whence they arrived at Zacualpan, after having walked about 46 days, and that they had him hidden in that village of Zacualpan about 40 days, wrapped in leaves from aromatic trees; and suddenly the leaders of the conquistadores and the soldiers approached and took Zacualpan, being in pursuit of the deserters; they found nothing as the same deserters had brought him by another route and they had hidden him in the same manner in a place called Tlapacolla; the group of men and women who adored that young king stayed there, growing in number; many families left their homes and stood together where the body of the young king lay; after many days they moved him to Alpichafia, where there was then a large and [well-]known village in that time, the body having remained in a spot which they called tescal, Tescal Tenancingo; they said that they drank water and all the people sighed without weeping, because some of the deserters told them how the king had died, this they told

f.5   to the people who were joining them, and then they climbed on foot to the highland which was called the Tecampana, where they spent a long time worshipping and playing ancient instruments of their times; there before them was a tribe which had risen; all of a sudden they received surprising news from the Sompanchagüitl and got up leaving behind many things, jewels and musical instruments which they lost in that place.

     Carrying the body in the same way as before, [they went] to a place in the highland called Chinaucla, where they were a long time, the people who were there worshipping their dead king were already many, when after many days that they were there in that place a dreadful plague struck which forced them to bury many bodies in that place; they told me that they did not know the place, that they only knew that it was on the way to Acatempa and that it had as an address the name Chinaucla, which was [means] stone snake and that there were in that place many tombs because of the plague.

     For this reason they returned to Sompancuagüitl which was the birthplace of this lord king; they carried him in the same manner and he was left in his own f.6   Palace in Cuayuatitla, where he was kept for a long time; and the people, after being as it were in peace for a while, guarding the remains of the king, according to what they told me, in 1529 the Indians, in fear of the plague which struck them in Cinaucla [*sic*], scattered and set off for their homes leaving the remains of the king in this his land; it was a place where many people lived. Some of the deserters having instructed the people, they went to the conquistadores, with whom there came some Friars who spent some time in this place; and then they say that they [the friars] buried the remains of the king and suffered the Indians to never reveal these secrets to anyone; they also told me that on leaving they took with them two Indians to Mexico where they remained a long time as slaves, and afterwards a missionary father took them to a place which they called de los Angeles; according to what they told me this was Puebla; there these [men] were taught to read, to do many things which the father who came to this place and went to los Angeles taught them; they only told me that he was very poor and a young man with great sympathy for the poor Indians; this is what the elders told me, that that missionary father was the same one who had come to these

f.7   lands [and] to whom we owe the favours of which they so much reminded me;[2] each time they spoke to me bathed in tears and weeping greatly, they were telling me the feelings of their heart, each time that they related me these things the old men had to cry and they made me cry with them as often as I had to hear these things; they said to me; my son, our fatherland, our race suffered greatly; they held us a long time, we know not how to count the years, that which the elders as we are [now] told us [in our turn], my son, was of the vast bitterness and pain which our race suffered, that they had us as dumb beasts; they branded our ancestors as one would brand an animal.

They told me these things and advised me that afterwards when I were old I should relate all these conversations to the young men; they told me many things which I do not remember any more; they told me how they brought the dead king from the place where they hanged him and all this they told me bathed in tears f.8 we used to finish the history in floods of tears which I did not understand, because such was the pain which pierced the soul of those old men.

I believed with all my heart; they told me; it was not one or two, they were many the elders who put their trust in me and I had the good fortune to know from the mouths of the elders this which astonished me, and I dare to write down the stories which they told me they knew as one knows a prayer.

f.9 They told me that on Shrove Tuesday the 26th of February 1525 the king died hanged in a place which I do not know by name.

They told me that on Shrove Tuesday, a moveable feast, being always a Tuesday, we pay the mass in honour of the soul of our king and thus have I always done until the present.

f.10 Because of my activities and the dangers of my situation I pay this mass today Shrove Tuesday in Ixcapuzalco and I hope, God willing, that it may be thus in years to come.

Note: Documents I, V, VI, and VII are written in pencil in a notebook, in handwriting that according to Salvador Rodríguez Juárez is that of Odilón Juárez, son of Don Florentino Juárez, whose signature appears at the end. Document II is written in ink on six pages, accompanied by a blank seventh page, which are sewn into a hide folder; document III is written in an invisible ink composed primarily of apple and lemon juice; document IV is written in ink on a half sheet of colonial-period paper, folded into a small reliquary.

Notes

Introduction

1. This has met, of course, with varying degrees of success. I call the nation-state a "thing" in the interest of simplicity; this does not endorse its reification. A Germanic compound noun—"idea-thing"?—might be more accurate. For the state as fiction rather than agency, see Derek Sayer, "Everyday Forms of State Formation: Some Dissident Remarks on 'Hegemony,'" in *Everyday Forms of State Formation: Revolution and the Negotiation of Rule in Modern Mexico*, ed. Gilbert M. Joseph and Daniel Nugent (Durham, N.C.: Duke University Press, 1994), 371.

2. For the recent and elite origins of genocidal nationalism in former Yugoslavia, see Noel Malcolm, *Bosnia: A Short History* (London: Macmillan, 1994); for a critique of British policy there, see Brendan Simms, *Unfinest Hour: Britain and the Destruction of Bosnia* (London: Allen Lane, 2001).

3. Darryl Li, "Echoes of Violence: Considerations on Radio and Violence in Rwanda," *Journal of Genocide Research* 6, no. 1 (March 2004): 9–27.

4. Anatol Lieven, *America Right or Wrong: An Anatomy of American Nationalism* (Oxford: Oxford University Press, 2005).

5. V. A. Schnirelman, "From Internationalism to Nationalism: Forgotten Pages of Soviet Archaeology in the 1930s and 1940s," in *Nationalism, Politics, and the Practice of Archaeology*, ed. P. L. Kohl and C. Fawcett (Cambridge: Cambridge University Press, 1995), 130–38.

6. Anthony D. Smith, "Nationalism and the Historian," in *Ethnicity and Nationalism*, ed. Anthony D. Smith (Leiden: E. J. Brill, 1992), 58–75.

7. Anthony D. Smith, *Nations and Nationalism in a Global Era* (Cambridge, U.K.: Polity Press, 1995); Ernst Gellner, *Culture, Identity, and Politics* (Cambridge: Cambridge University Press, 1987); Eric Hobsbawm and Terence Ranger, eds., *The Invention of Tradition* (Cambridge: Cambridge University Press, 1983); Eric Hobsbawm, *Nations and Nationalism since 1780: Programme, Myth, Reality* (Cambridge: Cambridge University Press, 1990); Benedict Anderson, *Imagined Communities: Reflections on the Origin and Spread of Nationalism* (London: Verso, 1991).

8. A minor variant of primordialism is sociobiological, positing that cultural markers function like phenotypic markers for extended kin, pushing individuals toward cooperative behaviour to maximise the transmission of common genes. Anthony D. Smith, *Nationalism: Theory, Ideology, History* (Cambridge, U.K.: Polity Press, 2001), 51–54.

9. Smith ("Nationalism and the Historian," 58–75) argues that this ignores long-term continuities of myth, landholding, and name.

10. Hobsbawm, *Nations and Nationalism since 1780*, 9–11; Eric Hobsbawm, "Introduction: Inventing Traditions," in *Invention of Tradition*, Hobsbawm and Ranger, 1–14.

11. Thomas Stearns Eliot, "Hamlet and His Problems," in *The Sacred Wood: Essays on Poetry and Criticism* (London: Methuen and Co. Ltd., 1920), 92.

12. Gellner, *Culture, Identity, and Politics*, 16.

13. Anderson, *Imagined Communities*, 6.

14. Anderson, *Imagined Communities*, 47–65; Sara Castro-Klarén and John Charles Chasteen, *Beyond Imagined Communities: Reading and Writing the Nation in Nineteenth-Century Latin America* (Washington, D.C.: Woodrow Wilson Center Press, 2003), xix–xx.

15. Francois-Xavier Guerra, "Forms of Communication, Political Spaces, and Cultural Identities in the Creation of Spanish American Nations," in *Beyond Imagined Communities*, Sarah Castro-Klarén and John Charles Chasteen, 6.

16. Claudio Lomnitz, *Deep Mexico, Silent Mexico: An Anthropology of Nationalism* (Minneapolis: University of Minnesota Press, 2001), 23, 29–32. For a comprehensive overview, see David Brading, *The First America: The Spanish Monarchy, Creole Patriots, and the Liberal State, 1492–1867* (Cambridge: Cambridge University Press, 1991).

17. Michiel Baud, "Beyond Benedict Anderson: Nation-Building and Popular Democracy in Latin America," *International Review of Social History* 50 (2005): 385–498.

18. Lomnitz, *Deep Mexico, Silent Mexico*, 3.

19. Benedict Anderson, cited in Ana María Alonso, "The Politics of Space, Time and Substance: State Formation, Nationalism, and Ethnicity," *Annual Review of Anthropology*, 1994: 379.

20. For Villa's ambivalent status, see Leticia Mayer, "El proceso de recuperación simbólica de cuatro héroes de la Revolución Mexicana de 1910 a través de la prensa nacional," *Historia Mexicana* 45, no. 2 (October–December 1995): 375–78.

21. Rafael Segovia, *La politización del niño mexicano* (Mexico City, 1975), 89–94; Ulises Beltrán, "El *ranking* de los héroes patrios," *Nexos*, September 2001: 93–94.

22. The Virgin of Guadalupe was not a master symbol for indigenous communities until comparatively recently. Brading deems seventeenth-century creole patriotism a protonationalism; Knight dates the "cultural revolution" underpinning Mexico's nation-state to the mid–eighteenth century. William B. Taylor, "The Virgin of Guadalupe in New Spain: An Inquiry into the Social History of Marian Devotion," *American Ethnologist* 14, no. 1 (February 1987): 9–33; David Brading, *The Origins of Mexican Nationalism* (Cambridge: Cambridge University Press, 1985), 1–24; Alan Knight, "Weapons and Arches in the Mexican Revolutionary

Landscape," in *Everyday Forms of State Formation*, Gilbert M. Joseph and Daniel Nugent, 54–65.

23. It can be seen as successful in comparison to earlier unifying ideologies in Meso-america and other Latin American nationalisms, though this success has, Alan Knight believes, been overstated. The urban populations surveyed by Almond and Verba had revealingly powerful "affective orientations" toward key components of Mexican nationalism such as the revolution. David Brading, *Prophecy and Myth in Mexican History* (Cambridge: Cambridge University Press, 1984); Rebecca Earle, "Creole Patriotism and the Myth of the 'Loyal Indian,'" *Past and Present* 172 (August 2001): 129; Alan Knight, "Peasants into Patriots: Thoughts on the Making of the Mexican Nation," *Mexican Studies/Estudios mexicanos* 10, no. 1 (Winter 1994): 141; Jacques Lafaye, *Quetzalcóatl y Guadalupe: La formación de la conciencia nacional en México* (Mexico City, 1995), 19, 418; Florencia Mallon, *Peasant and Nation: The Making of Postcolonial Mexico and Peru* (Berkeley: University of California Press, 1995), 15–19; Ilene O'Malley, *The Myth of the Revolution: Hero Cults and the Institutionalization of the Mexican State, 1920–1940* (New York: Greenwood Press, 1986); Guy P. C. Thomson, "Bulwarks of Patriotic Liberalism: The National Guard, Philharmonic Corps and Patriotic Juntas in Mexico, 1847–1888," *Journal of Latin American Studies* 22, no. 1 (1990): 31–68; Alan Knight, "The Weight of the State in Modern Mexico," in *Studies in the Formation of the Nation State in Latin America*, ed. James Dunkerley (London: Institute of Latin American Studies, 2002), 252; Nicola Miller, *In the Shadow of the State: Intellectuals and the Quest for National Identity in Twentieth-Century Spanish America* (London: Verso, 1999), 245; Gabriel Almond and Sidney Verba, *The Civic Culture: Political Attitude and Democracy in Five Nations* (Newbury Park, Calif.: Sage Publications, 1989), 41, 203, 310, 363.

24. Guillermo Prieto, cited in Agustín Basave Benítez, *México mestizo* (Mexico City, 1990), 23–28.

25. Enrique Florescano, *Etnia, estado y nación* (Mexico City, 1997), 370, 433–49.

26. Eyler Simpson, cited in Guillermo Palacios, "Postrevolutionary Intellectuals, Rural Readings and the Shaping of the 'Peasant Problem' in Mexico: El Maestro Rural, 1932–1934," *Journal of Latin American Studies* 30, no. 2 (May 1998): 322; Frank Tannenbaum, *Mexico: The Struggle for Peace and Bread* (New York: Alfred A. Knopf, 1950), 6, 15.

27. Octavio Paz, *The Labyrinth of Solitude* (New York: Grove Press, 1985), 7–28; Nathan Whetten, cited in Knight, "Weight of the State in Modern Mexico," 213.

28. Enrique Florescano, *El poder y la lucha por el poder en la historiografía mexicana* (Mexico City, 1980), 78–79.

29. Mauricio Tenorio-Trillo, cited in William French, "Imagining and the Cultural History of Nineteenth-Century Mexico," *Hispanic American Historic Review* 79, no. 2 (May 1999): 253; Adrian A. Bantjes, "The Eighth Sacrament: Nationalism and Revolutionary Political Culture in Mexico," in *Citizens of the Pyramid: Essays on Mexican Political Culture*, ed. Wil Pansters (Amsterdam: Thela Pub, 1997), 138.

30. Castro-Klarén and Chasteen, *Beyond Imagined Communities*, xviii–xix.

31. Although it is one with limits. Arjun Appadurai, "The Past as a Scarce Resource," *Man* 16, no. 2 (1981): 201–19.

32. Peter Guardino, *Peasants, Politics and the Formation of Mexico's National State: Guerrero, 1800–1857* (Stanford, Calif.: Stanford University Press, 1996), 82.

33. Michael T. Ducey, *A Nation of Villages: Riot and Rebellion in the Mexican Huasteca, 1750–1850* (Tucson: University of Arizona Press, 2004), 5, 9.

34. Thomson, "Bulwarks of Patriotic Liberalism"; Patrick McNamara, *Sons of the Sierra: Juárez, Díaz, and the People of Itxlán, Oaxaca, 1855–1920* (Chapel Hill: University of North Carolina Press, 2007), 17–20, 93–121.

35. Lomnitz, *Deep Mexico, Silent Mexico*, 263–86; Claudio Lomnitz-Adler, *Exits from the Labyrinth: Culture and Ideology in the Mexican National Space* (Berkeley: University of California Press, 1992), 24–227.

36. Mallon, *Peasant and Nation*, 5.

37. Knight, "Weight of the State in Modern Mexico," 242.

38. Eric Van Young, *The Other Rebellion*, 127–40, 497–504; Brading, *Prophecy and Myth in Mexican History*, 63–82; Knight, "Peasants into Patriots," 141–48.

39. Mallon, *Peasant and Nation*, 18, 96–98. Frank O'Gorman likewise suggests that a viable electoral culture can be a cornerstone of nationalism. Frank O'Gorman, "The Culture of Elections in England: From the Glorious Revolution to the First World War, 1688–1914," in *Elections before Democracy: The History of Elections in Europe and Latin America*, ed. Eduardo Posada Carbó (London: Institute of Latin American Studies, 1996), 28–30.

40. Ricardo Pérez Montfort, "Indigenismo, Hispanismo y Panamericanismo en la cultura popular Mexicana de 1920 a 1940," in *Cultura e identidad nacional*, ed. Roberto Blancarte (Mexico City, 1994), 364–67.

41. S. Hall, cited in *Everyday Forms of State Formation*, ed. Gilbert M. Joseph and Daniel Nugent, 17; Patrick Hutton, "The History of Mentalities: The New Map of Cultural History," *History and Social Theory* 2, no. 3 (October 1981): 247; Mikhail Bakhtin, cited in Carlo Ginzburg, *The Cheese and the Worms: The Cosmos of a Sixteenth-Century Miller* (Baltimore, Md.: Johns Hopkins University Press, 1992), xii.

42. Benjamin Smith, "Cardenismo, Caciques and Catholicism: The Politics of State-Building in Oaxaca" (D.Phil. thesis, Cambridge University, 2005), 188–89; Aaron Van Oosterhout and Benjamin T. Smith, "The Limits of Catholic Science and the Mexican Revolution," *Endeavour* 34, no. 2 (June 2010): 57.

43. Elsie Rockwell, "Schools of the Revolution: Enacting and Contesting State Forms in Tlaxcala, 1910–1930," in *Everyday Forms of State Formation*, ed. Gilbert M. Joseph and Daniel Nugent, 193–94; *Excélsior*, June 19, 1951; Benjamin Smith, "Inventing Tradition at Gunpoint: Culture, *Caciquismo* and State Formation in the Región Mixe, Oaxaca (1930–1959)," *Bulletin of Latin American Research* 27, no. 2 (2008): 224.

44. Secretaría de Educación Pública, *Los Hallazgos de Ichcateopan: Actas y dictámenes de la Comisión Investigadora* (Mexico City, 1962), 313.

45. Knight, "Weapons and Arches in the Mexican Revolutionary Landscape," 63.

46. Mayer, "El proceso de recuperación simbólica de cuatro héroes," 364–65; Friedrich Katz, *The Life and Times of Pancho Villa* (Stanford, Calif.: Stanford University Press, 1998), 769; Samuel Brunk, "Remembering Emiliano Zapata: Three Moments in the Posthumous Career of the Martyr of Chinameca," *Hispanic American Historical Review* 78, no. 3 (August 1998): 459–75.

47. Inspector Abel Bautista Reyes to Secretaría de Educación Pública, September 15, 1927, SEP caja 1668, ant. 1340, exp. 12-6-8-10.

48. Mary Kay Vaughan, "The Construction of the Patriotic Festival in Tecamachalco, Puebla, 1900–1946," in *Rituals of Rule, Rituals of Resistance: Public Celebrations and Popular Culture in Mexico*, ed. William H. Beezley, Cheryl E. Martin, and William E. French (Wilmington, Del.: Scholarly Resources, 1994), 216.

49. Vicente Riva Palacio and Juan de Dios Peza, *Tradiciones y Leyendas Mexicanas* (Mexico City, 1996), introduction; Claudia Fernández and Andrew Paxman, *El Tigre: Emilio Azcárraga y su imperio Televisa* (Mexico City, 2000), 62; Anne Rubenstein, *Bad Language, Naked Ladies, and Other Threats to the Nation: A Political History of Comic Books in Mexico* (Durham, N.C.: Duke University Press, 1998), 127–28; memos, August 14 and 17, 1948, AGN/DGIPS-111/2–1/260/82.

50. Subrata K. Mitra, "The Rational Politics of Cultural Nationalism: Subnational Movements of South Asia in Comparative Perspective," *British Journal of Political Science* 25, no. 1 (January 1995): 60.

51. Mitra, "Rational Politics of Cultural Nationalism," 63.

52. Miguel Angel Cevallos, *Excélsior*, October 17, 1949.

53. Arturo Arnáiz y Freg, *La Prensa*, September 26, 1949.

54. These include Eduardo Matos Moctezuma, Salvador Rueda, Guillermo Bonfil Batalla, and Gonzalo Aguirre Beltrán.

55. Harold Pinter, *Collected Works: One* (New York: Grove Weidenfeld, 1976), 11.

56. Clifford Geertz, "Thick Description: Towards an Interpretive Theory of Culture," in *The Interpretation of Cultures* (New York: Basic Books, 1973), 20.

57. Arthur Hocart argues that circumstantial evidence has been underrated: "Proof does not consist in seeing: it consists in providing so complete an explanation of the evidence of our senses that no better alternative can be thought of. . . . [C]ircumstantial evidence is not an inferior substitute for the evidence of eyes and ears: it is the very foundation of science" ("Evidence in Human History," in *Kings and Councillors*, ed. Rodney Needham [Chicago: University of Chicago Press, 1970], 28).

58. Dr. Watson, for example, is a classic unreliable narrator, clueless or wrong about events as they unfold; while Sherlock Holmes, Pierre Bayard argues, makes "countless mistakes" in the course of his career, "illustrating all the weaknesses of [his] method" (*Sherlock Holmes Was Wrong: Reopening the Case of the Hound of the Baskervilles* [New York: Bloomsbury, 2008], 45).

Chapter 1

1. Hernán Cortés, *Cartas de Relación*, 2 vols. (Madrid, 1940), 1:168–237, 2:1–65.

2. Bernal Díaz del Castillo, *The Conquest of New Spain* (Harmondsworth, U.K.: Penguin, 1963), 7, 44, 203. In 1540 Bernal Díaz himself would be deemed by one royal bureaucrat to have not been a conquistador at all. Miguel León-Portilla, "Presencia de Bernal Díaz del Castillo (1496–1584)," *Vuelta*, January 1985: 29.

3. Fernando Alvarado Tezozómoc, *Crónica Mexicáyotl* (Mexico City, 1975), 146.

4. José Luis Martínez, *Hernán Cortés* (Mexico City, 1990), 71–72, 109; Jacques Lafaye, *Quetzalcóatl y Guadalupe: La formación de la conciencia nacional en México* (Mexico City, 1995), 273.

5. Jacques Soustelle, *La vida cotidiana de los aztecas en vísperas de la Conquista* (Mexico City, 1998), 13, 132, 229.

6. Bernardino de Sahagún, *Historia general de las cosas de Nueva España* (Mexico City, 1989). Appreciation of his achievement was shown by the early colonial authorities, who twice seized his twelve-volume manuscript. Sahagún died in 1590 with his *meisterwerk* still unpublished.

7. This is the approach taken by other biographers of conquest-era indigenous figures such as La Malinche. Camilla Townsend, *Malintzin's Choices: An Indian Woman in the Conquest of Mexico* (Albuquerque: University of New Mexico Press, 2006). Biographies of Cuauhtémoc include Salvador Toscano, *Cuauhtémoc* (Mexico City, 1953); and Hector Pérez Martínez, *Cuauhtémoc: Vida y muerte de una cultura* (Mexico City, 1948).

8. Although this is disputed by partisans of the Ixcateopan tomb, who deem him the son of a different Ahuitzótl who was never emperor; Salvador Rodríguez Juárez, *Cuauhtémoc* (Taxco, 1987). This contradicts other written sources; see Tezozómoc, *Crónica Mexicáyotl*, 142–43; Fernando de Alva Ixtlilxóchitl, *Obras Históricas* (Mexico City, 1977), 2:177; Juan de Torquemada, *Monarquía Indiana* (Mexico City, 1975), 2:248; Sahagún, *Historia general*, 2:857.

9. Motolinía, *Historia de las cosas de la Nueva España* (Madrid, 1988), 174; Torquemada, *Monarquía Indiana*, 1:316.

10. Many of these must have been half brothers/sisters. For royal siblings to share the same mother was sufficiently rare for Tezozómoc to specifically remark. Tezozómoc, *Crónica Mexicáyotl*, 137–39, 143–46.

11. Bernal Díaz, *Conquest of New Spain*, 405; Alfredo Chavero, "Historia antigua y de la conquista," in *México a través de los siglos* (Mexico City, undated, first publication 1884), 1:716.

12. Ixtlilxóchitl, *Obras Históricas*, 2:177; Torquemada, *Monarquía Indiana*, 2:248.

13. Heinrich Berlin and Robert Barlow, eds., *Anales de Tlatelolco* (Mexico City, 1980), 6. One way of reconciling these two genealogies is to suggest that Bernal Díaz, who deems his version hearsay, misheard Moctezuma in place of Moquiquixtli. Cuauhtémoc is frequently deemed nephew to Moctezuma; this relationship seems to rest on Bernal Díaz's identification of his mother as Moctezuma's sister. Yet Tezozómoc's genealogies make no mention of a Tiyacapantzin among Moctezuma's sisters. It is more certain to describe him as Moctezuma's cousin, given that Moctezuma's father, Axacayatl, was unquestionably Ahuitzótl's elder brother. It would also seem sensible to prefer indigenous chroniclers to Spanish in the labyrinthine question of royal genealogy, and Ixtlilxóchitl, Tezozómoc, and Chimalpáhin all record Cuauhtémoc's mother as a Tlatelolca princess. But Mexica kinships are necessarily polyvalent, given their extended families and lax incest taboo; and Cuauhtémoc could also be classified as Moctezuma's brother-in-law (Moctezuma married one of Cuauhtémoc's sisters) and his son-in-law (Cuauhtémoc married one of Moctezuma's daughters). Tezozómoc, *Crónica Mexicáyotl*, 137–39, 142–44; Bernal Díaz, *Conquest of New Spain*, 405.

14. Francisco de Aguilar, *Relación breve de la conquista de la Nueva España* (Mexico City, 1977), 97; Cortés, *Cartas de Relación*, 2:33–34; Fernando de Alva Ixtlilxóchitl, *Historia de la nación chichimeca* (Madrid: Historia 16, 1985), 267.

15. Cuauhtémoc's youth is thus emphasised in both the *Ordenanza del señor Cuauhtémoc* of 1523 and the *Tira de Tepechpan*; see Salvador Rueda Smithers, "Cuauhtémoc: Iconografía del águila del crepúsculo," in *XVI Jornadas de Historia de Occidente: El ejercicio del poder* (Michoacán, 1995), 21, 24.
16. Bernal Díaz, *Conquest of New Spain*, 282, 405.
17. Robert Barlow, *The Extent of the Empire of the Culhua Mexica* (Berkeley: University of California Press, 1949).
18. Eric Wolf, *Sons of the Shaking Earth* (Chicago: University of Chicago Press, 1959), 132–35.
19. Soustelle, *La vida cotidiana*, 92, 131.
20. Population estimates for prehispanic central Mexico are notoriously varied, ranging from Rosenblat's 4.5 million to Borah and Cook's 25.2 million. A cautious sum, based on contemporary estimates of sixty thousand households, would give Tenochtitlán a population of under half a million people, still considerably larger than Seville, Toledo, or Granada, cities of fifty thousand at the most. W. George Lovell, "Heavy Shadows and Black Night: Disease and Depopulation in Colonial Spanish America," *Annals of the Association of American Geographers* 82, no. 3 (September 1992): 426–43; Francisco López de Gómara, *Historia general de las Indias* (Barcelona, 1965), 2:147; León Díaz Cárdenas, ed., *El Conquistador Anónimo* (Mexico City, 1941), 42; Martínez, *Hernán Cortés*, 54.
21. The great *cué* of Huitzilopochtli was started by Tizoc and inaugurated by his brother Ahuitzótl in 1487. Soustelle, *La vida cotidiana*, 36; Bernal Díaz, *Conquest of New Spain*, 238.
22. Wolf, *Sons of the Shaking Earth*, 132–35.
23. Cited in Soustelle, *La vida cotidiana*, 167.
24. See the 1504 war against Achiotlan and the 1511 or 1512 war against Taxiaco. Robert Barlow, "Las conquistas de Moctezuma Xocoyotzin," in *Los Mexica y la triple alianza*, ed. Robert Barlow (Mexico City, 1990), 115–27.
25. Sahagún, *Historia general*, 2:522.
26. Soustelle, *La vida cotidiana*, 67, 151.
27. Toscano, *Cuauhtémoc*, 30–38; Soustelle, *La vida cotidiana*, 173–76.
28. Berlin and Barlow, *Anales de Tlatelolco*, 6; Manuel Orozco y Berra, *Códice Ramírez: Relación del origen de los indios que habitan esta Nueva España según sus historias* (Mexico City, 1979), 202; Ixtlilxóchitl, *Historia*, 267.
29. Alfonso Caso, "Genealogía de Cuauhtémoc," in *Los Hallazgos de Ichcateopan*, Secretaría de Educación Pública, 507.
30. Toscano, *Cuauhtémoc*, 49–50; Díaz Cárdenas, *El Conquistador Anónimo*, 22.
31. Tezozómoc, *Crónica Mexicáyotl*, 137–46.
32. Torquemada, *Monarquía Indiana*, 1:270, 286–87, 2:257–58.
33. Ixtlilxóchitl, *Historia*, 267.
34. Sahagún, *Historia general*, 2:495–502.
35. This useful (for the Spanish) misidentificacán is vigorously disputed. Europeans clearly tend to attribute themselves godlike powers at first contact with indigenous societies; similar controversy attends the identification of Captain Cook with the god Lono during his fatal 1779 landing on Hawaii. In this case, however, the weight of evidence from Spanish and indigenous sources remains suggestive.

Bernal Díaz, *Conquest of New Spain*, 92, 220, 223, 271; Cortés, *Cartas de Relación*, 2:38–40; Sahagún, *Historia general*, 2:494, 821, 825, 834; Aguilar, *Relación breve de la conquista*, 81; Marshall Sahlins, *How "Natives" Think: About Captain Cook, for Example* (Chicago: University of Chicago Press, 1995), 1–15.

36. Sahagún, *Historia general*, 2:821, 827.
37. Torquemada, *Monarquía Indiana*, 1:268.
38. Nigel Davies, *The Aztecs* (London: Macmillan, 1973), 215.
39. Motolinía, *Historia*, 241–42.
40. Davies, *The Aztecs*, 222.
41. Jerónimo López to Charles V, cited in Hugh Thomas, *The Conquest of Mexico* (London: Hutchinson, 1993), 40.
42. Sahagún, *Historia general*, 2:831–32, 840; Motolinía, *Historia*, 242.
43. Bernal Díaz, *Conquest of New Spain*, 90.
44. Robert Moorman Denhardt, "The Equine Strategy of Cortés," *Hispanic American Historical Review* 18, no. 4 (1938): 550–55.
45. Bernal Díaz, *Conquest of New Spain*, 218; Sahagún, *Historia general*, 2:826, 831–32. The necromancers explained that the gods had abandoned Moctezuma because of his errors and cruelty, harnessing the sacrally protected mechanism of prophecy to the temporal end of political opposition.
46. Sahagún, *Historia general*, 2:833.
47. Martínez, *Hernán Cortés*, 208, 214; Bernal Díaz, *Conquest of New Spain*, 242–43.
48. Bernal Díaz, *Conquest of New Spain*, 245–49; Orozco y Berra, *Códice Ramírez*, 194. Francis Brooks's argument that the kidnapping and imprisonment are yet more inventions, and that Moctezuma remained a free agent, is questionable: the emperor remained in Cortés's quarters, and not his own palace, in his own capital. Francis J. Brooks, "Motecuzoma Xocoyotl, Hernán Cortés, and Bernal Díaz del Castillo: The Construction of an Arrest," *Hispanic American Historical Review* 75, no. 2 (May 1995): 149–83.
49. Torquemada, *Monarquía Indiana*, 2:174–75; Bernal Díaz, *Conquest of New Spain*, 249.
50. Bernal Díaz defines the hawks as "certain nephews" of Moctezuma, a description that applies, according to various of the (confused) genealogies, to Cuauhtémoc. He was also a leading member of the priesthood, whose hostility became overt when Cortés set up an altar on the main temple and who joined the militant faction in the 1521 power struggle. Bernal Díaz, *Conquest of New Spain*, 249, 255, 257, 278; Ixtlilxóchitl, *Historia*, 267; Berlin and Barlow, *Anales de Tlatelolco*, 65–66.
51. Bernal Díaz, *Conquest of New Spain*, 257–63, 271; Torquemada, *Monarquía Indiana*, 2:177–78.
52. Torquemada, *Monarquía Indiana*, 2:209. This sounds like Stockholm syndrome.
53. Bernal Díaz, *Conquest of New Spain*, 278–81.
54. He had effectively rebelled against Velázquez, his immediate superior, by turning the reconnaissance that governor ordered into conquest and settlement under independent authority.
55. Bernal Díaz, *Conquest of New Spain*, 282.

56. In their modes of empire building the Mexica and Spanish have attracted roughly similar descriptions. For Eric Wolf the Mexica were "in essence . . . little more than a band of pirates" (*Sons of the Shaking Earth*, 149), while, according to no lesser an authority than Cortés, "it is well known that the great part of Spanish people who come here [New Spain] are of low manner and type, and dissolute with assorted vices and sins" (private letter, Cortés to Charles V, October 15, 1524, reproduced in José Luis Martínez, ed., *Documentos Cortesianos* [Mexico City, 1991], 286).

57. Bernal Díaz, *Conquest of New Spain*, 286.

58. William Prescott, *History of the Conquest of Mexico* (London: Folio Society Ltd., 1994), 404; Orozco y Berra, *Códice Ramírez*, 114–15.

59. Torquemada, *Monarquía Indiana*, 2:205–6. While Bernal Díaz attributes this vital intervention by the emperor to his affection for the Spanish, Torquemada more cynically reports him acting under threat of death from Alvarado.

60. Bernal Díaz, *Conquest of New Spain*, 284–94; Torquemada, *Monarquía Indiana*, 2:209.

61. Orozco y Berra, *Códice Ramírez*, 115. Other sources record the formulaic insults but not Cuauhtémoc's authorship. Sahagún, *Historia general*, 2:838; Torquemada, *Monarquía Indiana*, 2:213.

62. Bernal Díaz, *Conquest of New Spain*, 294. Moctezuma's death was so unexpected that it generated the widespread belief that Cortés had surreptitiously garrotted or knifed him. Durán's and Sahagún's informants were adamant on the subject, as were historians including Tezozómoc, Chimalpahín, and the anonymous author of the Codex Ramírez, leading even Spanish writers such as Torquemada to admit the possibility. Cortés might well have murdered Moctezuma had it been in his interests; it was not. The emperor was the leading pro-Spanish figure among the Mexica and, given their internal divisions, could have proved useful even after the outbreak of war. A far more convincing accusation is that of Aguilar, who relates (albeit in an account tinged with senility) that Cortés killed the other captive lords before his retreat. Cortés took pains to deny this, alleging that they had been killed by their own people. Diego Durán, *Historia de las Indias de Nueva España e Islas de Tierra Firme*, 2 vols. (Mexico City, 1967), 2:556; Torquemada, *Monarquía Indiana*, 2:214–15; Tezozómoc, *Crónica Mexicáyotl*, 151; Francisco de San Antón Muñon Chimalpahín Cuauhtlehuanitzin, *Relaciones Originales de Chalco Amaquemecan* (Mexico City, 1965), 236; Orozco y Berra, *Códice Ramírez*, 119; Aguilar, *Relación breve de la conquista*, 89; Cortés, *Cartas de Relación*, 1:186.

63. Aside from his astrological skills, Botello had the misfortune to enter history as the owner of a leather dildo whose realism was "remarkable." Bernal Díaz, *Conquest of New Spain*, 302.

64. This estimate of the total strength of the Mexica and their allies is necessarily highly approximate. Sherburne Cook and Lesley Simpson, cited in Martínez, *Hernán Cortés*, 28; Bernal Díaz, *Conquest of New Spain*, 179, 284, 305.

65. For Aguilar the only weather that could form a fitting backdrop to the ensuing massacre was a storm, and so he provided one in which "it seemed as though the heavens were breaking" (*Relación breve de la conquista*, 90–91). But both Bernal

Díaz and the Florentine Codex have the less melodramatic, and for that more probable, memory of drizzle and mist. Bernal Díaz, *Conquest of New Spain*, 298; Miguel León-Portilla, *Visión de los vencidos: Relaciones indígenas de la conquista* (Mexico City, 1992), 91.

66. Bernal Díaz, *Conquest of New Spain*, 297–307; León-Portilla, *Visión de los vencidos*, 91–98; Cortés, *Cartas de Relación*, 1:140.

67. Prescott, *History of the Conquest of Mexico*, 452; Bernal Díaz, *Conquest of New Spain*, 305; Cortés, *Cartas de Relación*, 1:173.

68. Bernal Díaz, *Conquest of New Spain*, 282; Sahagún, *Historia general*, 2:846; Torquemada, *Monarquía Indiana*, 2:232; Lovell, "Heavy Shadows and Black Night," 430.

69. Motolinía, *Historia*, 54.

70. Cortés, *Cartas de Relación*, 1:171–72; Torquemada, *Monarquía Indiana*, 2:247.

71. He reigned for less than three months, being enthroned September 16 and dying December 3, 1520. At the same time smallpox killed the king of Tacuba, Totoquihuatzin. Tezozómoc, *Crónica Mexicáyotl*, 137, 159; Ixtlilxóchitl, *Historia*, 267.

72. Cited in Sahagún, *Historia general*, 2:338. According to Durán, however, little of the customary ritual was followed when Cuauhtémoc became emperor. Durán, *Historia*, 2:558.

73. Ixtlilxóchitl, *Historia*, 268; Torquemada, *Monarquía Indiana*, 2:248

74. Bernal Díaz, *Conquest of New Spain*, 324; Durán, *Historia*, 2:561.

75. Cortés, *Cartas de Relación*, 2:47.

76. Cortés, *Cartas de Relación*, 1:224–37, 2:1–19; Bernal Díaz, *Conquest of New Spain*, 380.

77. Cortés, *Cartas de Relación*, 1:4.

78. Bernal Díaz, *Conquest of New Spain*, 365, 395; Durán, *Historia*, 2:563–64.

79. Bernal Díaz, *Conquest of New Spain*, 380, 389.

80. Soustelle suggests that the Mexica were incapable of imagining the consequences of defeat and merely expected harsh negotiations over tribute should they lose. This underestimates their intelligence; nearly two years of dealing with Cortés had taught them that war with the Spanish would be sui generis. Soustelle, *La vida cotidiana*, 215.

81. León-Portilla, *Visión del los vencidos*, 105–6; Bernal Díaz, *Conquest of New Spain*, 341; Cortés, *Cartas de Relación*, 2:28; Durán, *Historia*, 2:561.

82. Díaz Cárdenas, *El Conquistador Anónimo*, 24.

83. Cortés, *Cartas de Relación*, 2:32.

84. The stones that the siege engine was supposed to hurl among the Mexica did not leave their sling, leaving Cortés greatly annoyed. Cortés, *Cartas de Relación*, 2:37; Bernal Díaz, *Conquest of New Spain*, 401.

85. Prescott, *History of the Conquest of Mexico*, 285; Bernal Díaz, *Conquest of New Spain*, 353.

86. Cortés, *Cartas de Relación*, 1:228.

87. Cortés, *Cartas de Relación*, 1:195.

88. Bernal Díaz, *Conquest of New Spain*, 325.

89. Bernal Díaz, *Conquest of New Spain*, 368, 390.

90. Bernal Díaz, *Conquest of New Spain*, 108, 175, 269, 179.

91. Cortés, *Cartas de Relación*, 1:223, 2:2.

92. If Xochimilco nursed a collective grudge against the Mexica, there was good cause. Moctezuma's father had once bet very heavily against the lord of Xochimilco and lost. He welched by having the ill-advised winner garrotted. Sahagún, *Historia general*, 2:850; Soustelle, *La vida cotidiana*, 163.

93. Cortés, *Cartas de Relación*, 2:8.

94. Cortés, *Cartas de Relación*, 1:187.

95. Sahagún, *Historia general*, 2:838; Tezozómoc, *Crónica Mexicáyotl*, 150–58; Berlin and Barlow, *Anales de Tlatelolco*, 65–66; Durán, *Historia*, 2:549.

96. Cortés, *Cartas de Relación*, 1:207, 2:2, 40; Aguilar, *Relación breve de la conquista*, 96. This Texcocan puppet, "Don Hernando," himself had close family (his uncle) fighting with the Mexica, while Cohuanacotzin's brother Ixtlilxóchitl fought on the Spanish side.

97. Sahagún, *Historia general*, 2:854.

98. Cortés, *Cartas de Relación*, 1:184.

99. Bernal Díaz, *Conquest of New Spain*, 365.

100. Cortés, *Cartas de Relación*, 1:184, 2:33, 45–46.

101. Gómara, *Historia general*, 2:273; Torquemada, *Monarquía Indiana*, 2:312.

102. John Gillingham, *The Wars of the Roses* (Baton Rouge: Louisiana State University Press, 1981), 252–53.

103. Motolinía, *Historia*, 54–58; Bernal Díaz, *Conquest of New Spain*, 405; Torquemada, *Monarquía Indiana*, 2:312.

104. Gómara, *Historia general*, 2:273.

105. Bernal Díaz, *Conquest of New Spain*, 393–94.

106. Cortés, *Cartas de Relación*, 2:33–34; Gómara, *Historia general*, 2:266, 268.

107. Cortés, *Cartas de Relación*, 2:39–40.

108. Sahagún, *Historia general*, 2:852; "Ms. Anónimo de Tlatelolco," cited in León-Portilla, *Visión de los vencidos*, 166; Bernal Díaz, *Conquest of New Spain*, 406–7.

109. Aguilar, *Relación breve de la conquista*, 97; Sahagún, *Historia general*, 2:857.

110. The Spanish never forgot this sight. Cortés, *Cartas de Relación*, 2:39, 43; Bernal Díaz, *Conquest of New Spain*, 405; Aguilar, *Relación breve de la conquista*, 97.

111. "Ms. Anónimo de Tlatelolco," cited in León-Portilla, *Visión de los vencidos*, 166.

112. Inga Clendinnen, "'Fierce and Unnatural Cruelty': Cortés and the Conquest of Mexico," *Representations* 33 (Winter 1991): 91.

113. Cortés, *Cartas de Relación*, 2:43.

114. Bernal Díaz, *Conquest of New Spain*, 402–3.

115. Expedition members paid for their own weapons and medical attention. With crossbows and swords changing hands for around fifty pesos, many of Cortés's men would find themselves indebted even if they accepted this derisory amount. Bernal Díaz, *Conquest of New Spain*, 404, 411–12.

116. Alderete was furthermore part of the household of Juan Rodríguez de Fonseca, bishop of Burgos, president of the Council of the Indies, and sworn enemy of Cortés. Bernal Díaz, *Conquest of New Spain*, 273–75, 384–85, 409; Cortés, *Cartas de Relación*, 2:13; Torquemada, *Monarquía Indian*, 2:314.

117. Bernal Díaz, *Conquest of New Spain*, 409; Gómara, *Historia general*, 2:275.

118. While it is usually held that the torture was confined to burning his feet, the most reliable version is that of the doctor who later treated him. This doctor, Cristóbal de Ojeda, described the torture during the 1529 *juicio de residencia* of Cortés: Cuauhtémoc's limbs were repeatedly coated with oil and heated over a brazier. "'Algunas respuestas de Cristóbal de Ojeda,' México, 27 de enero de 1529," in Martínez, *Documentos Cortesianos*, 2:47; Gómara, *Historia general*, 2:329–30.

119. Responsibility for the torture is variously attributed. Most contemporary chroniclers absolve Cortés from any direct blame; yet the incident, perceived as unjust even at the time, would form part of the accusations against him in multiple lawsuits of the 1520s. Martínez, *Hernán Cortés*, 376.

120. Bernal Díaz, *Conquest of New Spain*, 410.

121. Bernal Díaz, who witnessed the scene, who had a flair for the symbolic, and who was a faithful amanuensis of Cuauhtémoc's bons mots, would not have omitted the emperor's words had they actually been spoken. Torquemada backs him, reporting that "many said" the torture stopped following a confession by Cuauhtémoc. Bernal Díaz, *Conquest of New Spain*, 409–10; Torquemada, *Monarquía Indiana*, 2:314.

122. Bernal Díaz, *Conquest of New Spain*, 408–9.

123. Michoacán had, according to Ixtlilxóchitl, offered military support to the Mexica during the siege of Tenochtitlán. The supposed relief force was, however, never sent, due to the miraculous resurrection of the king's sister, four days dead, to warn her brother against such a costly mistake. *La Relación de Michoacán*, cited in Martínez, *Hernán Cortés*, 337; Ixtlilxóchitl, *Historia*, 269, 276–77.

124. Clendinnen, "'Fierce and Unnatural Cruelty,'" 94.

125. Gómara, *Historia general*, 2:300. The fear of indigenous rebellions against the new order is a recurrent theme in contemporary Spanish texts. See Motolinía, *Historia*, 61; Cortés, *Cartas de Relación*, 54, 56, 58–59, 221–22; Hernán Cortés, "Carta reservada de Hernán Cortés al emperador Carlos V, Tenochtitlán 15 de octubre de 1524," cited in Martínez, *Documentos Cortesianos*, 286.

126. The cihuacóatl's name is variously reported as Tlacotzin or Ahueltoctzin; Cortés later baptised him Don Juan Velázquez. When setting out Cuauhtémoc's refusal to surrender on the final day of the siege, he had informed Cortés that he regretted this decision; during Cortés's interrogation of the leading Mexica nobles on the subject of the gold, he had twice suggested, contradicting Cuauhtémoc, that there was in fact more gold and that either the Tlatelolcas or the commoners and women might be concealing it. Tezozómoc, *Crónica Mexicáyotl*, 165–66; Torquemada, *Monarquía Indiana*, 2:311; Cortés, *Cartas de Relación*, 2:45; Sahagún, *Historia general*, 2:861–62.

127. "Juan Velázquez, la serpiente femenina," in Barlow, *Los Mexica y la triple alianza*, 227–28; Gómara, *Historia general*, 2:300.

128. Gómara, *Historia general*, 2:330; Martínez, *Hernán Cortés*, 409; Barlow, *Los Mexica y la triple alianza*, 227–28.

129. Hernán Cortés, *Cartas de Relación* (Mexico City, 1973), 236.

130. Gómara, *Historia general*, 2:298–99; "Relación de gastos que hizo Hernán Cortés en la armada que envió al cabo de Honduras al mando de Cristóbal de Olid c. 1525," in Martínez, *Documentos Cortesianos*, 320.

131. Martínez, *Hernán Cortés*, 355–56.
132. "Carta de Hernán Cortés al emperador Carlos V, 1524," in *Documentos Cortesianos*, Martínez, 294.
133. Bernal Díaz del Castillo, *Historia verdadera de la conquista de la Nueva España*, 2 vols. (Mexico City, 1983), 686; "Carta de Hernán Cortés al emperador Carlos V, 1524," in *Documentos Cortesianos*, Martínez, 294.
134. Aguilar, *Relación breve de la conquista*, 99.
135. "The Spaniards who were there . . . were nothing but two hundred and had no more than fifty horses, and they had fallen out and were in factions" (Gómara, *Historia general*, 2:328; see also Aguilar, *Relación breve de la conquista*, 99; Durán, *Historia*, 2:574).
136. Cortés, *Cartas de Relación* (1973), 222, 225.
137. "Memoria de lo acaecido en la ciudad de México desde la salida de Hernán Cortés hasta la muerte de Rodrigo de Paz; Temixtitán, 1526," in Martínez, *Documentos Cortesianos*, 423.
138. Bernal Díaz, *Historia verdadera*, 695.
139. These numbers do not include some newly arrived Spaniards, whom Bernal Díaz contemptuously numbers apart from the battle-tried veterans. Cortés claimed to have taken a mere ninety-three horse, but it made sound political sense for him to underplay his abandonment of the city. Bernal Díaz, *Historia verdadera*, 691, 695; Cortés, *Cartas de Relación* (1973), 223, 233.
140. Cortés, *Cartas de Relación* (1973), 221; Gómara, *Historia general*, 2:328; Bernal Díaz, *Historia verdadera*, 691.
141. Bernal Díaz, *Historia verdadera*, 692.
142. Martínez, *Hernán Cortés*, 423–24.
143. Cortés, *Cartas de Relación* (1973), 223. Rainfall statistics for the Tabasco Plain are impressive, averaging some four inches a day. Comisión Nacional de Agua, *Registro Mensual de Precipitación Pluvial en mm* (unpublished MS, Biblioteca Daniel Cosío Villegas, 1992).
144. Cortés, *Cartas de Relación* (1973), 224.
145. Cortés, *Cartas de Relación* (1973), 225–29; Bernal Díaz, *Historia verdadera*, 696–98.
146. Cortés, *Cartas de Relación* (1973), 230.
147. Bernal Díaz, *Historia verdadera*, 699.
148. Bernal Díaz, *Historia verdadera*, 699–700; Martínez, *Hernán Cortés*, 431–32.
149. Bernal Díaz, *Historia verdadera*, 703.
150. Cortés, *Cartas de Relación* (1973), 233. "Never," wrote Gómara, "had Cortés seemed so confused" (*Historia general*, 2:325).
151. Bernal Díaz, *Historia verdadera*, 704.
152. While the precise location of Izankanac remains uncertain, Scholes, Gurría Lacroix, and B. Traven all suggest the modern municipality of Tenosique, Tabasco. Alicia Olivera de Bonfil, *La tradición oral sobre Cuauhtémoc* (Mexico City, 1980), 40–41; Karl S. Guthke, *B. Traven: The Life behind the Legends*, trans. Robert C. Sprung (Brooklyn: Lawrence Hill Books, 1991), 198–99.
153. Gómara, *Historia general*, 2:328. That the Mexica dancing caused fears of an imminent rising is also suggested in the eyewitness account of the Tlatelolca noble

Martín Ecatzin, cited in Jorge Gurría Lacroix, *Historiografía sobre la muerte de Cuauhtémoc* (Mexico City, 1976), 23.

154. Cortés, *Cartas de Relación* (1973), 236–37.

155. Alejandro Martínez Carbajal, *La muerte de Cuauhtémoc según fuentes escritas* (Mexico City, 1977), introduction.

156. Gurría Lacroix, *Historiografía sobre la muerte de Cuauhtémoc*, 64.

157. Tezozómoc, *Crónica Mexicáyotl*, 165–66; Fernando de Alva Ixtlilxóchitl, cited in Gurría Lacroix, *Historiografía sobre la muerte de Cuauhtémoc*, 42–43; Durán, *Historia*, 2:575; Torquemada, *Monarquía Indiana*, 2:316.

158. Bernal Díaz, *Historia verdadera*, 708. The only indigenous account to accuse Cuauhtémoc of conspiracy is Document III of the Chontal Text, an account of the history of Acalan-Tixchel from 1525 to 1604. The account, written in 1610, claims that Cuauhtémoc attempted to recruit the local cacique, Paxbolonacha, and that he warned the Spanish of the rebellion. Aside from diverse inaccuracies (dating the expedition to 1527, confusing Cortés with his son Martín), the text's version of events is evidently influenced by the author's desire to curry favour with the colonial administration by playing up the services of his ancestors; the text forms part of his claim to an *encomienda*. Francis V. Scholes and Ralph L. Roys, *The Maya Chontal Indians of Acalan-Tixchel* (Norman: University of Oklahoma Press, 1968), 359–66, 390–92.

159. Bernal Díaz, *Historia verdadera*, 707; Gurría Lacroix, *Historiografía sobre la muerte de Cuauhtémoc*, 25, 39.

160. Tezozómoc, *Crónica Mexicáyotl*, 166; Francisco de San Antón Muñon Chimalpahín Cuauhtlehuanitzin, cited in Barlow, *Los Mexica y la triple alianza*, 230.

161. Barlow, *Los Mexica y la triple alianza*, 230; Bernal Díaz, *Historia verdadera*, 707.

162. Tlacotzin/Juan Velázquez was Ahuitzótl's grandson and hence Cuauhtémoc's nephew. Barlow, *Los Mexica y la triple alianza*, 228.

163. Bernal Díaz, *Historia verdadera*, 709.

164. That the execution was a cynical expediency is proposed in various sources, most notably in the Texcocan tradition recorded by Ixtlilxóchitl and Torquemada. Fernando de Alva Ixtlilxóchitl, *Décima tercia relación de la venida de los españoles y principio de la ley evangélica* (Mexico City, 1938), 83; Torquemada, *Monarquía Indiana*, 2:317.

165. Among the eighteen assorted sixteenth- and early-seventeenth-century texts treating the execution of Cuauhtémoc there is considerable variation. The above version is a minimalist basis on which nearly all agree. Various Spanish and indigenous texts go on to talk of further hangings: several chroniclers claim that Cohuanacotzin, king of Texcoco, was also hanged, while Torquemada believes that a whole eight kings and nobles were killed, and Durán claims that none of the Mexica lords came back alive. All texts, save the late-sixteenth-century *Mapa de Tepechpan*, lámina III, and the Chontal Text, concur that the men were hanged and not decapitated. Finally, some sources record a last-minute baptism of Cuauhtémoc. This goes against everything we know about his character. Such a last-minute moral triumph would have been too attractive to Cortés's crusade mentality to have been omitted from his letters to Charles V; that it happened is highly improbable. Gurría Lacroix, *Historiografía sobre la muerte de Cuauhtémoc*,

44–45, 53, 61–62; Torquemada, *Monarquía Indiana*, 2:317; Durán, *Historia*, 2:575; Scholes and Roys, *Maya Chontal Indians of Acalan-Tixchel*, 392. For examples of the baptism trope, see Tezozómoc, *Crónica Mexicáyotl*, 165–66; and the Chontal Text, in Scholes and Roys, *Maya Chontal Indians of Acalan-Tixchel*, 392.
166. Bernal Díaz, *Historia verdadera*, 708.

Chapter 2

1. *Presidente municipal* Ixcateopan to Alemán, February 7, 1949, AGN/MAV-535/11; *El Universal*, February 7, 1949; *Excélsior*, February 8, 1949.
2. The main rival spelling is Ichcateopan. The difference is significant in the authenticity debate, as the debating sides used orthography and etymology to advance their views of the tomb's origin. *Ixcateopan* is usually translated as meaning "Temple of cotton," deriving from the Nahuatl stems *ichcatl* (cotton) and *teopan* (temple). Hopeful etymologists have traced Ixcateopan to a corruption of Ixcateimoteopan, which they translate as "Temple built on Cuauhtémoc" or "Here is your God"; or of Ichcateomopan, which is rendered as "Here is your lord king"; or of Ichtacateopan, which is taken to mean "Hidden temple"; or of Izcateopan, ambitiously translated as "Here is the temple of the great lord." There are then the archaic versions, such as Escateupa in the *Tasación de Ibarra*, Iscateupa or Izcateupa in volume 4 of the *Papeles de Nueva España*, and Ichcateupan in the eponymous *Relación*. The standard translation, "Temple of cotton," is put beyond doubt by the glyph used to represent the village in the Codex Mendocino: a temple topped by a cotton flower. Although "Ichcateopan" is the spelling of those sceptical of the tomb's authenticity, I have preferred "Ixcateopan," as this has been the villagers' version since the nineteenth century. Secretaría de Educación Pública, *Los Hallazgos de Ichcateopan*, 7, 439; Antonio Rodríguez, "Cuauhtémoc, símbolo de la defensa nacional," *Cultura Soviética*, no. 62 (December 1949): 33; the Florentino Juárez journals, in the appendix of this volume; *La Prensa*, November 2 and 30, 1949; Laura Espejel López and Salvador Rueda Smithers, *Reconstrucción histórica de una comunidad del norte de Guerrero: Ichcateopan* (Mexico City, 1979), 16; Lucas Pinto, "Relación de Ichateupan," in *Relaciones geográficas del siglo XVI: México*, 10 vols., ed. René Acuña (Mexico City, 1982), 6:257–68.
3. Moisés Ochoa Campos, *Guerrero: Análisis de un Estado problema* (Mexico City, 1964), 30–32; AHEG/AP/51/133.55 FIC.
4. *Excélsior*, February 20, 1949; General Baltasar Leyva Mancilla, second annual report, March 1, 1947, AHEG/AP/175/352.072.73 ETN.
5. Ochoa Campos, *Guerrero*, 53, 79; Moisés T. de la Peña, *Guerrero Económico*, 2 vols. (Mexico City, 1949), 2:612–14.
6. Pinto, "Relación de Ichateupan," 265–66.
7. "Tax return" is a loose translation of the "Manifestación de predios rústicos 1929," AMI-1929.
8. People in Ixcateopan today complain that "half the municipio has gone north," i.e., to the United States. "A los trabajadores que emigran a los Estados Unidos de América," AMI-1929; Secretaría de la Economía Nacional, Dirección General

de Estadística, *Estados Unidos Mexicanos 7° Censo de Población 1950 Guerrero* (Mexico City, 1952), 25, 73.

9. Secretaría de la Economía Nacional, *7° Censo de Población 1950 Guerrero*, 25.

10. Replies to *50 censo industrial*, AMI-1951; Secretaría de la Economía Nacional, *7° Censo de Población 1950 Guerrero*, 124.

11. Homicide rates revealed in the civil registry archive are low by comparative standards. *Libros de defunciones* 1930, 1940–52, IRC. For reports of violent crimes and a petition for professional policing, see *jefe de seguridad pública* to *presidente municipal*, September 28, 1948, AMI-1945 exp. 100; Manuel Rodríguez Juárez to *presidente municipal*, October 1, 1946, AMI-1946 exp. 41; petition to *ayuntamiento* Ixcateopan, December 10, 1948, AMI-1948.

12. The telephone arrived in 1888, and the town clock in 1893. A new clock was bought in 1928. Román Parra Terán, "Ixcateopan en el Siglo XIX" (Master's thesis, Universidad Autónoma de Guerrero, 1997), 99, 103; INAH/ASZ/1/1.

13. INAH/AS/PHO/CUAUH/5/3, 24.

14. INAH/AS/PHO/CUAUH/5/15, 72. This was remote even by the standards of a time when the journey from Mexico City to Chilpancingo took ten hours. INAH/AEG/9/2.

15. After the tomb find, General Baltasar Leyva Mancilla visited Ixcateopan every year. Baltasar Leyva Ventura, interview by the author, Chilpancingo, Guerrero, November 25, 1997; Governor's annual reports, AHEG/AP/51/352.072.73 ETN.

16. Telegram, Agrarian Committees and Municipio of Ixcateopan to Avila Camacho, November 11, 1944, AGN/DGG-2/311 G (9) 2/241.

17. INAH/AS/PHO/CUAUH/5/15, 18.

18. The priest "said what he felt as a man, as a Mexican, and . . . he said it with so much spirit, with so much enthusiasm that he enthused all the rest of us" (INAH/AS/PHO/CUAUH/5/5, 69).

19. INAH/AS/PHO/CUAUH/5/11, 21–22; INAH/AS/PHO/CUAUH/5/13, 20.

20. INAH/AS/PHO/CUAUH/5/18, 84; *Excélsior*, February 25, 1949.

21. *Excélsior*, February 25, 1949; Alicia Olivera de Bonfil, *La tradición oral sobre Cuauhtémoc* (Mexico City, 1980), 92; INAH/AS/PHO/CUAUH/5/38, 10.

22. Luis Reyes García, *Documentos manuscritos y pictóricos de Ichcateopan, Guerrero* (Mexico City, 1979), 18–19; INAH/AS/PHO/CUAUH/5/1, 12–13.

23. INAH/AS/PHO/CUAUH/5/18, 80, 83–84; INAH/AS/PHO/CUAUH/5/15, 56; Salvador Rueda Smithers, "De conspiradores y mitógrafos: Entre el mito, la historia y el hecho estético," *Historias: Revista de la Dirección de Estudios Históricos del INAH* 39 (April–September 1982): 17–27.

24. The notes were in what was supposed to be Motolinía's hand and interspersed with five Motolinía signatures. Cited in Reyes García, *Documentos manuscritos y pictóricos de Ichcateopan*, 198–200.

25. Reyes García, *Documentos manuscritos y pictóricos de Ichcateopan*, 11; Silvio Zavala, "Dictamen acerca de los hallazgos de Ichcateopan," *Revista Mexicana de Estudios Antropológicos* 2 (1950): 231–36, 242–43, 258.

26. *El Nacional*, February 3, 1950.

27. Hector Pérez Martínez, *Cuauhtémoc*; Salvador Toscano, *Cuauhtémoc* (Mexico City, 1953).

28. Thomas Benjamin, *La Revolución: Mexico's Great Revolution as Memory, Myth, and History* (Austin: University of Texas Press, 2000), 141–49.
29. *El Redondel*, March 9, 1947.
30. Wigberto Jiménez Moreno, "Los Hallazgos de Ichcateopan," *Historia Mexicana* 12 (October–December 1962): 161–62.
31. *Time*, March 4, 1946.
32. *Excélsior*, February 16, 1949.
33. Benjamin T. Smith, *Pistoleros and Popular Movements: The Politics of State Formation in Postrevolutionary Oaxaca* (Lincoln: University of Nebraska Press, 2009), 333; *La Prensa*, October 24, 1949.
34. Ruiz Cortines report 1947, in Carmen Blázquez Domínguez, Estado de Veracruz: Informes de sus gobernadores, 1826–1986, 20 vols. (Xalapa, 1986), 7521.
35. Secretaría de Educación Pública, *Memoria de la SEP 1949–1950* (Mexico City, 1950), 631.
36. AHEG informes del gobierno del Estado de Guerrero, 1950, AHEG/AP/161/350.73RAM.
37. Jiménez Moreno, "Los Hallazgos de Ichcateopan," 165–70; governor's annual report for 1950, AHEG/AP/51/352.072.73 ETN.
38. My analysis of AGN/DGG-2.311M(9) series.
39. AGN/DFS-Guerrero/48–8 H 69 L1.
40. Enrique Alba Calderón, "Report on possible candidates as Federal Deputies in the State of Guerrero," January 4, 1949, AGN/DGIPS-103 exp. EAC; *La Verdad*, February 24, 1949; *Excélsior*, March 20, 1949.
41. AGN/DFS-Guerrero/48–8/H69/L1; *La Verdad*, March 30 and April 6, 1949.
42. INAH/AS/PHO/CUAUH/5/11, 53–54; INAH/AS/PHO/CUAUH/5/13, 20; INAH/AS/PHO/CUAUH/5/2, 2–3.
43. AGN/DGIPS-800/2–1/49/444; INAH/AS/PHO/CUAUH/5/2, 2, 5–6; INAH/AS/PHO/CUAUH/5/9, 47–48; INAH/AEG/9/45; AGN/DGIPS-104/Orlando Delgado de Garay.
44. Both Leopoldo Carranco Cardoso, one of the governor's advisors, and Ignacio Marquina, then director of INAH, recall the specific request that Eulalia Guzmán be named. Whether this was before or after she had examined the documents is unclear. INAH/AS/PHO/CUAUH/5/34, 42; Ignacio Marquina, *Memorias* (Mexico City, 1994), 168.
45. INAH/AS/PHO/CUAUH/5/34, 42.
46. Julia Tuñón Pablos, *Women in Mexico: A Past Unveiled* (Austin: University of Texas Press, 1999), 81; *Enciclopedia de México* (Mexico City, 1977), 6:337; Eulalia Guzmán's obituary, *Novedades*, January 2, 1985; *La Antropología en México: Panorama histórico*, ed. Carlos García Mora (Mexico City, 1988), 10:255–70.
47. Benjamin Keen, *The Aztec Image in Western Thought* (New Brunswick, N.J.: Rutgers University Press, 1971), 481–85.
48. It has become a modern consensus. Inga Clendinnen, for example, describes Cortés's letters as "splendid fictions, marked by politic elisions, omissions, inventions, and a transparent desire to impress Charles of Spain" ("'Fierce and Unnatural Cruelty': Cortés and the Conquest of Mexico," *Representations* 33 [Winter 1991]: 68).

49. As one intellectual saw it, "[They] seem prepared to crush her by all means possible before allowing the book in which she unmasks Cortés to be published." The book finally emerged in a little-known imprint. *La Antropología en México*, 10:255–70; Salvador Novo, *La vida en México en el periodo presidencial de Miguel Alemán* (Mexico City, 1994), 349; Eulalia Guzmán, *Relaciones de Hernán Cortés a Carlos V sobre la invasión de Anáhuac: Aclaraciones y Rectificaciones por Eulalia Guzmán* (Mexico City, 1958).

50. Jorge Gurría Lacroix, *Hernán Cortés y Diego Rivera* (Mexico City, 1971), 29–45.

51. Eusebio Dávalos and Javier Romero reports, in Zavala, "Dictamen," 204.

52. Report, Eulalia Guzmán to Ignacio Marquina, February 28, 1949, INAH/AEG/9/4.

53. Zavala, "Dictamen," 242.

54. INAH/AEG/9/2, 4.

55. José Gómez Robleda later claimed that the tradition was supported by over fifty of Guzmán's interview informants; Guzmán herself registered under half this number. Arturo Monzón, "La Tradición Oral de Ichcateopan," in *Los Hallazgos de Ichcateopan*, Secretaría de Educación Pública, 417–19; Eulalia Guzmán, "El hallazgo de la tumba de Cuauhtémoc, Part I," *Cultura Soviética*, no. 66 (April 1950): 7–8. José Gómez Robleda, *Dictamen acerca de la Autenticidad de la tumba de Cuauhtémoc en Ichcateopan* (Mexico City, 1952); INAH/AEG/9/4, 23.

56. INAH/AS/PHO/CUAUH/5/13, 14–15; INAH/AS/PHO/CUAUH/5/71, 4.

57. Gómez Robleda, *Dictamen*, 44–45.

58. INAH/AS/PHO/CUAUH/5/18, 75–76; INAH/AS/PHO/CUAUH/5/10, 26; INAH/AS/PHO/CUAUH/5/1, 29; INAH/AS/PHO/CUAUH/5/4, 31; INAH/AS/PHO/CUAUH/5/13, 19. In support of her thesis that the dance depicted the return of Cuauhtémoc's body to Ichcateopan, Guzmán later suggested that *ahuiles* derived from the verb *aagüiltía*, to make pilgrimage. INAH/ASZ/1/2.

59. According to Tomás Espinosa, his grandmother used to pray on her knees in the street behind the church, propping a candle against the presbytery wall before leaving. She told him, "One prays inside the church to the saints, but here it's different, here one prays for our King, who is buried here" (Guzmán, "El hallazgo de la tumba de Cuauhtémoc, Part I," 10).

60. INAH/AEG/9/4; Bernardino de Sahagún, *Historia general de las cosas de Nueva España* (Mexico City, 1989), 2:894; Guzmán, "El hallazgo de la tumba de Cuauhtémoc, Part I," 10.

61. INAH/AEG/9/2, 8, 28; Instructions of Don Florentino Juárez to his children on leaving in their care the documents referring to Cuauhtémoc, in the appendix.

62. Instructions of Don Florentino Juárez, in the appendix.

63. Humberto Colín to Guzmán, March 7, 1949, INAH/AEG/9/5.

64. Report, Guzmán to Marquina, July 23, 1949, INAH/AEG/9/18.

65. Report, Banco de México to Guzmán, September 5, 1949, INAH/AEG/9/39.

66. The ink was a mixture of vegetable juices. Zavala, "Dictamen," 236–41; "Acta de la presidencia municipal de Ichcateopan May 27, 1949," INAH/AEG/9/10; report, Banco de México to Guzmán, September 5, 1949, INAH/AEG/9/39.

67. Florentino Juárez journal 1, in the appendix.

68. Manuscript of the hide folder, in the appendix; Zavala, "Dictamen," 232–33.

69. Florentino Juárez journal 1, in the appendix.

70. Letter of the reliquary, in the appendix.

71. Motolinía "suffered the Indians never to reveal these secrets to anyone," a repeated injunction. Manuscript of the hide folder, in the appendix.

72. The 1810 documents, packaged with the Juárez journals; for an example, see "Alleged court records from the late colony," in the appendix.

73. Letter of José Amado and José Francisco, reproduced in Zavala, "Dictamen," 260–61.

74. Florentino Juárez journal 1, in the appendix.

75. Salvador Rodríguez Juárez, *Cuauhtémoc* (Taxco, 1987), 11.

76. "I always had my doubts as to whether the tomb would be found there in the place indicated by the documents and the oral tradition" (Guzmán, "El hallazgo de la tumba de Cuauhtémoc, Part I," 11). INAH/AS/PHO/CUAUH/5/11, 53, 64; INAH/AS/PHO/CUAUH/5/2, 27.

77. Olivera de Bonfil, *La tradición oral*, 29. One Ixcateopan informant in 1998 compared Cuauhtémoc's resistance to the Spanish with the sporadic guerrilla war then being waged by the Maoist Ejército Popular Revolucionario. Interview by the author, Ixcateopan, February 23, 1998.

78. *Excélsior*, February 22, 1949.

79. *Excélsior*, February 22, 1949; INAH/AS/PHO/CUAUH/5/9, 48.

80. Espejel and Rueda, *Reconstrucción histórica*, 54.

81. "Acta del 4 de febrero de 1949," reproduced in Reyes García, *Documentos manuscritos y pictóricos de Ichcateopan*, 151–59.

82. INAH/AS/PHO/CUAUH/5/6, 4.

83. Cited in Olivera de Bonfil, *La tradición oral*, 129–31. Such Carnival questioning of the future is not unique to Ixcateopan. In Jamiltepec, Oaxaca, the end of the fiesta is ritually commented on in similar terms: "Perhaps we will not be able to dance next year; perhaps we'll die this year" (Veronique Flanet, *Viviré si Dios quiere* [Mexico City, 1990], 172).

84. Colín to Guzmán, March 7, 1949, INAH/AEG/9/5.

85. "This was a project of the Guerrero State Government," INAH/AS/PHO/CUAUH/5/2, 5; Marquina, *Memorias*, 168; Jorge Acosta, "Informe preliminar sobre las exploraciones arqueológicas llevadas al cabo en Ichcateopan, Guerrero, 1949," in *Los Hallazgos de Ichcateopan*, Secretaría de Educación Pública, 423; INAH/AS/PHO/CUAUH/5/34, 42–43; Jorge Enciso to Guzmán, February 16, 1949, INAH/AEG/9/1; *El Nacional*, October 1, 1949.

86. *Excélsior*, February 25, 1949; INAH/AS/PHO/CUAUH/5/9, 47.

87. Congressional Decree 30, *Periódico Oficial del Gobierno del Estado de Guerrero*, October 5, 1949.

88. INAH/AS/PHO/CUAUH/5/2, 5.

89. INAH/AS/PHO/CUAUH/5/34, 46, 64; INAH/AEG/9/3; Guzmán, "El hallazgo de la tumba de Cuauhtémoc, Part I," 9; Eduardo Matos Moctezuma, *Informe de la revisión de los trabajos arqueológicos realizados en Ichcateopan, Guerrero* (Mexico City, 1980), 23–35.

90. Guzmán to Marquina, September 21, 1949, INAH/AEG/9/45; Acosta, "Informe preliminar," 423.

91. Salvador Rueda Smithers, "La Fabula en la Historia: Los papeles de Ichcateopan," *El Nacional*, Suplemento Dominical, October 1992: 3–4.

92. Gudelia Guerra was a *maestra normalista*; the eight village labourers named in the official record of the discovery were Sidronio Parra, Abel Rodríguez Juárez, Antonio Flores Ramírez, Francisco Giles, Porfirio Reyna Ortíz, Custodio Barrera, Faustino Cuéllar, and Antonio Rodarte. INAH/AS/PHO/CUAUH/5/2, 6; "Acta Notarial del Descubrimiento de los Restos de Cuauhtémoc," reproduced in Luis Echeverría, *Cuauhtémoc es la luminaria sin ocaso que señala el camino de México en su marcha permanente hacía horizontes de superación* (Chilpancingo, 1970), 9–11.

93. Letters, Guzmán to Marquina, September 21 and 24, 1949, INAH/AEG/9/45, 48; Matos, *Informe*, 27.

94. For metropolitan contempt toward some of the architectural idiosyncrasies of Santa Maria de la Asunción, see Secretaría de Educación Pública, *Los Hallazgos de Ichcateopan*, 320, 444.

95. More than one eyewitness complained of Guzmán's blithely destructive approach to the church interior. Bernardo Salgado attributed it to her political beliefs, at the time broadly Stalinist. INAH/AS/PHO/CUAUH/5/11, 57–58; INAH/AS/PHO/CUAUH/5/15, 55.

96. *La Prensa*, September 21, 1949.

97. *La Prensa*, September 21, 1949; INAH/AS/PHO/CUAUH/5/13, 21.

98. Guzmán to Marquina, September 21, 1949, INAH/AEG/9/45.

99. *La Prensa*, September 24, 1949.

100. On September 25 she returned to her original plan, suggesting that the grave's integrity be preserved by tunnelling in from outside the church. But it was autumn in Mexico, and the pounding rains made such an approach unfeasible for weeks. *La Prensa*, September 24 and 26, 1949.

101. The dig was ad hoc from the start: when Guzmán gathered her team in the village it was discovered that there was no metal detector and that the team mustered between them one torch, whose batteries quickly died. Matos, *Informe*, 24–26; *El Nacional*, October 11, 1949; Lyman L. Johnson, "Digging Up Cuauhtémoc," in *Death, Dismemberment, and Memory: Body Politics in Latin America*, ed. Lyman L. Johnson (Albuquerque: University of New Mexico Press, 2004), 210.

102. Guzmán to Marquina, September 21, 1949, INAH/AEG/9/45; Acosta, "Informe preliminar," 423–26.

103. Report of Rafael Illescas Frisbie, Ignacio Diéz de Urdanivia Mora, and Rafael Molina Berbeyer, November 23, 1949, INAH/AEG/9/47. See also INAH/AS/PHO/CUAUH/5/11, 60; INAH/AS/PHO/CUAUH/5/2, 9; INAH/AS/PHO/CUAUH/5/15, 58.

104. Acosta, "Informe preliminar," 423–29; Eulalia Guzmán, "El hallazgo de la tumba de Cuauhtémoc, Part II," *Cultura Soviética*, no. 67 (May 1950): 40–41.

105. *El Nacional*, September 30, 1949.

106. There are two radically opposed accounts of the minutiae of the discovery. The official version has Eulalia Guzmán uncovering the entrance to the grave the evening of September 25 and then opening it in an orderly manner the afternoon of September 26. She herself gave this sequence of events in her verbal report to Jorge Acosta and later in her written report entitled "Aclaraciones" of October 19,

1949, to INAH. The other version—that she was not present when the break-through was made—is given by Anselmo Marino Flores (the state commission's anthropologist) and corroborated by Bernardo Salgado (*El Universal*'s correspondent), Sidronio Parra (the foreman of works), Juan Hernández Vielma (one of the soldiers guarding the tomb), and Leobarda Rivera, the bystander who was sent to fetch Guzmán. The resentment that most of the guerrerenses felt toward Guzmán after 1949 might conceivably have led them to play down her responsibility in the discovery and play up her incompetence; and Leobarda Rivera was in extreme old age when interviewed, while Sidronio Parra may not have been an entirely accurate witness. Marino Flores and Salgado, however, were neither particularly old nor unreliable. They had no overwhelming reason to lie, and had they done so, it would have been difficult to coordinate invented memories with the others. Guzmán's account, on the other hand, has the obvious motivation of self-promotion: that she was in control of the dig and that it was conducted with professional care and detachment. It was not, however; and had Guzmán been present she would presumably have stopped the workmen from going on to destroy the upper layers of the tomb. She would certainly not have waited nearly six hours on the morning of September 26, already aware of the grave's existence, before going ahead and blundering through its seal. See Guzmán's reports in *Los Hallazgos de Ichcateopan*, Secretaría de Educación Pública, 359–60, 426–29; INAH/AS/PHO/CUAUH/5/11, 60; INAH/AS/PHO/CUAUH/5/15, 58; INAH/AS/PHO/CUAUH/5/2, 13, 27; INAH/AS/PHO/CUAUH/5/7, 40; INAH/AS/PHO/CUAUH/5/14, 25.

107. INAH/AS/PHO/CUAUH/5/11, 60; INAH/AS/PHO/CUAUH/5/15, 58; *La Prensa*, September 27, 1949; Acosta, "Informe preliminar," 426–29, 434; INAH/AEG/9/47.

108. "Acta Notarial del Descubrimiento de los Restos de Cuauhtémoc," reproduced in Echeverría, *Cuauhtémoc*, 10.

109. *Excélsior*, September 27, 1949; INAH/AS/PHO/CUAUH/5/15, 59–60.

110. Salgado claims that the Río de los Sabinos rose five metres overnight; compare this to Bernal Díaz's elegiac ending to the siege of Tenochtitlán, "It rained and thundered that evening, and the lightning flashed, and up to midnight heavier rain fell than usual." INAH/AS/PHO/CUAUH/5/6, 49; Baltasar Leyva Ventura, interview by the author, Chilpancingo, November 25, 1997; INAH/AS/PHO/CUAUH/5/11, 61; Bernal Díaz del Castillo, *The Conquest of New Spain* (Harmondsworth, U.K.: Penguin, 1963), 404.

111. *Excélsior*, September 27, 1949; INAH/AS/PHO/CUAUH/5/2, 6; INAH/AS/PHO/CUAUH/5/7, 40; INAH/AS/PHO/CUAUH/5/9, 48.

112. "Acta Notarial del Descubrimiento de los Restos de Cuauhtémoc," reproduced in Echeverría, *Cuauhtémoc*, 11; INAH/AS/PHO/CUAUH/5/9, 48; INAH/AS/PHO/CUAUH/5/10, 46; INAH/AS/PHO/CUAUH/5/15, 59.

113. INAH/AS/PHO/CUAUH/5/4, 1–2; INAH/AS/PHO/CUAUH/5/35, 42.

114. Rueda, "De conspiradores y mitógrafos," 4.

115. *Excélsior*, September 27, 1949.

116. *Excélsior*, September 1949, 27; *La Prensa*, September 27, 1949.

117. INAH/AS/PHO/CUAUH/5/2, 11.

118. "Acta Notarial del Descubrimiento de los Restos de Cuauhtémoc," reproduced in Echeverría, *Cuauhtémoc*, 10.
119. Rueda, "De conspiradores y mitógrafos," 4; *Excélsior*, September 28, 1949.
120. *Excélsior*, September 29 and October 1, 1949; INAH/AS/PHO/CUAUH/5/5, 68.
121. The state government commissioners, Bernardo Salgado, and Salvador Rodríguez Juárez were awarded the Condecoración al Mérito. Decrees 26–30, *Periódico Oficial*, October 5, 1949.
122. *El Universal*, October 4, 1949.
123. *Excélsior*, October 25, 1949.

Chapter 3

1. *El Nacional*, September 27–28, 1949; *Excélsior*, September 27–28, 1949; Roderic Ai Camp, *Biografías de políticos mexicanos, 1935–1985* (Mexico City, 1992), 473.
2. *La Prensa*, September 22, 1949.
3. *Excélsior*, September 30, 1949; *Revista de Revistas*, March 25, 1951. Salvador Rodríguez Juárez welcomed Toscano's death, describing him as "Don Salvador Toscano, who thank God [has] already died because he could have worked against us" (INAH/AS/PHO/CUAUH/5/6, 33). The rumour may owe something to traditional, magical beliefs. It may, equally well, have been influenced by Hollywood "curse of the mummy" films or their Mexican counterparts, such as Chano Urueta's 1933 *Profanación* (in which a jade necklace recovered from an Aztec tomb bears a curse) or the 1939 *El Signo de la Muerte*.
4. INAH/AS/PHO/CUAUH/5/2, 6, 10; *Excélsior*, February 25–26, 1949; Ignacio Marquina, *Memorias* (Mexico City, 1994), 169; ". . . in '49 when we were in the fight," INAH/AS/PHO/CUAUH/5/11, 56.
5. Reyna to Alemán, February 12, 1949, and General Hermenegildo Cuenca Díaz to Reyna, February 25, 1949, AGN/MAV-535/11.
6. Acta, Ixcateopan, February 17, 1949, forming Comité Pro-Vigilancia Documentos Históricos, Nacimiento Sepulio Cuauhtémoc, in the longtime Ixcateopan schoolteacher Olivo Sotero's private papers.
7. *Excélsior*, March 1 and 27, 1949.
8. Lizardi, something of a specialist, never wrote about Ixcateopan again. Marquina, *Memorias*, 69; Cesar Lizardi Ramos, *Exploraciones en Quintana Roo* (Mexico City, 1940); Cesar Lizardi Ramos, *Copan y el jeroglífico de los sacrificios humanos* (Mexico City, 1948); *Excélsior*, March 12–13, 1949; *Impacto*, October 21, 1950.
9. INAH/AS/PHO/CUAUH/5/2, 7; INAH/AS/PHO/CUAUH/5/6, 22, 33, 35; INAH/AS/PHO/CUAUH/5/1ii, 26; INAH/AS/PHO/CUAUH/5/15, 66.
10. *Excélsior*, February 16 and March 10–11,1949.
11. Deputy Chief of Staff General Hermenegildo Cuenca Díaz to Reyna, February 25, 1949, AGN/MAV-535/11.
12. Lic. Francisco Villalón, interview by the author, Mexico City, May 13, 1998.
13. *La Prensa*, September 22–27, 1949.
14. *El Nacional*, October 1, 1949.
15. INAH/AEG/9/3; *La Prensa*, September 27, 1949. In an indicator of just how widely scepticism concerning Ixcateopan had spread by September 1949, the regional newspaper *Provincia Libre* did not send anyone to the village. Its man

was in the Iguala station of the Estrella de Oro bus company, trying to sell advertising space, when the Mexico City journalists arrived from Ixcateopan to phone in their copy. He eavesdropped on their reports, and *Provincia Libre* plagiarised them under the byline of a fictitious special correspondent. This was more enthusiastic than *La Verdad* of Acapulco, which kept silent about the discovery until October 1. Hermilo Castorena Noriega, interview by the author, Chilpancingo, November 18, 1997; *La Verdad*, October 1, 1949.

16. *El Nacional*, October 1, 1949.

17. *Excélsior*, September 27, 1949.

18. Jorge Acosta, "Informe preliminar sobre las exploraciones arqueológicas llevadas al cabo en Ichcateopan, Guerrero, 1949," in *Los Hallazgos de Ichcateopan*, Secretaría de Educación Pública, 422, 429, 434–35; British ambassador's report "Leading Personalities in Mexico, 1947," FO-371/60955/AN2144/2144/26, 3.

19. *Excélsior*, October 1, 1949; INAH/AS/PHO/CUAUH/5/6, 6, 22; Marquina, *Memorias*, 169.

20. *Excélsior*, October 1, 1949.

21. Carlos Margaín's preliminary report to INAH, October 12, 1949, INAH/ASZ/1/2, 166; Eduardo Matos Moctezuma, *Informe de la revisión de los trabajos arqueológicos realizados en Ichcateopan, Guerrero* (Mexico City, 1980), 23–35.

22. Acosta, "Informe preliminar," 431; Eulalia Guzmán, "El hallazgo de la tumba de Cuauhtémoc, Part II," *Cultura Soviética*, no. 67 (May 1950): 41.

23. Acosta, "Informe preliminar," 430.

24. *Excélsior*, October 1, 1949.

25. In his own words, "I was absolutely convinced that Señorita Guzmán had found Cuauhtémoc's tomb" (Secretaría de Educación Pública, *Los Hallazgos de Ichcateopan*, 339; INAH/AS/PHO CUAUH/5/2, 27).

26. Nelly Robles García, "La tumba 7 de Monte Albán," *Arqueología Mexicana* 5, no. 30 (1998): 42–44.

27. According to Eulalia Guzmán's (embittered) account of events, Marquina and Caso arrived, hypocritically congratulated her, and immediately asked the same question: where are the jewels? This was, however, a valid point. As Julio Jiménez Rueda puts it, the grave contents were pauperish for an emperor. It was customary across Mesoamerica to bury the dead accompanied by objects of high value; that the cultures in the Ixcateopan area were no exception is clearly shown in the *Relaciones de Oztuma*, about a village that came beneath Ixcateopan's jurisdiction in the sixteenth century. In this text indigenous royal burials are given the following description: "When the lord died they wept greatly and they buried him sat on a high-backed chair [with] much prepared food and they killed two men and two women that they might serve him, placing with him all that he possessed, even though they be precious things." Despite her bluster, Guzmán herself was disappointed in the tomb. "I had imagined it," she wrote wistfully, "as an elongated chamber, with its entrance at one end, as are many of the archaeological tombs" (*Una visión crítica de la historia de la conquista de México-Tenochtitlán* [Mexico City, 1989], 199–200). Julio Jiménez Rueda, "La intervención de Motolinía en el Entierro de Ichcateopan," in *Los Hallazgos de Ichcateopan*, Secretaría de Educación Pública, 453; Eulalia Guzmán, in report

of Rafael Illescas Frisbie, Ignacio Diéz de Urdanivia Mora, and Rafael Molina Berbeyer, November 23, 1949, INAH/AEG/9/47.

28. "It seems very probable," said Caso in one interview, "that the remains discovered are those of Cuauhtémoc," but at the same time "I think it's worthwhile to examine all the possibilities and then say yes or no" (*Excélsior*, October 2, 1949).

29. The commission was composed of the historian Dr. Silvio Zavala, the archaeologists Eusebio Dávalos and Carlos Margaín, the anthropologist Javier Romero, the architect Alfred Bishop, Lieutenant-Colonel Luis Tercero Urrutia, Major Roberto Tapía, the photographer Luis Limón, and Secretary of the INAH Alfonso Ortega Martínez. Wigberto Jiménez Moreno, "Los Hallazgos de Ichcateopan," *Historia Mexicana* 12 (October–December 1962): 161–81.

30. *Excélsior*, October 7, 1949.

31. *Excélsior*, October 7, 1949.

32. Eusebio Dávalos and Javier Romero, in Silvio Zavala, "Dictamen acerca de los hallazgos de Ichcateopan," *Revista Mexicana de Estudios Antropológicos* 2 (1950): 204–5.

33. Secretaría de Educación Pública, *Los Hallazgos de Ichcateopan*, 345.

34. INAH/AS/PHO/CUAUH/5/2, 22.

35. Dávalos and Romero, in Zavala, "Dictamen," 207–9.

36. Jiménez Moreno, "Los Hallazgos de Ichcateopan," 170. Margaín's behaviour, neither going to Ixcateopan for the dig nor putting his name to the INAH report, could be seen as politically astute or just craven.

37. *La Prensa*, October 28, 1949.

38. Marquina, *Memorias*, 170.

39. Zavala, "Dictamen," 229.

40. Dávalos and Romero, in Zavala, "Dictamen," 212.

41. Zavala, "Dictamen," 250–57.

42. Telegram, Dra. Esther Chapa to Alemán, October 19, 1949, and letter, José María Sandoval and *vecinos* to Alemán, October 22, 1949, AGN/MAV-535/11.

43. *La Prensa*, October 21 and 28, 1949.

44. *Excélsior*, October 1, 1949.

45. *La Prensa*, October 28, 1949.

46. *Excélsior*, October 19, 1949.

47. Lic. Francisco Villalón, interview by the author, Mexico City, May 13, 1998. Examples of debate being conducted with beatings are not hard to find. Abel Quezada's acid cartoon of one bullfight caused a bullfighter and two *pistoleros* to corner his paper's bullfight critic in the Café Tupinamba and beat him up. This was remarkable only for their poor choice of victim; as memoirs show, violence against and between members of the press was frequent. Rodolfo Usigli took a fist in the face from an anonymous critic on the opening night of his politically courageous play *El Gesticulador*. *Ovaciones*, March 1, 1950; Roberto Blanco Moheno, *Memorias de un reportero* (Mexico City, 1965); Rodolfo Usigli, *Teatro Completo*, 5 vols. (Mexico City, 1979), 3:552.

48. *Todo*, January 4, 1951.

49. *Excélsior*, October 22, 1949.

50. Marquina, *Memorias*, 170; Jiménez Moreno, "Los Hallazgos de Ichcateopan," 171.
51. The commission was formed by Professor Arturo Arnáiz y Freg of the Colegio de México; Dr. Alfonso Caso of the Instituto Nacional Indigenista; Dr. Manuel Gamio of the Instituto Indigenista Interamericano; Rafael Illescas Frisbie of the Comisión Impulsora y Coordinadora de la Investigación Científica; Dr. José Joaquín Izquierdo of the Comisión Impulsora y Coordinadora de la Investigación Científica; Professor Wigberto Jiménez Moreno of the Seminario de Cultura Mexicana; Dr. Julio Jiménez Rueda of the Archivo General de la Nación; Dr. Pablo Martínez del Río of the Instituto de Historia de la Universidad Nacional Autónoma de México (UNAM); Pedro C. Sánchez, director of the Instituto Panamericano de Geografía e Historia; Professor Manuel Toussaint of the Colegio Nacional; and Dr. José Gómez Robleda of the Instituto de Investigaciones Sociales of the UNAM. Secretaría de Educación Pública, *Los Hallazgos de Ichcateopan*, x–xv.
52. Roderic Ai Camp, *Mexican Political Biographies 1935–1981* (Tucson: University of Arizona Press, 1982), 55; FO-371/74077/AN0105.
53. Eduardo Matos, introduction to Manuel Gamio, *Arqueología e Indigenismo* (Mexico City, 1972).
54. See, for example, the Kafkaesque debate over the validity of using oxide analysis to date the grave's copper artefacts. Halfway through the long-winded argument between Caso and Gómez Robleda, Gamio interrupted: "I understand that the chemists' report means that they can't determine the antiquity of these objects . . . why are we discussing it? It's useless." The historian Edmundo O'Gorman apparently held a similar opinion of the commission's worth, politely excusing himself from participation. Secretaría de Educación Pública, *Los Hallazgos de Ichcateopan*, 40, 92.
55. Ignacio Marquina had, according to one florid account, tried to sabotage her from the outset: when the guerrerenses, wanting to hire Guzmán, asked for her telephone number, he gave them three. One was the national newspaper archive, one was a corner shop, and one was a Chinese laundry. INAH/AS/PHO/CUAUH/5/34, 44.
56. Roderic Ai Camp, *Intellectuals and the State in Twentieth Century Mexico* (Austin: University of Texas Press, 1985), 123–44.
57. *Excélsior*, October 4, 1949.
58. Robert S. Wicks and Roland H. Harrison, *Buried Cities, Forgotten Gods: William Niven's Life of Discovery and Revolution in Mexico and the American Southwest* (Lubbock: Texas Tech University Press, 1999), 173–74, 196, 205.
59. Marquina, *Memorias*, 53–54, 64. Such accusations were believed by at least some of Caso's enemies, such as José Vasconcelos, and they still cropped up in the press in 1950. Toro, an outspoken nationalist, later enthusiastically joined public debate on Ixcateopan by calling Silvio Zavala incompetent. José Vasconcelos, *Obras Completas*, 4 vols. (Mexico City, 1957), 3:1476; *Excélsior*, September 8, 1950; *El Nacional*, October 26, 1949.
60. Rapp to Bevin, November 1, 1949, FO-371/74108/AN3448.
61. *El Signo de la Muerte* (Mexico City, 1939), directed by Chano Urueta, written by Salvador Novo, starring Mario Moreno "Cantinflas" and Manuel Medel.

62. "My first idea concerning that discovery [the tomb] was that we were confronted with the burial of a sacrificial offering or that of the guardians of the
lord [Cuauhtémoc]" (Guzmán, in report of Rafael Illescas Frisbie, Ignacio Diéz
de Urdanivia Mora, and Rafael Molina Berbeyer, November 23, 1949, INAH/
AEG/9/47, 16; see also Acosta, "Informe preliminar," 431–32; Jorge Acosta's letter to *Excélsior*, March 2, 1951). Although Guzmán never publicly suggested that
she had ever believed the remains to be anything but those of Cuauhtémoc, her
earliest statements are ambiguous. In the telegram that she sent to the president,
the governor, and INAH on the afternoon of September 26 she did not claim to
have found the emperor himself but, rather, signs of his tomb; it read, "Today
unequivocal signs of tomb of Cuauhtémoc discovered, consisting among others, copper disc with dates and name, found subsoil of church." One of her first
reports further illustrates her lack of authentic conviction, reading, "The more I
have thought about it, the more I have modified my first impression to the point
of believing that it really is the burial of the remains of Cuauhtémoc." The clear
implication is that her first impression was that the tomb was not that of the
emperor, a reading reinforced by a conversation Josefina Jaimes reports in which
Guzmán said that she believed the remains of Cuauhtémoc had not yet been
found. Telegram, Guzmán to Marquina and others, September 26, 1949, INAH/
AEG/9/49; Eulalia Guzmán, "Aclaraciones," October 19, 1949, INAH/ASZ/1/2;
INAH/AS/PHO/CUAUH/5/1, 24.

63. Dávalos and Romero, in Zavala, "Dictamen," 213; Eulalia Guzmán, in *Excélsior*,
February 27, 1951; Guzmán to General Baltazar Leyva Mancilla, December 20,
1949, INAH/AEG/9/81; Matos, *Informe*, 28–29.

64. Telegrams, Leyva Mancilla to Alemán, October 21 and December 3, 1949, AGN/
MAV-535/11.

65. For examples of this conviction, widespread among Guzmán's supporters, see,
among others, Eulalia Guzmán, *La Genealogía y Biografía de Cuauhtémoc*
(Culiacán, 1954), 1–4; José Gómez Robleda, *Dictamen acerca de la Autenticidad
de la tumba de Cuauhtémoc en Ichcateopan* (Mexico City, 1952), 7–8; Antonio
Rodríguez, "Cuauhtémoc, símbolo de la defensa nacional," *Cultura Soviética*,
no. 62 (December 1949): 33; INAH PHO/CUAUH/5/34, 42.

66. Guzmán, *Una visión crítica de la historia de la conquista*, 135; Benjamin Keen, *The
Aztec Image in Western Thought* (New Brunswick, N.J.: Rutgers University Press,
1971), 481–82.

67. Jorge Gurría Lacroix, *Hernán Cortés y Diego Rivera* (Mexico City, 1971), 29–45;
Eulalia Guzmán, "El Hernán Cortés que Pinta Diego Rivera," *Excélsior*, August 11,
1952.

68. He was sufficiently important to be invited to a presidential reception, an opportunity he took to canvass Alemán's support for the tomb. In one informant's pithy
description, he belonged to "the governing mafia." Quiroz Cuarón to Guzmán,
December 2, 1949, INAH/AEG/9/79; Lic. Francisco Villalón, interview by the
author, Mexico City, May 13, 1998.

69. This was no inspired guess; immediately after returning from Ixcateopan Ignacio
Marquina had personally told Guzmán, the governor of Guerrero, and the secretary of education that the grave was not authentic. Guzmán to Marquina,

August 16, 1949, INAH/AEG/9/29; Guzmán, in report of Rafael Illescas Frisbie, Ignacio Diéz de Urdanivia Mora, and Rafael Molina Berbeyer, November 23, 1949, INAH/AEG/9/47, 16–17.

70. Salvador Rueda Smithers, "De conspiradores y mitógrafos: Entre el mito, la historia y el hecho estético," *Historias: Revista de la Dirección de Estudios Históricos del INAH* 39 (April–September 1982): 8.

71. Eulalia Guzmán, *La Autenticidad de la tumba de Cuauhtémoc* (Mexico City, 1951), 204–15; INAH/AEG/9/40.

72. Alejandro von Wuthenau, "El templo de Ichcateopan. Historia de su construcción. Las siete intervenciones primordiales," INAH/AEG/9/40, 70–107.

73. José A. Cuevas, "Edad del entierro de Ichcateopan, de acuerdo con el examen constructivo de las estructuras superpuestas," *Cultura Soviética*, no. 68 (June 1950); Secretaría de Educación Pública, *Los Hallazgos de Ichcateopan*, 346–49.

74. A. M. Cortés Herrera, "La inscripción de la tumba de Ichcateopan fue grabada en el siglo XVI," in *Los Hallazgos de Ichcateopan*, Secretaría de Educación Pública, 271–80.

75. Enrique Bustamante Llaca, "Sobre la edad de las placas de cobre," in *Los Hallazgos de Ichcateopan*, Secretaría de Educación Pública, 357–58.

76. Alfonso Quiroz Cuarón, José Gómez Robleda, and Liborio Martínez, "Estudio de los restos oseos de Cuauhtémoc," in *Los Hallazgos de Ichcateopan*, Secretaría de Educación Pública, 186–211; *Excélsior*, February 9, 1951.

77. *Excélsior*, December 12, 1949.

78. Secretaría de Educación Pública, *Los Hallazgos de Ichcateopan*, 346–47.

79. Secretaría de Educación Pública, *Los Hallazgos de Ichcateopan*, 273–75, 283–85.

80. Carlos Graef to the Comisión Investigadora de los hallazgos de Ichcateopan, cited in Secretaría de Educación Pública, *Los Hallazgos de Ichcateopan*, 357–58.

81. Joaquín Roncal y Gómez del Palacio, "Los Huesos de Cuauhtémoc, un esqueleto elástico," *Excélsior*, February 3, 9, 16, and 21, 1951.

82. Roncal, "Los Huesos de Cuauhtémoc," *Excélsior*, February 3, 1951.

83. "Nos están tomando el pelo," *Excélsior*, March 2, 1950.

84. Secretaría de Educación Pública, *Los Hallazgos de Ichcateopan*, 190.

85. Secretaría de Educación Pública, *Los Hallazgos de Ichcateopan*, 215–16, 219–20, 224.

86. Secretaría de Educación Pública, *Los Hallazgos de Ichcateopan*, 104, 158–59; *Excélsior*, December 30, 1949, and February 3, 13, 20, and 27, 1951; *La Prensa* series, 2–24 November 1950; *Cultura Soviética*, nos. 66–68, 71, 73 (all 1950).

87. *Excélsior*, February 3, 1951. José Cuevas was another aficionado of the superlative, variously describing his evidence as "unmistakable," "definitive," "authentic proof," and "indispensable." Matos, *Informe*, 23–35.

88. Secretaría de Educación Pública, *Los Hallazgos de Ichcateopan*, 532.

89. Guzmán, *La Autenticidad de la tumba de Cuauhtémoc*, 199, 216.

90. Ixcateopan was important enough for Gual Vidal to consult Alemán before making any major decisions; he met with the president before releasing the INAH and the Gran Comisión reports. Secretaría de Educación Pública, *Los Hallazgos de Ichcateopan*, 121; Marquina, *Memorias*, 170; *Excélsior*, February 13, 1951.

91. This is the version consecrated by generations of textbooks since 1883. Revisionists question its factual basis. Only half the cadets are documented as having been in the castle at the time; the gesture of suicide before surrender was variously attributed to Melgar and Montes de Oca before settling on Juan Escutia, the cadet about whom we know nothing and whose passage through the Colegio Militar left no documental trace whatsoever; in General Pillow's report of the battle, Major Seymour of the Ninth Regiment is recorded as seizing the Mexican flag from its post; and most suggestive of all, the cadets are not even mentioned in the 1849 commemoration of the war dead. Such doubts led to the omission of their names from the revised primary school history textbooks of 1992. This omission formed part of a generalised attempt to empiricise what is termed in Mexico "official history," an attempt that sparked the political scandal known as the textbook crisis. Enrique Plasencia de la Parra, "Conmemoración de la hazaña épica de los niños héroes: Su origen, desarrollo y simbolismos," *Historia Mexicana* 45 (1995): 247–50, 274; Ernesto Fritsche Aceves, "Los Niños Héroes o el olvido," *Nexos* 285 (September 2001): 78–80.

92. Plasencia de la Parra, "Conmemoración de la hazaña épica de los niños héroes," 264–67.

93. *Excélsior*, September 10, 1947.

94. Salvador Rueda, interview by the author, Mexico City, October 1995; Plasencia de la Parra, "Conmemoración de la hazaña épica de los niños héroes," 267–68.

95. Eulalia Guzmán's obituary, *Novedades*, January 2, 1985; *La Antropología en México: Panorama histórico*, ed. Carlos García Mora (Mexico City, 1988), 10:255–70.

96. He had been director of the Department of Scientific Research, 1940–41, and secretary of the Technical Studies Commission in 1948. He had also coauthored a politically sensitive critique of the National University. Miguel Alemán, *Remembranzas y testimonios* (Mexico City, 1987), 59; Camp, *Mexican Political Biographies*, 125; Lucio Mendieta y Núñez and José Gómez Robleda, *Problemas de la universidad* (Mexico City, 1948).

97. See, for example, the minutes of the January 17 and 19, 1951, meetings. When Arnáiz y Freg identifies an evident logical inconsistency in the Banco de México pathology report, Gómez Robleda declares that the session is out of time and that the discussion should continue at the next reunion. At the beginning of the following meeting he then suggests that the committee consider the palaeography report. Secretaría de Educación Pública, *Los Hallazgos de Ichcateopan*, 195–96, 198.

98. Telegram, de la Selva to Guzmán, January 26, 1950, AGN/MAV-535/11; Guzmán to Gual Vidal, October 18, 1949, INAH/AEG/9/68.

99. Guzmán to Gual Vidal, December 22, 1949, INAH/AEG/9/82; Secretaría de Educación Pública, *Los Hallazgos de Ichcateopan*, 81, 93, 95, 112, 145, 149–53, 158–59.

100. Letters, Quiroz Cuarón to Alemán, October 21, 1949, March 13 and 29, 1950, and April 23, 1950, INAH/AEG/1/76, 89, 96, 103.

101. Gual Vidal met Manuel Gamio socially in September 1950 and asked for his opinion of the case. When Gamio told him that the Gran Comisión's report would probably go against the tomb's authenticity, the secretary "appeared a little surprised" (Secretaría de Educación Pública, *Los Hallazgos de Ichcateopan*, 111).

102. *Excélsior*, November 23, 1949, and August 15, 1950, cited in Alejandra Moreno Toscano, *Los hallazgos de Ichcateopan, 1949–1951* (Mexico City, 1976), 135, 186; Secretaría de Educación Pública, *Los Hallazgos de Ichcateopan*, 90.

103. Although the books contained a footnote stating that the grave was still being studied. Joaquín Jara Díaz and Elias G. Torres Natterman, *Primer Ciclo 1º y 2º años Historia Gráfica de México* (Mexico City, 1952), 132.

104. For samples of such schemes, see INAH/AEG/9/107; AGN/MAV-535/11.

105. *Excélsior*, August 15, 1950; Enrique Mesta, president of Ateneo de Torreón, to Guzmán, April 4, 1950, and Luis Garciá Galindo, president of Cuerpo Alpinista de México, to Guzmán, March 29, 1950, INAH/AEG/9/98–99; Luis Reyes García, *Documentos manuscritos y pictóricos de Ichcateopan, Guerrero* (Mexico City, 1979), 62.

106. *Diario de Xalapa*, January 4, 1950.

107. *Excélsior*, October 4 and 12, 1949; Comité de Homenaje a Cuauhtémoc, petition circular, November 1949, AMI-1949.

108. Salvador Rodríguez Juárez met Gual Vidal in late February 1951. *Novedades*, February 27, 1951; *La Prensa*, December 2, 1950; *Excélsior*, March 3, 1951.

109. Jorge Hernández to Guzmán, October 28, 1949, INAH/AEG/9/73.

110. *Gachupín* is a pejorative popular term for a Spaniard. "Cuauhtémoc, corrido mexicano," mimeograph, AGN/DGIPS-320/2–1/360/207.

111. *Excélsior*, February 3 and 13, 1951.

112. "The fact of being attacked by this señorita Guzmán . . . is beginning to have, in the public eye, the status of a reward. The reward which in our day, after a life dedicated exclusively to intellectual endeavour, every Mexican specialised in this area, and who has won some distinction, should receive" (*Excélsior*, February 26, 1951).

113. Salvador Novo, *La vida en México en el periodo presidencial de Miguel Alemán* (Mexico City, 1994), 566.

114. Secretaría de Educación Pública, *Los Hallazgos de Ichcateopan*, 357–81; *Excélsior*, February 27, 1951.

115. Gómez Robleda to the Gran Comisión, February 7, 1951, reproduced in Secretaría de Educación Pública, *Los Hallazgos de Ichcateopan*, 382–83.

116. Secretaría de Educación Pública, *Los Hallazgos de Ichcateopan*, 270, 288, 404.

117. *Excélsior*, February 15, 1951; Lyman L. Johnson, "Digging Up Cuauhtémoc," in *Death, Dismemberment, and Memory*, ed. Lyman L. Johnson, 238.

118. *Excélsior*, February 27, 1951.

Chapter 4

1. Secretaría de Educación Pública, *Los Hallazgos de Ichcateopan*, 191–92; a 1976 commission source, interview by the author, Mexico City, August 2, 2000.

2. The most persuasive argument for the historiographical sophistication of the Juárez texts is Luis Chávez Orozco, *Don Florentino Juárez no pudo ser el creador de la tradición de Ichcateopan acerca de los restos de Cuauhtémoc* (Mexico City, 1950).

3. These take place particularly in the last week of February, in the course of which, one informant estimated, an average of two to three thousand visitors pass through Ixcateopan to celebrate the conveniently adjacent festivals of Cuauhtémoc's birth (February 23) and death (February 28). Interview by the author, Ixcateopan, February 23, 1998.

4. "Mexicanists predisposed to dismiss the discovery as a falsification may well be surprised at the powerful evidence marshalled for the defense" (Charles Gibson, review of Salvador Toscano, *Cuauhtémoc, Hispanic American Historical Review* 35, no. 1 [February 1955]: 108).

5. Silvio Zavala, "Dictamen acerca de los hallazgos de Ichcateopan," *Revista Mexicana de Estudios Antropológicos* 2 (1950): 295.

6. Zavala, "Dictamen," 252, 256–57. The idea foreshadows Bonfil Batalla's influential dichotomy between *México imaginario* and *México profundo*. Guillermo Bonfil Batalla, *México Profundo: Una civilización negada* (Mexico City, 1987), 9–17.

7. Zavala, "Dictamen," 256.

8. *Don nadie* is an ironic term for an everyman.

9. The strength of the *leyenda negra* concerning the nineteenth century can be seen in its perpetuation in relatively recent work; see, for an example, the rough literacy estimates of Carlos Monsiváis for the 1860s and 1870s at 0.1 percent of the population. This would have given a total literate population of about eight thousand, which, at a time when popular novels could reach print runs of six thousand, is evidently wrong. Cited critically in José Ortiz Monasterio, *Historia y Ficción: Los dramas y novelas de Vicente Riva Palacio* (Mexico City, 1993), 140, 183, 186.

10. Chávez Orozco, *Don Florentino Juárez.*

11. Zavala, "Dictamen," 295; Alicia Olivera de Bonfil, *La tradición oral sobre Cuauhtémoc* (Mexico City, 1980), 14.

12. Alan Knight, *The Mexican Revolution*, 2 vols. (Lincoln: University of Nebraska Press, 1990), 1:559.

13. *La Prensa*, September 28, 1949.

14. Secretaría de Educación Pública, *Los Hallazgos de Ichcateopan*, 18.

15. A 1976 commission source, interview by the author, Mexico City, August 2, 2000.

16. Sonia Lombardo de Ruiz, *La iglesia de la Asunción en relación a la autenticidad de los restos de Cuauhtémoc* (Mexico City, 1978), 78.

17. Olivera de Bonfil, *La tradición oral*, 49–55, 124.

18. H. Legislatura del Estado de Guerrero to Alemán, October 4, 1949, AGN/MAV-535/11.

19. Wigberto Jiménez Moreno, "Los Hallazgos de Ichcateopan," *Historia Mexicana* 12 (October–December 1962): 161–81; Bateman to Bevin, "Report on leading personalities in Mexico for the year 1946," FO-371/60955 AN 1816/1656/26; Roderic Ai Camp, *Mexican Political Biographies 1935–1981* (Tucson: University of Arizona Press, 1982), 138.

20. INAH/AS/PHO/CUAUH/5/1, 32; INAH/AS/PHO/CUAUH/5/34, 49–50. Riva Palacio was first listed as a potential master forger by Silvio Zavala, while Rodríguez Juárez was suspected by Eulalia Guzmán before the tomb was even

opened. Zavala, "Dictamen," 295; Guzmán to Rodríguez Juárez, August 26, 1949, INAH/AEG/9/34.
21. Josefina García Quintana, *Cuauhtémoc en el siglo XIX* (Mexico City, 1977), 71.
22. Secretaría de Educación Pública, *Los Hallazgos de Ichcateopan*, 4–19; C. Díaz y de Ovando, *Vicente Riva Palacio y la identidad nacional* (Mexico City, 1985), 11.
23. *Novedades*, August 21–23, 1956.
24. I am indebted to the scholarship and generous advice of José Ortiz Monasterio, who knows more than anyone else about Vicente Riva Palacio and who passionately rebuts the suggestion that Riva Palacio could have masterminded the Ixcateopan forgery.
25. García Quintana, *Cuauhtémoc en el siglo XIX*, 54.
26. Peter Guardino, *Peasants, Politics and the Formation of Mexico's National State*, 134–35.
27. García Quintana, *Cuauhtémoc en el siglo XIX*, 66–67.
28. García Quintana, *Cuauhtémoc en el siglo XIX*, 54.
29. Ortiz Monasterio, *Historia y Ficción*, 148.
30. José Ortiz Monasterio, *"Patria," tu ronca voz me repetía . . . biografía de Vicente Riva Palacio y Guerrero* (Mexico City, 1999), 186–89, 201–10, 222, 242.
31. Ortiz Monasterio, *Historia y Ficción*, 183.
32. Six out of Riva Palacio's seven novels are set in the colony; the exception is his first, *Calvario y Tabor*, which is loosely based on Riva Palacio's experiences during the French Intervention. García Quintana, *Cuauhtémoc en el siglo XIX*, 55–56.
33. Raymond Chandler, *Trouble Is My Business* (New York: Vintage, 1992), viii.
34. Ortiz Monasterio, *Historia y Ficción*, 188, 250, 297.
35. García Quintana, *Cuauhtémoc en el siglo XIX*, 56; Ortiz Monasterio, *Historia y Ficción*, 313.
36. Gonzalo N. Santos, *Memorias* (Mexico City, 1987), 455.
37. This impression was reinforced by the joking collapse of his last novel into self-parody. Ortiz Monasterio, *Historia y Ficción*, 149.
38. Riva Palacio himself described the book as "a monument." Mauricio Tenorio-Trillo, *Mexico at the World's Fairs* (Berkeley: University of California Press, 1996), 71.
39. Ortiz Monasterio, *"Patria," tu ronca voz me repetía*, 227–36.
40. Enrique Krauze, "Los diarios espiritistas de Francisco I. Madero," *Letras Libres*, February 1999: 10–15.
41. Cited in Ortiz Monasterio, *"Patria," tu ronca voz me repetía*, 233–34.
42. Vicente Riva Palacio, *México a través de los siglos*, 6 vols. (Mexico City, undated edition), 2:12.
43. Ignacio Altamirano, cited in Díaz y de Ovando, *Vicente Riva Palacio y la identidad nacional*, 22.
44. Cited in Ortiz Monasterio, *"Patria," tu ronca voz me repetía*, 211.
45. Overlapping political and literary careers were hardly exceptional at the time: Altamirano was briefly governor of Guerrero in 1868, and José Maria Lafragua, head of the Liberal Party, was also the author of *Netzula*, one of the first Mexican novels set in the prehispanic period. Men such as Guillermo Prieto openly announced their ambition to "deliver a national identity through literature."

Carlos Illades and Miguel Ortega, *Guerrero: Una historia compartida* (Mexico City, 1989), 79–80; J. Rojas Garciadueñas, "El Indigenismo en la literatura de Mexico del siglo XVIII al XIX," in *La Polémica del Arte Nacional en Mexico, 1850–1910,* ed. Daniel Schávelzon (Mexico City, 1988), 71–80; Díaz y de Ovando, *Vicente Riva Palacio y la identidad nacional,* 15.

46. Fernando Unzueta, "Scenes of Reading: Imagining Nations/Romancing History in Spanish America," in *Beyond Imagined Communities,* Sara Castro-Klarén and John Charles Chasteen, 115–60.

47. He coedited a collection of popular verses relating such traditions, with titles such as "La Llorona," "El Llano del Diablo," "El Callejón del Muerto," and "La Cita en la Catedral." Vicente Riva Palacio and Juan de Dios Peza, *Tradiciones y Leyendas Mexicanas* (Mexico City, 1996).

48. J. Rojas Garciadueñas, "Carlos de Sigüenza y Góngora y el primer ejemplo de arte neoprehispánico en América," in Schávelzon, *La Polémica del Arte Nacional,* 49–51; Enrique Florescano, *Memoria Mexicana* (Mexico City, 1987), 299; David Brading, *The Origins of Mexican Nationalism* (Cambridge: Cambridge University Press, 1985), 57.

49. Enrique Florescano, *Etnia, estado y nación* (Mexico City, 1997), 436.

50. Rebecca Earle, *The Return of the Native: Indians and Myth-Making in Spanish America, 1810–1930* (Durham, N.C.: Duke University Press, 2007), 33, 77.

51. Fanny Calderón de la Barca, *Life in Mexico* (Berkeley: University of California Press, 1982), 416.

52. Francisco Xavier Clavijero, *Historia antigua de México* (London, 1826); Benjamin Keen, *The Aztec Image in Western Thought* (New Brunswick, N.J.: Rutgers University Press, 1971), 414; Manuel Rivera Cambas, *Los gobernantes de Mexico* (Mexico City, 1962 [1872]), 3–29.

53. The same legitimating link between prehispanic royalty and creole rebels is made in another Riva Palacio novel, *Memorias de un impostor,* in which the hero's Indian lover owns a codex with directions to Moctezuma's hidden treasure. This, the codex commands, "may only be used to obtain Mexico's liberty." Ortiz Monasterio, *Historia y Ficción,* 289.

54. Riva Palacio, *México a través de los siglos,* 2:12.

55. Cited in Ortiz Monasterio, *Historia y Ficción,* 236.

56. Riva Palacio, *México a través de los siglos,* 2:107–11.

57. The first royal letter, dated "Seville 14 April 1523," consists of an extensive grant of lands, political sinecures, and a coat of arms from Charles V to Don Diego Mendoza de Austria Moctezuma, described as Cuauhtémoc's legitimate heir; the second royal letter, dated "Madrid, 2 October 1525," consists of a reprimand for the execution of Cuauhtémoc and again the royal instruction to grant "all the lands, houses and haciendas together with everything else from his [Cuauhtémoc's] kingdom" to Don Diego. Putative descendants of Cuauhtémoc used the letters in an eighteenth-century claim to ownership of the barrio of Tlatelolco. Neither is genuine: the 1523 letter, for example, charges Phillip II and his descendants to honour the land grant, four years before Phillip II was born, while in the 1525 letter the signature of the viceroy, Don Antonio de Mendoza, is falsified. Furthermore, the latter assumes that the emperor could have known

of Cuauhtémoc's death by October 1525. Cortés did not arrive in Hibueras until early summer, did not manage to get a messenger to Mexico City until the end of January 1526, and usually experienced delays of at least a year between sending dispatches and receiving replies from Spain. The chronology is consequently extremely improbable. A colonial official declared the 1523 letter fraudulent in 1753. Riva Palacio, however, argued that neither document could be considered false as they had been used in litigation over the ownership of Tlatelolco. That a lawyer like Riva Palacio could believe all evidence produced in a court genuine seems improbable. Riva Palacio, *México a través de los siglos*, 2:107–10; Secretaría de Educación Pública, *Los Hallazgos de Ichcateopan*, 7; Hector Pérez Martínez, *Cuauhtémoc*, 261–63; José Luis Martínez, *Hernán Cortés* (Mexico City, 1990), 441, 452; José Luis Martínez, ed., *Documentos Cortesianos* (Mexico City, 1991), 1:275, 345.

58. The first modern indigenista novel was written with Xicoténcatl as its hero rather than Cuauhtémoc. Rojas Garciadueñas, "El Indigenismo en la literatura de Mexico del siglo XVIII al XIX," 74–77.

59. Salvador Novo, *La vida en México en el periodo presidencial de Miguel Alemán* (Mexico City, 1994), 356–62; Daniel Schávelzon, "El primer monumento a Cuauhtémoc (1869)," in *La Polémica del Arte Nacional*, Daniel Schávelzon, 109–11; Keen, *Aztec Image in Western Thought*, 453.

60. Jeffrey M. Pilcher, *Cantinflas and the Chaos of Mexican Modernity* (Wilmington, Del.: Scholarly Resources, 2001), 14.

61. Cited in Díaz y de Ovando, *Vicente Riva Palacio y la identidad nacional*, 27–28.

62. Keen, *Aztec Image in Western Thought*, 423, 455–58; Schávelzon, *La Polémica del Arte Nacional*, 125–26; Barbara A. Tenenbaum, "Streetwise History: The Paseo de la Reforma and the Porfirian State, 1876–1910," in *Rituals of Rule, Rituals of Resistance*, ed. William H. Beezley, Cheryl E. Martin, and William E. French, 138–39.

63. Novo, *La vida en México*, 356–62.

64. Cited in Tenenbaum, "Streetwise History," 139. A common trope had the colony as a parenthesis in the otherwise continuous history of independent Mexico; see, for example, Vicente Reyes writing of "a mournful parenthesis of three centuries in the independence of the land of Anáhuac" in his 1887 review of the Cuauhtémoc monument. Schávelzon, *La Polémica del Arte Nacional*, 118.

65. Guy P. C. Thomson and David G. LaFrance, *Patriotism, Politics, and Popular Liberalism in Nineteenth-Century Mexico: Juan Francisco Lucas and the Puebla Sierra* (Wilmington, Del.: Scholarly Resources, 1998), 230.

66. The labels were printed with an image of Cuauhtémoc lifted wholesale from that monument. Enrique Krauze, *Mexico, Biography of Power: A History of Modern Mexico, 1810–1996* (New York: Harper Collins, 1997), 27.

67. Tenenbaum, "Streetwise History," 138–39.

68. A statue of Columbus was already in place, a gift from the owner of the Veracruz–Mexico City railroad. The other three monuments were to represent Hidalgo, Juárez, and Zaragoza, flanked by the symbolic runners-up of their respective times. Tenenbaum, "Streetwise History," 129; Ortiz Monasterio, *"Patria," tu ronca voz me repetía*, 195–96.

69. Daniel Schávelzon, "El concurso del monumento a Cuauhtémoc (1876–1882)," in *La Polémica del Arte Nacional*, Daniel Schávelzon, 127–31.

70. Tenenbaum, "Streetwise History," 138. A rural labourer (in Ixcateopan, San José de Gracia, Michoacán, and Naranja, Michoacán, at least) was paid twenty-five centavos a day in the 1880s. INAH/AS/PHO/CUAUH/5/18, 11–12; INAH/AS/PHO/CUAUH/5/15, 22; INAH/AS/PHO/CUAUH/5/3, 2–3; Luis González y González, *Pueblo en Vilo* (Mexico City, 1995), 69; Paul Friedrich, *Agrarian Revolt in a Mexican Village* (Englewood Cliffs, N.J.: Prentice Hall, 1970), 44.

71. The unveiling of the statue decisively propelled Cuauhtémoc clear of competing symbols to stand alone (in part due to budgetary constraints) as Mexico's indigenous master symbol. As late as 1884 his status was not so clear cut; to Altamirano, writing in one almanac, Xicoténcatl was equally significant. Manuel Caballero, *Primer almanaque histórico, artístico y monumental de la República Mexicana para 1884–1885* (Mexico City, 1884), 9.

72. Carl Shuchhardt, *Schliemann's Discoveries of the Ancient World* (New York: Avenel Books, 1979 [1891]), 8–15.

73. The Tizoc stone was discovered in 1791 during the installation of a water pipe in the atrium of the Mexico City cathedral; while it was preserved, the accompanying stones were broken up for builders' rubble. The Coatlicue, discovered a year earlier, was reburied, while the Piedra del Sol was left propped against the cathedral wall until 1900. Foreign workers could be equally insensitive to their discoveries; Marshall Howard Saville, for example, destroyed the immaculate facade of a Zapotec tomb to take its decorative urns. Alfredo Chavero, *México a través de los siglos* (Mexico City, undated, first publication 1884), 1:680; Daniel Schávelzon, "El reconocimiento del arte prehispánico en el siglo XVIII," in *La Polémica del Arte Nacional*, Daniel Schávelzon, 60; Ignacio Bernal, *A History of Mexican Archaeology* (London: Thames and Hudson, 1980), 156.

74. R. Tripp Evans, *Romancing the Maya: Mexican Antiquity in the American Imagination, 1820–1915* (Austin: University of Texas Press, 2004), 3–4.

75. David A. Brading, "Manuel Gamio and Official *Indigenismo* in Mexico," *Bulletin of Latin American Research* 7, no. 1 (1988): 77.

76. "There is a great need for archaeologists," Riva Palacio wrote, ". . . in this country so full of antiquities" (*Los Ceros. Galeria de Contemporaneos*, cited in Díaz y de Ovando, *Vicente Riva Palacio y la identidad nacional*, 27–28; see also Ortiz Monasterio, *"Patria," tu ronca voz me repetía*, 198).

77. Cited in Ortiz Monasterio, *"Patria," tu ronca voz me repetía*, 211.

78. Bernal, *History of Mexican Archaeology*, 126.

79. Earle, *Return of the Native*, 184–85; Alexander S. Dawson, *Indian and Nation in Revolutionary Mexico* (Tucson: University of Arizona Press, 2004), xiv–xvii; Brading, "Manuel Gamio and Official *Indigenismo*," 76.

80. Agustín Basave Benítez, *México mestizo* (Mexico City, 1990), 29.

81. In Mexican Spanish attaining "the age of reason" is a common periphrasis for growing up. José López Papantla to Secretaría de Educación Pública, August 31, 1935, SEP DGEP caja 1347, ant. 208, exp. 16; "Monografía de la 13a zona escolar del estado de Guerrero," in *Centenario* (Chilpancingo, 1949), 56–57; Dawson, *Indian and Nation in Revolutionary Mexico*, xvi, 13–16, 143–51; Guillermo Palacios,

"Postrevolutionary Intellectuals, Rural Readings and the Shaping of the 'Peasant Problem' in Mexico: *El Maestro Rural*, 1932–1934," *Journal of Latin American Studies* 30, no. 2 (May 1998): 316–17; Rafael Molina Betancourt, cited in Jorge Mora Forero, "Los maestros y la práctica de la educación socialista," *Historia Mexicana* 29, no. 1 (1979): 134; Alan Knight, "Racism, Revolution and *Indigenismo*: Mexico, 1910–1940," in *The Idea of Race in Latin America, 1870–1940*, ed. Richard Graham (Austin: University of Texas Press, 1990), 87–92.

82. In 1857 Ignacio Ramírez proposed bilingual state education for Nahuatl, Tarascan, Otomí, Zapotec, and Maya communities. Shirley Brice Heath, *La política del lenguaje en México* (Mexico City, 1972).

83. Instituto Nacional de Economía, Geografía e Informática, *Estadísticas históricas de México*, CD-ROM (Mexico City, 2000); Manuel Gamio, cited in Rick A. López, *Crafting Mexico: Intellectuals, Artisans, and the State after the Revolution* (Durham, N.C.: Duke University Press, 2010), 8.

84. This was, admittedly, the only specific reference to Indians in 161 pages. Porfirio Díaz, *Informe del Ciudadano General . . . a sus compatriotas* (Mexico City, 1896), 64.

85. Moisés González Navarro, conclusion in *Métodos y resultados de la política indigenista en México*, edited by Alfonso Caso (Mexico City, 1954), 165.

86. Guillermo Bonfil Batalla, *Obras escogidas* (Mexico City, 1995), 183–204.

87. Arturo Warman, *De eso que llaman antropología mexicana* (Mexico City, 1970), 22–29.

88. This was done by force when necessary. Jaime Salazar Adame, et al., *Historia de la cuestión agraria mexicana: Estado de Guerrero, 1867–1940* (Chilpancingo, 1987), 40–41; González Fernández, "Memoria . . . de Los Tuxtlas . . . 28 de Junio de 1890," and Rosas Landa, "Memoria . . . de Acayucán . . . 15 de Abril de 1891," in *Memorias e informes de jefes políticos y autoridades del régimen porfirista 1883–1911 Estado de Veracruz*, ed. Soledad García Morales and José Velasco Toro (Xalapa, 1997), 6:44–45, 110.

89. Mary Kay Vaughan, *The State, Education, and Social Class in Mexico, 1880–1928* (De Kalb: Northern Illinois University Press, 1982), 22–39; Brice Heath, *La política del lenguaje*.

90. Knight, "Racism, Revolution and *Indigenismo*," 79; Warman, *De eso que llaman antropología mexicana*, 18–22.

91. Ortiz Monasterio, *Historia y Ficción*, 183, 193, 277–78, 293.

92. Cited in José Ortiz Monasterio, "Introducción," in Riva Palacio and Peza, *Tradiciones y Leyendas Mexicanas*, 21.

93. Pierre Nora, *Rethinking France: Les lieux de mémoire*, 3 vols. (Chicago: University of Chicago Press, 2001), 3.

94. Ortiz Monasterio, *Historia y Ficción*, 44, 275–76, 315; García Quintana, *Cuauhtémoc en el siglo XIX*, 55–56.

95. Riva Palacio, *México a través de los siglos*, 2:60, 62, 74–75, 165, 224.

96. Vicente Riva Palacio and Manuel Payno, *El libro rojo* (Mexico City, 1870), 10; Florentino Juárez journal 1, in the appendix.

97. C. Díaz y de Ovando, "Prólogo," in Vicente Riva Palacio, *Cuentos del General* (Mexico City, 1968), xxvi.

98. Guardino, *Peasants, Politics and the Formation of Mexico's National State*, 136–39.
99. García Quintana, *Cuauhtémoc en el siglo XIX*, 53–54, 65–70.
100. García Quintana, *Cuauhtémoc en el siglo XIX*, 70. He was well known; his wife's death was covered in the state government's gazette. *Periódico Oficial* 17, no. 79 (November 22, 1893).

Chapter 5

1. INAH/AS/PHO/CUAUH/5/6, 1; Alicia Olivera de Bonfil, *La tradición oral sobre Cuauhtémoc* (Mexico City, 1980), 99.
2. Olivera de Bonfil, *La tradición oral*, 26.
3. ADC/LG/XII/1192, XIII/470; INAH/AS/PHO/CUAUH/5/18, 89; Román Parra Terán, "Ixcateopan en el Siglo XIX" (Master's thesis, Universidad Autónoma de Guerrero, 1997), 101.
4. INAH/AS/PHO/CUAUH/5/1ii, 16–17; Josefina García Quintana, *Cuauhtémoc en el siglo XIX* (Mexico City, 1977), 40, 84.
5. Román Parra Terán, interview by the author, Chilpancingo, November 25, 2002.
6. INAH/AS/PHO/CUAUH/5/3, 5; INAH/AS/PHO/CUAUH/5/14, 13.
7. INAH/AS/PHO/CUAUH/5/27, 59; Livestock certificate, Ixcateopan, October 26, 1918, AMI-1929; licence to exhume body of Primitivo Rodríguez Juárez, AMI-1945.
8. John Womack, *Zapata and the Mexican Revolution* (London: Thames and Hudson, 1969), 138–40, 310–11, 370.
9. Secretaría de Fomento, Dirección General de Estadística, *Censo y división territorial del Estado de Guerrero, verificados en 1900* (Mexico City, 1905); Padrón General del municipio de Ixcateopan, 1921, AMI-fragmentos 1865–1929, caja 1.
10. This was done by Castrejón's zapatistas, quartered in Ixcateopan. "Ixcapuzalco," *Así Somos . . .* 6, no. 106 (February 15, 1996).
11. INAH/AS/PHO/CUAUH/5/3, 7.
12. Laura Espejel López and Salvador Rueda Smithers, *Reconstrucción histórica de una comunidad del norte de Guerrero*, 35.
13. As Josefina Jaimes and his uncle Odilón did. Espejel and Rueda, *Reconstrucción histórica*, 40; Parra Terán, "Ixcateopan," 78.
14. It is possible that he went to primary school, as many in the village did, after 1919. INAH/AS/PHO/CUAUH/5/3, 10; INAH/AS/PHO/CUAUH/5/4, 18; INAH/AS/PHO/CUAUH/5/15, 24; INAH/AS/PHO/CUAUH/5/19, 16; INAH/AS/PHO/CUAUH/5/13, 6.
15. Olivera de Bonfil, *La tradición oral*, 10; INAH/AS/PHO/CUAUH/5/1, 3; INAH/AS/PHO/CUAUH/5/34, 57.
16. Luis Reyes García, *Documentos manuscritos y pictóricos de Ichcateopan, Guerrero* (Mexico City, 1979), 44.
17. INAH/AS/PHO/CUAUH/5/15, 39–45.
18. INAH/AS/PHO/CUAUH/5/1, 12–13.
19. Olivera de Bonfil, *La tradición oral*, 27.
20. Rodríguez Juárez disconcerted most visitors to Ixcateopan. They expected him to appear indigenous, and he looked like a very pale mestizo; he styled himself "doctor" and was obviously no such thing. *El Nacional*, October 9, 1950; Roberto

Blanco Moheno, "Conjura en el caso de Cuauhtémoc," *Impacto*, October 21, 1949; Román Parra Terán, interview by the author, Chilpancingo, November 25, 2002.

21. Certificate of health, Salvador Rodríguez Juárez to Anciano Trinidad and Leobarda Velázquez, November 19, 1945, AMI-1945.

22. See, for example, Rodríguez Juárez on Cortés: "As I have always said we the ancient families have been the fodder and the murdered meat of the vile and specifically of the scoundrel, alias *el conquistador* Fernando de Cortés; I don't like him, I want to let you know that I hate him, if he'd been a gladiator I wouldn't have pardoned that evil man" (INAH/AS/PHO/CUAUH/5/6, 10).

23. During the strongly contested local elections of 1933 they were among a handful of signatories, headed by Manuel Rodríguez, to a Partido Nacional Revolucionario letter of protest at Governor Castrejón's municipal election-rigging. PNR Comité Ixcateopan to Gobernación, January 1, 1933, AGN/DGG-2.311M(9)/5B.

24. *Periódico Oficial*, September 21, 1932; "Relación de presidentes municipales de Ixcateopan," Olivo Sotero private papers, Ixcateopan.

25. *Presidente municipal* to the Health and Assistance Centre, July 16, 1946, AMI-1946; actas, Ixcateopan, August 6 and November 17, 1948, AMI-1948; expediente de la junta de acciones cívicas, AMI-1951.

26. Eric Wolf, "Kinship, Friendship and Patron–Client Relations," in *Pathways of Power: Building an Anthropology of the Modern World* (Berkeley: University of California Press, 2001 [1966]), 181.

27. Salvador Rueda Smithers, "De conspiradores y mitógrafos: Entre el mito, la historia y el hecho estético," *Historias: Revista de la Dirección de Estudios Históricos del INAH* 39 (April–September 1982): 2, 7.

28. INAH/AS/PHO/CUAUH/5/18, 80; INAH/AS/PHO/CUAUH/5/11, 21; Guzmán to Rodríguez Juárez, March 14, 1949, INAH/AEG/9/8.

29. Parra Terán, "Ixcateopan," 75; INAH/AS/PHO/CUAUH/5/17, 16; INAH/AS/PHO/CUAUH/5/22, 8; INAH/AS/PHO/CUAUH/5/18, 61.

30. INAH/AS/PHO/CUAUH/5/19, 20; INAH/AS/PHO/CUAUH/5/28, 14.

31. INAH/AS/PHO/CUAUH/5/26, 8; INAH/AS/PHO/CUAUH/5/32, 13–14; INAH/AS/PHO/CUAUH/5/3, 18; INAH/AS/PHO/CUAUH/5/30, 8.

32. Reyes García, *Documentos manuscritos y pictóricos de Ichcateopan*, 18–19; INAH/AS/PHO/CUAUH/5/18, 83–84; Olivera de Bonfil, *La tradición oral*, 97; Alvaro López Miramontes, "Panorama historiográfica del estado de Guerrero," in Alvaro López Miramontes et al., *Ensayos para la historia del estado de Guerrero* (Chilpancingo, 1985), 25.

33. Guzmán to Rodríguez Juárez, June 8, 1949, INAH/AEG/9/11.

34. "The oral tradition according to Salvador Rodríguez Juárez" (1949), reproduced in Silvio Zavala, "Dictamen acerca de los hallazgos de Ichcateopan," *Revista Mexicana de Estudios Antropológicos* 2 (1950): 278–83.

35. Eulalia Guzmán, "El hallazgo de la tumba de Cuauhtémoc, Part I," *Cultura Soviética*, no. 66 (April 1950): 11.

36. *La Nación*, October 10, 1949.

37. Rodríguez Juárez's statement of January 1, 1973, reproduced in Reyes García, *Documentos manuscritos y pictóricos de Ichcateopan*, 205–9. In the words of one of the tomb's partisans in the 1970s, Rodríguez Juárez's first story of the

documents—one in which he was a passive, and unknowing, recipient—"disagreed with 90% of what he says today" (INAH/AS/PHO/CUAUH/5/34, 50).

38. Salvador Rodríguez Juárez, *Cuauhtémoc* (Taxco, 1987); INAH/AS/PHO/CUAUH/5/71, 5–6.

39. One commentator described Rodríguez Juárez and his followers as "ignorant old men of lamentable mental infirmity" (R. Loza, "Cuauhtémoc multiplicado," *Novedades*, August 30, 1956).

40. AGN/DGIPS-102; unnumbered file "Romualdo Vadilla Sanoguera," INAH/AS/PHO/CUAUH/5/13, 20; Carlos Monsiváis, "La nación de unos cuantos y las esperanzas románticas: Notas sobre la historia del término 'cultura nacional' en México," in *En torno a la cultura nacional*, ed. José Emilio Pacheco (Mexico City, 1982), 127, 213; Barry Carr, "The Fate of the Vanguard Party under a Revolutionary State: Marxism's Contribution to the Construction of the Great Arch," in *Everyday Forms of State Formation*, ed. Gilbert M. Joseph and Daniel Nugent, 347; *Excélsior*, March 13, 1952.

41. *Novedades*, February 27, 1951.

42. *Cultura Soviética*, no. 68 (June 1950). Judging by his "private" notes, Cárdenas was convinced by Rodríguez Juárez, who showed him the church and the documents. Lázaro Cárdenas, *Obras: I—Apuntes 1941–1956*, vol. 2 (Mexico City, 1973), 391.

43. Ruíz Cortines, López Mateos, Díaz Ordaz, and Echeverría all visited Ixcateopan. Alfonso Treviño and others to Ruíz Cortines, December 10, 1952, AMI-1952; *Excélsior*, January 18, 1964; Luis Echeverría, *Cuauhtémoc es la luminaria sin ocaso que señala el camino de México en su marcha permanente hacía horizontes de superación* (Chilpancingo, 1970).

44. Maurice Bloch, *The Royal Touch: Sacred Monarchy and Scrofula in England and France*, trans. J. E. Anderson (London: Routledge and Kegan Paul, 1973).

45. *El Universal*, April 1, 1951.

46. Jorge Ibargüengoitía, *Instrucciones para Vivir en México* (Mexico City, 2000), 164–66.

47. *Periódico Oficial*, August 1950; *Excélsior*, August 11 and 15, 1950.

48. Reyes García, *Documentos manuscritos y pictóricos de Ichcateopan*, 159, 162, 167, 169, 171, 177–87.

49. Modesto Jaimes Alvarez, interview by the author, Ixcateopan, June 12, 2002; Baltasar Leyva Mancilla informe 1951, AP-175/352.072.073ETN.

50. Comité Pro-Autenticidad de los Restos de Cuauhtémoc to Juan Reyna, September 19, 1950, AMI-1950/174. Such pressure worked, and in 1976 (and well after) villagers were afraid to deny the tomb's authenticity. When Alicia Miranda was asked if the village believed in the bones, she replied that it was dinnertime. Dario Álvarez sworn statement to the Ixcateopan ayuntamiento, January 3, 1950, INAH/AEG/9/83; INAH/AS/PHO/CUAUH/5/32, 20.

51. Olivera de Bonfil, *La tradición oral*, 147–58.

52. Receipt for half purchase price of house, Florencio Juárez to Rosendo Rodríguez, July 25, 1946, AMI-1946.

53. "Acta del 4 de febrero de 1949," reproduced in Reyes García, *Documentos manuscritos y pictóricos de Ichcateopan*, 151–59.

54. Inventory of municipal property, 1951, AMI-1951 caja 1; INAH/AS/PHO/ CUAUH/5/6, 44; Decree no. 37 of the Congress of Guerrero, October 24, 1951, and Quintana to Rodríguez Juárez, Ixcateopan, January 22, 1952, both in Reyes García, *Documentos manuscritos y pictóricos de Ichcateopan*, 160–62.
55. Román Parra Terán, interview by the author, Chilpancingo, November 25, 2002.
56. J. Mayagoitía to Rodríguez Juárez, May 18, 1950, in Reyes García, *Documentos manuscritos y pictóricos de Ichcateopan*, 181–82.
57. Olivera de Bonfil, *La tradición oral*, 157.
58. Swearing in of Rodríguez Juárez as tomb guardian, Ixcateopan, February 27, 1950, AMI-1950.
59. INAH/AS/PHO/CUAUH/5/34, 49.
60. Pierre Bourdieu, *Outline of a Theory of Practice* (Cambridge: Cambridge University Press, 1977), 179.
61. *La Prensa*, October 11, 1949.
62. Reyes García, *Documentos manuscritos y pictóricos de Ichcateopan*, 43–45.
63. Thirteen other strips of paper contained sketches of hanged men, trails marked by footprints, and pyramids. Reyes García, *Documentos manuscritos y pictóricos de Ichcateopan*, 17–18, 22–25.
64. Reyes García, *Documentos manuscritos y pictóricos de Ichcateopan*, 16, 26, 29.
65. The supposed author of the Rome manuscript's pidgin Spanish was Martín Jacobita, a distinguished trilingual grammarian. The two "living letters" referred to a physically disfigured Cortés, a description only imaginable after the Guzmán/ Quiroz Cuarón report of 1947; one of them contained the gothic prophecy that the tomb would appear only when the "five talents coin" was minted, a clear reference to the 1947 release of the Cuauhtémoc five peso coin. The extensive notes in *Catechismi Romani* were signed by a Padre Retellín, who never existed. (There had been a Padre Retiquin in Ixcateopan in the 1850s. The forger, however, believed erratic spelling an infallible sign of documental antiquity and consequently distorted the orthography of the priest's notes to the point of meaninglessness.) Reyes García, *Documentos manuscritos y pictóricos de Ichcateopan*, 16–17, 26, 28–30, 194–98.
66. Reyes García, *Documentos manuscritos y pictóricos de Ichcateopan*, 33–36.
67. INAH/AS/PHO/CUAUH/5/15, 36.
68. Florentino Juárez journals 2 and 4, reproduced in Zavala, "Dictamen," 265–73, 276–77.
69. Reyes García, *Documentos manuscritos y pictóricos de Ichcateopan*, 36–37.
70. Guzmán to Rodríguez Juárez, August 26, 1949, INAH/AEG/9/34.
71. "Sr. Rodríguez has said to me that he is really annoyed because you took away the documents, and he doesn't know why" (Colín to Guzmán, August 27, 1949, INAH/AEG/9/35).
72. INAH/AS/PHO/CUAUH/5/28, 24; Espejel and Rueda, *Reconstrucción histórica*, 49–50.
73. INAH/AS/PHO/CUAUH/5/7, 31–33; INAH/AS/PHO/CUAUH/5/10, 46; INAH/ AS/PHO/CUAUH/5/19, 29.
74. Florentino Juárez journal 5, in Zavala, "Dictamen," 278.

75. Salvador Rueda Smithers, "La Fábula en la Historia: Los papeles de Ichcateopan," *El Nacional*, Suplemento Dominical, October 1992: 10; Ian Jacobs, *Ranchero Revolt: The Mexican Revolution in Guerrero* (Austin: University of Texas Press, 1982), 92.
76. Florentino Juárez journal 4, in Zavala, "Dictamen," 276–77.
77. General Neri to Florentino Juárez, August 28, 1893, in Reyes García, *Documentos manuscritos y pictóricos de Ichcateopan*, 141–42.
78. He claimed to have dismissed it as a fraud. Roberto Cervantes-Delgado, "Viajeros y cronistas del estado de Guerrero (1550–1946)," in *Ensayos para la historia del estado de Guerrero*, ed. López Miramontes et al., 68; J. Aviles Solares, "Destierro de Ignorancias," *Excélsior*, September 9, 1950.
79. Florentino Juárez journal 2, in Zavala, "Dictamen," 272.
80. Florentino Juárez journal 5, in Zavala, "Dictamen," 278.
81. Florentino Juárez journal 2, in Zavala, "Dictamen," 273.
82. INAH/AS/PHO/CUAUH/5/5, 11.
83. NASA directory of bright comets, http://encke.jpl.nasa.gov/bright_comet.html.
84. Disraeli to Sarah Brydges Willyams, June 7, 1857, cited in William F. Monypenny and George E. Buckle, *The Life of Benjamin Disraeli* (London: J. Murray, 1910–20), 4:83; Donald K. Yeomans, *Comets: A Chronological History of Observation, Science, Myth, and Folklore* (New York: John Wiley and Sons, 1991), 178–79, 186–87.
85. Luis González y González, *Pueblo en Vilo* (Mexico City, 1995), 61; Miguel Alemán, *Remembranzas y testimonios* (Mexico City, 1987), 22.
86. Bernardino de Sahagún, *Historia general de las cosas de Nueva España* (Mexico City, 1989), 2:495–502; William B. Taylor, "The Virgin of Guadalupe in New Spain: An Inquiry into the Social History of Marian Devotion," *American Ethnologist* 14, no. 1 (February 1987): 12.
87. Charles Flandrau, *Viva Mexico!* (London: Elan, 1990), 267.
88. NASA directory of bright comets, http://encke.jpl.nasa.gov/bright_comet.html.
89. There were also the convenient returns of Comet Brorsen, which did appear in 1857 and was predicted to return in 1890, 1895, and 1901. This was, however, a relatively small comet and is unlikely to have received the publicity surrounding the other two events. Gary W. Kronk, *Comets: A Descriptive Handbook* (Berkeley Heights, N.J.: Enslow Publishers, Inc., 1984), 47–48, 259; Yeomans, *Comets*, 200–201, 260–61.
90. León Medel y Alvarado, *Historia de San Andrés Tuxtla*, 3 vols. (Xalapa, 1993), 1:449–52.
91. The geography of knowledge for late-nineteenth-century rural Mexico is poorly mapped, and how Juárez might have learned of astronomical predictions is unclear. The *Periódico Oficial* published a detailed weekly weather forecast, which may have included news of exceptional astronomical events; from a minute in the Ixcateopan municipal archive, it seems that by 1889 at least the ayuntamiento was sending regular meteorological data to Mexico City. Another potential source would be almanacs. These contained extremely varied information, including essays on scientific themes, and were popular and ubiquitous; some businesses

gave them as presents to clients. Minute, Flores, Ixcateopan, to Salgado, Teloloapan, October 1, 1889, AMI-1889 bundle.

92. James Lockhart, *The Nahuas after the Conquest: A Social and Cultural History of the Indians of Central Mexico, Sixteenth through Eighteenth Centuries* (Stanford, Calif.: Stanford University Press, 1992), 414.

93. Reyes García, *Documentos manuscritos y pictóricos de Ichcateopan*, 39–43, 51.

94. He also issued numerous medical exemption certificates citing "anaemia," "cardiac problems," and "high blood pressure" for peasants called up for military service. Expediente de solicitudes, August 20, 1944, AMI-1944.

95. Guzmán to Rodríguez Juárez, June 8, 1949, INAH/AEG/9/11; INAH/AS/PHO/CUAUH/5/6, 44.

96. Guzmán to *El Universal*, August 16, 1949; INAH/AEG/9/28.

97. INAH/AS/PHO/CUAUH/5/34, 64.

98. Zavala, "Dictamen," 237; Olivera de Bonfil, *La tradición oral*, 92.

99. Report, Guzmán to Marquina, September 5, 1949, INAH/AEG/9/3.

100. "The scion will save the critical situation of the mysterious secret with his prophetic words; finally and at the appointed time he will be triumphant albeit with sacrifices, sorrows and great adversity"; and "One of my offspring will fulfil his mission. . . . [H]is friends will see with warm acclaim that which he has within, and he will come to fulfil this mission; it is he who will save the situation from time and that which he will write should be the last word on this secret" (Florentino Juárez journals 4–5, in Zavala, "Dictamen," 276–78; INAH/AS/PHO/CUAUH/5/22, 13).

101. Report, Guzmán to Marquina, September 5, 1949, INAH/AEG/9/41.

102. Hugh Trevor-Roper, *The Hermit of Peking: The Hidden Life of Sir Edmund Backhouse* (London: Elan Press, 1993), 352.

103. *El Nacional*, October 22, 1949; Guzmán to General Leyva Mancilla, December 20, 1949, INAH/AEG/9/81; *Impacto*, October 21, 1950.

104. INAH/AS/PHO/CUAUH/5/2, 17.

105. The earliest possible date for the church's construction is 1550. This aside, no other sixteenth-century church has a date on the keystone of the doorway; the writing is more art deco than sixteenth century; the cross section of the numerals is a "v" shape, consistent with hurried use of a chisel, as opposed to the "u" form of other sixteenth-century dates carved by a mason; and ultraviolet photography revealed a marked difference between the weathering of the stone inside the numerals and the rest of the arch. As for the imperial coat of arms, it was anachronistic, remarkably clear cut, and did not square with the design of the entrance to the eyes of even von Wuthenau, the pro-authenticity architect. Sonia Lombardo de Ruiz, *La iglesia de la Asunción en relación a la autenticidad de los restos de Cuauhtémoc* (Mexico City, 1978), 82–83; Alejandro von Wuthenau, "El templo de Ichcateopan. Historia de su construcción. Las siete intervenciones primordiales," INAH/AEG/9/40, 98.

106. Guzmán to Reyna, August 26, 1949, INAH/AEG/9/33.

107. Leopoldo Carranco Cardoso, Bernardo Salgado, and Eulalia Guzmán, all of whom were Rodríguez Juárez's allies, were all ironically enough convinced that he was a forger. In Carranco Cardoso's words, Rodríguez Juárez had "invented

many things and at the end of the day has really put his foot in it, unfortunately." Even *El Nacional*, the newspaper of the party line, found Rodríguez Juárez a charlatan. INAH/AS/PHO/CUAUH/5/34, 49; INAH/AS/PHO/CUAUH/5/11, 29; *Impacto*, October 21, 1949; *El Nacional*, October 1, 1949.

108. This is one of several such confessions. Florentino Juárez journal 1, in the appendix.

109. Florentino Juárez journal 1, in the appendix.

110. In the eighth century BC, for example, forgers in Memphis created the Shabaka Stone: a black basalt slab that made Ptah, patron god of Memphis, creator of the world. The slab "purports to be a copy of an ancient worm-eaten document which the pharaoh [Shabaka] ordered to be transcribed for posterity, and the compiler of the text has reproduced the layout of early documents and introduced a number of archaic spellings and grammatical usages to lend the piece an air of antiquity.... [I]t is now generally accepted that the text in its present form was composed in Shabaka's own time" (John Taylor, "The Shabaka Stone," in *Fake? The Art of Deception*, ed. Mark Jones [Berkeley: University of California Press, 1990], 60).

111. Rodríguez Juárez's statement of January 1, 1973, in Reyes García, *Documentos manuscritos y pictóricos de Ichcateopan*, 205–9.

112. Compare Florentino Juárez journal 1, in the appendix, with Rodríguez Juárez's statement of 1949, reproduced in Zavala, "Dictamen," 278–83.

113. Rodríguez Juárez, *Cuauhtémoc*, 5.

114. It was not just the conquistadores whom Rodríguez Juárez disliked but also their descendants. Notebook 7 calls for students of the Ixcateopan tradition "to be Mexicans because other types of people who are mixed up with *gachupines* they're evil bad and our nation would perish." This xenophobia echoes Eulalia Guzmán's protests to the Instituto Nacional de Antropología e Historia over the planned assignment of Pedro Armillas, a Spanish archaeologist, to her team in 1949, a xenophobia that also ran strongly through *El Nacional*'s reporting of the tomb find. That Rodríguez Juárez should fulminate against the clergy in the 1976 documents is unsurprising, given his decade-long conflict with the priest over possession and use of Nuestra Señora de la Asunción. Notebook 7, in Reyes García, *Documentos manuscritos y pictóricos de Ichcateopan*, 137; Guzmán to Alfonso Caso, July 26, 1949, INAH/AEG/9/21; *El Nacional*, September 27, 1949. For attacks on the clergy ("proud ambitious and bad"), see notebooks 6–7, in Reyes García, *Documentos manuscritos y pictóricos de Ichcateopan*, 129, 133, 136.

115. Rodríguez Juárez, *Cuauhtémoc*, 7.

116. Undated clipping from regional press, reproduced in Blanca Jiménez and Samuel Villela, *Los Salmerón: Un siglo de fotografía en Guerrero* (Mexico City, 1998), 144.

117. Notebook 6, in Reyes García, *Documentos manuscritos y pictóricos de Ichcateopan*, 125–36.

118. It is also noteworthy that while the first five notebooks are reasonably well punctuated, notebooks 6 and 7 are a comma-free stream of consciousness.

119. The only document whose authorship seems questionable is the invisible ink letter. Its melodrama, its claim to sixteenth-century provenance, and its passable

Motolinía signature all suggest Rodríguez Juárez's hand. The fragmentary text, the lack of references to the Juárez family, and its cataloguing in Florentino Juárez's testament all tend, however, to place this letter as one of the original documents.

120. Ernest Hemingway, *Death in the Afternoon* (London: Arrow Books, 1994), 168.
121. Jorge Acosta, "Informe preliminar sobre las exploraciones arqueológicas llevadas al cabo en Ichcateopan, Guerrero, 1949," in *Los Hallazgos de Ichcateopan*, Secretaría de Educación Pública, 427; Eulalia Guzmán, "El hallazgo de la tumba de Cuauhtémoc, Part II," *Cultura Soviética*, no. 67 (May 1950): 38–39.
122. Guzmán to Marquina, September 21, 1949, INAH/AEG/9/45; report of Rafael Illescas Frisbie, Ignacio Diéz de Urdanivia Mora, and Rafael Molina Berbeyer, November 23, 1949, INAH/AEG/9/47.
123. Secretaría de Educación Pública, *Los Hallazgos de Ichcateopan*, 319–20.
124. Lombardo, *La iglesia de la Asunción*, 77–79.
125. Secretaría de Educación Pública, *Los Hallazgos de Ichcateopan*, 320.
126. ADC/LG/XIII/728.
127. Lombardo, *La iglesia de la Asunción*, 77–79; ADC/LG/XIII/180.
128. The tomb was created to be discovered; the means by which it was to be located were the documents and the village tradition; and that tradition was invented in the last third of the nineteenth century. Olivera de Bonfil, *La tradición oral*, 125.
129. Notably José Jaimes, Tranquilino Mendoza, and Felipe Terán. INAH/AS/PHO/CUAUH/5/28, 9–10; INAH/AS/PHO/CUAUH/5/71, 4; Olivera de Bonfil, *La tradición oral*, 28, 52, 70.
130. These jefes were Perfecto Beltrán and Cipriano Salgado. Florentino Juárez notebook 4, in the appendix; *Periódico Oficial* 21, no. 39 (1897); INAH/AS/PHO/CUAUH/5/11, 29; Aviles Solares, "Destierro de Ignorancias," *Excélsior*, September 9, 1950.
131. Receipt issued by ayuntamiento to Florencio Juárez for sale of house in Plaza Riva Palacio, July 25, 1946, AMI-1945/121.
132. That the rooms existed was confirmed by Román Parra Terán, a student at the time. *Excélsior*, February 25, 1949; INAH/AS/PHO/CUAUH/5/34, 65; Román Parra Terán, interview by the author, Chilpancingo, November 25, 2002.

Chapter 6

1. *Periódico Oficial* 1 (May 4 and June 5, 1876).
2. INAH/AS/PHO/CUAUH/5/10, 38.
3. INAH/AS/PHO/CUAUH/5/32, 3–5.
4. INAH/AS/PHO/CUAUH/5/15, 25.
5. This was Josefina García Quintana's team's experience in 1976 and my own in 1998. Josefina García Quintana, *Cuauhtémoc en el siglo XIX* (Mexico City, 1977), 90.
6. Luis González y González, *Invitación a la microhistoria* (Mexico City, 1997), 128; Felipe Solís Olguín, "Family Histories: The Ancestors of Moctezuma II," in *Moctezuma: Aztec Ruler*, ed. Colin McEwan and Leonardo López Luján (London: British Museum Press, 2009), 35.

7. Guzmán's account of the dig, in report of Rafael Illescas Frisbie, Ignacio Diéz de Urdanivia Mora, and Rafael Molina Berbeyer, November 23, 1949, INAH/ AEG/9/47. *Excélsior*, September 30 and October 19, 1949; *La Prensa*, September 21, 1949; *El Nacional*, September 27, 1949; INAH/AS/PHO/CUAUH/5/11, 18.
8. Such dichotomies survived into the textbooks of the 1920s; "all which is called civilisation," one instructed, came from Spain. Mary Kay Vaughan, *The State, Education, and Social Class in Mexico, 1880–1928* (De Kalb: Northern Illinois University Press, 1982), 214–23.
9. The list of diggers in Ixcateopan included Ninfo Ibarra, Abel Rodríguez, Juan Blanco Álvarez, and Sidronio Parra. "Relación, peones empleados en la excavación en Santa María de la Asunción," Olivo Sotero private papers, Ixcateopan.
10. *Chilango* is a pejorative term for a person from Mexico City. For ethnic self-labelling as creole, see INAH/AS/PHO/CUAUH/5/71, 13; INAH/AS/PHO/CUAUH/ 5/15, 4.
11. Dirección General de Estadística, Estados Unidos Mexicanos, *6º Censo de Población 1940 Guerrero* (Mexico City, 1942), 72; Secretaría de la Economía Nacional, Dirección General de Estadística, *Estados Unidos Mexicanos 7º Censo de Población 1950 Guerrero* (Mexico City, 1952), 124; INAH/AS/PHO/CUAUH/5/33, 37.
12. Robert Barlow, *The Extent of the Empire of the Culhua Mexica* (Berkeley: University of California Press, 1949), 18.
13. Laura Espejel López and Salvador Rueda Smithers, *Reconstrucción histórica de una comunidad del norte de Guerrero*, 21.
14. Lucas Pinto, "Relación de Ichcateupan," in *Relaciones geográficas del siglo XVI*, ed. René Acuña, 6:261–68.
15. AGN/BN-216–48/30; "Matrícula de 1768," reproduced in Román Parra Terán, *La Provincia de Ichcateopan* (Chilpancingo, 1992), 116–20.
16. The principal coastal industry, cotton and associated textile production, similarly declined. Peter Guardino, *Peasants, Politics and the Formation of Mexico's National State*, 115, 123; Espejel and Rueda, *Reconstrucción histórica*, appendix on Taxco mining.
17. Eduardo Miranda Arrieta, *Economía y Comunicaciones en el Estado de Guerrero 1877–1910* (Michoacán, 1994), 137–68.
18. Mario Gill, "Los Escudero, de Acapulco," *Historia Mexicana* 3, no. 4 (October–December 1953): 292; Tomás Bustamante Álvarez, *Las transformaciones de la agricultura o las paradojas del desarrollo regional: Tierra Caliente, Guerrero* (Mexico City, 1996), 94.
19. Robert S. Wicks and Roland H. Harrison, *Buried Cities, Forgotten Gods*, 135–40.
20. Ministerio de Fomento, *Censo del Estado de Guerrero* (Mexico City, 1899), 50.
21. The diocesan archives are filled with petitions for dispensations that parishioners might marry relatives or minors, "the cause the low number of inhabitants of this place"; local societies were clearly very endogamous. See, for example, the priest of Ixcateopan to the Bishop of Chilapa, August 11, 1894, ADC/LG/XIII/572.
22. Román Parra Terán, "Ixcateopan en el Siglo XIX" (Master's thesis, Universidad Autónoma de Guerrero, 1997), 36–44.
23. Ian Jacobs, *Ranchero Revolt*, 43.
24. Parra Terán, "Ixcateopan," 80–81.

25. Ian Jacobs, *Ranchero Revolt*, 41–59. Recent studies by Raymond Craib and Emilio Kourí have demonstrated how in Veracruz the mapping critical to redistributing land could be successfully resisted and how some indigenous communities that underwent land privatisation developed endogenous capitalist farmers. Raymond B. Craib, *Cartographic Mexico: A History of State Fixations and Fugitive Landscapes* (Durham, N.C.: Duke University Press, 2004), 55–90; Emilo Kourí, *A Pueblo Divided: Business, Property and Community in Papantla, Mexico* (Stanford, Calif.: Stanford University Press, 2004).

26. These were in El Puente, Pipincatla, Tenanguillo, Teucizapan, Simatel, and Ixcateopan. Parra Terán, "Ixcateopan," 82.

27. There were by 1900 461 ranches in Guerrero. Jaime Salazar Adame, et al., *Historia de la cuestión agraria mexicana*, 16; Moisés González Navarro, *Estadísticas sociales del Porfiriato* (Mexico City, 1956), 41.

28. Petition for the establishment of the state of Guerrero, in Parra Terán, "Ixcateopan," 57–58.

29. Between 1856 and 1861 various government orders attempted to qualify the bald terms of the Ley Lerdo in favour of preexisting tenancies. Their efficacy is plain from the shifts in tenure that nevertheless occurred. Thirty years on the legislation was still being debated, as an 1885 appeal from the jefe político of Teloloapan shows. "Various cases," he wrote, "are being brought in front of this jefatura política concerning denunciations of indigenous community lands in this District, made by individuals who are not residents of the said localities, whose processing is suspended due to the diverse interpretations which they give to the relevant laws and circulars which they cite of 9 October and 7, 8 and 11 November 1856" (AGN/BN-101/152, 212–101/95).

30. Given that Miller's estimate is based on maize cultivation in areas with more *temporal* land, this is a conservative estimate. There is no useful universal definition of what constitutes a ranch in nineteenth-century Mexico; I have defined a rancher as one whose total holdings sum above thirty hectares. This is a strictly regional estimate, founded on the generally poor quality of agricultural land around Ixcateopan. This low quality meant that thirty hectares seems to have been a functional minimum to fulfil three essential criteria of "rancherhood": the regular production of surplus, the regular employment of wage labour, and the social capital to obtain office in local government. Simon Miller, *Landlords and Haciendas in Modernizing Mexico: Essays in Radical Reappraisal* (Amsterdam: CEDLA, 1995), 31. Secretaría de Fomento, Dirección General de Estadística, *Censo y división territorial del Estado de Guerrero, verificados en 1900* (Mexico City, 1905), 48–69; Padrón de predios agrícolas, Ixcateopan 1939, AMI-1939/I; Manifestación de predios rústicos, Ixcateopan 1929, AMI-1929.

31. INAH/AS/PHO/CUAUH/5/15, 16.

32. "Circular de 9 de octubre de 1856," in Francisco González de Cossío, ed., *Legislación Indigenista de México* (Mexico City, 1958), 51.

33. Secretaría de Fomento, *Censo y división territorial del Estado de Guerrero*, 50–53, 63, 67.

34. Moisés T. de la Peña, *Guerrero Económico*, 2 vols. (Mexico City, 1949), 2:159.

35. *Periódico Oficial* 15 (November 4, 1891, and September 30, 1893).

36. INAH/AS/PHO/CUAUH/5/15, 3; INAH/AS/PHO/CUAUH/5/27, 49.

37. INAH/AS/PHO/CUAUH/5/10, 3; INAH/AS/PHO/CUAUH/5/15, 19; INAH/AS/PHO/CUAUH/5/3,2–3;INAH/AS/PHO/CUAUH/5/27,4;INAH/AS/PHO/CUAUH/5/30, 1–3; INAH/AS/PHO/CUAUH/5/35, 9–10.

38. INAH/AS/PHO/CUAUH/5/4, 3–7.

39. INAH/AS/PHO/CUAUH/5/18, 22; Bustamante, *Las transformaciones de la agricultura*, 90.

40. Espejel and Rueda, *Reconstrucción histórica*, 36. For out-migration, see, for example, the petition of the vecinos of Tenanguillo to the state finance minister, November 24, 1885: "We are one of the poorest villages in our district, we have almost no lands on which to labour for which reason many of our brothers have had to emigrate to provide the subsistence of their families in other places" (AGN/BN-218–101/152).

41. Parra Terán, "Ixcateopan," 83.

42. James Scott concludes just this for villages in Malaysia before the Green Revolution. On the *costa chica*, if we believe the rancher-friendly Vázquez Añorve, the sharecrop rate was 4 percent, and a common property regime applied to fruit, firewood, and *zacate* grass. Francisco Vázquez Añorve, *El ayer de mi costa* (Puebla, 1974), 19, 106; James Scott, *Weapons of the Weak: Everyday Forms of Peasant Resistance* (New Haven: Yale University Press, 1985), 177.

43. Antonio Mercenario to Gobernación, January 3, 1895, AGN/BN-214–48/48.

44. INAH/AS/PHO/CUAUH/5/27, 24; INAH/AS/PHO/CUAUH/5/1, 8; INAH/AS/PHO/CUAUH/5/15, 15.

45. Both documents are reproduced in Luis Reyes García, *Documentos manuscritos y pictóricos de Ichcateopan, Guerrero* (Mexico City, 1979), 138–39.

46. Parra Terán, "Ixcateopan," 53, 93.

47. INAH/AS/PHO/CUAUH/5/27, 24–26; INAH/AS/PHO/CUAUH/5/38, 4, 7; Román Parra Terán, interview by the author, Chilpancingo, November 25, 2002.

48. INAH/AS/PHO/CUAUH/5/12, 1–5; INAH/AS/PHO/CUAUH/5/11, 5–6.

49. INAH/AS/PHO/CUAUH/5/1, 5; INAH/AS/PHO/CUAUH/5/16, 11–12; INAH/AS/PHO/CUAUH/5/27, 23.

50. Scott, *Weapons of the Weak*, xviii.

51. INAH/AS/PHO/CUAUH/5/29, 18; INAH/AS/PHO/CUAUH/5/1, 7; García Quintana, *Cuauhtémoc en el siglo XIX*, 36.

52. Florencio Juárez was "de armas tomar." *Periódico Oficial* 26, no. 28 (July 10, 1903).

53. García Quintana, *Cuauhtémoc en el siglo XIX*, 40; *Periódico Oficial* 16, no. 39 (May 25, 1893).

54. This was egregiously low even by the standards of the rest of the district: in Teloloapan 7.8 percent were literate, and no other municipio fell below a 5 percent literacy rate. Secretaría de Fomento, *Censo y división territorial del Estado de Guerrero*, 16–17, 76–77.

55. INAH/AS/PHO/CUAUH/5/17, 20. This was an informal manifestation of a more universal phenomenon, the codification of literacy as a qualification for access to citizenship. In contemporary Brazil and Chile, for example, literacy was a legal prerequisite for the right to vote. Eduardo Posada Carbó, "Latin American

Elections, Parties and State Formation, 1850–1880" (research seminar, Oxford University Latin American Centre, March 2003).

56. INAH/AS/PHO/CUAUH/5/5, 5; INAH/AS/PHO/CUAUH/5/7, 11.

57. INAH/AS/PHO/CUAUH/5/5, 16; INAH/AS/PHO/CUAUH/5/28, 11.

58. Claude Lévi-Strauss, *Tristes Tropiques* (Paris: Gallimard, 1990), 343–44.

59. García Quintana, *Cuauhtémoc en el siglo XIX*, 32–36; Parra Terán, "Ixcateopan," 93.

60. Florentino Juárez journal 1, in the appendix; INAH/AS/PHO/CUAUH/5/11, 29; ADC/LG/XIII/264; Reyes García, *Documentos manuscritos y pictóricos de Ichcateopan*, 140–42; García Quintana, *Cuauhtémoc en el siglo XIX*, 35–36.

61. The conflict was resolved in 1933 by the Comisión Nacional Agraria's decision to move half of Teuzizapan's population to a new agrarian colony in Cocula, leaving the disputed lands largely in possession of Temaxcalapa. INAH/AS/PHO/CUAUH/5/218, 37; Peña, *Guerrero Económico*, 1:443.

62. Parra Terán, "Ixcateopan," 17–21; Tomás Bustamante, interview by the author, Chilpancingo, June 27, 2002.

63. Guardino, *Peasants, Politics and the Formation of Mexico's National State*, 104–6; Bustamante, *Las transformaciones de la agricultura*, 65.

64. Real Audiencia ruling, Mexico City, January 7, 1794, Pachivia *papeles del pueblo*, unclassified box, comisaría municipal de Pachivia, Guerrero.

65. Peña, *Guerrero Económico*, 1:434–35.

66. Salazar Adame et al., *Historia de la cuestión agraria mexicana*, 27–28, 53; Hacienda Guerrero to Hacienda Federal, March 3, 1884, AGN/BN-218–101/152; *Periódico Oficial* 25, no. 12 (April 4, 1902).

67. Parra Terán, "Ixcateopan," 88; Adolfo Dollero, *México al día (impresiones y notas de viaje)* (Paris, 1911), 586.

68. INAH/AS/PHO/CUAUH/5/17, 3, 5.

69. This started eight years of disputes over its rightful ownership. The legitimacy of the 1906 sale by Odilón to his father can be judged from the immediate revocation order issued by the prefecto político. García Quintana, *Cuauhtémoc en el siglo XIX*, 74–75.

70. Manifestación de predios rústicos, Ixcateopan 1929, AMI-1929; Pinto, "Relación de Ichcateupan," 6:266.

71. INAH/AS/PHO/CUAUH/5/18, 14; Padrón de predios agrícolas, Ixcateopan 1939, AMI-1939, caja 1; INAH/AS/PHO/CUAUH/5/27, 25–26; INAH/AS/PHO/CUAUH/5/16, 5; Danièle Dehouve, *Cuando los banqueros eran santos: Historia económica y social de la provincia de Tlapa, Guerrero* (Chilpancingo, 2001), 72; Parra Terán, "Ixcateopan," 86; Dollero, *México al día*, 907–8; *Periódico Oficial* 14, no. 13 (August 23, 1890); INAH/AS/PHO/CUAUH/5/21, 19–23; INAH/AS/PHO/CUAUH/5/27, 22–23; INAH/AS/PHO/CUAUH/5/28, 8.

72. INAH/AS/PHO/CUAUH/5/27, 29–30.

73. Namely, Rafael Rodríguez del Olmo, Salvador Rodríguez Juárez's son, and Josefina Jaimes, José Jaimes's daughter.

74. Michael Taussig, *The Devil and Commodity Fetishism in South America* (Chapel Hill: University of North Carolina Press, 1980), 13–18; Román Parra Terán, interview by the author, Chilpancingo, November 25, 2002; Miguel Angel Gutiérrez

Avila, *La Conjura de los Negros: Cuentos de la Tradición Afromestiza de la Costa Chica de Guerrero y Oaxaca* (Chilpancingo, 1993); Luz de Guadalupe Joseph, *En el viejo Acapulco* (Mexico City, n.d.), 53–60; Claudio Lomnitz-Adler, *Exits from the Labyrinth*, 202.

75. Manifestación de predios rústicos, Ixcateopan 1929, AMI-1929; Padrón de predios agrícolas, Ixcateopan 1939, AMI-1939, caja 1.

76. Pedro Flores owned the Triunfo del Comercio and was the Banco de Morelos's local agent; Ignacio Flores owned El Puerto de V Cruz and was agent for the Banco Nacional de México and the Banco de Guerrero; one Lauro Flores, in addition, was the town's doctor. Parra Terán, "Ixcateopan," 105–6; Secretaría de Fomento, *Censo y división territorial del Estado de Guerrero*, 50–51; García Quintana, *Cuauhtémoc en el siglo XIX*, 80–81; Dollero, *México al día*, 907; INAH/AS/PHO/CUAUH/5/35, 17; INAH/AS/PHO/CUAUH/5/18, 16.

77. Despite tax breaks the state government awarded sugar producers, his seems to have been the only distillery in the immediate region. Parra Terán, "Ixcateopan," 47; *Periódico Oficial* 14, no. 74 (1890).

78. INAH/AS/PHO/CUAUH/5/27, 21.

79. Silvio Zavala, "Dictamen acerca de los hallazgos de Ichcateopan," *Revista Mexicana de Estudios Antropológicos* 2 (1950): 241; García Quintana, *Cuauhtémoc en el siglo XIX*, 38; INAH/AS/PHO/CUAUH/5/5, 4.

80. INAH/AS/PHO/CUAUH/5/1, 36–37.

81. Román Parra Terán, interview by the author, Chilpancingo, November 25, 2002; Parra Terán, "Ixcateopan," 78; INAH/AS/PHO/CUAUH/5/15, 44; INAH/AS/PHO/CUAUH/5/5, 5.

82. Secretaria de Educación Pública to *presidente municipal*, Ixcateopan, September 5, 1922, AMI-pre-1929.

83. Nearly eighty years after his death, José Jaimes is well remembered in Ixcateopan; in the diner next to the ayuntamiento, the owner proudly showed me a framed portrait. INAH/AS/PHO/CUAUH/5/6, 19.

84. Eric Wolf, "Closed Corporate Peasant Communities in Mesoamerica and Central Java," in *Pathways of Power*, 148.

85. INAH/AS/PHO/CUAUH/5/22, 21; INAH/AS/PHO/CUAUH/5/1, 18, 39.

86. INAH/AS/PHO/CUAUH/5/8, 27; INAH/AS/PHO/CUAUH/5/5, 23–25, 37; Román Parra Terán, interview by the author, Chilpancingo, November 25, 2002.

87. INAH/AS/PHO/CUAUH/5/5, 21; INAH/AS/PHO/CUAUH/5/13, 29–30.

88. Assorted numbers for 1890, 1891, *Periódico Oficial*; AHEG-AP/659/917.273 DAT.

89. ADC/LG/XII/760, 918, 1117.

90. Manuel Gamio, *La población del valle de Teotihuacán*, 5 vols. (Mexico City, 1979), 4:264–69.

91. Luis González y González, *Pueblo en Vilo* (Mexico City, 1995), 56. For examples from the eastern highlands of Guerrero, see Dehouve, *Cuando los banqueros eran santos*, 273–375.

92. Eric Van Young, "Conclusion: The State as Vampire—Hegemonic Projects, Public Ritual, and Popular Culture in Mexico, 1600–1990," in *Rituals of Rule, Rituals of Resistance*, ed. William H. Beezley, Cheryl E. Martin, and William E. French, 360.

93. Enrique Florescano, *Etnia, estado y nación* (Mexico City, 1997), 345.
94. Michael T. Ducey, *A Nation of Villages*, 12, 108, 112.
95. Parra Terán, "Ixcateopan," 97.
96. Lucas Pinto, "Relación de Tzicaputzalco," in *Relaciones geográficas del siglo XVI*, ed. René Acuña, 6:271; Florentino Juárez, "Instructions to his children," in the appendix.
97. Reports are "shadowy" because he shows up in greatest detail in the unreliable memories of Salvador Rodríguez Juárez and in no written sources. Trujillo is, however, vouched for by Josefina Jaimes, who further claimed that the woman whose lover he killed was Anita Sales, Florentino Juárez's eventual wife, and that her family had ambushed and killed Trujillo. Espejel and Rueda, *Reconstrucción histórica*, 31; INAH/AS/PHO/CUAUH/5/1ii, 6–7.
98. Espejel and Rueda, *Reconstrucción histórica*, 49.
99. Román Parra Terán, interview by the author, Chilpancingo, November 25, 2002; INAH/AS/PHO/CUAUH/5/15, 19.
100. Dollero, *México al día*, 586.
101. Secretaría de Fomento, *Censo y división territorial del Estado de Guerrero*, 48–69.
102. Francisco Arce, *Memoria presentada al X Congreso Constitucional del Estado* (Chilpancingo, 1888), xxiv–xxv; Ian Jacobs, *Ranchero Revolt*, 39.
103. Guardino, *Peasants, Politics and the Formation of Mexico's National State*, 87.
104. Leopoldo Carranco Cardoso, *Geografía del Estado de Guerrero: Para el uso de las escuelas primarias* (Mexico City, 1942), 12.
105. Report for Aldama, December 1890, *Periódico Oficial* 15, no. 7 (February 18, 1891).
106. *Periódico Oficial* 17, no. 65 (November 22, 1894). The prefecto político repeatedly called Ixcateopan to account for this over the 1890s. *Periódico Oficial* 17, no. 19 (March 31, 1894), and 26, no. 42 (October 16, 1903).
107. ADC/LG/XII/1965.
108. INAH/AS/PHO/CUAUH/5/15, 14–15, 40; INAH/AS/PHO/CUAUH/5/26, 7; Parra Terán, "Ixcateopan," 98–99.
109. INAH/AS/PHO/CUAUH/5/17, 22; INAH/AS/PHO/CUAUH/5/27, 23; Parra Terán, "Ixcateopan," 88.
110. García Quintana, *Cuauhtémoc en el siglo XIX*, 74–75.
111. These included Naranja, Michoacán, albeit in the mid–twentieth century. Paul Friedrich, *The Princes of Naranja: An Essay in Anthrohistorical Method* (Austin: University of Texas Press, 1986), 34, 73, 95.
112. González y González, *Pueblo en Vilo*, 61.
113. INAH/AS/PHO/CUAUH/5/15, 45.
114. General Neri to Florentino Juárez, December 18, 1893, in Reyes García, *Documentos manuscritos y pictóricos de Ichcateopan*, 139–40; ADC/LG/XIII/265.
115. Silvio Zavala, unfiled notes, INAH/ASZ/1.
116. The petition was conciliatory, offering Ixcapuzalco the status of "town" and proposing a neutral name, "Rayón," for the reunited municipio, but it was rejected. *Periódico Oficial* 19, no. 43 (October 9, 1895, and May 9, 1896).

Chapter 7

1. The chronology of the fraud is, for obvious reasons, debated. The 1949 dig established that the tomb could not have been inserted after the altar was built; the lack of foundations made any tunnelling underneath the altar impossible. Guzmán to Marquina, September 21, 1949, INAH/AEG/9/45; report of Rafael Illescas Frisbie, Ignacio Diéz de Urdanivia Mora, and Rafael Molina Berbeyer, November 23, 1949, INAH/AEG/9/47.

2. Sonia Lombardo de Ruíz, *La iglesia de la Asunción en relación a la autenticidad de los restos de Cuauhtémoc* (Mexico City, 1978), 77–79.

3. INAH/AS/PHO/CUAUH/5/11, 29; *Periódico Oficial* 17, no. 84 (December 16, 1893).

4. INAH/AS/PHO/CUAUH/5/1, 35–36; INAH/AS/PHO/CUAUH/5/33, 38–39.

5. For example, he wrote a hymn in 1921 to celebrate the centenary of the *abrazo de Acatempan*, the reconciliation between Agustín Iturbide and Vicente Guerrero. Alicia Olivera de Bonfil, *La tradición oral sobre Cuauhtémoc* (Mexico City, 1980), 20, 23–25; INAH/AS/PHO/CUAUH/5/28, 9; Jesús Guzmán Urióstegui, *Evila Franco Nájera, a pesar del olvido* (Mexico City, 1995), 59.

6. INAH/AS/PHO/CUAUH/5/34, 49, 65; INAH/AS/PHO/CUAUH/5/1ii, 24.

7. The petition was unsuccessful. ADC/LG/XIII/264.

8. And once Juárez was dead, no one else seems to have done much to "discover" the tomb. Olivera de Bonfil, *La tradición oral*, 19–20.

9. Monthly report Ixcateopan to jefe político, October 1889, AMI-"fragmentos pre-1952."

10. INAH/AS/PHO/CUAUH/5/8, 9.

11. Florentino Juárez journals 2 and 3, in the appendix. Reproduced in Silvio Zavala, "Dictamen acerca de los hallazgos de Ichcateopan," *Revista Mexicana de Estudios Antropológicos* 2 (1950): 265–76.

12. Claudio Lomnitz-Adler, *Exits from the Labyrinth*, 224–37; Claudio Lomnitz, *Deep Mexico, Silent Mexico*, 263–86; Trevor Stack, "Citizens of Towns, Citizens of Nations: The Knowing of History in Mexico," *Critique of Anthropology* 23, no. 2 (2003): 193–208; Samuel Brunk, "The Mortal Remains of Emiliano Zapata," in *Death, Dismemberment, and Memory*, ed. Lyman L. Johnson, 161.

13. While Josefina Jaimes remembered him as being "an Indian type," her testimony seems coloured by bitter family rivalry; Ninfo Ibarra's memory of a "medio trigueño" Juárez is more reliable. INAH/AS/PHO/CUAUH/5/21, 16; *El Nacional*, October 9, 1950.

14. Secretaría de Fomento, Dirección General de Estadística, *Censo y división territorial del Estado de Guerrero, verificados en 1900* (Mexico City, 1905), 72–73; INAH/AS/PHO/CUAUH/5/15, 1; INAH/AS/PHO/CUAUH/5/1, 46; INAH/AS/PHO/CUAUH/5/28, 16–17; INAH/AS/PHO/CUAUH/5/33, 26.

15. Florentino Juárez journal 3, in Zavala, "Dictamen," 274–76.

16. Florentino Juárez journal 2, in Zavala, "Dictamen," 269, 273.

17. Florentino Juárez journal 2, in Zavala, "Dictamen," 273.

18. I am indebted to Salvador Rueda of the Dirección de Estudios Históricos, Instituto Nacional de Antropología e Historia, whose idea this is.

19. "Our basis of knowledge for estimating the yield ten years hence of a railway, a copper mine, a textile factory, the goodwill of a patent medicine, a building in the City of London amounts to little and sometimes to nothing," hence some decisions to act "can only be taken as a result of animal spirits—of a spontaneous urge to action rather than inaction" (John Maynard Keynes, *The General Theory of Employment, Interest and Money* [Orlando: Harcourt Brace, 1991], 161).

20. *Periódico Oficial* 15, no. 37 (September 30, 1891).

21. Bernal Díaz del Castillo, *The Conquest of New Spain* (Harmondsworth, U.K.: Penguin, 1963), 404; José Luis Martínez, *Hernán Cortés* (Mexico City, 1990), 92.

22. Claudio Lomnitz, *Death and the Idea of Mexico* (New York: Zone Books, 2005), 41. The ghost of Cuauhtémoc is the narrator of Ignacio Rodríguez Galván's 1839 lament for the French attack on Veracruz, "Profecía de Cuauhtémoc"; his spirit also appeared in a 1947 schoolteacher's ode and to at least one medium to give details of his burial in the aftermath of the 1949 discovery. Luis Monroy, "Cuauhtemotzin," AGN/MAV-135/21/10; V. Retana, letter to the editor, *La Prensa*, October 25, 1949.

23. Enrique Krauze, "Los diarios espiritistas de Francisco I. Madero," *Letras Libres*, February 1999: 10–15.

24. Suzanne B. Pasztor, *The Spirit of Hidalgo: The Mexican Revolution in Coahuila* (Calgary: University of Calgary and Michigan State University Press, 2002), 18. The undead are not wholly absent from modern Mexican politics. The Partido Revolucionario Institucional's candidate for the governorship of Michoacán in the mid-1990s claimed personal endorsement from the spirit voice of President Cárdenas, while a psychic nicknamed "La Paca" claimed that spirits had led her to the corpse of a murdered PRIísta congressman. (She had in reality buried the remains herself.)

25. Marshall Sahlins, *How "Natives" Think*, 14; Michael Shortland, review of Janet Oppenheim, *The Other World: Spiritualism and Psychical Research in England, 1850–1914*, *British Journal for the History of Science* 19, no. 2 (July 1986): 219–21.

26. John Womack, *Zapata and the Mexican Revolution* (London: Thames and Hudson, 1969), 298; Manuel Gamio, *Forjando Patria (Pro-Nacionalismo)* (Mexico City, 1916), 171.

27. I use the term loosely, at a remove from its original theoretical context of "prior science" and the antinomy with "the engineer" as a type. A bricoleur is literally a jack-of-all-trades; in a selective quotation of Lévi-Strauss's definition, it is "someone who works with their hands and uses devious means compared to those of a craftsman. . . . The 'bricoleur' is adept at performing a large number of diverse tasks. . . . His universe of instruments is closed and the rules of his game are always to make do with 'whatever is at hand,' that is to stay with a set of tools and materials which is always finite and is also heterogeneous because what it contains bears no relation to the current project, or indeed to any particular project, but is the contingent result of all the occasions there have been to renew or enrich the stock or to maintain it with the remains of previous constructions or destructions." When Lévi-Strauss specifies that "mythical thought is therefore a kind of intellectual 'bricolage,'" the utility of the concept for thinking about

Juárez is clear. Claude Lévi-Strauss, *The Savage Mind* (Chicago: University of Chicago Press, 1966), 16–18.

28. AHEG-AP/659/917.273 DAT.

29. "A national map," Raymond Craib observes, "had as much iconographic as instrumental power" ("A Nationalist Metaphysics: State Fixations, National Maps, and the Geo-historical Imagination in Nineteenth-Century Mexico," *Hispanic American Historical Review* 82, no. 1 [February 2002]: 37).

30. Peter Guardino, *Peasants, Politics and the Formation of Mexico's National State*, 85–86, 100.

31. This took place from 1850 to 1962. AHEG-AP/659/917.273 DAT.

32. Guy P. C. Thomson, "Bulwarks of Patriotic Liberalism: The National Guard, Philharmonic Corps and Patriotic Juntas in Mexico, 1847–1888," *Journal of Latin American Studies* 22, no. 1 (1990): 43.

33. Fray Servando Teresa de Mier and Carlos María de Bustamante would later try to have Mexico's name changed to Anáhuac. David Brading, *The Origins of Mexican Nationalism* (Cambridge: Cambridge University Press, 1985), 51–52, 83; Enrique Florescano, *Memoria Mexicana* (Mexico City, 1987), 305–6.

34. David Brading and Charles Hale have argued for a rapid decline in indigenismo after independence; Rebecca Earle's rich collection of references to the prehispanic past after 1821 qualifies that analysis. Rebecca Earle, "'Padres de la Patria' and the Ancestral Past: Commemorations of Independence in Nineteenth-Century Spanish America," *Journal of Latin American Studies* 34, no. 4 (November 2002): 788, 797–98.

35. Robert H. Duncan, "Embracing a Suitable Past: Independence Celebrations under Mexico's Second Empire, 1864–1866," *Journal of Latin American Studies* 30 (1998): 263.

36. Juan A. Ortega y Medina, "Indigenismo e Hispanismo en la conciencia historiográfica mexicana," in *Cultura e identidad nacional*, ed. Roberto Blancarte (Mexico City, 1994), 65–66.

37. Alan Knight, "The Several Legs of Santa Anna: A Saga of Secular Relics," in *Relics and Remains: Past and Present Supplement 5*, ed. Alex Walsham (Oxford: Oxford University Press, 2010), 227–55.

38. Florencia Mallon, "Los campesinos y la formación del Estado en el México del siglo XIX: Morelos, 1848–1858," in *Secuencia* no. 15 (Mexico City, 1989), 54.

39. Terry Rugeley, "The Outsider: Federalism, Filibusters, and the Tabascan Military Empire of Francisco Semanat, 1835–1844," paper presented at the meeting of the American Historical Association, Washington, D.C., January 2008.

40. Irving W. Levinson, *Wars within Wars: Mexican Guerrillas, Domestic Elites, and the United States of America, 1846–1848* (Fort Worth: Texas Christian University Press, 2005), 57–85, 114.

41. Cited in Enrique Florescano, *Etnia, estado y nación* (Mexico City, 1997), 369; Luis Villoro, *Los grandes momentos del indigenismo en México* (Mexico City, 1997), 167.

42. M. E. Salas Cuesta, *Molino del Rey: Historia de un monumento* (Mexico City, 1997), 99–104, 117; Raymond B. Craib, *Cartographic Mexico*, 50; Enrique Plasencia

de la Parra, "Conmemoración de la hazaña épica de los niños héroes: Su origen, desarrollo y simbolismos," *Historia Mexicana* 45 (1995): 241–81.

43. M. Rodríguez, "El 12 de octubre: Entre el IV y el V Centenario," in Blancarte, *Cultura e identidad nacional*, 127; Matthew Esposito, "Memorializing Modern Mexico: The State Funerals of the Porfirian Era, 1876–1911" (unpublished Ph.D. diss., Texas Christian University, 1997), 383.

44. Shirley Brice Heath, *La política del lenguaje en México* (Mexico City, 1972).

45. *Periódico Oficial* 26, no. 33 (August 14, 1903).

46. Alan Knight, "Peasants into Patriots: Thoughts on the Making of the Mexican Nation," *Mexican Studies/Estudios mexicanos* 10, no. 1 (Winter 1994): 141.

47. According to Rebecca Earle, "The heritage of modern, nineteenth-century Mexico began to be described as essentially Spanish, even if its history included the preconquest era," which enjoyed a "complex place" in elite nationalism (*The Return of the Native*, 92).

48. *El album de la juventud*, August 1893, August 1894, reproduced respectively in Josefina García Quintana, *Cuauhtémoc en el siglo XIX* (Mexico City, 1977), 104–27; Daniel Schávelzon, ed., *La Polémica del Arte Nacional en México, 1850–1910* (Mexico City, 1988), 126; and Rebecca Earle, "*Sobre Héroes y Tumbas*: National Symbols in Nineteenth-Century Spanish America," *Hispanic American Historical Review* 85, no. 3 (2005): 401.

49. E. García Barragán, "Escultura y arquitectura neoindígena," in *La Polémica del Arte Nacional*, ed. Daniel Schávelzon, 182.

50. I. R. Prampolini, "La figura del indio en la pintura del siglo XIX: Fondo ideológico," in *La Polémica del Arte Nacional*, ed. Daniel Schávelzon, 202–17.

51. Luis Salazar, "La arqueología y la arquitectura" (1895), in *La Polémica del Arte Nacional*, ed. Daniel Schávelzon, 139–51; García Barragán, "Escultura y arquitectura neoindígena," 182–83.

52. M. F. Alvarez, "Creación de una arquitectura nacional," reproduced in *La Polémica del Arte Nacional*, ed. Daniel Schávelzon, 155–61.

53. García Barragán, "Escultura y arquitectura neoindígena," 182.

54. Francisco Rodríguez, "Bellas Artes: Arquitectura y arqueología mexicanas" (1899), reproduced in *La Polémica del Arte Nacional*, ed. Daniel Schávelzon, 152–54.

55. Reproduced in *La Polémica del Arte Nacional*, ed. Daniel Schávelzon, 37.

56. The storm of protest this evinced is telling. Cited in Agustín Basave Benítez, *México mestizo* (Mexico City, 1990), 33–42.

57. Enthusiastic participation in Universal Expositions was a Latin American, not a purely Mexican, phenomenon. As Beatriz González-Stephens observes, "The wobbly and only recently consolidated national states of Latin America were staking a claim to rough parity with those at the metropolitan centre of the international economy. They had history. They had literature. And they had abundant material goods to exchange." Mexico, furthermore, was not alone in sending an indigenous-themed pavilion; Ecuador sent an "Inca Palace." Beatriz González-Stephens, "Showcases of Consumption: Historical Panoramas and Universal Expositions," in *Beyond Imagined Communities*, Sara Castro-Klarén and John Charles Chasteen, 231; Earle, *Return of the Native*, 5–6.

58. *Periódico Oficial* 17, no. 72 (October 28, 1893).

59. Mauricio Tenorio-Trillo, *Mexico at the World's Fairs* (Berkeley: University of California Press, 1996), 49, 54; Instituto Nacional de Economía, Geografía e Informática, *Estadísticas históricas de México*, CD-ROM (Mexico City, 2000).

60. Salazar, "La arqueología y la arquitectura," Rodríguez, "Bellas Artes," and Alvarez, "Creación de una arquitectura nacional," all in *La Polémica del Arte Nacional*, ed. Daniel Schávelzon, 139–61; Tenorio-Trillo, *Mexico at the World's Fairs*, 65.

61. Jesús Galindo y Villa, "Exposición histórico-americana de Madrid de 1892; Nota relativa a la Sección de la República Mexicana," *Periódico Oficial* 17, no. 74 (November 4, 1893).

62. Contributors ruled out extermination as "scientific" but repugnant, endorsing instead miscegenation, indigenous-language literacy programmes, and enforced education in "relative tyranny." Guillermo Bonfil Batalla, *Obras escogidas* (Mexico City, 1995), 183–204.

63. Schávelzon, *La Polémica del Arte Nacional*, 173; Tenorio-Trillo, *Mexico at the World's Fairs*, 54.

64. *El Universal*, August 23, 1890, cited in Teresa Rojas Rabiela, ed., *El indio en la prensa nacional mexicana del siglo XIX: Catálogo de noticias*, 3 vols. (Mexico City, 1987), 3:190.

65. *Periódico Oficial* 17, no. 53 (August 23, 1893).

66. *Periódico Oficial* 15, no. 28 (May 5, 1894).

67. The ceremonies were meant to commemorate the opening of the State Congress, Porfirio Díaz's and Nicolas Bravo's birthdays, the installation of the first Mexican Congress, the Declaration of Independence, the birth of Morelos, and the death of ex-governor Arce. *Periódico Oficial* 26, no. 47 (November 20, 1903).

68. Román Parra Terán, "Ixcateopan en el Siglo XIX" (Master's thesis, Universidad Autónoma de Guerrero, 1997), 94; *Periódico Oficial* 15, no. 42 (November 4, 1891).

69. Luis Reyes García, *Documentos manuscritos y pictóricos de Ichcateopan, Guerrero* (Mexico City, 1979), 18–19; INAH/AS/PHO/CUAUH/5/18, 83–84; Olivera de Bonfil, *La tradición oral*, 97; Alvaro López Miramontes, "Panorama historiográfico del estado de Guerrero," in *Ensayos para la historia del estado de Guerrero*, ed. Alvaro López Miramontes et al. (Chilpancingo, 1985), 25.

70. Christopher Fulton, "Cuauhtémoc Regained," *Estudios de Historia Moderna y Contemporánea de México* 36 (July–December 2008): 6.

71. Cuauhtémoc was, Juan Ortega y Medina writes, "almost a god for the liberal group" ("Indigenismo e Hispanismo," 58).

72. *Periódico Oficial* 11, no. 54 (September 10, 1887).

73. *Periódico Oficial* 14, no. 60 (August 23, 1890). See also *Periódico Oficial* 11, no. 54 (September 10, 1887); 14, no. 59 (August 20, 1890); 17, no. 74 (November 4, 1893).

74. Cited in Nicole Girón, "La idea de la cultura nacional en el siglo XIX: Altamirano y Ramírez," in *En torno a la cultura nacional*, ed. José Emilio Pacheco (Mexico City, 1982), 66.

75. An exception is Saudi Arabia, where kings are buried with deliberate simplicity beneath piles of stones. Peter Metcalf and Richard Huntingdon, *Celebrations of Death: The Anthropology of Mortuary Ritual* (Cambridge: Cambridge University Press, 1991), 134, 141.

76. *Herodotus: The Histories*, trans. Robin Waterfield (Oxford: Oxford University Press, 1998), 29–30.

77. Plutarch, *Vies*, vol. 7 (Paris: Bude, 1972), 24–25.

78. Katherine Verdery, *The Political Lives of Dead Bodies: Reburial and Postsocialist Change* (New York: Columbia University Press, 1996), 1–3, 11–14.

79. Laura Silber and Alan Little, *The Death of Yugoslavia* (London: Penguin, 1996), 72.

80. See Matthew Esposito, *Funerals, Festivals, and Cultural Politics in Porfirian Mexico* (Albuquerque: University of New Mexico Press, 2010).

81. Esposito, "Memorializing Modern Mexico," 231–73, 375.

82. For a list of translations, see Antonio Barbosa Heldt, *Hombres ilustres de México y lugares donde reposan sus restos* (Mexico City, 1972), 19–33, 59–128.

83. *Periódico Oficial* 26, no. 34 (August 21, 1903).

84. Epigmenio López Barroso, *Diccionario Geográfico, Histórico y Estadístico del Distrito de Abasolo, del Estado de Guerrero: Hechos históricos propios de esa región* (Mexico City, 1967), 57–61.

85. Timothy J. Henderson, *The Worm in the Wheat: Rosalie Evans and Agrarian Struggle in the Puebla-Tlaxcala Valley of Mexico, 1906–1927* (Durham, N.C.: Duke University Press, 1998), 110–11.

86. Brunk, "The Mortal Remains of Emiliano Zapata," 154–61.

87. Lyman L. Johnson, introduction of *Death, Dismemberment, and Memory*, ed. Lyman Johnson, 1–26.

88. As were the dates: Republican festivals in the 1850s were often scheduled to coincide with Church festivals such as Corpus Christi. Earle, "'Padres de la Patria' and the Ancestral Past," 780–81.

89. *Periódico Oficial* 26, no. 34 (August 21, 1903).

90. Lomnitz, *Death and the Idea of Mexico*, 246–47.

91. Danièle Dehouve, "Santos viajeros e identidad regional en el estado de Guerrero," in *Encuentros antropológicos: Power, Identity and Mobility in Mexican Society*, ed. Valentina Napolitano and Xochitl Leyva Solano (London: Institute of Latin American Studies, 1998), 182–91.

92. Guzmán Urióstegui, *Evila Franco Nájera*, 48.

93. This parallel was reinforced by the religious tone and imagery employed by later villagers in speaking of Cuauhtémoc, who is compared to Christ in ceremonies such as his *anniversario luctuoso* in Ixcateopan. The teacher Juan Campuzano wrote a prayer to Cuauhtémoc in which he is called an "adolescent Christ." The extent to which this discourse draws on Octavio Paz—"The Mexican venerates a bleeding and humiliated Christ . . . And this brings to mind Cuauhtémoc"—is unclear. Juan Campuzano, *Cinco Héroes de Guerrero: Galeana, Guerrero, Cuauhtémoc, Alvarez, Altamirano* (Mexico City, 1961), 23; Octavio Paz, *The Labyrinth of Solitude* (New York: Grove Press, 1985), 83. For an overview of the links between sacred and secular relics in Latin America, see Paul Gillingham, "The Strange Business of Memory: Relic Forgery in Latin America," in *Relics and Remains*, ed. Alex Walsham, 199–226.

94. Sigüenza y Góngora had even tried to drill into the base of the Pyramid of the Sun in Teotihuacán in the late seventeenth century. Florescano, *Memoria Mexicana*,

265; Ignacio Bernal, *Arqueología ilustrada y mexicanista en el siglo XVIII* (Mexico City, 1975), 16.

95. Ignacio Bernal, *A History of Mexican Archaeology* (London: Thames and Hudson, 1980), 59.

96. Florescano, *Memoria Mexicana*, 264–65; Bernal, *Arqueología ilustrada*, 22; Earle, *Return of the Native*, 137; Antonio de León y Gama, *Descripción histórica y cronológica de las dos piedras que con ocasión del nuevo empedrado que se está formando en la plaza principal de México, se hallaron en ella el año de 1790* (Mexico City, 1792).

97. Earle, *Return of the Native*, 138.

98. Christina Bueno, "*Forjando Patrimonio*: The Making of Archaeological Patrimony in Porfirian Mexico," *Hispanic American Historical Review* 90, no. 2 (2010): 229.

99. Florescano, *Etnia, estado y nación*, 447–49; Arturo Warman, *De eso que llaman antropología mexicana* (Mexico City, 1970), 22–29.

100. Earle, *Return of the Native*, 139–40; José Ortiz Monasterio, "*Patria*," tu ronca voz me repetía . . . *biografía de Vicente Riva Palacio y Guerrero* (Mexico City, 1999), 211.

101. Bueno, "*Forjando Patrimonio*," 229–32, 239–45.

102. And complete with stunning illustrations. Leopoldo Batres, *Cuadro arqueológico y etnográfico de la República Mexicana* (Mexico City, 1885).

103. Robert H. K. Marett, *An Eye-Witness of Mexico* (London: Oxford University Press, 1939), 52.

104. James Lockhart, *The Nahuas after the Conquest*, 413–15; Stephanie Wood, "The Techialoyan Codices," in *Sources and Methods for the Study of Postconquest Mesoamerican History*, ed. James Lockhart, Lisa Sousa, and Stephanie Wood (Eugene: University of Oregon, 2007), http://whp.uoregon.edu/Lockhart/Wood. pdf, 1–3. With thanks to Aaron Van Oosterhout for the former reference.

105. Mark Jones, "Why Fakes?" in *Fake? The Art of Deception*, ed. Mark Jones (Berkeley: University of California Press, 1990), 12.

106. Hector Pérez Martínez, *Cuauhtémoc*, 262.

107. Manuel Gamio, *La población del valle de Teotihuacán*, 5 vols. (Mexico City, 1979), 4:266.

108. Real Audiencia ruling, Mexico City, January 7, 1794, and Don Juan José Sevilla resolution, 1789, both Pachivia *papeles del pueblo*, unclassified box, comisaría municipal de Pachivia, Guerrero.

109. William Henry Holmes, "The Trade in Spurious Mexican Antiquities," *Science* 7, no. 159 (February 19, 1886): 170; Bernal, *A History of Mexican Archaeology*, 160–67.

110. Cited in Jane MacLaren Walsh, "What Is Real? A New Look at PreColumbian Mesoamerican Collections," *Anthronotes* 26, no. 1 (Spring 2005): 2.

111. L. P. Gratacap, "An Archaeological Fraud," *Science* 8, no. 196 (November 5, 1886): 403–4.

112. F. Plancarte, "Archaeologic Explorations in Michoacán, Mexico," *American Anthropologist* 6, no. 1 (January 1893): 84.

113. John F. Finerty, *John F. Finerty Reports Porfirian Mexico, 1879* (El Paso: Texas Western Press, 1974), 143.

114. Leopoldo Batres, *Antigüedades Mejicanas Falsificadas: Falsificación y Falsificadores* (Mexico City, 1910), 5, 24.
115. Batres, *Antigüedades Mejicanas Falsificadas*, 1, 10.
116. Thomas Hoving, *False Impressions: The Hunt for Big-Time Art Fakes* (New York: Touchstone, 1997), 26, 65–73.
117. Batres, *Antigüedades Mejicanas Falsificadas*, 24.
118. Holmes, "The Trade in Spurious Mexican Antiquities," 171; Batres, *Antigüedades Mejicanas Falsificadas*, 15–30.
119. Batres, *Antigüedades Mejicanas Falsificadas*, 23; Jane MacLaren Walsh, "Crystal Skulls and Other Problems; Or, 'Don't Look It in the Eye,'" in *Exhibiting Dilemmas: Issues of Representation at the Smithsonian*, ed. Amy Henderson and Adrienne L. Kaeppler (Washington, D.C.: Smithsonian Institution Press, 1997), 127.
120. Batres, *Antigüedades Mejicanas Falsificadas*, 6.
121. The crystal was seemingly Brazilian. Walsh, "Crystal Skulls and Other Problems," 132.
122. Michael D. Coe, "From *Huaquero* to Connoisseur: The Early Market in Pre-Columbian Art," in *Collecting the Pre-Columbian Past: A Symposium at Dumbarton Oaks, 6th and 7th October 1990*, ed. Elizabeth Hill Boone (Washington, D.C.: Dumbarton Oaks Research Library and Collection, 1993), 288; Jones, "Why Fakes?," 13.
123. Walsh, "Crystal Skulls and Other Problems," 124–29.
124. Holmes, "The Trade in Spurious Mexican Antiquities," 171.
125. Robert S. Wicks and Roland H. Harrison, *Buried Cities, Forgotten Gods*, 213–25.
126. Luis González y González, *El indio en la era liberal* (Mexico City, 1996), 408, 412; *Periódico Oficial* 17, no. 64 (September 30, 1893).
127. William Spratling, *Little Mexico* (New York: J. Cape and H. Smith, 1932), 39.
128. Batres, *Antigüedades Mejicanas Falsificadas*, 24.
129. *Periódico Oficial* 21, no. 34 (August 25, 1897). For more on the "great and unknown prehistoric city" of Quechmietoplican and the treasures Niven found there, see Marie Robinson Wright, *Picturesque Mexico* (Philadelphia: J. B. Lippincott Co., 1897), 333–34.
130. Spratling, *Little Mexico*, 65.
131. Jones, "Why Fakes?," 13, 19.
132. This was something of a forger's peer review. Frederick Peterson, "Faces That Are Really False," *Natural History*, April 1953: 176–80.
133. Coe, "From *Huaquero* to Connoisseur," 273, 279, 283–84; William Spratling, *File on Spratling: An Autobiography* (Boston: Little, Brown and Co., 1967), 175–87; Guzmán Urióstegui, *Evila Franco Nájera*, 68.
134. Quoted in González y González, *El indio en la era liberal*, 108.
135. *Revista de revistas*, October 8, 1899; AGN/BN-30/223/7271/14082.
136. Weber, cited in Lomnitz, *Deep Mexico, Silent Mexico*, 266. In Gramscian terms Juárez was an "organic intellectual," one of those that "every social group . . . creates within itself . . . [to] . . . give it homogeneity and an awareness of its own function not only in the economic but also in the social and political fields" (Antonio Gramsci, *Selections from the Prison Notebooks* [London: Lawrence and Wishart, 1996], 9).

137. Only seventy-nine novels were produced in the decade between 1867 and 1876. Manuel Payno, *Los bandidos de Río Frío* (Mexico City, 1964), 373; José Ortiz Monasterio, *Historia y Ficción*, 140. I am grateful to Ben Smith for bringing this to my attention.

138. Payno, *Los bandidos de Río Frío*, 1.

139. Payno, *Los bandidos de Río Frío*, 5.

140. Payno, *Los bandidos de Río Frío*, 5, 371. Payno never states outright that Lamparilla forges the documents; the key verb, *compulsar*, can mean either to make a copy or to force. The satirical tone with which he describes the claim (and the character of Lamparilla) makes a reading of fraud an obvious option.

141. Payno, *Los bandidos de Río Frío*, 6, 215–16, 368–79.

142. Payno, *Los bandidos de Río Frío*, 618, 743, 758.

143. Payno, *Los bandidos de Río Frío*, 1, 6.

144. David Brading, "The Rebirth of Ancient Mexico," in *Moctezuma*, ed. Colin McEwan and Leonardo López Luján, 272.

145. AHSH-1/28/40; AHSH-113/1159/23; AHSH-113/1178/100; AHSH-113/1187/57; AHSH-S/N/3085/12.

146. Secretaría de Educación Pública, *Los Hallazgos de Ichcateopan*, 264.

147. Lévi-Strauss, *The Savage Mind*, 18–19.

148. Armando Salmerón Jr., "Cuauhtémoc," in *Centenario* (Chilpancingo, 1949), 2, 11; *Periódico Oficial* 21, no. 39 (1897); INAH/AS/PHO/CUAUH/5/11, 29; Olivera de Bonfil, *La tradición oral*, 38; J. Aviles Solares, "Destierro de Ignorancias," *Excélsior*, September 9, 1950; Florentino Juárez journal 4, reproduced in Zavala, "Dictamen," 276–77.

149. J. Mirabal Lausan, Orizaba, to Guzmán, October 14, 1949, INAH/AEG/9/64.

150. *Revista de revistas*, October 8, 1899.

151. Julia Tuñón Pablos, *Women in Mexico*, 91.

152. Ian Jacobs, *Ranchero Revolt*, chap. 1.

153. A main thoroughfare is now named for Dr. Camerino Jaimes. Guzmán Urióstegui, *Evila Franca Nájera*, 53, 59.

154. Reyes García, *Documentos manuscritos y pictóricos de Ichcateopan*, 33–36.

Chapter 8

1. José Vasconcelos, *Obras Completos*, 4 vols. (Mexico City, 1957) 3:1312, 1476; Christopher Fulton, "Cuauhtémoc Regained," *Estudios de Historia Moderna y Contemporánea de México* 36 (July–December 2008): 10.

2. This was not the only time Vasconcelos made instrumental use of the prehispanic past; in 1929 he proclaimed himself the reincarnation of Quetzalcóatl. José Vasconcelos, *Obras Completas*, 2, 3:1336–37.

3. Jacques Lafaye, *Quetzalcóatl y Guadalupe*, 118; J. Rojas Garcidueñas, "Carlos de Sigüenza y Góngora y el primer ejemplo de arte neoprehispanico en América," in *La Polémica del Arte Nacional en México, 1850–1910*, ed. Daniel Schávelzon (Mexico City, 1988), 50–51.

4. Heriberto Frías, *Biblioteca del niño mexicano: El Grito de Libertad ó Viva la Independencia* (Mexico City, 1901), 10. See also Heriberto Frías, *Biblioteca del*

niño mexicano: ¡Once años de guerra! ó El pueblo contra el tírano (Mexico City, 1901), 14.

5. Mary Kay Vaughan, *The State, Education, and Social Class in Mexico, 1880–1928* (De Kalb: Northern Illinois University Press, 1982), 22–39.

6. Heriberto Frías, *Biblioteca del niño mexicano: El Sol de la Paz* (Mexico City, 1901), 8.

7. Fulton, "Cuauhtémoc Regained," 8.

8. Carlos Fuentes, *La región más transparente del aire* (Mexico City, 1996), 197; Mario Appelius, *El Aguila de Chapultepec: Méjico bajo los aspectos geográfico, histórico, étnico, político, natural, social y económico* (Barcelona: Casa Editorial Maucci, 1931), 179.

9. Enrique Krauze, *Mexico, Biography of Power*, 208; Mariano Azuela, *The Flies*, trans. Lesley Byrd Simpson (Berkeley: University of California Press, 1956), 15–16.

10. Martín Luis Guzmán, *El Aguila y la Serpiente* (Mexico City, 1949), 84.

11. Cited in Josefina Vázquez de Knauth, *Nacionalismo y Educación en México* (Mexico City, 1970), 198.

12. Vasconcelos, *Obras Completas*, 3:1311.

13. Alan Knight, "Racism, Revolution and *Indigenismo*: Mexico, 1910–1940," in *The Idea of Race in Latin America, 1870–1940*, ed. Richard Graham (Austin: University of Texas Press, 1990), 81–83.

14. Manuel Gamio, *Forjando Patria (Pro-Nacionalismo)* (Mexico City, 1916), 33, 14, 170.

15. Rick A. López, "The India Bonita Competition of 1921 and the Ethnicization of Mexican National Culture," *Hispanic American Historical Review* 82, no. 2 (2002): 293–94; Knight, "Racism, Revolution and *Indigenismo*," 79–82; Vasconcelos, *Obras Completas*, 3:1288–31.

16. Ilene O'Malley, *The Myth of the Revolution*, 113–32; Stephen E. Lewis, "Revolution and the Rural Schoolhouse: Forging State and Nation in Chiapas, Mexico, 1913–1948" (unpublished Ph.D. diss., University of California, San Diego, 1997), 424.

17. Guillermo Palacios, "Postrevolutionary Intellectuals, Rural Readings and the Shaping of the 'Peasant Problem' in Mexico: *El Maestro Rural*, 1932–1934," *Journal of Latin American Studies* 30, no. 2 (May 1998): 318.

18. Guillermo Bonfil Batalla, *Obras escogidas* (Mexico City, 1995), 296. For variations on the theme, see Arturo Warman, *De eso que llaman antropología mexicana* (Mexico City, 1970); David A. Brading, "Manuel Gamio and Official *Indigenismo* in Mexico," *Bulletin of Latin American Research* 7, no. 1 (1988): 77, 88.

19. Manuel Gamio, *Arqueología e Indigenismo* (Mexico City, 1972), 123.

20. Brading, "Manuel Gamio and Official *Indigenismo* in Mexico," 75–76.

21. Andrés Molina Enríquez and José Vasconcelos also saw mestizaje in terms of defence against the United States: Spain's defeats in Cuba and the Philippines in 1898 had been, Vasconcelos wrote, military and ideological defeats for the entire Latin race. Gamio, *Forjando Patria*, 10–12, 190; Molina Enríquez, cited in Luis Villoro, *Los grandes momentos del indigenismo en México* (Mexico City, 1997), 266; José Vasconcelos, *La raza cósmica* (Mexico City, 1948), 18.

22. Gamio, *Forjando Patria*, 31.

23. Fukuzawa Yukichi, "Good-Bye Asia," in *Worlds of History, vol. 2: Since 1400: A Comparative Reader*, ed. Kevin Reilly (Boston: Bedford St. Martin's, 2007), 318–20.
24. Vasconcelos, *La raza cósmica*, 25.
25. Instituto Nacional de Economía, Geografía e Informática, *Estadísticas históricas de México*, CD-ROM (Mexico City, 2000).
26. Gamio, *Forjando Patria*, 23.
27. López, "The India Bonita Competition of 1921," 307.
28. To congress in the 1923 presidential report. Vasconcelos, *Obras Completas*, 3:1228, 1321; Hector Aguilar Camín, "Nociones Presidenciales de Cultura Nacional de Alvaro Obregón a Gustavo Díaz Ordaz, 1920–1968," in *En torno a la cultura nacional*, ed. José Emilio Pacheco (Mexico City, 1982), 127.
29. Vaughan, *State, Education and Social Class in Mexico*, 214; Vasconcelos, *Obras Completas*, 1:1231.
30. "Indias" proved reluctant to apply, driving *El Universal* to search them out; the contest sparked a heated racialist debate in the newspapers; and the winner, Maria Bibiana, turned out to be pregnant, forfeiting the private education promised her and ending up cleaning houses. López, "The India Bonita Competition of 1921."
31. Ricardo Pérez Montfort, "Indigenismo, Hispanismo y Panamericanismo en la cultura popular Mexicana de 1920 a 1940," in *Cultura e identidad nacional*, ed. Roberto Blancarte (Mexico City, 1994), 358–61.
32. In Chiapas, for example, census data show little change in literacy rates between 1930 and 1950. Lewis, "Revolution and the Rural Schoolhouse," 31, 431–32.
33. López, "The India Bonita Competition of 1921," 327; Agustín Victor Casasola and David Elliott, eds., *Tierra y Libertad! Photographs of Mexico, 1900–1935 from the Casasola Archive* (Oxford: Oxford University Press, 1986).
34. Fulton, "Cuauhtémoc Regained," 8.
35. Friedrich Katz, *The Life and Times of Pancho Villa* (Stanford, Calif.: Stanford University Press, 1998), 426.
36. Carlos Pellicer, "Ode to Cuauhtémoc," in *The Mexico Reader: History, Culture, Politics*, ed. Gilbert M. Joseph and Timothy Henderson (Durham, N.C.: Duke University Press, 2002), 407–10; Salvador Rueda Smithers, "Rethinking Moctezuma," in *Moctezuma*, ed. Colin McEwan and Leonardo López Luján, 288.
37. Alfonso Reyes, foreword to *Canto a Cuauhtémoc, con un juicio de Alfonso Reyes* by José López Bermúdez (Tuxtla Gutiérrez, 1951), 12.
38. This is according to his widow and to a typed note that reads, "What is more I found the tomb of Cuauhtémoc. . . . But I followed T.'s advice and let that great warrior rest in peace where he fell" (cited in Karl S. Guthke, *B. Traven: The Life behind the Legends*, trans. Robert C. Sprung [Brooklyn: Lawrence Hill Books, 1991], 194).
39. This was curiously apt: a man who didn't exist finding a tomb that didn't exist. See Guthke, *B. Traven*, xi.
40. Roderic Ai Camp, "Mexican Governors since Cárdenas: Education and Career Contacts," *Journal of Interamerican Studies and World Affairs* 16, no. 4 (November 1974): 455.

41. At his 1945 inauguration the governor who oversaw the tomb find was told by the president's representative that, like Cuauhtémoc, he was not going to lie on a bed of roses. Lic. Trujillo Gurría speech transcript, Chilpancingo, April 1, 1945, AGN/MAC-544.2/11–4. See also Francisco Múgica's 1949 speech on the tribute to Benito Juárez, JNM and EAC to Gobernación, February 6, 1949, AGN/DGIPS-102/JNM. For the Plan del Veladero, see Jaime Salazar Adame, et al., *Historia de la cuestión agraria mexicana*, 320. For a conference on Cuauhtémoc, see Secretaría de Educación Pública, *Memoria que indica el estado que guarda el ramo de educación pública el 31 de agosto de 1930* (Mexico City, 1930), 214.
42. Thomas Rath, "Army, State and Nation in Mexico, 1920–1958" (unpublished Ph.D. diss., Columbia University, 2009), 60.
43. These are asserted in part—echoing Gamio—by the adoption of their arms, symbolised by horses, armour, and atom symbols. Christopher Fulton, "Siqueiros against the Myth: Paeans to Cuauhtémoc, Last of the Aztec Emperors," *Oxford Art Journal* 32, no. 1 (2009): 67–93.
44. Fulton, "Cuauhtémoc Regained," 15–18, 41–42.
45. Luis González y González, *Pueblo en Vilo* (Mexico City, 1995), 279.
46. María López, "El capote de paseillo," *Matador* 4, no. 1 (1999).
47. Profesor Luis Monroy, San Luis Potosí, to Alemán, January 30, 1947, AGN/MAV-135/21/10.
48. "Programa de acción," 1950, AGN/DGIPS-19/12.
49. Assorted reports, AGN/DGIPS-128/2–1/268.2/4; assorted correspondence, Barrat to Gobernación, 1947–48, AHEG-1552/159/0.
50. *El Sol de Acapulco*, June 9, 1951.
51. Steven R. Niblo, *Mexico in the 1940s: Modernity, Politics and Corruption* (Wilmington, Del.: Scholarly Resources, 1999), 343–44, 352–53; General Electric advertisement, *Impacto*, August 5, 1950.
52. Robert H. K. Marett, *An Eye-Witness of Mexico* (London: Oxford University Press, 1939), 207; Oscar Lewis, *The Children of Sánchez: Autobiography of a Mexican Family* (New York: Random House, 1963), xvi–xvii.
53. *Diario de Xalapa*, May 1 and June 7, 1945; Governor Carvajal report 1949, reproduced in Carmen Blázquez Domínguez, *Estado de Veracruz: Informes de sus gobernadores, 1826–1986*, 20 vols. (Xalapa, 1986), 14:7753; Claudia Fernández and Andrew Paxman, *El Tigre*, 53, 201.
54. Gobernación to *presidentes municipales*, August 23, 1947, AHEG-ramo ejecutivo/51/"Gobernación y justicia 1947"; Dirección General de Información to Chilpancingo, November 22, 1952, AMI-1952.
55. Fernández and Paxman, *El Tigre*, 54.
56. Vasconcelos, *Obras Completas*, 3:1247–49.
57. Ian Jacobs, *Ranchero Revolt*, 120; INAH/AS/PHO/CUAUH/5/18, 67–68; INAH/AS/PHO/CUAUH/5/9, 26–27; INAH/AS/PHO/CUAUH/5/34, 41.
58. *Excélsior*, October 5, 1949.
59. *El Popular*, October 4, 1949.
60. *El Nacional*, October 14, 1949; *Excélsior*, October 14, 1949.
61. Reyes, foreword to *Canto a Cuauhtémoc*, by José López Bermúdez, 11.
62. *Excélsior*, October 9, 10, 11, and 13, and November 19 and 21, 1949.

63. One letter from Monterrey suggested changing the capital's name to Ciudad Cuauhtémoc. *La Antropología en México: Panorama histórico*, ed. Carlos García Mora, 10:255; José García Jiménez, Monterrey, to Alemán, November 17, 1949, AGN/MAV-535/11.

64. *El Universal*, October 4, 1949.

65. Notably Manuel López Dávila (Chih.) and Ruffo Figueroa (Gro.). *La Prensa*, October 13, 1949; *Excélsior*, October 19, 1949.

66. *Excélsior*, October 5 and 19, 1949; *La Prensa*, October 12, 1949.

67. *La Prensa*, September 1, 1950.

68. Manuel Gual Vidal, speech on inauguration of monument to the Niños Héroes, November 27, 1952, SEP/Manuel Gual Vidal-G3/14. "May you be praised, Lord, for your smile, / Because it flourished above the flames, / And kindled your fire for the people" (López Bermúdez, *Canto a Cuauhtémoc*, 72–73).

69. Jorge Ibargüengoitía, *Excélsior*, June 1, 1974.

70. This line was also followed by President Salinas when he ended agrarian reform in 1992. Samuel Brunk, "Remembering Emiliano Zapata: Three Moments in the Posthumous Career of the Martyr of Chinameca," *Hispanic American Historical Review* 78, no. 3 (August 1998): 470–71.

71. Benjamin Smith, "Inventing Tradition at Gunpoint: Culture, *Caciquismo* and State Formation in the Region Mixe, Oaxaca (1930–1959)," *Bulletin of Latin American Research* 27, no. 2 (2008): 221.

72. Cited in O'Malley, *Myth of the Revolution*, 113.

73. Eric Hobsbawm, "Introduction: Inventing Traditions," in *The Invention of Tradition*, ed. Eric Hobsbawm and Terence Ranger (Cambridge: Cambridge University Press, 1983), 10–11.

74. Florencia Mallon, *Peasant and Nation*, 98.

75. For examples, see *La Prensa*, September 28, 1949; and *Excélsior*, October 20, 1949 (where congressmen interviewed said off the record that, as in other cases, "a pious lie would have been preferable" to INAH's negative report).

76. *Excélsior*, October 19, 1949.

77. *La Prensa*, December 10, 1950.

78. *Excélsior*, February 16, 1949.

79. *La Prensa*, September 26, 1949.

80. *El Nacional*, September 27, 1949.

81. *Excélsior*, October 6, 1949.

82. *La Prensa*, September 30, 1949.

83. Burrows to State Department, November 18, 1949, NARG-812.00/11–1949.

84. Cárdenas to Leyva Mancilla, April 14, 1950, AMI-1950.

85. Press clipping, April 1950, AGN/DGIPS-803–1; list of Communist Party members, 1949, AGN/DGIPS-21/1; Delgado de Garay to Gobernación, November 22, 1949, AGN/DGIPS-104/Orlando Delgado de Garay; Salazar Adame et al., *Historia de la cuestión agraria mexicana*, 47.

86. Press clipping, April 1950, AGN/DGIPS-803–1.

87. *La Prensa*, October 19, 1949.

88. Roderic Ai Camp, *Mexican Political Biographies 1935–1981* (Tucson: University of Arizona Press, 1982), 125; profile of Chávez Orozco, 1949, AGN/DGIPS-21/1;

La Antropología en México, 10:255–70; *Cultura Soviética*, nos. 61–68 (November 1949–June 1950).

89. *El Nacional*, September 28, 1949; Vasconcelos, *Obras Completas*, 2:43.
90. These became part of the epic *canto general*. Pablo Neruda, "Cuauhtémoc," *Cultura Soviética*, no. 61 (November 1949).
91. Luis Córdova, "Cuauhtémoc, Soldier of Liberty," *Cultura Soviética*, no. 61 (November 1949).
92. Burrows to State Department, November 18, 1949, NARG-812.00/11–1949.
93. Although set to attend, Guzmán pulled out at the last minute. Burrows to State Department, November 18, 1949, NARG-812.00/11–1949.
94. EAC to Gobernación, February 27, 1950, AGN/DGIPS-320/2–1/360/207.
95. FFM and JGV to Gobernación, March 19, 1950, AGN/DGIPS-98/4.
96. Cited in Barry Carr, "The Fate of the Vanguard Party under a Revolutionary State: Marxism's Contribution to the Construction of the Great Arch," in *Everyday Forms of State Formation*, ed. Gilbert M. Joseph and Daniel Nugent, 347.
97. *La Nación*, October 17, 1949.
98. Monthly reports, January 6 and February 3, 1949, FO-371/74077; *Excélsior*, October 7, 1949.
99. RVS to Gobernación, June 30, 1950, AGN/DGIPS-102/RVS.
100. Burrows to State Department, November 18, 1949, NARG-812.00/11–1949.
101. Though it was not opposed to keeping the Spaniards and the Israelis. Miguel Galán Balboa to Alemán, January 1, 1950, AGN/MAV-535/11.
102. Burrows to State Department, November 18, 1949, NARG-812.00/11–1949; Rapp to Bevin, October 8, 1949, FO-371/74077/AN3139.
103. Cited in Arjun Appadurai, "The Past as a Scarce Resource," *Man* 16, no. 2 (1981): 202.
104. *El Nacional*, October 15, 1949; *Excélsior*, October 20, 1949.
105. "Lista de personas invitadas de honor," AMI-1950/168.
106. Assorted correspondence, September 1950, AMI-1950/168.
107. INAH/AS/PHO/CUAUH/5/11, 56.
108. Assorted correspondence, September 1950, AMI-1951/72.
109. Roberto Blanco Moheno, "Conjura en el caso de Cuauhtémoc," *Impacto*, October 21, 1950.
110. It was then remaindered by the library and given to me by Anvy Guzmán. Thanks very much.
111. Thomas Philip Terry, *Terry's Guide to Mexico* (New York: Doubleday, 1962), 238.
112. Armando Bartra, *Guerrero Bronco: Campesinos, ciudadanos y guerrilleros en la Costa Grande* (Mexico City, 1996), 107–16.
113. Eduardo Matos Moctezuma, interview by the author, Mexico City, July 20, 2000.
114. Echeverría decree forming the third commission on Cuauhtémoc's bones, January 14, 1976, reproduced in *El Día*, January 15, 1976.
115. Echeverría speech, Ixcateopan, March 12, 1970, reproduced in Luis Echeverría, *Cuauhtémoc es la luminaria sin ocaso que señala el camino de México en su marcha permanente hacia horizontes de superación* (Chilpancingo, 1970), 3–8. The point was repeated in the decree reopening the Ixcateopan case, in which Cuauhtémoc

was dubbed "a paradigm of youth." Echeverría returned to Cuauhtémoc in a rambling 1998 press conference on Tlatelolco, in which he seemingly lamented that 1960s youth had adopted Castro and Guevara as icons of resistance in place of the "national concept" of the last emperor. *Proceso*, no. 1110 (February 8, 1998).

116. The new investigation was solicited by Vicente Fuentes Díaz, a lifelong leftist whose political journey took him from the Communist Party through the Partido Popular to end up as PRIísta senator for Guerrero. Echeverría decree forming the third commission on Cuauhtémoc's bones, January 14, 1976, in *El Día*, January 15, 1976.

117. V. A. Schnirelman, "From Internationalism to Nationalism: Forgotten Pages of Soviet Archaeology in the 1930s and 1940s," in *Nationalism, Politics, and the Practice of Archaeology*, ed. P. L. Kohl and C. Fawcett (Cambridge: Cambridge University Press, 1995), 125–30.

118. See, for example, Guzmán's series in *Excélsior*, February 6–15, 1976.

119. Eduardo Matos Moctezuma, interview by the author, Mexico City, July 20, 2000.

120. Jaime Castañeda Iturbide, *Cuauhtémoc* (Mexico City, 1985), 168; *Excélsior*, February 24, 1986.

121. Camp, *Mexican Political Biographies*, 125.

122. *La Antropología en México*, 10:255–70; Michael D. Coe, "From *Huaquero* to Connoisseur: The Early Market in Pre-Columbian Art," in *Collecting the Pre-Columbian Past*, ed. Elizabeth Hill Boone, 273.

123. Rebecca Earle, "'Padres de la Patria' and the Ancestral Past: Commemorations of Independence in Nineteenth-Century Spanish America," *Journal of Latin American Studies* 34, no. 4 (November 2002): 801.

124. EAC to Gobernación, February 27, 1950, AGN/DGIPS-320/2–1/360/207; PS-16 and PS-20 to Gobernación, March 18, 1949, AGN/DGIPS-94/2–1/131/802.

125. *El Nacional*, October 14, 1949; *Excélsior*, October 14 and 19, 1949.

126. ". . . ya no se dice osamenta, sino osamentira . . . ," *Excélsior*, October 23, 1949.

127. See AGN/MAV-535/11; AGN/MAV-135.21/10; and AGN/MAV-533.31/4.

128. Visitor's book, Ixcateopan church, 1949–51, AMI-1950.

129. José Vasconcelos, "El Desastre," in *Obras Completas*, 3:1336–37; Fuentes, *La región más transparente*, 289.

130. This despite continuing promotion in the school curriculum. See, for example, the recent textbook biography of Cuauhtémoc published by the Instituto de Estudios Históricos de la Revolución Mexicana. Rafael Segovia, *La politización del niño mexicano* (Mexico City, 1975); Ulises Beltrán, "El *ranking* de los héroes patrios," *Nexos*, September 2001: 94; Ruth Solís Vicarte and Mario A. Pérez, *Cuauhtémoc* (Mexico City, 1992).

131. *La Jornada*, February 15, 2008.

132. "Today, the 16th September 1997, we the zapatistas of the EZLN come to tell the bad government that it has no right to shout in the name of our fighters in our country, in the name of Miguel Hidalgo, of Morelos, of Guerrero or of Allende" (Ejército Zapatista de Liberación Nacional communiqué, September 16, 1997, reproduced in *La Jornada*, September 17, 1997).

133. *El insurgente* 2, no. 19 (March 1998); *Proceso*, no. 1197 (October 10, 1999); interview by the author, Ixcateopan, February 22, 1998.

134. Alvaro López Zapata, *La muerte de Cuauhtémoc: ¿Dónde? ¿Cómo?¿Cuándo? y ¿Por qué?* (Campeche, 2001).

135. Claudio Lomnitz, *Death and the Idea of Mexico* (New York: Zone Books, 2005), 469; César Chávez, speech at Austin, Texas, February 6, 1971, in César Chávez, Richard J. Jensen, and John C. Hammerback, *The Words of César Chávez* (College Station: Texas A&M University Press, 2002), 54–61.

136. Lyman L. Johnson, "Digging Up Cuauhtémoc," in *Death, Dismemberment, and Memory*, ed. Lyman L. Johnson, 219.

137. *Excélsior*, October 16, 1949.

Chapter 9

1. Eric Hobsbawm, "Introduction: Inventing Traditions," in *The Invention of Tradition*, ed. Eric Hobsbawm and Terence Ranger (Cambridge: Cambridge University Press, 1983), 1–14.

2. Edmundo O'Gorman, *El proceso de la invención de América* (Mexico City, 1995), 85–86.

3. Rodolfo Usigli, *El Gesticulador* (Mexico City, 1985), 11; Rodolfo Usigli, *Teatro Completo*, 5 vols. (Mexico City, 1979), 3:547–50.

4. Manuel Gómez Morín, *Diez Años de México: Informes del Jefe de Acción Nacional* (Mexico City, 1950), 281.

5. *La Prensa*, December 27, 1950. This substantially predated Enrique Florescano's conclusion that the elite use of the past was "the most powerful tool in the creation of a nationalist conscience, and the most ubiquitous resource in the Legitimisation of Power" (*El poder y la lucha por el poder en la historiografía mexicana* [Mexico City, 1980], 78–79).

6. *El Nacional*, October 3, 1949.

7. Antonio Gramsci, *Selections from the Prison Notebooks* (London: Lawrence and Wishart, 1996), 167.

8. His secretary, Rogelio de la Selva, took two weeks to reply to her request for an interview; the reply, moreover, said that she could come any Wednesday after ten o'clock and de la Selva would, "should his official business permit," see her. The rebuff was unmistakable. De la Selva to Guzmán, January 26, 1950, AGN/MAV-535/11.

9. *Excélsior*, October 7, 1949; *El Nacional*, October 7, 1949.

10. *La Prensa*, October 13, 1949.

11. *Excélsior*, November 21, 1949.

12. *El Nacional*, October 6, 1949.

13. EAC to Gobernación, February 21 and 27, 1950, AGN/DGIPS-320/2–1/360/207.

14. "Cuauhtémoc, corrido mexicano," mimeograph, AGN/DGIPS-320/2–1/360/207.

15. Visitor's book, Ixcateopan church, 1949–51, AMI-1950.

16. *Excélsior*, September 30, 1949.

17. *El Nacional*, October 13, 1949.

18. *El Nacional*, October 21, 1949.

19. The ahuiles was traditionally danced during Carnival. Reyna to Benjamín Roa and Audifaz García, September 19, 1950, AMI-1950/168.

20. Christopher Fulton, "Cuauhtémoc Regained," *Estudios de Historia Moderna y Contemporánea de México* 36 (July–December 2008): 37–38; Norberto Valdez, *Ethnicity, Class, and Struggle for Land in Guerrero, Mexico* (New York: Routledge, 1998), 43.

21. *El Nacional*, October 3, 1949.

22. *La Prensa*, October 13, 1949.

23. He asked the president to decide whether to repress or release the first commission's report. Ignacio Marquina, *Memorias* (Mexico City, 1994), 170.

24. Profesora Adelia Carro, Tlaxcala, to Guzmán, April 19, 1950, INAH/AEG-9/102.

25. Again, this was an imitation of Catholic practice. Various letters, A. M. del Castillo, September 27, 1949–May 31, 1950, INAH/AEG-9/107.

26. RVS to Gobernación, April 24, 1950, AGN/DGIPS-102/RVS; arrangements for teachers' visit, AMI-1950/129.

27. Profesor Salvador Mateos Higuera to Alemán, November 17, 1949, AGN/MAV-533.31/4.

28. Visitor's book, Ixcateopan church, 1949–51, AMI-1950.

29. *El Universal*, October 4, 1949.

30. *La Verdad*, October 8, 1949.

31. On the relationship between education and nationalism in this period, see Mary Kay Vaughan, *Cultural Politics in Revolution: Teachers, Peasants, and Schools in Mexico, 1930–1940* (Tucson: University of Arizona Press, 1997); Josefina Vázquez de Knauth, *Nacionalismo y Educación en México* (Mexico City, 1970); Elsie Rockwell, "Schools of the Revolution: Enacting and Contesting State Forms in Tlaxcala, 1910–1930," in *Everyday Forms of State Formation*, ed. Gilbert M. Joseph and Daniel Nugent, 170–208; Stephen E. Lewis, *The Ambivalent Revolution: Forging State and Nation in Chiapas, 1910–1945* (Albuquerque: University of New Mexico Press, 2005); Guillermo Palacios, "Postrevolutionary Intellectuals, Rural Readings and the Shaping of the 'Peasant Problem' in Mexico: *El Maestro Rural*, 1932–1934," *Journal of Latin American Studies* 30, no. 2 (May 1998): 309–39.

32. Hugo Meza, Jefe de Zona del Banco Nacional de Crédito Ejidal, to Alemán, December 26, 1949, AGN/MAV-533.31/4.

33. Cervantes Díaz to Alemán, November 8, 1949, and Carlos Jinesta's analysis of same, December 7, 1949, AGN/MAV-535/11.

34. Marcos Mena Gordoa to Alemán, November 23, 1949, and February 15, 1950, AGN/MAV-535/11.

35. Comité Coordinador de Unidad Proletaria del DF to Alemán, December 19, 1949, AGN/MAV-535/11.

36. Eduardo Cataño to Alemán, December 31, 1949, AGN/MAV-535/11.

37. For details, see Paul Gillingham, "Force and Consent in Mexican Provincial Politics: Guerrero and Veracruz, 1945–1953" (D.Phil. thesis, Oxford University, 2005), 248–51.

38. *Diario de Guerrero* to *presidente municipal*, Ixcateopan, 1948, AMI-1948; March 8, 1952, AMI-1952; *El Nacional* to *presidente municipal*, February 20, 1948, AMI-1948.

39. President, Club de Leones de Ameca, Jalisco, to *presidente municipal*, April 14, 1952, AMI-1952. Governors were also subject to such pressure; see, for example,

Miguel Casasola's marketing campaign of 1947. "I hope," he wrote to Guerrero's governor, "that like all the other State Governors you help me by buying a certain quantity [of the six volumes of *Historia gráfica de la Revolución*] to distribute in schools, Libraries and other agencies." This added to pressure from the very top of the state to buy and disseminate nationalist materials. President Cárdenas urged governors to buy everything from histories of *zapatismo* to *El Periquillo Estudiantil*, a morally instructive comic. Casasola to Leyva Mancilla, June 5, 1947, AHEG-ramo ejecutivo/51/4; Samuel Brunk, "Remembering Emiliano Zapata: Three Moments in the Posthumous Career of the Martyr of Chinameca," *Hispanic American Historical Review* 78, no. 3 (August 1998): 471–72; Anne Rubenstein, *Bad Language, Naked Ladies, and Other Threats to the Nation*, 87.

40. Bloque de Periodistas Revolucionarios to presidente municipal, October 22, 1951, AMI-1951.

41. *Impacto*, October 21, 1950.

42. R. Arles entry, October 2, 1949, visitor's book, Ixcateopan church, 1949–51, AMI-1950.

43. Acta de protesta, Ixcateopan, February 27, 1950, AMI-1950.

44. "One doubts, of course, that he is a doctor, because he talks all kind of nonsense and is in general uncultivated" (*Impacto*, October 21, 1950).

45. The influx caused a "massacre" of the village dogs, unused to cars. *El Nacional*, October 11, 1949; *La Verdad*, October 11–12, 1949; visitor's book, Ixcateopan church, 1949–51, AMI-1950.

46. Román Parra Terán, interview by the author, Chilpancingo, November 25, 2002; JNM to Gobernación, October 11, 1948, AGN/DGIPS-102/JNM.

47. Manifestación de predios rústicos 1929, AMI-1929.

48. Gonzalo Parr to presidente municipal, Ixcateopan, August 1, 1938, AMI-1938; case vs. Abel Rodríguez Juárez, July 1, 1970, *libro de gobierno*, Ministerio Público Ixcateopan 1970, AMI-post 1952.

49. PNR comité Ixcateopan to Gobernación, January 1, 1933, AGN/DGG-2.311M (9)/5B.

50. Cuestas had been the village secretary when Rodríguez Juárez was mayor in 1932. *Periódico Oficial*, September 21, 1932; Frente Cuauhtémoc Ixcateopan to Gobernación, December 5, 1952, AGN/DGG-2.311M(9)/3B.

51. Sales Juárez was the committee's Secretario de Finanzas; he was also the *compadre* of Rodríguez Juárez's uncle Odilón. Birth certificate of José Anastacio Júarez, November 11, 1922, IRC *libro de nacimientos* 1922.

52. Modesto Jaimes, interview by the author, Ixcateopan, June 12, 2002.

53. Acta, formation of the comité pro-carretera, January 10, 1951, AMI-1951.

54. Acta, meeting of villagers and Prof. Saturnino Monterrosa Avendaño, May 19, 1952, AMI-1952.

55. Alicia Olivera de Bonfil, *La tradición oral sobre Cuauhtémoc* (Mexico City, 1980), 147–58.

56. Rafael Catalán Calvo, governor's report, 1944, AP-158/350.003.73INF; Andres Morelos, Gonzalo Torres, and Carmen Reifa to presidente municipal, August 8, 1944, AMI-1944; acta, December 31, 1944, AMI-1944; presidente municipal

to Ministerio Público, August 19, 1948, AMI-1948; Andres Morelos et al. to presidente municipal, August 8, 1944, AMI-1944.

57. *La Prensa*, October 11 and 14, 1949.

58. Manuel Rodríguez Juárez to Ministerio Público, December 19, 1954, AMI-post 1952/1.

59. José Landa, "A Summary of Facts Concerning the Hostility of the Municipal Authorities toward the Priests and Catholics of the Village of Ixcateopan, 1949 to 1956," reproduced in *La tradición oral*, Olivera de Bonfil, 152.

60. Juan Cano Calderón to presidente municipal, February 27, 1952, AMI-1952; assorted correspondence, AMI-1951 and AMI-1952; Olivera de Bonfil, *La tradición oral*, 116, 152.

61. Rodríguez Juárez to presidente municipal, September 19, 1950, AMI-1950.

62. Acta, Ixcateopan, January 3, 1950, INAH/AEG-83.

63. Román Parra Terán, interview by the author, Chilpancingo, November 25, 2002; Manuel Rodríguez Juárez to Ministerio Público, December 19, 1954, AMI-post 1952/1; Manuel Rodríguez Juárez to Ministerio Público, undated, AMI-post 1952/2.

64. INAH/AS/PHO/CUAUH/5/34, 60.

65. Stephen E. Lewis, "Revolution and the Rural Schoolhouse: Forging State and Nation in Chiapas, Mexico, 1913–1948" (unpublished Ph.D. diss., University of California, San Diego, 1997), 29, 198–201.

66. Paul Gillingham, "Ambiguous Missionaries: Rural Teachers and State Facades in Guerrero, 1930–1950," *Mexican Studies/Estudios mexicanos* 22, no. 2 (Summer 2006): 331–60; Departamento de Educación Federal del Estado de Guerrero to school inspectors, November 6, 1943, SEP/DGEP-488 ant. 76, exp. Leyes 1941.

67. They did not in 1920s Tlaxcala. Rockwell, "Schools of the Revolution," 173, 202.

68. Presidente municipal to Samuel Fuentes, January 31, 1945, AMI-1945.

69. Assorted letters, junta patriótica to villagers, April 7 and 17, 1948, AMI-1948.

70. Román Parra Terán, interview by the author, Chilpancingo, November 25, 2002.

71. This was a standard incentive for public works. Presidente municipal to Ygnacio Quijano and others, September 6, 1951, AMI-1951.

72. Román Parra Terán, interview by the author, Chilpancingo, November 25, 2002.

73. Román Parra Terán, interview by the author, Chilpancingo, November 25, 2002.

74. Emmanuel LeRoy-Ladurie, *Carnival: A People's Uprising at Romans, 1579–1580*, trans. Mary Feeney (London: Scolar Press, 1980), 316.

75. Quintana to block inspectors, May 2, 1944, AMI-1944; acta, April 30, 1947, AMI-1947; Román Parra Terán, interview by the author, Chilpancingo, November 25, 2002.

76. Circular, Departamento de Acción Cívica, Cultural y Social, September 10, 1951, AMI-1951; schoolteacher of Tenanguillo to presidente municipal, Ixcateopan, February 19, 1948, AMI-1948.

77. Quintana to block inspectors, May 2, 1944, AMI-1944.

78. Comisariado municipal Pachivia to presidente municipal, May 1, 1947, AMI-1947.

79. Presidente municipal to Ministerio Público, Ixcateopan, August 30, 1945, AMI-1945.

80. Reyna to Benjamín Roa et al., September 18, 1950, AMI-1950/168.
81. INAH/AS/PHO/CUAUH/5/18, 71; INAH/AS/PHO/CUAUH/5/5, 42.
82. INAH/AS/PHO/CUAUH/5/30, 20.
83. Landa, "A Summary of Facts Concerning the Hostility of the Municipal Authorities toward the Priests and Catholics of the Village of Ixcateopan, 1949 to 1956," in *La tradición oral*, Olivera de Bonfil, 152; Román Parra Terán, interview by the author, Chilpancingo, November 25, 2002.
84. Report, "Códice Cuauhtémoc," INAH/AEG-84; *El Nacional*, September 28, 1949; *La Prensa*, September 24, 1949.
85. Villagers of Ixcateopan to Alemán, February 28, 1950, AGN/MAV-535/11.
86. INAH/AS/PHO/CUAUH/5/5, 21, 80; INAH/AS/PHO/CUAUH/5/22, 16; INAH/AS/PHO/CUAUH/5/38, 18; *La Prensa*, September 24, 1949. In the highlands of faraway eastern Guerrero, the villagers of Ixcateopan de San Lucas began claiming that in reality they harboured the bones of Cuauhtémoc. Padre Humberto Cervantes, personal communication, September 20, 2000.
87. For a conflict over road building, see actas, March 21–22, 1947, AMI-1947; presidente municipal's report 1947–48, AMI-1948.
88. Josefina Jaimes, "El secreto de Ixcateopan," reproduced in INAH/AS/PHO/CUAUH/5/1, 21.
89. *50 censo industrial*, AMI-1951.
90. INAH/AS/PHO/CUAUH/5/5, 19.
91. These were the Comité Pro-Autenticidad de los Restos de Cuauhtémoc, which provided mayors in 1952 and 1954, and the Frente Cuauhtémoc, their *agrarista* opponents. Modesto Jaimes Alvarez, interview by the author, Ixcateopan, June 12, 2002; Frente Cuauhtémoc Ixcateopan to Gobernación, December 5, 1952, AGN/DGG-2.311M(9)/3B.
92. Open letter members of the Instituto Nacional de Antropología e Historia, *Excélsior*, March 6, 1951.
93. Comité Pro-Autenticidad de los Restos de Cuauhtémoc to Reyna, September 19, 1950, AMI-1950/174; Dario Álvarez's sworn statement to the Ixcateopan village council, Ixcateopan, January 3, 1950, INAH/AEG/9/83.
94. Politician/historian Leopoldo Carranco Cardoso, INAH/AS/PHO/CUAUH/5/34.

Conclusion

1. Jürgen Buchenau, "The Arm and Body of a Revolution: Remembering Mexico's Last Caudillo, Alvaro Obregón," in *Death, Dismemberment, and Memory*, ed. Lyman L. Johnson, 198–99; Governor Muñoz report 1952, reproduced in Carmen Blázquez Domínguez, *Estado de Veracruz*, 15:8292; *El Nacional*, March 4 and 6, 1951; *Excélsior*, October 13, 1950, and February 25, 1951.
2. It is in itself symbolic that popular celebrations of everything from football to election victories eschew the statue of Cuauhtémoc, people crowding in preference around the Angel of Independence.
3. *Time*, March 4, 1946; *La Jornada*, May 25, 2005.
4. See Mary Kay Vaughan, *Cultural Politics in Revolution*; Jeffrey W. Rubin, *Decentering the Regime: Ethnicity, Radicalism, and Democracy in Juchitán, Mexico* (Durham, N.C.: Duke University Press, 1997); Benjamin T. Smith, *Pistoleros and Popular*

Movements, chap. 7; Paul Gillingham, "Maximino's Bulls: Popular Protest after the Mexican Revolution, 1940–1952," *Past and Present* 206 (February 2010): 175–211; Thomas Rath, "'Que el cielo un soldado en cada hijo te dio . . .': Conscription, Recalcitrance and Resistance in Mexico in the 1940s," *Journal of Latin American Studies* 37, no. 3 (2005); Paul Gillingham, "Ambiguous Missionaries: Rural Teachers and State Facades in Guerrero, 1930–1950," *Mexican Studies/Estudios mexicanos* 22, no. 2 (Summer 2006): 357–61; Eric Zolov, *Refried Elvis: The Rise of the Mexican Counterculture* (Berkeley: University of California Press, 1999), 56–71.

5. Katherine Verdery, *The Political Lives of Dead Bodies*, 125.

6. Arjun Appadurai, "The Past as a Scarce Resource," *Man* 16, no. 2 (1981): 201–19.

7. Even folk art, which Rick López argues was shunned by the Porfirian elite, was to some extent promoted as part of Mexican identity before the revolution: the Development Ministry tried to collect *artesanía* from across the country to represent Mexico at the Chicago World Fair. Rick A. López, *Crafting Mexico*, 2; *Periódico Oficial* 17, no. 72 (October 28, 1893).

8. José Vasconcelos, *Obras Completas*, 4 vols. (Mexico City, 1957), 1:1311; Paul Friedrich, *Agrarian Revolt in a Mexican Village* (Englewood Cliffs, N.J.: Prentice Hall, 1970), 73; Gonzalo N. Santos, *Memorias* (Mexico City, 1987), 17.

9. Smith, *Pistoleros and Popular Movements*, 51.

10. Judith Friedlander, *Being Indian in Hueyapan: A Study of Forced Identity in Contemporary Mexico* (New York: St. Martin's Press, 1975).

11. Benjamin Smith, "Inventing Tradition at Gunpoint: Culture, *Caciquismo* and State Formation in the Region Mixe, Oaxaca (1930–1959)," *Bulletin of Latin American Research* 27, no. 2 (2008): 215–16.

12. Arturo Warman, *De eso que llaman antropología mexicana* (Mexico City, 1970), 11, 31.

13. Steve Lewis dates the federal government's loss of interest in indigenista development projects to the mid-1960s. Stephen E. Lewis, "Chronicle of a Debacle; or, What Happened to the INI's Pilot Coordinating Center in Chiapas, Mexico, 1951–1976?," *Latin American Perspectives*, forthcoming.

14. Rafael Segovia, *La politización del niño mexicano* (Mexico City, 1975), 89–94; Ulises Beltrán, "El *ranking* de los héroes patrios," *Nexos*, September 2001.

15. Fernando Benítez, Agustín Yañez, and Rosario Castellanos constitute obvious exceptions.

16. Lewis, "Chronicle of a Debacle."

17. The number of languages is an estimate calculated by the geographer Orozco y Berra in the mid–nineteenth century (cited in Luis González y González, *El indio en la era liberal* [Mexico City, 1996], 163).

18. Mauricio Tenorio-Trillo, *Mexico at the World's Fairs* (Berkeley: University of California Press, 1996), 54; Manuel Gamio, *Forjando Patria (Pro-Nacionalismo)* (Mexico City, 1916), 172, 183–90; *Excélsior*, February 8, 1949.

19. This was measured by the crude indicator of language. Speakers of indigenous languages stayed roughly constant at circa one million from 1930 to 1960, while Mexico's overall population boomed. Anne Doremus, "Indigenism, *Mestizaje*, and National Identity in Mexico during the 1940s and the 1950s," *Mexican Studies/Estudios mexicanos* 17, no. 1 (Summer 2001): 380–82; Instituto Nacional de

Economía, Geografía e Informática, *Estadísticas históricas de México*, CD-ROM (Mexico City, 2000).

20. Ricardo Pérez Montfort, "Indigenismo, Hispanismo y Panamericanismo en la cultura popular Mexicana de 1920 a 1940," in *Cultura e identidad nacional*, ed. Roberto Blancarte (Mexico City, 1994), 353.

21. Leticia Sánchez, "Revaloran legado de Manuel Rodríguez," *Reforma*, March 10, 1998.

22. Guillermo Sheridan, "Entre la casa y la calle: La polémica de 1932 entre nacionalism y cosmopolitismo literario," in *Cultura e identidad nacional*, ed. Roberto Blancarte, 385–413.

23. *Excélsior*, March 6, 1951.

24. Octavio Paz, *The Labyrinth of Solitude* (New York: Grove Press, 1985), 87.

25. Deborah Cohn, "The Mexican Intelligentsia, 1950–1968: Cosmopolitanism, Nationalism and the State," *Mexican Studies/Estudios mexicanos* 21, no. 1 (Winter 2005): 175–76.

26. Zolov, *Refried Elvis*, 8–11.

27. Cohn, "The Mexican Intelligentsia"; Pérez Montfort, "Indigenismo, Hispanismo y Panamericanismo," 343–44; Zolov, *Refried Elvis*, 63–68.

28. Eduardo Matos Moctezuma, interview by the author, Mexico City, July 20, 2000.

29. Salvador Rueda, interview by the author, Mexico City, October 1995; Enrique Plasencia de la Parra, "Conmemoración de la hazaña épica de los niños héroes: Su origen, desarrollo y simbolismos," *Historia Mexicana* 45 (1995): 267–68.

30. Stafford Poole, *Our Lady of Guadalupe: The Origins and Sources of a Mexican National Symbol, 1531–1797* (Tucson: University of Arizona Press, 1996), 60–64; Serge Gruzinski, *La guerra de las imágenes: De Cristóbal Colón a "Blade Runner" (1492–2019)* (Mexico City, 1995), 111; David A. Brading, *Mexican Phoenix: Our Lady of Guadalupe: Image and Tradition across Five Centuries* (Cambridge: Cambridge University Press, 2001), 56–57.

31. Robert Fisk, "Some Talk of Alexander's Tomb Starts to Ring Hollow," *The Independent* (February 7, 1995).

32. J. L. Hazelton, "Japanese Archaeologist Who Fooled Many Leaves Dark Legacy," Associated Press, August 19, 2001.

33. John Bohannon, "Researchers Helpless as Bosnian Pyramid Bandwagon Gathers Pace," *Science* 314, no. 5807 (September 22, 2006): 1862.

34. See P. L. Kohl and C. Fawcett's "Introduction," Bettina Arnold and Henning Hassman's "Archaeology in Nazi Germany: The Legacy of the Faustian Bargain," V. A. Schnirelman's "From Internationalism to Nationalism: Forgotten Pages of Soviet Archaeology in the 1930s and 1940s," Evgeni Chernyk's "Postscript: Russian Archaeology after the Collapse of the USSR–Infrastructural Crisis and the Resurgence of Old Nationalisms," and Neil A. Silberman's "Promised Lands and Chosen Peoples: The Politics and Poetics of Archaeological Narrative," all in *Nationalism, Politics, and the Practice of Archaeology*, ed. P. L. Kohl and C. Fawcett (Cambridge: Cambridge University Press, 1995), 3–18, 70–81, 130–37, 141–44, 256.

35. Although its results are frequently undemocratic.

36. This can be seen in terms of historiography, too: in Europe medieval millers or late-eighteenth-century journeymen printers are classed as representatives of popular culture, voices for history's silent masses, while in their contemporaries' eyes they were certainly a cut above those masses. Carlo Ginzburg, *The Cheese and the Worms*; and Robert Darnton, *The Great Cat Massacre: And Other Episodes in French Cultural History* (New York: Vintage Books, 1985).

37. Mary Kay Vaughan, *The State, Education, and Social Class in Mexico, 1880–1928* (De Kalb: Northern Illinois University Press, 1982); Hector Aguilar Camín, "Nociones Presidenciales de Cultura Nacional de Alvaro Obregón a Gustavo Díaz Ordaz, 1920–1968," in *En torno a la cultura nacional*, ed. José Emilio Pacheco (Mexico City, 1982), 127; Rick A. López, "The India Bonita Competition of 1921 and the Ethnicization of Mexican National Culture," *Hispanic American Historical Review* 82, no. 2 (2002): 298; Samuel Brunk, "Remembering Emiliano Zapata: Three Moments in the Posthumous Career of the Martyr of Chinameca," *Hispanic American Historical Review* 78, no. 3 (August 1998): 475.

38. Anne Rubenstein, *Bad Language, Naked Ladies, and Other Threats to the Nation*, 112–21.

39. This then attracted an investor who bought land and brought tourists to the "Posada de Quetzalcóatl." Claudio Lomnitz, *Deep Mexico, Silent Mexico*, 272–73.

40. Claudio Lomnitz, *Death and the Idea of Mexico* (New York: Zone Books, 2005), 483; Lomnitz, *Deep Mexico, Silent Mexico*, 3–34; Claudio Lomnitz-Adler, *Exits from the Labyrinth*, 221–34.

41. Peter H. Smith, *Labyrinths of Power: Political Recruitment in Twentieth-Century Mexico* (Princeton: Princeton University Press, 1979), 265.

42. For more on this useful way of conceptualizing the articulation of local and national cultures, see Claudio Lomnitz, "Center, Periphery, and the Connections between Nationalism and Local Discourses of Distinction," in *Deep Mexico, Silent Mexico*, 165–93.

43. Florentino Juárez journals, in the appendix.

44. Clifford Geertz, "Ideology as a Cultural System," in *The Interpretation of Cultures* (New York: Basic Books, 1973), 193–233.

45. Joanne Rappaport, *The Politics of Memory: Native Historical Interpretation in the Colombian Andes* (Cambridge: Cambridge University Press, 1990), 179–80.

46. Brooke Larson, *Trials of Nation Making: Liberalism, Race, and Ethnicity in the Andes, 1810–1910* (Cambridge: Cambridge University Press, 2004), 248.

47. Paz, *The Labyrinth of Solitude*, 84.

48. Norberto Valdez, *Ethnicity, Class, and the Indigenous Struggle for Land in Guerrero, Mexico* (New York: Routledge, 1998), 43.

49. Lomnitz-Adler, *Exits from the Labyrinth*, 224–27; Lomnitz, *Deep Mexico, Silent Mexico*, 170–71, 272–73.

50. Defining which modern populations are Indian and which are not is contentious. In brief, there are three accepted methods for such definitions: linguistic, self-defining, and cultural. As far as we can tell, most villagers by the late nineteenth century neither saw themselves as Indians nor spoke an indigenous language. The principal features of their culture—patterns of land tenure, social organisation, production, and consumption—had likewise become mestizo.

51. E. Gabrielle Kuenzli, "Acting Inca: The Parameters of National Belonging in Early-Twentieth Century Bolivia," *Hispanic American Historical Review* 90, no. 2 (2010): 247–81.
52. Pierre L. van den Berghe, *The Ethnic Phenomenon* (New York: Elsevier, 1981), 254.
53. López, "The India Bonita Competition of 1921," 301.
54. INAH/AS/PHO/CUAUH/5/18, 66.
55. Acta, Ixcateopan, September 1, 1950, AMI-1950/175.
56. Such gazettes are ideal manifestations of the role of print capitalism in Gellner's and Anderson's theories of nationalism; only the chronology, in the latter case, is wrong. Ernst Gellner, *Culture, Identity, and Politics* (Cambridge: Cambridge University Press, 1987); Benedict Anderson, *Imagined Communities*.

Appendix

1. The last two digits of this date have been rectified to read 1810.
2. The original reads "los favores que tanto me reciolataban."

Bibliography

Archival Sources

ADC/LG/*volume/ document number*
Archivo Diocesano de Chilapa, Chilapa, Guerrero

AHEG-*series name/box number/ file name*
Archivo Histórico del Estado de Guerrero, Chilpancingo, Guerrero

AHEG-AP/*box number/ file name*
Archivo Histórico del Estado de Guerrero, Archivo Paucic, Chilpancingo, Guerrero

AHSH-*volume/file number/ folios*
Archivo Histórico de la Secretaría de Hacienda

AGN/BN-*file number*
Archivo General de la Nación, Fondo Bienes Nacionalizados

AGN/DFS-*Guerrero/ file number*
Archivo General de la Nación, Fondo Dirección Federal de Seguridad

AGN/DGG-*series number/ box number/file number*
Archivo General de la Nación, Fondo Dirección General de Gobierno

AGN/DGIPS-*box number/ file number*
Archivo General de la Nación, Fondo Dirección General de Investigaciones Políticas y Sociales

AGN/MAC-*file number*
Archivo General de la Nación, Fondo Presidente Manuel Avila Camacho

AGN/MAV-*file number*
Archivo General de la Nación, Fondo Presidente Miguel Alemán Valdés

AMI-*box number/file number*
Archivo Municipal de Ixcateopan, Guerrero

FO-*series number/file number/ paper number*	National Archives, Papers of the Foreign Office
INAH/AEG/*box number/ file number*	Instituto Nacional de Antropología e Historia, Archivo Eulalia Guzmán
INAH/AS/PHO/CUAUH/5/ *file number/page number*	Instituto Nacional de Antropología e Historia, Archivo Sónoro Programa de Historia Oral Cuauhtémoc
INAH/ASZ/*box number/ file number*	Instituto Nacional de Antropología e Historia, Archivo Silvio Zavala
IRC	Ixcateopan Registro Civil, Ixcateopan, Guerrero
NARG-*series number/file number*	U.S. National Archives Record Group
SEP/*box number/file number*	Secretaría de Educación Pública

Periodicals

Así Somos . . .
Cultura Soviética
Diario de Xalapa
El Día
El Insurgente
El Nacional
El Popular
El Redondel
El Sol de Acapulco
El Universal
Excélsior
Impacto
La Jornada
La Nación
La Prensa
La Verdad, agil, audaz, dinámico, un diario al servicio del estado de Guerrero
Novedades
Ovaciones
Periódico Oficial del Gobierno del Estado de Guerrero
Proceso
Revista de Revistas
Time
Todo

Primary Sources

Aguilar, Francisco de. *Relación breve de la conquista de la Nueva España*. Mexico City, 1977.

Alemán, Miguel. *Remembranzas y testimoniosi*. Mexico City, 1987.

Alvarez, M. F. "Creación de una arquitectura nacional." Reproduced in *La Polémica del Arte Nacional*, edited by Daniel Schávelzon. Mexico City, 1988.

Appelius, Mario. *El Aguila de Chapultepec: Méjico bajo los aspectos geográfico, histórico, étnico, político, natural, social y económico*. Barcelona: Casa Editorial Maucci, 1931.

Arce, Francisco. *Memoria presentada al X Congreso Constitucional del Estado*. Chilpancingo, 1888.

Azuela, Mariano. *The Flies*. Translated by Lesley Byrd Simpson. Berkeley: University of California Press, 1956.

Batres, Leopoldo. *Antigüedades Mejicanas Falsificadas: Falsificación y Falsificadores*. Mexico City, 1910.

———. *Cuadro arqueológico y etnográfico de la República Mexicana*. Mexico City, 1885.

Berlin, Heinrich, and Robert Barlow, eds. *Anales de Tlatelolco*. Mexico City, 1980.

Bernal Díaz del Castillo. *The Conquest of New Spain*. Harmondsworth, U.K.: Penguin, 1963.

———. *Historia verdadera de la conquista de la Nueva España*. 2 vols. Mexico City, 1983.

Blanco Moheno, Roberto. *Memorias de un reportero*. Mexico City, 1965.

Blázquez Domínguez, Carmen. *Estado de Veracruz: Informes de sus gobernadores, 1826–1986*. 20 vols. Xalapa, 1986.

Caballero, Manuel. *Primer almanaque histórico, artístico y monumental de la República Mexicana para 1884–1885*. Mexico City, 1884.

Calderón de la Barca, Fanny. *Life in Mexico*. Berkeley: University of California Press, 1982.

Campuzano, Juan. *Cinco Héroes de Guerrero: Galeana, Guerrero, Cuauhtémoc, Alvarez, Altamirano*. Mexico City, 1961.

Cárdenas, Lázaro. *Obras: I—Apuntes 1941–1956*. Vol. 2. Mexico City, 1973.

Carranco Cardoso, Leopoldo. *Geografía del Estado de Guerrero: Para el uso de las escuelas primarias*. Mexico City, 1942.

Casasola, Agustín Victor, and David Elliott, eds. *Tierra y Libertad! Photographs of Mexico, 1900–1935 from the Casasola Archive*. Oxford: Oxford University Press, 1986.

Castañeda Iturbide, Jaime. *Cuauhtémoc*. Mexico City, 1985.

Cervantes-Delgado, Roberto. "Viajeros y cronistas del estado de Guerrero (1550–1946)." In *Ensayos para la historia del estado de Guerrero*, edited by Alvaro López Miramontes et al. Chilpancingo, 1985.

Chavero, Alfredo. *México a través de los siglos*. Mexico City, undated, first publication 1884.

Chávez, César, Richard J. Jensen, and John C. Hammerback. *The Words of César Chávez*. College Station: Texas A&M University Press, 2002.

Chimalpahín Cuauhtlehuanitzin, Francisco de San Antón Muñon. *Relaciones Originales de Chalco Amaquemecan*. Mexico City, 1965.

Clavijero, Francisco Xavier. *Historia antigua de México*. London, 1826.

Cortés, Hernán. *Cartas de Relación*. 2 vols. Madrid, 1940.

————. *Cartas de Relación.* Mexico City, 1973.

Díaz, Porfirio. *Informe del Ciudadano General . . . a sus compatriotas.* Mexico City, 1896.

Díaz Cárdenas, León, ed. *El Conquistador Anónimo.* Mexico City, 1941.

Dirección General de Estadística, Estados Unidos Mexicanos. *6° Censo de Población 1940 Guerrero.* Mexico City, 1942.

Dollero, Adolfo. *México al día (impresiones y notas de viaje).* Paris, 1911.

Durán, Diego. *Historia de las Indias de Nueva España e Islas de Tierra Firme.* 2 vols. Mexico City, 1967.

Echeverría, Luis. *Cuauhtémoc es la luminaria sin ocaso que señala el camino de México en su marcha permanente hacía horizontes de superación.* Chilpancingo, 1970.

Finerty, John F. *John F. Finerty Reports Porfirian Mexico, 1879.* El Paso: Texas Western Press, 1974.

Flandrau, Charles. *Viva Mexico!* London: Elan, 1990.

Frías, Heriberto. *Biblioteca del niño mexicano: El Grito de Libertad ó Viva la Independencia.* Mexico City, 1901.

————. *Biblioteca del niño mexicano: El Sol de la Paz.* Mexico City, 1901.

————. *Biblioteca del niño mexicano: ¡Once años de guerra! ó El pueblo contra el tírano.* Mexico City, 1901.

Fuentes, Carlos. *La región más transparente del aire.* Mexico City, 1996.

Gamio, Manuel. *Forjando Patria (Pro-Nacionalismo).* Mexico City, 1916.

————. *La población del valle de Teotihuacán.* 5 vols. Mexico City, 1979.

García Barragán, E. "Escultura y arquitectura neoindígena." In *La Polémica del Arte Nacional,* edited by Daniel Schávelzon. Mexico City, 1988.

García Morales, Soledad, and José Velasco Toro, eds. *Memorias e informes de jefes políticos y autoridades del régimen porfirista 1883–1911 Estado de Veracruz.* Xalapa, 1997.

Gómez Morín, Manuel. *Diez Años de México: Informes del Jefe de Acción Nacional.* Mexico City, 1950.

Gratacap, L. P. "An Archaeological Fraud." *Science* 8, no. 196 (November 5, 1886).

Gruzinski, Serge. *La guerra de las imágenes: De Cristóbal Colón a "Blade Runner" (1492–2019).* Mexico City, 1995.

Guadalupe Joseph, Luz de. *En el viejo Acapulco.* Mexico City, n.d.

Guzmán, Martín Luis. *El Aguila y la Serpiente.* Mexico City, 1949.

Guzmán Urióstegui, Jesús. *Evila Franco Nájera, a pesar del olvido.* Mexico City, 1995.

Herodotus: The Histories. Translated by Robin Waterfield. Oxford: Oxford University Press, 1998.

Holmes, William Henry. "The Trade in Spurious Mexican Antiquities." *Science* 7, no. 159 (February 19, 1886).

Instituto Nacional de Economía, Geografía e Informática. *Estadísticas históricas de México,* CD-ROM. Mexico City, 2000.

Ixtlilxóchitl, Fernando de Alva. *Décima tercia relación de la venida de los españoles y principio de la ley evangélica.* Mexico City, 1938.

————. *Historia de la nación chichimeca.* Madrid: Historia 16, 1985.

————. *Obras Históricas.* Mexico City, 1977.

Jara Díaz, Joaquín, and Elias G. Torres Natterman. *Primer Ciclo 1° y 2° años Historia Gráfica de México.* Mexico City, 1952.

Krauze, Enrique. "Los diarios espiritistas de Francisco I. Madero." *Letras Libres*, February 1999.

León-Portilla, Miguel. *Visión de los vencidos: Relaciones indígenas de la conquista.* Mexico City, 1992.

León y Gama, Antonio de. *Descripción histórica y cronológica de las dos piedras que con ocasión del nuevo empedrado que se está formando en la plaza principal de México, se hallaron en ella el año de 1790.* Mexico City, 1792.

López Bermúdez, José. *Canto a Cuauhtémoc, con un juicio de Alfonso Reyes.* Tuxtla Gutiérrez, 1951.

López de Gómara, Francisco. *Historia general de las Indias.* Barcelona, 1965.

López Miramontes, Alvaro. "Panorama historiográfica del estado de Guerrero." In *Ensayos para la historia del estado de Guerrero*, edited by Alvaro López Miramontes et al. Chilpancingo, 1985.

Marett, Robert H. K. *An Eye-Witness of Mexico.* London: Oxford University Press, 1939.

Marquina, Ignacio. *Memorias.* Mexico City, 1994.

Martínez, José Luis, ed. *Documentos Cortesianos.* Mexico City, 1991.

Mendieta y Nuñez, Lucio, and José Gómez Robleda. *Problemas de la universidad.* Mexico City, 1948.

Ministerio de Fomento. *Censo del Estado de Guerrero.* Mexico City, 1899.

Motolinía. *Historia de las cosas de la Nueva España.* Madrid, 1988.

Novo, Salvador. *La vida en México en el periodo presidencial de Miguel Alemán.* Mexico City, 1994.

Orozco y Berra, Manuel. *Códice Ramírez: Relación del origen de los indios que habitan esta Nueva España según sus historias.* Mexico City, 1979.

Paz, Octavio. *The Labyrinth of Solitude.* New York: Grove Press, 1985.

Pellicer, Carlos. "Ode to Cuauhtémoc." In *The Mexico Reader: History, Culture, Politics*, edited by Gilbert M. Joseph and Timothy Henderson. Durham, N.C.: Duke University Press, 2002.

Pinter, Harold. *Collected Works: One.* New York: Grove Weidenfeld, 1976.

Pinto, Lucas. "Relación de Ichateupan." In *Relaciones geográficas del siglo XVI: México.* Edited by René Acuña. 10 vols. Mexico City, 1982–.

———. "Relación de Tzicaputzalco." In *Relaciones geográficas del siglo XVI: México.* Edited by René Acuña. 10 vols. Mexico City, 1982–.

Riva Palacio, Vicente. *México a través de los siglos.* 6 vols. Mexico City, undated edition.

———, and Manuel Payno. *El libro rojo.* Mexico City, 1870.

———, and Juan de Dios Peza. *Tradiciones y Leyendas Mexicanas.* Mexico City, 1996.

Rivera Cambas, Manuel. *Los gobernantes de Mexico.* Mexico City, 1962 [1872].

Robinson Wright, Marie. *Picturesque Mexico.* Philadelphia: J. B. Lippincott Co., 1897.

Rodríguez, Francisco. "Bellas Artes: Arquitectura y arqueología mexicanas" (1899). Reproduced in *La Polémica del Arte Nacional*, edited by Daniel Schávelzon. Mexico City, 1988.

Rodríguez Juárez, Salvador. *Cuauhtémoc.* Taxco, 1987.

Sahagún, Bernardino de. *Historia general de las cosas de Nueva España.* Mexico City, 1989.

Salazar, Luis. "La arqueología y la arquitectura" (1895). In *La Polémica del Arte Nacional*, edited by Daniel Schávelzon. Mexico City, 1988.

Salmerón, Armando, Jr. "Cuauhtémoc." In *Centenario*. Chilpancingo, 1949.

Sánchez, Leticia. "Revaloran legado de Manuel Rodríguez." *Reforma*, March 10, 1998.

Santos, Gonzalo N. *Memorias*. Mexico City, 1987.

Secretaría de Educación Pública. *Memoria de la SEP 1949-1950*. Mexico City, 1950.

Secretaría de Educación Pública. *Memoria que indica el estado que guarda el ramo de educación pública el 31 de agosto de 1930*. Mexico City, 1930.

Secretaría de Fomento, Dirección General de Estadística. *Censo y división territorial del Estado de Guerrero, verificados en 1900*. Mexico City, 1905.

Secretaría de la Economía Nacional, Dirección General de Estadística. *Estados Unidos Mexicanos 7° Censo de Población 1950 Guerrero*. Mexico City, 1952.

Shuchhardt, Carl. *Schliemann's Discoveries of the Ancient World*. New York: Avenel Books, 1979 [1891].

Spratling, William. *File on Spratling: An Autobiography*. Boston: Little, Brown and Co., 1967.

———. *Little Mexico*. New York: J. Cape and H. Smith, 1932.

Tezozómoc, Fernando Alvarado. *Crónica Mexicáyotl*. Mexico City, 1975.

Torquemada, Juan de. *Monarquía Indiana*. Mexico City, 1975.

Usigli, Rodolfo. *El Gesticulador*. Mexico City, 1985.

———. *Teatro Completo*. 5 vols. Mexico City, 1979.

Vasconcelos, José. *La raza cósmica*. Mexico City, 1948.

———. *Obras Completas*. 4 vols. Mexico City, 1957.

Secondary Sources

Acosta, Jorge. "Informe preliminar sobre las exploraciones arqueológicas llevadas al cabo en Ichcateopan, Guerrero, 1949." In *Los Hallazgos de Ichcateopan: Actas y dictámenes de la Comisión Investigadora*, edited by Secretaría de Educación Pública. Mexico City, 1962.

Aguilar Camín, Hector. "Nociones Presidenciales de Cultura Nacional de Alvaro Obregón a Gustavo Díaz Ordaz, 1920-1968." In *En torno a la cultura nacional*, edited by José Emilio Pacheco. Mexico City, 1982.

Almond, Gabriel, and Sidney Verba. *The Civic Culture: Political Attitude and Democracy in Five Nations*. Newbury Park, Calif.: Sage Publications, 1989.

Alonso, Ana María. "The Politics of Space, Time and Substance: State Formation, Nationalism, and Ethnicity." *Annual Review of Anthropology*, 1994.

Anderson, Benedict. *Imagined Communities: Reflections on the Origin and Spread of Nationalism*. London: Verso, 1991.

Appadurai, Arjun. "The Past as a Scarce Resource." *Man* 16, no. 2 (1981).

Arnold, Bettina, and Henning Hassman. "Archaeology in Nazi Germany: The Legacy of the Faustian Bargain." In *Nationalism, Politics, and the Practice of Archaeology*, edited by P. L. Kohl and C. Fawcett. Cambridge: Cambridge University Press, 1995.

Bantjes, Adrian A. "The Eighth Sacrament: Nationalism and Revolutionary Political Culture in Mexico." In *Citizens of the Pyramid: Essays on Mexican Political Culture*, edited by Wil Pansters. Amsterdam: Thela Pub, 1997.

Barbosa Heldt, Antonio. *Hombres ilustres de México y lugares donde reposan sus restos.* Mexico City, 1972.

Barlow, Robert. *The Extent of the Empire of the Culhua Mexica.* Berkeley: University of California Press, 1949.

——, ed. *Los Mexica y la triple alianza.* Mexico City, 1990.

Bartra, Armando. *Guerrero Bronco: Campesinos, ciudadanos y guerrilleros en la Costa Grande.* Mexico City, 1996.

Basave Benítez, Agustín. *México mestizo.* Mexico City, 1990.

Baud, Michiel. "Beyond Benedict Anderson: Nation-Building and Popular Democracy in Latin America." *International Review of Social History* 50 (2005).

Bayard, Pierre. *Sherlock Holmes Was Wrong: Reopening the Case of the Hound of the Baskervilles.* New York: Bloomsbury, 2008.

Beezley, William H., Cheryl E. Martin, and William E. French, eds. *Rituals of Rule, Rituals of Resistance: Public Celebrations and Popular Culture in Mexico.* Wilmington, Del.: Scholarly Resources, 1994.

Beltrán, Ulises. "El *ranking* de los héroes patrios." *Nexos,* September 2001.

Benjamin, Thomas. *La Revolución: Mexico's Great Revolution as Memory, Myth, and History.* Austin: University of Texas Press, 2000.

Berghe, Pierre L. van den. *The Ethnic Phenomenon.* New York: Elsevier, 1981.

Bernal, Ignacio. *Arqueología ilustrada y mexicanista en el siglo XVIII.* Mexico City, 1975.

——. *A History of Mexican Archaeology.* London: Thames and Hudson, 1980.

Blancarte, Roberto, ed. *Cultura e identidad nacional.* Mexico City, 1994.

Bloch, Maurice. *The Royal Touch: Sacred Monarchy and Scrofula in England and France.* Translated by J. E. Anderson. London: Routledge and Kegan Paul, 1973.

Bohannon, John. "Researchers Helpless as Bosnian Pyramid Bandwagon Gathers Pace." *Science* 314, no. 5807 (September 22, 2006).

Bonfil Batalla, Guillermo. *México Profundo: Una civilización negada.* Mexico City, 1987.

——. *Obras escogidas.* Mexico City, 1995.

Bourdieu, Pierre. *Outline of a Theory of Practice.* Cambridge: Cambridge University Press, 1977.

Brading, David A. *The First America: The Spanish Monarchy, Creole Patriots, and the Liberal State, 1492–1867.* Cambridge: Cambridge University Press, 1991.

——. "Manuel Gamio and Official *Indigenismo* in Mexico." *Bulletin of Latin American Research* 7, no. 1 (1988).

——. *Mexican Phoenix: Our Lady of Guadalupe: Image and Tradition across Five Centuries.* Cambridge: Cambridge University Press, 2001.

——. *The Origins of Mexican Nationalism.* Cambridge: Cambridge University Press, 1985.

——. *Prophecy and Myth in Mexican History.* Cambridge: Cambridge University Press, 1984.

——. "The Rebirth of Ancient Mexico." In *Moctezuma: Aztec Ruler,* edited by Colin McEwan and Leonardo López Luján. London: British Museum Press, 2009.

Brice Heath, Shirley. *La política del lenguaje en México.* Mexico City, 1972.

Brooks, Francis J. "Motecuzoma Xocoyotl, Hernán Cortés, and Bernal Díaz del Castillo: The Construction of an Arrest." *Hispanic American Historical Review* 75, no. 2 (May 1995).

Brunk, Samuel. "The Mortal Remains of Emiliano Zapata." In *Death, Dismemberment, and Memory: Body Politics in Latin America*, edited by Lyman L. Johnson. Albuquerque: University of New Mexico Press, 2004.

——. "Remembering Emiliano Zapata: Three Moments in the Posthumous Career of the Martyr of Chinameca." *Hispanic American Historical Review* 78, no. 3 (August 1998).

Buchenau, Jürgen. "The Arm and Body of a Revolution: Remembering Mexico's Last Caudillo, Alvaro Obregón." In *Death, Dismemberment, and Memory: Body Politics in Latin America*, edited by Lyman L. Johnson. Albuquerque: University of New Mexico Press, 2004.

Bueno, Christina. "*Forjando Patrimonio*: The Making of Archaeological Patrimony in Porfirian Mexico." *Hispanic American Historical Review* 90, no. 2 (2010).

Bustamante Álvarez, Tomás. *Las transformaciones de la agricultura o las paradojas del desarrollo regional: Tierra Caliente, Guerrero*. Mexico City, 1996.

Bustamante Llaca, Enrique. "Sobre la edad de las placas de cobre." In *Los Hallazgos de Ichcateopan: Actas y dictámenes de la Comisión Investigadora*, edited by Secretaría de Educación Pública. Mexico City, 1962.

Camp, Roderic Ai. *Biografías de políticos mexicanos, 1935–1985*. Mexico City, 1992.

——. *Intellectuals and the State in Twentieth Century Mexico*. Austin: University of Texas Press, 1985.

——. "Mexican Governors since Cárdenas: Education and Career Contacts." *Journal of Interamerican Studies and World Affairs* 16, no. 4 (November 1974).

——. *Mexican Political Biographies 1935–1981*. Tucson: University of Arizona Press, 1982.

Carr, Barry. "The Fate of the Vanguard Party under a Revolutionary State: Marxism's Contribution to the Construction of the Great Arch." In *Everyday Forms of State Formation: Revolution and the Negotiation of Rule in Modern Mexico*, edited by Gilbert M. Joseph and Daniel Nugent. Durham, N.C.: Duke University Press, 1994.

Caso, Alfonso. "Genealogía de Cuauhtémoc." In *Los Hallazgos de Ichcateopan: Actas y dictámenes de la Comisión Investigadora*, edited by Secretaría de Educación Pública. Mexico City, 1962.

——, ed. *Métodos y resultados de la política indigenista en México*. Mexico City, 1954.

Castro-Klarén, Sara, and John Charles Chasteen, eds. *Beyond Imagined Communities: Reading and Writing the Nation in Nineteenth-Century Latin America*. Washington, D.C.: Woodrow Wilson Center Press, 2003.

Chandler, Raymond. *Trouble Is My Business*. New York: Vintage, 1992.

Chávez Orozco, Luis. *Don Florentino Juárez no pudo ser el creador de la tradición de Ichcateopan acerca de los restos de Cuauhtémoc*. Mexico City, 1950.

Chernyk, Evgeni. "Postscript: Russian Archaeology after the Collapse of the USSR– Infrastructural Crisis and the Resurgence of Old Nationalisms." In *Nationalism, Politics, and the Practice of Archaeology*, edited by P. L. Kohl and C. Fawcett. Cambridge: Cambridge University Press, 1995.

Clendinnen, Inga. "'Fierce and Unnatural Cruelty': Cortés and the Conquest of Mexico." *Representations* 33 (Winter 1991).

Coe, Michael D. "From *Huaquero* to Connoisseur: The Early Market in Pre-Columbian Art." In *Collecting the Pre-Columbian Past: A Symposium at Dumbarton Oaks, 6th and 7th October 1990*, edited by Elizabeth Hill Boone. Washington, D.C.: Dumbarton Oaks Research Library and Collection, 1993.

Cohn, Deborah. "The Mexican Intelligentsia, 1950–1968: Cosmopolitanism, Nationalism and the State." *Mexican Studies/Estudios mexicanos* 21, no. 1 (Winter 2005).

Córdova, Luis. "Cuauhtémoc, Soldier of Liberty." *Cultura Soviética*, no. 61 (November 1949).

Cortés Herrera, A. M. "La inscripción de la tumba de Ichcateopan fue grabada en el siglo XVI." In *Los Hallazgos de Ichcateopan: Actas y dictámenes de la Comisión Investigadora*, edited by Secretaría de Educación Pública. Mexico City, 1962.

Craib, Raymond B. *Cartographic Mexico: A History of State Fixations and Fugitive Landscapes*. Durham, N.C.: Duke University Press, 2004.

———. "A Nationalist Metaphysics: State Fixations, National Maps, and the Geohistorical Imagination in Nineteenth-Century Mexico." *Hispanic American Historical Review* 82, no. 1 (February 2002).

Cuevas, José A. "Edad del entierro de Ichcateopan, de acuerdo con el examen constructivo de las estructuras superpuestas." *Cultura Soviética*, no. 68 (June 1950).

Darnton, Robert. *The Great Cat Massacre: And Other Episodes in French Cultural History*. New York: Vintage Books, 1985.

Davies, Nigel. *The Aztecs*. London: Macmillan, 1973.

Dawson, Alexander S. *Indian and Nation in Revolutionary Mexico*. Tucson: University of Arizona Press, 2004.

Dehouve, Danièle. *Cuando los banqueros eran santos: Historia económica y social de la provincia de Tlapa, Guerrero*. Chilpancingo, 2001.

———. "Santos viajeros e identidad regional en el estado de Guerrero." In *Encuentros antropológicos: Power, Identity and Mobility in Mexican Society*, edited by Valentina Napolitano and Xochitl Leyva Solano. London: Institute of Latin American Studies, 1998.

Denhardt, Robert M. "The Equine Strategy of Cortés." *Hispanic American Historical Review* 18, no. 4 (1938).

Doremus, Anne. "Indigenism, *Mestizaje*, and National Identity in Mexico during the 1940s and the 1950s." *Mexican Studies/Estudios mexicanos* 17, no. 1 (Summer 2001).

Díaz y de Ovando, C. "Prólogo." In *Cuentos del General*, edited by Vicente Riva Palacio. Mexico City, 1968.

———. *Vicente Riva Palacio y la identidad nacional* (Mexico City, 1985).

Ducey, Michael T. *A Nation of Villages: Riot and Rebellion in the Mexican Huasteca, 1750–1850*. Tucson: University of Arizona Press, 2004.

Duncan, Robert H. "Embracing a Suitable Past: Independence Celebrations under Mexico's Second Empire, 1864–1866." *Journal of Latin American Studies* 30 (1998).

Earle, Rebecca. "Creole Patriotism and the Myth of the 'Loyal Indian.'" *Past and Present* 172 (August 2001).

———. "'Padres de la Patria' and the Ancestral Past: Commemorations of Independence in Nineteenth-Century Spanish America." *Journal of Latin American Studies* 34, no. 4 (November 2002).

———. *The Return of the Native: Indians and Myth-Making in Spanish America, 1810–1930*. Durham, N.C.: Duke University Press, 2007.

———. "*Sobre Héroes y Tumbas*: National Symbols in Nineteenth-Century Spanish America." *Hispanic American Historical Review* 85, no. 3 (2005).

Eliot, Thomas Stearns. "Hamlet and His Problems." In *The Sacred Wood: Essays on Poetry and Criticism*. London: Methuen and Co. Ltd., 1920.

Enciclopedia de México. Mexico City, 1977.

Espejel López, Laura, and Salvador Rueda Smithers. *Reconstrucción histórica de una comunidad del norte de Guerrero: Ichcateopan*. Mexico City, 1979.

Esposito, Matthew. *Funerals, Festivals, and Cultural Politics in Porfirian Mexico*. Albuquerque: University of New Mexico Press, 2010.

———. "Memorializing Modern Mexico: The State Funerals of the Porfirian Era, 1876–1911." Unpublished Ph.D. diss., Texas Christian University, 1997.

Evans, R. Tripp. *Romancing the Maya: Mexican Antiquity in the American Imagination, 1820–1915*. Austin: University of Texas Press, 2004.

Fernández, Claudia, and Andrew Paxman. *El Tigre: Emilio Azcárraga y su imperio Televisa*. Mexico City, 2000.

Fisk, Robert. "Some Talk of Alexander's Tomb Starts to Ring Hollow." *The Independent*, February 7, 1995.

Flanet, Veronique. *Viviré si Dios quiere*. Mexico City, 1990.

Florescano, Enrique. *El poder y la lucha por el poder en la historiografía mexicana*. Mexico City, 1980.

———. *Etnia, estado y nación*. Mexico City, 1997.

———. *Memoria Mexicana*. Mexico City, 1987.

French, William. "Imagining and the Cultural History of Nineteenth-Century Mexico." *Hispanic American Historic Review* 79, no. 2 (May 1999).

Friedlander, Judith. *Being Indian in Hueyapan: A Study of Forced Identity in Contemporary Mexico*. New York: St. Martin's Press, 1975.

Friedrich, Paul. *Agrarian Revolt in a Mexican Village*. Englewood Cliffs, N.J.: Prentice Hall, 1970.

———. *The Princes of Naranja: An Essay in Anthrohistorical Method*. Austin: University of Texas Press, 1986.

Fritsche Aceves, Ernesto. "Los Niños Héroes o el olvido." *Nexos* 285 (September 2001).

Fulton, Christopher. "Cuauhtémoc Regained." *Estudios de Historia Moderna y Contemporánea de México* 36 (July–December 2008).

———. "Siqueiros against the Myth: Paeans to Cuauhtémoc, Last of the Aztec Emperors." *Oxford Art Journal* 32, no. 1 (2009).

Gamio, Manuel. *Arqueología e Indigenismo*. Mexico City, 1972.

García Quintana, Josefina. *Cuauhtémoc en el siglo XIX*. Mexico City, 1977.

Geertz, Clifford. *The Interpretation of Cultures*. New York: Basic Books, 1973.

Gellner, Ernst. *Culture, Identity, and Politics*. Cambridge: Cambridge University Press, 1987.

Gibson, Charles. Review of *Cuauhtémoc. Hispanic American*, by Salvador Toscano. *Historical Review* 35, no. 1 (February 1955).

Gill, Mario. "Los Escudero, de Acapulco." *Historia Mexicana* 3, no. 4 (October–December 1953).

Gillingham, John. *The Wars of the Roses*. Baton Rouge: Louisiana State University Press, 1981.

Gillingham, Paul. "Ambiguous Missionaries: Rural Teachers and State Façades in Guerrero, 1930–1950." *Mexican Studies/Estudios mexicanos* 22, no. 2 (Summer 2006).

———. "Force and Consent in Mexican Provincial Politics: Guerrero and Veracruz, 1945–1953." D.Phil. thesis, Oxford University, 2005.

———. "Maximino's Bulls: Popular Protest after the Mexican Revolution, 1940–1952." *Past and Present* 206 (February 2010).

———. "The Strange Business of Memory: Relic Forgery in Latin America." In *Relics and Remains: Past and Present Supplement 5*, edited by Alex Walsham. Oxford: Oxford University Press, 2010.

Ginzburg, Carlo. *The Cheese and the Worms: The Cosmos of a Sixteenth-Century Miller*. Baltimore, Md.: Johns Hopkins University Press, 1992.

Girón, Nicole. "La idea de la cultura nacional en el siglo XIX: Altamirano y Ramírez." In *En torno a la cultura nacional*, edited by José Emilio Pacheco. Mexico City, 1982.

Gómez Robleda, José. *Dictamen acerca de la Autenticidad de la tumba de Cuauhtémoc en Ichcateopan*. Mexico City, 1952.

González de Cossío, Francisco, ed. *Legislación Indigenista de México*. Mexico City, 1958.

González Navarro, Moisés. *Estadísticas sociales del Porfiriato*. Mexico City, 1956.

González-Stephens, Beatriz. "Showcases of Consumption: Historical Panoramas and Universal Expositions." In *Beyond Imagined Communities: Reading and Writing the Nation in Nineteenth-Century Latin America*, edited by Sara Castro-Klarén and John Charles Chasteen. Washington, D.C.: Woodrow Wilson Center Press, 2003.

González y González, Luis. *El indio en la era liberal*. Mexico City, 1996.

———. *Invitación a la microhistoria*. Mexico City, 1997.

———. *Pueblo en Vilo*. Mexico City, 1995.

Gramsci, Antonio. *Selections from the Prison Notebooks*. London: Lawrence and Wishart, 1996.

Guardino, Peter. *Peasants, Politics and the Formation of Mexico's National State: Guerrero, 1800–1857*. Stanford, Calif.: Stanford University Press, 1996.

Guerra, Francois-Xavier. "Forms of Communication, Political Spaces, and Cultural Identities in the Creation of Spanish American Nations." In *Beyond Imagined Communities: Reading and Writing the Nation in Nineteenth-Century Latin America*, edited by Sara Castro-Klarén and John Charles Chasteen. Washington, D.C.: Woodrow Wilson Center Press, 2003.

Gurría Lacroix, Jorge. *Hernán Cortés y Diego Rivera*. Mexico City, 1971.

———. *Historiografía sobre la muerte de Cuauhtémoc*. Mexico City, 1976.

Guthke, Karl S. *B. Traven: The Life behind the Legends*. Translated by Robert C. Sprung. Brooklyn: Lawrence Hill Books, 1991.

Gutiérrez Avila, Miguel Angel. *La Conjura de los Negros: Cuentos de la Tradición Afromestiza de la Costa Chica de Guerrero y Oaxaca*. Chilpancingo, 1993.

Guzmán, Eulalia. "El hallazgo de la tumba de Cuauhtémoc, Part I." *Cultura Soviética*, no. 66 (April 1950).

———. "El hallazgo de la tumba de Cuauhtémoc, Part II." *Cultura Soviética*, no. 67 (May 1950).

———. *La Autenticidad de la tumba de Cuauhtémoc*. Mexico City, 1951.

———. *La Genealogía y Biografía de Cuauhtémoc*. Culiacán, 1954.

———. *Relaciones de Hernán Cortés a Carlos V sobre la invasión de Anáhuac: Aclaraciones y Rectificaciones por Eulalia Guzmán*. Mexico City, 1958.

———. *Una visión crítica de la historia de la conquista de México-Tenochtitlán*. Mexico City, 1989.

Hemingway, Ernest. *Death in the Afternoon*. London: Arrow Books, 1994.

Henderson, Timothy J. *The Worm in the Wheat: Rosalie Evans and Agrarian Struggle in the Puebla-Tlaxcala Valley of Mexico, 1906–1927*. Durham, N.C.: Duke University Press, 1998.

Hobsbawm, Eric. "Introduction: Inventing Traditions." In *The Invention of Tradition*, edited by Eric Hobsbawm and Terence Ranger. Cambridge: Cambridge University Press, 1983.

———. *Nations and Nationalism since 1780: Programme, Myth, Reality*. Cambridge: Cambridge University Press, 1990.

———, and Terence Ranger, eds. *The Invention of Tradition*. Cambridge: Cambridge University Press, 1983.

Hocart, Arthur M. "Evidence in Human History." In *Kings and Councillors*, edited by Rodney Needham. Chicago: University of Chicago Press, 1970.

Hoving, Thomas. *False Impressions: The Hunt for Big-Time Art Fakes*. New York: Touchstone, 1997.

Hutton, Patrick. "The History of Mentalities: The New Map of Cultural History." *History and Social Theory* 2, no. 3 (October 1981).

Ibargüengoitía, Jorge. *Instrucciones para Vivir en México*. Mexico City, 2000.

Illades, Carlos, and Manuel Ortega. *Guerrero: Una historia compartida*. Mexico City, 1989.

Jacobs, Ian. *Ranchero Revolt: The Mexican Revolution in Guerrero*. Austin: University of Texas Press, 1982.

Jiménez, Blanca, and Samuel Villela. *Los Salmerón: Un siglo de fotografía en Guerrero*. Mexico City, 1998.

Jiménez Moreno, Wigberto. "Los Hallazgos de Ichcateopan." *Historia Mexicana* 12 (October–December 1962).

Jiménez Rueda, Julio. "La intervención de Motolinía en el Entierro de Ichcateopan." In *Los Hallazgos de Ichcateopan: Actas y dictámenes de la Comisión Investigadora*, edited by Secretaría de Educación Pública. Mexico City, 1962.

Johnson, Lyman L. "Digging Up Cuauhtémoc." In *Death, Dismemberment, and Memory: Body Politics in Latin America*, edited by Lyman L. Johnson. Albuquerque: University of New Mexico Press, 2004.

———, ed. *Death, Dismemberment, and Memory: Body Politics in Latin America*. Albuquerque: University of New Mexico Press, 2004.

Jones, Mark. "Why Fakes?" In *Fake? The Art of Deception*, edited by Mark Jones. Berkeley: University of California Press, 1990.

Joseph, Gilbert M., and Daniel Nugent, eds. *Everyday Forms of State Formation: Revolution and the Negotiation of Rule in Modern Mexico*. Durham, N.C.: Duke University Press, 1994.

Katz, Friedrich. *The Life and Times of Pancho Villa*. Stanford, Calif.: Stanford University Press, 1998.

Keen, Benjamin. *The Aztec Image in Western Thought*. New Brunswick, N.J.: Rutgers University Press, 1971.

Keynes, John Maynard. *The General Theory of Employment, Interest and Money*. Orlando: Harcourt Brace, 1991.

Knight, Alan. *The Mexican Revolution*. 2 vols. Lincoln: University of Nebraska Press, 1990.

———. "Peasants into Patriots: Thoughts on the Making of the Mexican Nation." *Mexican Studies/Estudios mexicanos* 10, no. 1 (Winter 1994).

———. "Racism, Revolution and *Indigenismo*: Mexico, 1910–1940." In *The Idea of Race in Latin America, 1870–1940*, edited by Richard Graham. Austin: University of Texas Press, 1990.

———. "The Several Legs of Santa Anna: A Saga of Secular Relics." In *Relics and Remains: Past and Present Supplement 5*, edited by Alex Walsham. Oxford: Oxford University Press, 2010.

———. "Weapons and Arches in the Mexican Revolutionary Landscape." In *Everyday Forms of State Formation: Revolution and the Negotiation of Rule in Modern Mexico*, edited by Gilbert M. Joseph and Daniel Nugent. Durham, N.C.: Duke University Press, 1994.

———. "The Weight of the State in Modern Mexico." In *Studies in the Formation of the Nation State in Latin America*, edited by James Dunkerley. London: Institute of Latin American Studies, 2002.

Kohl, P. L., and C. Fawcett. "Introduction." In *Nationalism, Politics, and the Practice of Archaeology*, edited by P. L. Kohl and C. Fawcett. Cambridge: Cambridge University Press, 1995.

———, eds. *Nationalism, Politics, and the Practice of Archaeology*. Cambridge: Cambridge University Press, 1995.

Kourí, Emilo. *A Pueblo Divided: Business, Property and Community in Papantla, Mexico*. Stanford, Calif.: Stanford University Press, 2004.

Krauze, Enrique. *Mexico, Biography of Power: A History of Modern Mexico, 1810–1996*. New York: Harper Collins, 1997.

Kronk, Gary W. *Comets: A Descriptive Handbook*. Berkeley Heights, N.J.: Enslow Publishers, Inc., 1984.

Kuenzli, E. Gabrielle. "Acting Inca: The Parameters of National Belonging in Early-Twentieth Century Bolivia." *Hispanic American Historical Review* 90, no. 2 (2010).

La Antropología en México: Panorama histórico. Edited by Carlos García Mora. Mexico City, 1988.

Lafaye, Jacques. *Quetzalcóatl y Guadalupe: La formación de la conciencia nacional en México*. Mexico City, 1995.

Larson, Brooke. *Trials of Nation Making: Liberalism, Race, and Ethnicity in the Andes, 1810–1910*. Cambridge: Cambridge University Press, 2004.

León-Portilla, Miguel. "Presencia de Bernal Díaz del Castillo (1496–1584)." *Vuelta*, January 1985.

LeRoy-Ladurie, Emmanuel. *Carnival: A People's Uprising at Romans, 1579–1580*. Translated by Mary Feeney. London: Scolar Press, 1980.

Levinson, Irving W. *Wars within Wars: Mexican Guerrillas, Domestic Elites, and the United States of America, 1846–1848*. Fort Worth: Texas Christian University Press, 2005.

Lévi-Strauss, Claude. *The Savage Mind*. Chicago: University of Chicago Press, 1966.

———. *Tristes Tropiques*. Paris: Gallimard, 1990.

Lewis, Oscar. *The Children of Sánchez: Autobiography of a Mexican Family*. New York: Random House, 1963.

Lewis, Stephen E. *The Ambivalent Revolution: Forging State and Nation in Chiapas, 1910–1945*. Albuquerque: University of New Mexico Press, 2005.

———. "Chronicle of a Debacle; or, What Happened to the INI's Pilot Coordinating Center in Chiapas, Mexico, 1951–1976?" *Latin American Perspectives*, forthcoming.

———. "Revolution and the Rural Schoolhouse: Forging State and Nation in Chiapas, Mexico, 1913–1948." Unpublished Ph.D. diss., University of California, San Diego, 1997.

Li, Darryl. "Echoes of Violence: Considerations on Radio and Violence in Rwanda." *Journal of Genocide Research* 6, no. 1 (March 2004): 9–27.

Lieven, Anatol. *America Right or Wrong: An Anatomy of American Nationalism*. Oxford: Oxford University Press, 2005.

Lizardi Ramos, César. *Copan y el jeroglífico de los sacrificios humanos*. Mexico City, 1948.

———. *Exploraciones en Quintana Roo*. Mexico City, 1940.

Lockhart, James. *The Nahuas after the Conquest: A Social and Cultural History of the Indians of Central Mexico, Sixteenth through Eighteenth Centuries*. Stanford, Calif.: Stanford University Press, 1992.

Lombardo de Ruiz, Sonia. *La iglesia de la Asunción en relación a la autenticidad de los restos de Cuauhtémoc*. Mexico City, 1978.

Lomnitz-Adler, Claudio. *Death and the Idea of Mexico*. New York: Zone Books, 2005.

———. *Deep Mexico, Silent Mexico: An Anthropology of Nationalism*. Minneapolis: University of Minnesota Press, 2001.

———. *Exits from the Labyrinth: Culture and Ideology in the Mexican National Space*. Berkeley: University of California Press, 1992.

López, María. "El capote de paseillo." *Matador* 4, no. 1 (1999).

López, Rick A. *Crafting Mexico: Intellectuals, Artisans, and the State after the Revolution*. Durham, N.C.: Duke University Press, 2010.

———. "The India Bonita Competition of 1921 and the Ethnicization of Mexican National Culture." *Hispanic American Historical Review* 82, no. 2 (2002).

López Barroso, Epigmenio. *Diccionario Geográfico, Histórico y Estadístico del Distrito de Abasolo, del Estado de Guerrero: Hechos históricos propios de esa región*. Mexico City, 1967.

López Zapata, Alvaro. *La muerte de Cuauhtémoc: ¿Dónde? ¿Cómo?¿Cuándo? y ¿Por qué?* Campeche, 2001.

Lovell, W. George. "Heavy Shadows and Black Night: Disease and Depopulation in Colonial Spanish America." *Annals of the Association of American Geographers* 82, no. 3 (September 1992).

Malcolm, Noel. *Bosnia: A Short History*. London: Macmillan, 1994.

Mallon, Florencia. "Los campesinos y la formación del Estado en el México del siglo XIX: Morelos, 1848–1858." In *Secuencia*, no. 15 (Mexico City, 1989).

———. *Peasant and Nation: The Making of Postcolonial Mexico and Peru*. Berkeley: University of California Press, 1995.

Martínez, José Luis. *Hernán Cortés*. Mexico City, 1990.

Martínez Carbajal, Alejandro. *La muerte de Cuauhtémoc según fuentes escritas*. Mexico City, 1977.

Matos Moctezuma, Eduardo. *Informe de la revisión de los trabajos arqueológicos realizados en Ichcateopan, Guerrero*. Mexico City, 1980.

Mayer, Leticia. "El proceso de recuperación simbólica de cuatro héroes de la Revolución Mexicana de 1910 a través de la prensa nacional." *Historia Mexicana* 45, no. 2 (October–December 1995).

McNamara, Patrick. *Sons of the Sierra: Juárez, Díaz, and the People of Itxlán, Oaxaca, 1855–1920*. Chapel Hill: University of North Carolina Press, 2007.

Medel y Alvarado, León. *Historia de San Andrés Tuxtla*. 3 vols. Xalapa, 1993.

Metcalf, Peter, and Richard Huntingdon. *Celebrations of Death: The Anthropology of Mortuary Ritual*. Cambridge: Cambridge University Press, 1991.

Miller, Nicola. *In the Shadow of the State: Intellectuals and the Quest for National Identity in Twentieth-Century Spanish America*. London: Verso, 1999.

Miller, Simon. *Landlords and Haciendas in Modernizing Mexico: Essays in Radical Reappraisal*. Amsterdam: CEDLA, 1995.

Miranda Arrieta, Eduardo. *Economía y Comunicaciones en el Estado de Guerrero 1877–1910*. Michoacán, 1994.

Mitra, Subrata K. "The Rational Politics of Cultural Nationalism: Subnational Movements of South Asia in Comparative Perspective." *British Journal of Political Science* 25, no. 1 (January 1995).

Monsiváis, Carlos. "La nación de unos cuantos y las esperanzas románticas: Notas sobre la historia del término 'cultura nacional' en México." In *En torno a la cultura nacional*, edited by José Emilio Pacheco. Mexico City, 1982.

Monypenny, William F., and George E. Buckle. *The Life of Benjamin Disraeli*. London: J. Murray, 1910–20.

Monzón, Arturo. "La Tradición Oral de Ichcateopan." In *Los Hallazgos de Ichcateopan: Actas y dictámenes de la Comisión Investigadora*, edited by Secretaría de Educación Pública. Mexico City, 1962.

Mora Forero, Jorge. "Los maestros y la práctica de la educación socialista." *Historia Mexicana* 29, no. 1 (1979).

Moreno Toscano, Alejandra. *Los hallazgos de Ichcateopan, 1949–1951*. Mexico City, 1976.

Neruda, Pablo. "Cuauhtémoc." *Cultura Soviética*, no. 61 (November 1949).

Niblo, Steven R. *Mexico in the 1940s: Modernity, Politics and Corruption*. Wilmington, Del.: Scholarly Resources, 1999.

Nora, Pierre. *Rethinking France: Les lieux de mémoire*. 3 vols. Chicago: University of Chicago Press, 2001.

Ochoa Campos, Moisés. *Guerrero: Análisis de un Estado problema*. Mexico City, 1964.

O'Gorman, Edmundo. *El proceso de la invención de América*. Mexico City, 1995.

O'Gorman, Frank. "The Culture of Elections in England: From the Glorious Revolution to the First World War, 1688–1914." In *Elections before Democracy: The History of Elections in Europe and Latin America*, edited by Eduardo Posada Carbó. London: Institute of Latin American Studies, 1996.

Olivera de Bonfil, Alicia. *La tradición oral sobre Cuauhtémoc*. Mexico City, 1980.

O'Malley, Ilene. *The Myth of the Revolution: Hero Cults and the Institutionalization of the Mexican State, 1920–1940*. New York: Greenwood Press, 1986.

Ortega y Medina, Juan A. "Indigenismo e Hispanismo en la conciencia historiográfica mexicana." In *Cultura e identidad nacional*, edited by Roberto Blancarte. Mexico City, 1994.

Ortiz Monasterio, José. *Historia y Ficción: Los dramas y novelas de Vicente Riva Palacio*. Mexico City, 1993.

———. "Introducción." In *Tradiciones y Leyendas Mexicanas*, edited by Vicente Riva Palacio and Juan de Dios Peza. Mexico City, 1996.

———. *"Patria," tu ronca voz me repetía . . . biografía de Vicente Riva Palacio y Guerrero*. Mexico City, 1999.

Palacios, Guillermo. "Postrevolutionary Intellectuals, Rural Readings and the Shaping of the 'Peasant Problem' in Mexico: *El Maestro Rural*, 1932–1934." *Journal of Latin American Studies* 30, no. 2 (May 1998).

Parra Terán, Román. "Ixcateopan en el Siglo XIX." Master's thesis, Universidad Autónoma de Guerrero, 1997.

———. *La Provincia de Ichcateopan*. Chilpancingo, 1992.

Pasztor, Suzanne B. *The Spirit of Hidalgo: The Mexican Revolution in Coahuila*. Calgary: University of Calgary and Michigan State University Press, 2002.

Payno, Manuel. *Los bandidos de Río Frío*. Mexico City, 1964.

Peña, Moisés T. de la. *Guerrero Económico*. 2 vols. Mexico City, 1949.

Pérez Martínez, Hector. *Cuauhtémoc: Vida y muerte de una cultura*. Mexico City, 1948.

Pérez Montfort, Ricardo. "Indigenismo, Hispanismo y Panamericanismo en la cultura popular Mexicana de 1920 a 1940." In *Cultura e identidad nacional*, edited by Roberto Blancarte. Mexico City, 1994.

Peterson, Frederick. "Faces That Are Really False." *Natural History*, April 1953.

Pilcher, Jeffrey M. *Cantinflas and the Chaos of Mexican Modernity*. Wilmington, Del.: Scholarly Resources, 2001.

Plancarte, F. "Archaeologic Explorations in Michoacán, Mexico." *American Anthropologist* 6, no. 1 (January 1893).

Plasencia de la Parra, Enrique. "Conmemoración de la hazaña épica de los niños héroes: Su origen, desarrollo y simbolismos." *Historia Mexicana* 45 (1995).

Plutarch. *Vies*. Vol. 7. Paris: Bude, 1972.

Poole, Stafford. *Our Lady of Guadalupe: The Origins and Sources of a Mexican National Symbol, 1531–1797*. Tucson: University of Arizona Press, 1996.

Prampolini, I. R. "La figura del indio en la pintura del siglo XIX: Fondo ideológico." In *La Polémica del Arte Nacional*, edited by Daniel Schávelzon. Mexico City, 1988.

Prescott, William. *History of the Conquest of Mexico*. London: Folio Society Ltd., 1994.

Quiroz Cuarón, Alfonso, José Gómez Robleda, and Liborio Martínez. "Estudio de los restos oseos de Cuauhtémoc." In *Los Hallazgos de Ichcateopan: Actas y dictámenes de la Comisión Investigadora*, edited by Secretaría de Educación Pública. Mexico City, 1962.

Rappaport, Joanne. *The Politics of Memory: Native Historical Interpretation in the Colombian Andes*. Cambridge: Cambridge University Press, 1990.

Rath, Thomas. "Army, State and Nation in Mexico, 1920–1958." Unpublished Ph.D. diss., Columbia University, 2009.

———. "'Que el cielo un soldado en cada hijo te dio . . .': Conscription, Recalcitrance and Resistance in Mexico in the 1940s." *Journal of Latin American Studies* 37, no. 3 (2005).

Reyes García, Luis. *Documentos manuscritos y pictóricos de Ichcateopan, Guerrero.* Mexico City, 1979.

Robles García, Nelly. "La tumba 7 de Monte Albán." *Arqueología Mexicana* 5, no. 30 (1998).

Rockwell, Elsie. "Schools of the Revolution: Enacting and Contesting State Forms in Tlaxcala, 1910–1930." In *Everyday Forms of State Formation: Revolution and the Negotiation of Rule in Modern Mexico,* edited by Gilbert M. Joseph and Daniel Nugent. Durham, N.C.: Duke University Press, 1994.

Rodríguez, Antonio. "Cuauhtémoc, símbolo de la defensa nacional." *Cultura Soviética,* no. 62 (December 1949).

Rodríguez, M. "El 12 de octubre: Entre el IV y el V Centenario." In *Cultura e identidad nacional,* edited by Roberto Blancarte. Mexico City, 1994.

Rojas Garcidueñas, J. "Carlos de Sigüenza y Góngora y el primer ejemplo de arte neo-prehispánico en América." In *La Polémica del Arte Nacional,* edited by Daniel Schávelzon. Mexico City, 1988.

———. "El Indigenismo en la literatura de Mexico del siglo XVIII al XIX." In *La Polémica del Arte Nacional,* edited by Daniel Schávelzon. Mexico City, 1988.

Rojas Rabiela, Teresa, ed. *El indio en la prensa nacional mexicana del siglo XIX: Catálogo de noticias.* 3 vols. Mexico City, 1987.

Rubenstein, Anne. *Bad Language, Naked Ladies, and Other Threats to the Nation: A Political History of Comic Books in Mexico.* Durham, N.C.: Duke University Press, 1998.

Rubin, Jeffrey W. *Decentering the Regime: Ethnicity, Radicalism, and Democracy in Juchitán, Mexico.* Durham, N.C.: Duke University Press, 1997.

Rueda Smithers, Salvador. "Cuauhtémoc: Iconografía del águila del crepúsculo." In *XVI Jornadas de Historia de Occidente: El ejercicio del poder.* Michoacán, 1995.

———. "De conspiradores y mitógrafos: Entre el mito, la historia y el hecho estético." *Historias: Revista de la Dirección de Estudios Históricos del INAH* 39 (April–September 1982).

———. "Rethinking Moctezuma." In *Moctezuma: Aztec Ruler,* edited by Colin McEwan and Leonardo López Luján. London: British Museum Press, 2009.

Sahlins, Marshall. *How "Natives" Think: About Captain Cook, for Example.* Chicago: University of Chicago Press, 1995.

Salas Cuesta, M. E. *Molino del Rey: Historia de un monumento.* Mexico City, 1997.

Salazar Adame, Jaime, Renato Ravelo Lecuona, Daniel Molina Alvarez, and Tomás Bustamante. *Historia de la cuestión agraria mexicana: Estado de Guerrero, 1867–1940.* Chilpancingo, 1987.

Sayer, Derek. "Everyday Forms of State Formation: Some Dissident Remarks on 'Hegemony.'" In *Everyday Forms of State Formation: Revolution and the Negotiation of Rule in Modern Mexico,* edited by Gilbert M. Joseph and Daniel Nugent. Durham, N.C.: Duke University Press, 1994.

Schávelzon, Daniel. "El concurso del monumento a Cuauhtémoc (1876–1882)." In *La Polémica del Arte Nacional,* edited by Daniel Schávelzon. Mexico City, 1988.

———. "El primer monumento a Cuauhtémoc (1869)." In *La Polémica del Arte Nacional,* edited by Daniel Schávelzon. Mexico City, 1988.

———. "El reconocimiento del arte prehispánico en el siglo XVIII." In *La Polémica del Arte Nacional,* edited by Daniel Schávelzon. Mexico City, 1988.

———, ed. *La Polémica del Arte Nacional en México, 1850–1910.* Mexico City, 1988.

Schnirelman, V. A. "From Internationalism to Nationalism: Forgotten Pages of Soviet Archaeology in the 1930s and 1940s." In *Nationalism, Politics, and the Practice of Archaeology*, edited by P. L. Kohl and C. Fawcett. Cambridge: Cambridge University Press, 1995.

Scholes, Francis V., and Ralph L. Roys. *The Maya Chontal Indians of Acalan-Tixchel*. Norman: University of Oklahoma Press, 1968.

Scott, James. *Weapons of the Weak: Everyday Forms of Peasant Resistance*. New Haven: Yale University Press, 1985.

Secretaría de Educación Pública. *Los Hallazgos de Ichcateopan: Actas y dictámenes de la Comisión Investigadora*. Mexico City, 1962.

Segovia, Rafael. *La politización del niño mexicano*. Mexico City, 1975.

Sheridan, Guillermo. "Entre la casa y la calle: La polémica de 1932 entre nacionalismo y cosmopolitismo literario." In *Cultura e identidad nacional*, edited by Roberto Blancarte. Mexico City, 1994.

Shortland, Michael. Review of *The Other World: Spiritualism and Psychical Research in England, 1850–1914*, by Janet Oppenheim. *British Journal for the History of Science* 19, no. 2 (July 1986).

Silber, Laura, and Alan Little. *The Death of Yugoslavia*. London: Penguin, 1996.

Silberman, Neil A. "Promised Lands and Chosen Peoples: The Politics and Poetics of Archaeological Narrative." In *Nationalism, Politics, and the Practice of Archaeology*, edited by P. L. Kohl and C. Fawcett. Cambridge: Cambridge University Press, 1995.

Simms, Brendan. *Unfinest Hour: Britain and the Destruction of Bosnia*. London: Allen Lane, 2001.

Smith, Anthony D. "Nationalism and the Historian." In *Ethnicity and Nationalism*, edited by Anthony D. Smith. Leiden: E. J. Brill, 1992.

———. *Nationalism: Theory, Ideology, History*. Cambridge, U.K.: Polity Press, 2001.

———. *Nations and Nationalism in a Global Era*. Cambridge, U.K.: Polity Press, 1995.

Smith, Benjamin T. "*Cardenismo*, Caciques and Catholicism: The Politics of State-Building in Oaxaca." D.Phil. thesis, Cambridge University, 2005.

———. "Inventing Tradition at Gunpoint: Culture, *Caciquismo* and State Formation in the Region Mixe, Oaxaca (1930–1959)." *Bulletin of Latin American Research* 27, no. 2 (2008).

———. *Pistoleros and Popular Movements: The Politics of State Formation in Postrevolutionary Oaxaca*. Lincoln: University of Nebraska Press, 2009.

Smith, Peter H. *Labyrinths of Power: Political Recruitment in Twentieth-Century Mexico*. Princeton: Princeton University Press, 1979.

Solís Olguín, Felipe. "Family Histories: The Ancestors of Moctezuma II." In *Moctezuma: Aztec Ruler*, edited by Colin McEwan and Leonardo López Luján. London: British Museum Press, 2009.

Solís Vicarte, Ruth, and Mario A. Pérez. *Cuauhtémoc*. Mexico City, 1992.

Soustelle, Jacques. *La vida cotidiana de los aztecas en vísperas de la Conquista*. Mexico City, 1998.

Stack, Trevor. "Citizens of Towns, Citizens of Nations: The Knowing of History in Mexico." *Critique of Anthropology* 23, no. 2 (2003).

Tannenbaum, Frank. *Mexico: The Struggle for Peace and Bread*. New York: Alfred A. Knopf, 1950.

Taussig, Michael. *The Devil and Commodity Fetishism in South America*. Chapel Hill: University of North Carolina Press, 1980.

Taylor, John. "The Shabaka Stone." In *Fake? The Art of Deception*, edited by Mark Jones. Berkeley: University of California Press, 1990.

Taylor, William B. "The Virgin of Guadalupe in New Spain: An Inquiry into the Social History of Marian Devotion." *American Ethnologist* 14, no. 1 (February 1987).

Tenenbaum, Barbara A. "Streetwise History: The Paseo de la Reforma and the Porfirian State, 1876–1910." In *Rituals of Rule, Rituals of Resistance: Public Celebrations and Popular Culture in Mexico*, edited by William H. Beezley, Cheryl E. Martin, and William E. French. Wilmington, Del.: Scholarly Resources, 1994.

Tenorio-Trillo, Mauricio. *Mexico at the World's Fairs*. Berkeley: University of California Press, 1996.

Terry, Thomas Philip. *Terry's Guide to Mexico*. New York: Doubleday, 1962.

Thomas, Hugh. *The Conquest of Mexico*. London: Hutchinson, 1993.

Thomson, Guy P. C. "Bulwarks of Patriotic Liberalism: The National Guard, Philharmonic Corps and Patriotic Juntas in Mexico, 1847–1888." *Journal of Latin American Studies* 22, no. 1 (1990).

———, and David G. LaFrance. *Patriotism, Politics, and Popular Liberalism in Nineteenth-Century Mexico: Juan Francisco Lucas and the Puebla Sierra*. Wilmington, Del.: Scholarly Resources, 1998.

Toscano, Salvador. *Cuauhtémoc*. Mexico City, 1953.

Townsend, Camilla. *Malintzin's Choices: An Indian Woman in the Conquest of Mexico*. Albuquerque: University of New Mexico Press, 2006.

Trevor-Roper, Hugh. *The Hermit of Peking: The Hidden Life of Sir Edmund Backhouse*. London: Elan Press, 1993.

Tuñón Pablos, Julia. *Women in Mexico: A Past Unveiled*. Austin: University of Texas Press, 1999.

Unzueta, Fernando. "Scenes of Reading: Imagining Nations/Romancing History in Spanish America." In *Beyond Imagined Communities: Reading and Writing the Nation in Nineteenth-Century Latin America*, edited by Sara Castro-Klarén and John Charles Chasteen. Washington, D.C.: Woodrow Wilson Center Press, 2003.

Valdez, Norberto. *Ethnicity, Class, and the Indigenous Struggle for Land in Guerrero, Mexico*. New York: Routledge, 1998.

Van Oosterhout, Aaron, and Benjamin T. Smith. "The Limits of Catholic Science and the Mexican Revolution." *Endeavour* 34, no. 2 (June 2010).

Van Young, Eric. "Conclusion: The State as Vampire—Hegemonic Projects, Public Ritual, and Popular Culture in Mexico, 1600–1990." In *Rituals of Rule, Rituals of Resistance: Public Celebrations and Popular Culture in Mexico*, edited by William H. Beezley, Cheryl E. Martin, and William E. French. Wilmington, Del.: Scholarly Resources, 1994.

Vaughan, Mary Kay. "The Construction of the Patriotic Festival in Tecamachalco, Puebla, 1900–1946." In *Rituals of Rule, Rituals of Resistance: Public Celebrations and Popular Culture in Mexico*, edited by William H. Beezley, Cheryl E. Martin, and William E. French. Wilmington, Del.: Scholarly Resources, 1994.

———. *Cultural Politics in Revolution: Teachers, Peasants, and Schools in Mexico, 1930–1940*. Tucson: University of Arizona Press, 1997.

————. *The State, Education, and Social Class in Mexico, 1880–1928.* De Kalb: Northern Illinois University Press, 1982.

Vázquez Añorve, Francisco. *El ayer de mi costa.* Puebla, 1974.

Vázquez de Knauth, Josefina. *Nacionalismo y Educación en México.* Mexico City, 1970.

Verdery, Katherine. *The Political Lives of Dead Bodies: Reburial and Postsocialist Change.* New York: Columbia University Press, 1996.

Villoro, Luis. *Los grandes momentos del indigenismo en México.* Mexico City, 1997.

Viscount Kingsborough. *Antiquities of Mexico: Comprising facsimiles of ancient Mexican paintings and hieroglyphics.* Vol. 2. London, 1830–48.

Walsh, Jane MacLaren. "Crystal Skulls and Other Problems; Or, 'Don't Look It in the Eye.'" In *Exhibiting Dilemmas: Issues of Representation at the Smithsonian,* edited by Amy Henderson and Adrienne L. Kaeppler. Washington, D.C.: Smithsonian Institution Press, 1997.

————. "What Is Real? A New Look at PreColumbian Mesoamerican Collections." *Anthronotes* 26, no. 1 (Spring 2005).

Warman, Arturo. *De eso que llaman antropología mexicana.* Mexico City, 1970.

Wicks, Robert S., and Roland H. Harrison. *Buried Cities, Forgotten Gods: William Niven's Life of Discovery and Revolution in Mexico and the American Southwest.* Lubbock: Texas Tech University Press, 1999.

Wolf, Eric. *Pathways of Power: Building an Anthropology of the Modern World.* Berkeley: University of California Press, 2001 [1966].

Wolf, Eric. *Sons of the Shaking Earth.* Chicago: University of Chicago Press, 1959.

Womack, John. *Zapata and the Mexican Revolution.* London: Thames and Hudson, 1969.

Wood, Stephanie. "The Techialoyan Codices." In *Sources and Methods for the Study of Postconquest Mesoamerican History,* edited by James Lockhart, Lisa Sousa, and Stephanie Wood. Eugene: University of Oregon, 2007; http://whp.uoregon.edu/Lockhart/Wood.pdf.

Yeomans, Donald K. *Comets: A Chronological History of Observation, Science, Myth, and Folklore.* New York: John Wiley and Sons, 1991.

Yukichi, Fukuzawa. "Good-Bye Asia." In *Worlds of History, vol. 2: Since 1400: A Comparative Reader,* edited by Kevin Reilly. Boston: Bedford St. Martin's, 2007.

Zavala, Silvio. "Dictamen acerca de los hallazgos de Ichcateopan." *Revista Mexicana de Estudios Antropológicos* 2 (1950).

Zolov, Eric. *Refried Elvis: The Rise of the Mexican Counterculture.* Berkeley: University of California Press, 1999.

Index

Page numbers in italic text indicate illustrations.

abigeo, cattle rustling, 135
Acalán, 39–41
Acapulco, 46, 47, 50, 88, 130, 133, 137, 139, 169, 201
Acción Revolucionaria Mexicana, 190
Acosta, Jorge, 68, 69, 74, 256, 262
Aguirre Beltrán, Gonzalo, 193
ahuiles, 53, 57, 146, 200, 211, 254
Ahuitzótl, 14, 19–20, 23, 34, 123, 152–53, 242
Aldama, district of, 125, 130, 131
Alemán, Miguel, 109; decisions regarding Cuauhtémoc's tomb, 70, 72, 79, 81, 86–87, 111, 187, 200; failed personality cult of, 215; and Halley's Comet, 119; and nationalism, 182, 186, 190–91, 221; and violence in Guerrero, 50, 67
Altamirano, Ignacio, 92, 96, 267, 270
Alvarado, Pedro de, 27, 32, 34, 37; and *noche triste*, 23–24
Alvarez, Dario, 111
Alvarez, Diego, 137
Alvarez, Juan, 104, 137, 155
Alvarez, Santiago, 134
Alzate, José Antonio, 159
Amador, José Amado, 114
La América, 208–9
Anáhuac, 137, 150, 269, 288
Anales de Tlatelolco, 12, 29

Anderson, Benedict, 3–4
anticlericalism, 205–6
Appadurai, Arjun, 6, 216
Arce, Governor Francisco, 131, 137, 140, 152, 290
archaeology: colonial, 159; factionalism within, 73–74; and fraud in Bosnia, Egypt, and Japan, 123, 220; and fraud in Mexico, 163–68, 219–20; and nationalism, 216, 219–20; in Nazi Germany, 220; Porfirian, 98–99, *100*, *101*, 149, 159, *160*, *161*, 162–63; in Soviet Union, 193, 220
archives, destruction thereof, 106, 127–28
Arnaíz y Freg, Arturo, 68, 82, 88, 187, 261, 264
Arrieta, Toribio de, 115–17
Azcárraga, Emilio, 8
Azuela, Mariano, 175

Banco de México group, 75–79, 82, 264
bands, 8, 37, 76, 92, 155, 207–8
Bantjes, Adrian, 5
Barrera, Jesús, 133
Barrera Rodríguez, Rafael, 211
Barthes, Roland, 185
Bastille Day, 207
Batres, Leopoldo, 161, 163–66, 219
Beltrán, Modesto, 106, 127
Beltrán, Perfecto, 117, 137, 279
Bernal, Arias, 187, *188*

tions of history, 127–28; and Vicente Riva Palacio, 102, 104

Guerrero, Vicente, 88, 152, 209, 286

Guillén, Luis, 155

Guzmán, Eulalia, 51–53, 219; in Ixcateopan, 52–54, 58–65, 67–69, 74; pro-authenticity campaign, 73–82, 193

Haley, Bill, 219

hegemony, 28, 85, 111, 131

Helguera, Jesús, 180, *181*

Hemingway, Ernest, 124

Henríquez Guzmán, Miguel, 190

Hernández, Ignacio, 139

Hibueras expedition, 36–43

Hidalgo, Miguel, 7, 150, 152, 175, 194, 202, 208–9, 216

hispanismo, 153–54, 173, 185–87

historia patria, 78, 94, 220

history as a natural resource, 109, 199, 222

history textbooks, 78, *80*, 108, 142, 174, 175, 176, 185, 221, 223, 264, 280, 301

Hobsbawm, Eric, 185, 197, 215

Holmes, William Henry, 166–67

Huerta, Victoriano, 51, 117, 175

Huerta Molina, Mauro, 51, 58

Humboldt, Alexander von, 176

Ibargüengoitía, Jorge, 110, 184–85

Ibarra, Ninfo, 134

Iguala, 47, 60, 130, 147, 157, 168, 212, 259

Incas, 224, 290

Independence Day, 8, 93, 150, 153, 155, 217, 221

"India Bonita" competition, 178, 221, 296–97

indigenismo, 56, 72, 74, 81, 83, 85, 95–97, 128, 173–78, 183, 185–87, 192–93; 212; definition of and Porfirian origins, 99–102, 152–54, 174–75; rise and fall of, 216–18

indios verdes, 152–53, 215

Inquisition, 55, 90, 103

Instituto Nacional de Antropología e Historia (INAH), 51–52, 58, 60, 68–75, 79, 84, 182, 186, 193

Instituto Nacional Indigenista (INI), 72, 193, 217, 218

Instituto Politécnico Nacional (IPN), 201

instrumentalism, 3–5, 9, 98, 147, 168, 180–82, 194, 197–204, 210–14, 220–26

invisible ink, 54, 55, 123, 230

Iturbide, Agustín, 7, 150, 198, 286

Ixcapuzalco, 106, 129, 137, 139, 140–44, 145, 148, 149, 172, 212, 223, 225, 235, 286

Ixcateopan, 44–47, 128–44, 163, 211–12; and church/state conflict, 205–6; culture of, 52–53, 56–57, 66–67, 138–40, 145–47, 191–92, 202–14; etymology of, 251; land reform, 57, 130–32; politics, nineteenth-century, 135–36, 140–44; politics, twentieth-century, 105–11, 203–6, 211; tensions with outsiders, 67; traditions and ceremonies, 53, 57, 83–84, 125, 140, 154–55, 207–14, 223

Ixcateopan de San Lucas, 149, 306

Ixtlilxóchitl, Fernando de Alva, 12, 14, 15, 25, 40, 41

Izaguirre, Leandro, 155

Izankanac, capital of Acalán, 1, 39–42, 123

Izquierdo, Joaquín, 86, 261

Jaimes, Arnulfo Fuentes, 81

Jaimes, Camerino, 140, 172, 295

Jaimes, José, 118, 172; and Ixcateopan oral tradition, 125; political networks, 135; relationship with Florentino Juárez, 135, 137, 145; strategies of estate formation, 138–39; as village doctor and intellectual, 138–40, 284

Jaimes, Josefina, 134, 206, 262, 272, 284, 285, 287

Jaimes, Modesto, 111, 205, 206

Jalisco, 105, 180, 202

jefes políticos, 125, 136, 137, 140, 155, 159, 171, 279, 281

Johnson, Lyman, xi, 35, 126, 143, 181, 196

Jones, Mark, 168

Juárez, Alberta, 105, 145, 231

Juárez, Benito, 4, 8, 93, 148, 190

Juárez, Florencio, 106, 112, 135, 144, 204, 231

Juárez, Florentino, 54, 134–39, 143–44, 203; as *bricoleur* and forger, 85–86, 125–26, 145–72, 220–21; death of, 172; and ethnic identity, 146–47, 224–25; and family, 56, 204, 222–23; memory of, 134–35; political networks and power, 117, 135–36, 143–45, 171, 203; and spiritualism, 118, 147–48; and village culture, 139–40, 146–49, 155, 169, 225–26

**Other titles in the Diálogos series available from the
University of New Mexico Press:**

*Independence in Spanish America:
Civil Wars, Revolutions, and Underdevelopment* (revised edition)
—Jay Kinsbruner

Heroes on Horseback: A Life and Times of the Last Gaucho Caudillos—John Charles Chasteen

The Life and Death of Carolina Maria de Jesus
—Robert M. Levine and José Carlos Sebe Bom Meihy

¡Que vivan los tamales! Food and the Making of Mexican Identity—Jeffrey M. Pilcher

The Faces of Honor: Sex, Shame, and Violence in Colonial Latin America
—Edited by Lyman L. Johnson and Sonya Lipsett-Rivera

The Century of U.S. Capitalism in Latin America—Thomas F. O'Brien

Tangled Destinies: Latin America and the United States—Don Coerver and Linda Hall

Everyday Life and Politics in Nineteenth Century Mexico: Men, Women, and War
—Mark Wasserman

Lives of the Bigamists: Marriage, Family, and Community in Colonial Mexico—Richard Boyer

*Andean Worlds: Indigenous History, Culture,
and Consciousness Under Spanish Rule, 1532–1825*—Kenneth J. Andrien

The Mexican Revolution, 1910–1940—Michael J. Gonzales

Quito 1599: City and Colony in Transition—Kris Lane

A Pest in the Land: New World Epidemics in a Global Perspective—Suzanne Austin Alchon

The Silver King: The Remarkable Life of the Count of Regla in Colonial Mexico
—Edith Boorstein Couturier

National Rhythms, African Roots: The Deep History of Latin American Popular Dance
—John Charles Chasteen

The Great Festivals of Colonial Mexico City: Performing Power and Identity
—Linda A. Curcio-Nagy

*The Souls of Purgatory:
The Spiritual Diary of a Seventeenth-Century Afro-Peruvian Mystic, Ursula de Jesús*
—Nancy E. van Deusen

Dutra's World: Wealth and Family in Nineteenth-Century Rio de Janeiro—Zephyr L. Frank

Death, Dismemberment, and Memory: Body Politics in Latin America
—Edited by Lyman L. Johnson

Plaza of Sacrifices: Gender, Power, and Terror in 1968 Mexico—Elaine Carey

*Women in the Crucible of Conquest:
The Gendered Genesis of Spanish American Society, 1500–1600*
—Karen Vieira Powers

— continued on next page —

Beyond Black and Red: African-Native Relations in Colonial Latin America
—Edited by Matthew Restall

Mexico OtherWise: Modern Mexico in the Eyes of Foreign Observers
—Edited and translated by Jürgen Buchenau

Local Religion in Colonial Mexico—Edited by Martin Austin Nesvig

Malintzin's Choices: An Indian Woman in the Conquest of Mexico—Camilla Townsend

From Slavery to Freedom in Brazil: Bahia, 1835–1900—Dale Torston Graden

Slaves, Subjects, and Subversives: Blacks in Colonial Latin America
—Edited by Jane G. Landers and Barry M. Robinson

Private Passions and Public Sins: Men and Women in Seventeenth-Century Lima
—María Emma Mannarelli

*Making the Americas: The United States and Latin America
from the Age of Revolutions to the Era of Globalization*—Thomas F. O'Brien

*Remembering a Massacre in El Salvador:
The Insurrection of 1932, Roque Dalton, and the Politics of Historical Memory*
—Héctor Lindo-Fuentes, Erik Ching, and Rafael A. Lara-Martínez

Raising an Empire: Children in Early Modern Iberia and Colonial Latin America
—Ondina E. González and Bianca Premo

Christians, Blasphemers, and Witches: Afro-Mexican Rituals in the Seventeenth Century
—Joan Cameron Bristol

Art and Architecture of Viceregal Latin America, 1521–1821—Kelly Donahue-Wallace

Rethinking Jewish-Latin Americans—Edited by Jeffrey Lesser and Raanan Rein

True Stories of Crime in Modern Mexico—Edited by Robert Buffington and Pablo Piccato

Aftershocks: Earthquakes and Popular Politics in Latin America
—Edited by Jürgen Buchenau and Lyman L. Johnson

Black Mexico: Race and Society from Colonial to Modern Times
—Edited by Ben Vinson III and Matthew Restall

The War for Mexico's West: Indians and Spaniards in New Galicia, 1524–1550—Ida Altman

Damned Notions of Liberty: Slavery, Culture, and Power in Colonial Mexico, 1640–1769
—Frank Proctor

*Irresistible Forces:
Latin American Migration to the United States and its Effects on the South*
—Gregory B. Weeks and John R. Weeks